JAMES HILLMAN UNIFORM EDITION

6

Uniform Edition of the Writings of James Hillman
Volume 6: *Mythic Figures*

Series Editor: Klaus Ottmann

Published by Spring Publications
www.springpublications.com

Second edition 2021 (2.7)

First published in 2007

Cover illustration:
James Lee Byars, *Untitled,* ca.1960. Black ink on Japanese paper.
Estate of James Lee Byars, courtesy Michael Werner Gallery,
New York, London, and Berlin

ISBN: 978-0-88214-951-6

Library of Congress Control Number: 2021917693

JAMES HILLMAN

MYTHIC
FIGURES

With an Introduction by
JOANNE H. STROUD

SPRING PUBLICATIONS
THOMPSON, CONN.

Gentlemen, I need hardly say that every god
must command our homage.
—Plato, *Symposium* 180*e*

Contents

AUTHOR'S NOTE

Here and there in the following pages I have inserted a few emendations and deleted some remarks appropriate only for the audience of the occasion for which the text was originally prepared. Wherever several variations of the same lecture occurred, I have collapsed them into the present final version.

Dr. Markus McKinney took great pains with a preliminary editing of many of these chapters, for which I am more than grateful.

Further disquisition on the psychological effects of mythic figures, or what might be called "clinical mythology," can be found in several of my other published works: *UE 3: Senex & Puer* (Ulysses, Saturn, Chronos/Kronos); *The Myth of Analysis* (Eros, Psyche, Dionysus); *Pan and the Nightmare* (Pan, Selene, Nymphs); *Re-Visioning Psychology* (Persephone); and *The Dream and the Underworld* (Hades, Hercules, Demeter, Gaia, Nyx, Persephone).

The Uniform Edition of the Writings of James Hillman
is published in conjunction with

Dallas Institute Publications, Joanne H. Stroud, Director

The Dallas Institute of Humanities and Culture
Dallas, Texas

as an integral part of its publications program concerned with
the imaginative, mythic, and symbolic sources of culture

⌒◦⫘◦⌒

Additional support for this publication has been provided by

Elisabeth and Willem Peppler

The Fertel Foundation, New Orleans, Louisiana

Pacifica Graduate Institute, and
Joseph Campbell Archives and Library,
Carpinteria, California

INTRODUCTION

James Hillman brings an uncommon acuity to the current study of mythology. He explores how ancient myths can provide insights for present day issues: "I am attempting to show how antiquity can be relevant to the life of the psyche and how psychic life can vivify antiquity." The focus of these papers, then, is not to offer a better understanding of the classical, academic structures of myths. Nor is the intention to provide personal help that these larger-than-life archetypes can offer as models for personal development, or, on the other hand, to warn against shadow characteristics that cause obsessions and behavior problems. Instead, Hillman links myth to history and daily events. He reminds us of deeper connections: "Besides our aim of tying a human mess to a wider myth, we are attempting to connect present experience to historical culture."

The primary reason, Hillman explains, that Greek mythology has relevance, especially for Westerners, is: "They [the Greeks] had no depth psychology and psychopathology such as we have. They had myths. And we have no myths as such—instead, depth psychology and psychopathology. Therefore, ... psychology shows myths in modern dress and myths show our depth psychology in ancient dress."

Hillman teaches his readers how to regain the mythical perspective so lacking in our current all-too-literal approach to both friends and foes—black versus white, good guys versus evil empire. We fail to see our own shadows while refusing to see a stranger's virtue. Hillman applies the wisdom of myth that demonstrates that what we consider positive casts shadows just as the darkness has its redeeming light. Hillman's work demonstrates the verity of this principle, which is like the image of the curving, interpenetrating symbol of Yin and Yang in Chinese thought.

Hillman asks: "Have the gods truly fled?" Or are we just not able to see them? His implication is that they are still there for us to see. Other eras could rely on original myths to ground both the perspective of the individual and national ambitions. In the narratives of myth we are shown the unexpected, unforeseen consequences of even the most noble intentions, because "each god is a way in which we are shadowed."

In most past and some present cultures, myths provide explanations for the mysterious. With most of the gods of mythology dead or unavailable to us, we have insufficient containers for the numinous. Hillman proposes that "Mysteries are best accounted for by myths." Without these supporting vessels, we begin substituting for the worship of the gods the worship of fame—film personalities, athletes, and rock stars. In America in particular, we have developed to a considerable degree the craven adulation of transitory celebrity.

Another of our current excesses is the one of excess itself, too much of everything. We need to recall that the most famous of the Titans (the predecessors of the Olympians) was Prometheus, who not only gave mortals the gift of fire but also taught them to circumvent the allegiance of the gods. Our society has become subject to the dangers of an expanded Prometheism, of a kind of titanism unknown in past ages. In "Huge is Ugly," an appropriate title, Hillman points out: "We are not Titans nor can we become titanic—only when the gods are absent can titanism return to earth." He follows with this question: "Do you see why we must keep the gods alive and well? Small is beautiful requires a prior step: the return of the gods."

During the twentieth century, beauty almost became a bad word, or at least one that we were embarrassed to use. As a result of the scientific revolution, even the body became an object to be perfected. Hillman wryly remarks: "Remember, social Darwinism says survival of the *fittest*, not of the loveliest." Like Sir Herbert Read, the English art critic who wrote an important analysis of the way in which beauty has disappeared in art, Hillman addresses the loss of that quality in our society in general. His chapter on "Pink Madness or Why Does Aphrodite Drive Men Crazy With Pornography?" helps to explain why we have so little of beauty and so much pornography in our culture. It began, like all splits in the personality that we blame on Descartes, with the wedge between head and heart, or between the thinking brain and natural instincts. It is a split that has yet to be healed. Hillman prompts us to remember: "Pornography is where the pagan gods have fallen and how they force themselves back into our minds."

In the chapter on "War, Arms, Rams, Mars," Hillman speaks of the power of Mars, which should not be forgotten. In the same instance he says that "we have lost the overwhelming essence of war, now more of a nightly news event than any kind of heroic undertaking." He includes this provocative warning: "We do not know much nowadays about imagining divinities. We have lost the angelic imagination and its angelic protection. It has disappeared from all curricula—theological, philosophical, aesthetic. That loss may be more of a danger than either war or apocalypse because that loss results in literalism, the cause of both."

Even though "psychoanalysts are the myth-preservers in our culture," Hillman brings to our attention the shocking fact that the very practice of psychoanalysis is based on what he calls "the myth in the method." By this he means that the founding myth of psychoanalysis can hold its practitioners in the binds of its inevitable end. Hilllman's psychoanalysis of psychoanalysis is instructive. While Freud highlighted the myth of Oedipus as a way into understanding the central dynamic in family relationships, the Greek tragedy bearing his name also gives insights into the life of the city. Self-knowledge, to the extent possible, is a noble achievement, but "To find one's father and the truth of oneself is not enough." The whole emphasis in analysis is on a search for identity, the uncovering of one's early life with parents, which limits the psychoanalytical method to an ongoing Oedipal approach. Hillman further declares: "Whatever myths may operate in the psyche, whatever contents we might disclose, as long as our method remains *search for self,* these other tales will yield only Oedipal results because we turn to them with the same old intention." And therefore this method of attempting cure is doomed to recurring tragedy. Even though it sounds as if there is no way out, for Sophocles, the tragedian, the city, "the *polis,* is central to the play." Hillman shows us this pathway: we have learned that substituting another myth or any number of myths will only lead back to Oedipus because of the analytical method. Fortunately, the very same myth offers us a way forward. Freud stops in Thebes, with the *Tyrannus*. Sophocles dreams the myth along, as Jung advised us all to do. Let us move then from Freud to Jung by going with Oedipus to *Colonus*, the second Oedipus, written by Sophocles in his nineties, soon before his death in this same city, Colonus.

Whether as a psychologist, or equally as a participant in any exchange, we are called to examine our culpability, our blindness to the contributing part we play. It is not an acceptable excuse to be unaware. However, even this move toward awakened consciousness is not the ultimate one. With increased self-knowledge, the movement is back into the world. Hillman reminds us of what Jung always says: that the rocky path of individuation leads to the return to the world, where our talents ultimately need to be engaged. Hillman's final word: "Unless we let go of subjectivism, how will the soul ever return to the world, to things as they are so that they receive the attention they need from us? There are other pursuits, other urgencies than those of Self. What is it to make beauty? To serve my city? Be a friend, die with dignity, love the world, remember the gods?"

In the chapter on Orpheus, Hillman reveals an abiding interest in the French philosopher Gaston Bachelard, who could expand and bring together multiple associations for even a simple image. Hillman speaks of an "'Orpheus complex,' to use the language of Gaston Bachelard," that connects or disconnects us to the environment. Hillman, always concerned with words, remarks that Orpheus "may be present in their [environmentalists'] ideals, their practices, but lacking in their language." In this case, "If environmentalism does not awaken nature's sublimity, its beauty and its terror, if rocks and trees do not speak, they themselves become mere objects, not ensouled subjects with whom the human is bound."

I cannot resist adding that the Dallas Institute of Humanities and Culture, of which Hillman is a Founding Fellow, is engaged in a twenty-five-year love affair with Gaston Bachelard, having sponsored the translation of seven, soon to be eight, of his works from French to English. Hillman was also a keynote speaker and major contributor at two conferences on Bachelard at the Institute.

Hillman succeeds here, as usual, in provoking the reader's imagination. With his multifaceted perspective and his metaphysical wit, his work has influenced a number of thinkers and spawned an important school of thought.

JOANNE H. STROUD

ABBREVIATIONS

CP = Sigmund Freud, *Collected Papers*. Authorized translation under the supervision of Joan Riviere, 5 vols. (London: The Hogarth Press and The Institute of Psycho-Analysis, 1924–50)

CW = *Collected Works of C. G. Jung*, edited and translated by Gerhard Adler and R. F. C. Hull, 20 vols. (Princeton, N.J.: Princeton University Press, 1953–79), cited by paragraph number

NIL = Sigmund Freud, *New Introductory Lectures on Psycho-Analysis*, translated by W. J. H. Sprott (London: The Hogarth Press and The Institute of Psycho-Analysis, 1933)

SE = *The Standard Edition of the Complete Psychological Works of Sigmund Freud*, translated by James Strachey, 24 vols. (London: The Hogarth Press and The Institute of Psycho-Analysis, 1953–73)

UE = *Uniform Edition of the Writings of James Hillman*, edited by Klaus Ottmann, 12 vols. (Putnam and Thompson, Conn.: Spring Publications, 2004–)

1

DIONYSUS IN JUNG'S WRITINGS

An examination of C.G. Jung's view of Dionysus and the Dionysian is the subject of this note. Elsewhere[1] I suggested with some detail that analytical consciousness has been governed by an archetypal structure that favors the principles of light, order, and distance over emotional involvement, or what has, in short, been called the Apollonic over the Dionysian. There I also examined the notion of Dionysus, exposing prejudices in both classical psychiatry and Classical scholarship, prejudices that hinder the transformation of consciousness and resolution of fundamental analytical problems. I made the case that the fields of psychiatry and mythology by using each others arguments[2] have been, for the most part, in collusion against the Dionysian, resulting in a repression, and thus a distortion, of all Dionysian phenomena, so that they have come to be regarded as inferior, hysterical, effeminate, unbridled, and dangerous. I suggested a rectification of our appreciation of this archetypal structure and also a means to move toward this rectification. After all, Dionysus was the lord of souls (as Rohde called him), so that psychotherapy can hardly afford to labor under misleading notions of him.

First published in Spring: An Annual of Archetypal Psychology and Jungian Thought (1972).

1. The Myth of Analysis: Three Essays in Archetypal Psychology (Evanston, Ill.: Northwestern University Press, 1972).

2. The psychiatrist Paul Julius Möbius used for his diagnostic view of Dionysus Erwin Rohde's work in mythology, while Rohde's discussion of the wilder Dionysian cult, in turn, refers to the psychiatric work of Justus F.K. Hecker on dancing hysteria and to Pierre Janet on hysterical dissociation. The books to be consulted are: Paul Julius Möbius, Über das Pathologische bei Nietzsche (Wiesbaden: Bergmann, 1902); Erwin Rohde, Psyche (Tübingen: Mohr, 1925); J.F.K. Hecker, Die Tanzwuth: Eine Volks-krankheit im Mittelalter (Berlin: Enslin 1832), translated as The Epidemics of the Middle Ages by B.G. Babington (London, Trubner & Co., 1859); Pierre Janet, The Major Symptoms of Hysteria (London and New York: Macmillan, 1920).

This note is a postscript to that argument. I ought to add here that objections to the usage of "Apollonic" and "Dionysian" and to their opposition were there, in part, rehearsed, and I believe satisfactorily answered. We may, therefore, have a freer hand in using the term "Dionysian" for an archetypal structure of consciousness, much as Nietzsche introduced it in *The Birth of Tragedy* (1872), which Cornford called "a work of profound imaginative insight, which left the scholarship of a generation toiling in the rear."[3] We are also following Jung (who followed Nietzsche) in employing "Dionysian" as a term for a basic structure of consciousness.[4]

The First Dionysus

The following selection of passages represents the dominant notion of the Dionysian in the *Collected Works*:

> Dionysus is the abyss of impassioned dissolution...[5]
> Seldom or never have I had a patient who did not go back to neolithic art forms or revel in evocation of Dionysian orgies.[6]

> No reason guides him, only the Dionysian *libido effrenata*.[7]

> "Before dinner I am a Kantian, but after dinner a Nietzschean." In his habitual attitude, that is to say, he is an intellectual, but under the stimulating influence of a good dinner a Dionysian wave breaks through his conscious attitude.[8]

> The "terrible Mother" is the *mater saeva cupidinum*, unbridled and unbroken Nature, represented by the most paradoxical god of the Greek Pantheon, Dionysus...[9]

> ...Dionysian orgies that surged over from the East...Dionysian licentiousness...[10]

---

3. Francis Macdonald Cornford, *From Religion to Philosophy: A Study in the Origins of Western Speculation* (New York: Harper Torchbooks, 1957), 111n.

4. *CW* 6: 223–42; *CW* 10: p. 181n.

5. *CW* 12: 118 (2nd ed.).

6. *CW* 15: 212.

7. *CW* 5: 624.

8. *CW* 6: 908.

9. *CW* 5: 623.

10. *CW* 7: 17 (2nd ed.).

He delivers himself up unresistingly to the animal psyche. That is the moment of the Dionysian frenzy, the overwhelming manifestation of the "blond beast"...[11]
...an outburst of bestial greed and the tearing of living animals with the teeth were part of the Dionysian orgy.[12]

In Jung's alchemical writings, Dionysus is associated with the ape and the Black Mass,[13] an atavistic identification with animal ancestors,[14] and the Lord of Darkness (devil).[15] The association of Dionysus with the devil continues in both Jung's alchemical study of transference[16] and in his late opus, *Mysterium Coniunctionis.*[17] Another group of passages, fewer in number and lesser in power, give us another connotation—a second Dionysus. But we shall put off these passages until later because there is still more to say about the first Dionysus in Jung's writings.

Despite the many references to Dionysus and the long "Zarathustra Seminar," Dionysus was never central to Jung's focus. Dionysus had been given ample attention by Jung's earlier contemporaries in both classical psychiatry and in the history of religions, so that perhaps this avenue of mythology and pathology was less open to original exploration. Rohde and Nietzsche had forced Dionysus upon the consciousness of Classical scholarship. Freud and Janet had done the same for hysteria, which had already in the nineteenth century been associated with Dionysus.[18] Then there was the literary-philosophical psychologizing of

---

11. Ibid., 40.

12. *CW* 13: 91; cf. *CW* 11: 353.

13. *CW* 12: 191 (2nd ed.).

14. Ibid., 171.

15. Ibid., 119, 181. Cf. ETH Lectures, "Alchemy," vol. 1 (17 January 1941), 78, and (6 June 1941), 181 (Edition 1960, privately printed, C. G. Jung Institute, Zurich).

16. "The Church has the doctrine of the devil, of an evil principle, whom we like to imagine complete with cloven hoofs, horns, and tail, half man, half beast, a chthonic deity apparently escaped from the rout of Dionysus, the sole surviving champion of the sinful joys of paganism." *CW* 16: 388 (2nd ed.)

17. *CW* 14: 420.

18. Two letters from Freud to Fliess relate hysteria with "dancing epidemics of the Middle Ages," with "extremely primitive devil religion and the remnants of a primitive sexual cult which...may once have been a religion." Although Dionysus is not mentioned directly, he is implicated through the phallus ("great Lord Penis"),

Stefan George and Ludwig Klages, which Jung would not go near and in which he saw a poetic cult of the irrational in the name of Dionysus.[19]

Thus, as Jung's attention was only peripherally engaged with hysteria,[20] likewise was he only occasionally occupied with Dionysus. Schizophrenia and Hermes-Mercurius, however, received his full interest from the start and into his late work. He wrote separate studies on both schizophrenia and on Hermes-Mercurius (and Trickster), making extraordinary psychological contributions to both psychopathology and mythology. His basic insights into the nature of the psyche owe more to this work on schizophrenia than to hysteria and more to his investigation of the archetypal complexities of Hermes-Mercurius-Trickster than to those of Dionysus.

Although Dionysus was not in the foreground, Nietzsche was. There is probably a direct and causal relation between the presence of Nietzsche in Jung's consciousness and the absence of Dionysus, as if the more deeply Jung entered into Nietzsche, the more he was dissuaded from the Dionysian.

Jung says in his autobiography[21] that in his youth (around 1890), "I was unconsciously caught up by this spirit of the age, and had no methods at hand for extricating myself from it." This spirit he describes:
The archetypes of Wagner were already knocking at the gates, and along with them came the Dionysian experience of Nietzsche—which might better be ascribed to the god of ecstasy, Wotan.[22]

Jung displays already in his doctoral thesis his familiarity with Nietzsche's work.[23] But it is Nietzsche as "case" that seems uppermost in Jung's mind already in 1901-1902. Jung writes that Nietzsche's "poetic ecstasy at more than one point verges on the pathological."[24]

---

the dancing, the secret rites, seduction, and the devil (cf. below for the identity of Dionysus with the devil in earlier Christianity). Sigmund Freud, *The Origins of Psycho-Analysis. Letters to Wilhelm Fliess, Drafts and Notes, 1887–1902* (New York: Basic Books, 1954).

19. *CW* 10: 375.

20. *CW* 2, 3, 4, 6, 7, *passim.*

21. C.G. Jung, *Memories, Dreams, Reflections,* recorded and edited by Aniela Jaffé (London: Collins and Routledge, 1963). Referred hereafter as *MDR.*

22. *MDR,* 222.

23. *CW* 1: 141.

24. Ibid., 142.

Perhaps the history of psychiatry and of ideas will one day examine more closely the effects of the "case" of Nietzsche upon the spirit of the 1890s and turn of the century. It must certainly have been vividly felt in Basel, city of both Nietzsche and Jung, and especially in psychiatric circles, owing to the questions about Nietzsche's diagnosis and to the patholography on Nietzsche written by Möbius.

At least we do know that the "case" of Nietzsche had a profound effect upon Jung. During his student years he harbored "a secret fear that I might be like him [Nietzsche], at least in regard to the 'secret' which had isolated him from his environment."[25] And Jung imagined his "personality Number 2" to correspond with Zarathustra.[26] Let us remember that at the core of Nietzsche's catastrophe was his identification with Dionysus-Zagreus. Evidently, the fate of Nietzsche was a *Vorbild* of possession by an archetypal power, neither the idea of which nor a means of extrication from which were then available to Jung. This power was called Dionysus, even if it should have been called Wotan.[27] "In Nietzsche's biography you will find irrefutable proof that the god he originally meant was really Wotan, but being a philologist and living in the seventies and eighties of the nineteenth century, he called him Dionysus."[28]

---

25. *MDR*, 105.

26. *MDR*, 106.

27. Jung's prolonged occupation with Nietzsche's *Zarathustra* in the 1934–39 Seminars (*Nietzsche's Zarathustra: Notes of the Seminar by C. G. Jung*, edited by James L. Jarrett, 2 vols. [Princeton, N.J.: Princeton University Press, 1988]) attempts to come to terms not only with the case of Nietzsche but perhaps also with Jung's own other half. Jung speaks of "the panthers of Dionysus [that] jump upon you" (874); "the bliss of the Dionysian revelation" (144), and of the danger of the introverted descent: "Nietzsche describes how he was digging down into himself...till he suddenly produced the explosion of the most original form of spirit, the Dionysian" (369). Elsewhere, Jung equates Dionysus with Shiva (289). As the Seminar proceeds, Jung does give the explosive force its right name. Of Nietzsche he says: "The archetype of Wotan was in his blood" (1076). "It is Wotan who gets him, the old wind god breaking forth, the god of inspiration, of madness, intoxication and wildness, the god of the Berserkers, those wild people who run amok... It is a horrible forboding of insanity" (1227). "Dionysus could be assimilated, while Wotan is an unassimilable element" (898).

28. *CW* 11: 44.

We find this proof not only in Nietzsche's biography. *The Birth of Tragedy* opens with a dedicatory foreword to Wagner in which Nietzsche relates his essay to the "German problem" and "German hopes." At the end of the book, he warms again to his German theme:

...the German spirit has remained whole, in magnificent health, depth, and Dionysiac strength, resting and dreaming in an inaccessible abyss like a knight who has sunk into slumber; now the Dionysiac song rises from this abyss to tell us that, at this very moment, this German knight still dreams his ancient Dionysiac myth in blissfully grave visions.[29]

The paragraph ends with Brunnhilde and Wotan's spear. This is not Greek, not antiquity, but the return of Wotan in modern Germany. The restitution of the Dionysian in modern Western consciousness was from the very beginning entangled in Wotan.

In 1911, Thomas Mann recapitulated the disastrous mess of this archetypal contamination by means of a dream, which turns the fate of Gustav von Aschenbach in the novella *Death in Venice.* It must be read. There we see Dionysus, Pan, and the Maenads in a Germanic inscape informed by a Wotanic spirit. The facet of Dionysus that is revealed is altogether an enemy to dignity and self-control. But is this "stranger god" not more likely Wotan than the one depicted in antique vase paintings, where he appears so dignified and self-possessed. Or, even if there is a Dionysus as obscene and exuberant as Aschenbach's dream, that obscenity meant a death of another sort than the one in Venice. Heraclitus[30] pointed out in regard to the obscene Lenean rites of the Dionysian cult that they must be understood in the light of the unity of Hades and Dionysus. They may not be taken on the literal level of concrete enactment, but have an invisible meaning for the soul in terms of its underworld psychic life. Thus, though the images presented to Aschenbach seem authentically

---

29. *Nietzsche: The Birth of Tragedy and Other Writings,* translated by Ronald Speirs; edited by Raymond Geuss and Ronald Speirs (Cambridge: Cambridge University Press, 1999), 114–15.

30. Heraclitus, fr. 15 (Diels-Kranz). "If it were not in honor of Dionysus that they conducted the procession and sang the hymn to the male organ (*the phallic hymn*), their activity would be completely shameless. But Hades is the same as Dionysus, in whose honor they rave and perform the Bacchic revels." Kathleen Freeman, *Ancilla to The Pre-Socratic Philosophers* (Cambridge, Mass.: Harvard University Press, 2003), 25n.15.

Dionysian, the structure of his consciousness in which they perform provides a stage for literalism that is Wagnerian, Nietzschean, Wotanic, and where Hades becomes literal death, rather than the invisible realm of souls. The case of Nietzsche repeats in Mann's Aschenbach where "Dionysus" means enantiodromia, disease, and death.

Unlike Nietzsche, Jung saw through to the Wotan shadow of what Nietzsche called Dionysus.[31] Yet Jung insists that the "two gods have much in common." He speaks of them as "cousins."[32] He brings them into juxtapositions that are mytholographically strained, as, for instance, Jung's amplification of the horse and horse's hoof motifs[33] appropriate to Wotan, but where Dionysus is suddenly introduced by means of the *bull's* foot. Another peculiar—and Nietzschean—instance is the apposition of "Dionysian frenzy" and "blond beast."[34] It is as if, despite himself, Jung had difficulty extricating his perception of Dionysus from the Wotanic distortion shared by his generation and their transalpine, Germanic view of pagan Mediterranean culture. He observes this himself, saying: "Hence the Christian Weltanschauung, when reflected in the ocean of the (Germanic) unconscious, logically takes on the features of Wotan."[35] As Kerényi points out, "in that which concerns the image of Dionysus, researchers and scholars have submitted to the influence of German philosophy to a much higher degree than they themselves realize."[36] In other words, Jung's first view of Dionysus is distorted not only by the influence of nineteenth-century northern European scholarship but also by a dominant in the background of that scholarship: Wotan. More specifically, Jung's view is crucially affected by the model of Nietzsche who not only was the first to formulate and thus give his personal stamp to what has become our popular notion of this divinity, but who chose him as his god. Jung asks and answers what Dionysus signifies by means of Nietzsche. The first Dionysus of whom Jung writes is thus neither a figure of antiquity nor a figure in Jung's own life but one

---

31. E.g., *CW*5: 623; *CW*10: 375, 391; *CW*9.1: 442).
32. *CW*11: 44; cf. *CW*10: 386.
33. *CW*5: 421.
34. *CW*7: 40 (2nd. ed.).
35. *CW*9.1: 442.
36. Karl Kerényi, "Dionysus le Cretois," *Diogenes* 20 (1957): 4 (my translation).

who is vicariously known to Jung through Nietzsche. The key passage illustrating this is in *Psychology and Alchemy*:

It needed a Nietzsche to expose in all its feebleness Europe's school-boy attitude to the ancient world. But what did Dionysus mean to Nietzsche? What he says about it must be taken seriously; what it did to him still more so. There can be no doubt that he knew, in the preliminary stages of his fatal illness, that the dismal fate of Zagreus was reserved for him. Dionysus is the abyss of impassioned dissolution, where all human distinctions are merged in the animal divinity of the primordial psyche—a blissful and terrible experience.[37]

That Nietzsche's experience—eleven years of degenerating madness—should have provided the Virgil for the underworld descent in *Psychology and Alchemy* is of no minor importance for everyone who uses the model of individuation described in that book. Let us return to that text to see exactly where and how the Nietzschean Dionysus enters and how it affects the course of psychic movement.

The passage occurs at the end of part 2, chapter 2. The initial dreams and visions of the case have led to a climax. An elephant, an apeman or bear or caveman with a club, and a man with a pointed beard appear. The text is accompanied by three terrifying pictures of a skeleton, a wild-man, and a devil.

These visual images may be referred to "the Dionysian experience" as Jung does in paragraphs 118–19, but strictly they are not images of Dionysus. Mythographically, Dionysus was not a cave god (like Pan), nor were the ape or elephant in his train. The vision finds its lysis in a voice saying, "Everything must be ruled by the light." Jung concludes that the *nekyia* is now reversing and that the light refers to that "of the discerning, conscious mind."[38] The chapter ends with the "active intervention of the intellect" and the "symbols of the self."[39] Immediately thereafter, we turn to the study of the mandala while the pictures accompanying the text turn from horrid images of human shapes to abstract contemplative forms.

---

37. *CW* 12: 118.
38. Ibid., 120.
39. Ibid., 121.

Of course, Jung was following material of a case and not his own visions and dreams—neither was the case one of his.[40] Also, the accompanying pictures were not chosen and placed there by him. Yet the *selection* of the material, the *amplifications,* and the elaboration of the case into the *sequences* of the book are Jung's. How are we to understand this sudden return to the upper world via the light of intellect to the mandala? Does not the pattern presented in this movement indicate a direct relation between the Dionysian and the mandala?

We may remember that in Jung's life the mandala played a similar role. Jung's discovery of it came toward the end of his *nekyia*[41] when he "began to emerge from the darkness" of that long phase of intense psychological disturbance (1913–1919),[42] which Ellenberger calls "a creative illness."[43] He had painted his first mandala in 1916 and began to understand it in 1918.

Something similar to the mandala coincided with this emergence from the darkness: *Psychological Types.* This work was the first major fruit to be published after this dark phase.[44] We may look at the typological system with its eightfold structure within the psychological context of Jung's life. *Psychological Types* is also a mandala in conceptual form, performing a similarly ordering—and defensive—function.[45] Autobiographically, in

---

40. Cf. *Atom and Archetype: The Jung/Pauli Letters, 1932–1958,* edited by C.A. Meier (Princeton, N.J.: Princeton University Press, 2001).

41. Jung read the *nekyia* episode of the *Odyssey* during a sailing trip with friends on the Lake of Zurich. This is left out of the English version of *MDR,* but see the account in Henri F. Ellenberger, *The Discovery of the Unconscious* (New York: Basic Books, 1970), 670, and also the German original of *MDR,* 103–4.

42. *MDR,* 186.

43. Ellenberger, *The Discovery of the Unconscious,* 672.

44. *MDR,* 185n. Cf. Aniela Jaffé, "The Creative Phases in Jung's Life," in her *Jung's Last Years* (Dallas: Spring Publications, 1984).

45. "The need for the defensive aspect of mandalas [is] to be recognized and interpreted" (J.W.T. Redfearn, "Mandala Symbols and the Individuation Process," unpublished paper presented at the 4th International Congress for Analytical Psychology, London, 1971). He also notes, in connection with the mandala, that Jung's theory of the four functions "developed at a time when chaotic psychotic forces were threatening him." Jung points to the protective function of mandalas in *CW* 9.1: 16, 710, and 387–88.

Jung's case and in the sequence presented in *Psychology and Alchemy*, the mandala appears against the background of the "Dionysian experience" (i.e., Nietzschean Wotanic experience) and is a response to it.

The upshot of all this can be put in a series of conclusions. First, the experience—as Jung himself observes in several places that we cited—should not be named "Dionysian," but "Wotanic." Second, as Dionysus and Wotan differ, so must our psychological measures for connecting with them differ. A defensive order against Wotan may be appropriate; against Dionysus, it may be altogether inappropriate, as the tales of Lycurgus and Pentheus show. Third, although the mandala and typology may serve as useful defenses against Wotan and Nietzschean disintegration, these very same abstractions may block an appreciation of the "Dionysian experience." For psychotherapy to misperceive Dionysus would be worse than folly. After all, this god plays a central role in tragedy, in the transformational mysteries of Eleusis, in the instinctual and communal levels of the soul, and in the development of the kind of culture related to wine.[46] Moreover, there is the profound importance of Dionysus for the feminine psyche. Fourth, if this god is the archetypal dominant express-

---

46. On the cultural significance of wine, see Plato, *Laws* 672a–d, where "the gift of Dionysus, even including "Bacchic possession and all its frenzied dancing" is made a source of music. "...the gift was meant...as a medicine, to produce modesty of soul, and health and strength of the body." This "gift of Dionysus" belongs with ageing, for it shall be prohibited to "boys under eighteen," allowed moderately to "men under thirty." "But when a man is verging on the forties, we shall tell him, after he has finished banqueting at the general table, to invoke the gods and, more particularly, to ask the presence of Dionysus in that sacrament and pastime of advancing years—I mean the wine cup..." (666a–b). Plato's most impressive dialogue—with a vision of love that has been the main cultural influence (excepting the Gospels) upon the eros of our Western psyche—is a drinking party. The god who rules that dialogue, and is hinted at in the last episodes and through Silenos, is Dionysus. On the cultural significance of wine education and wine in education, see Paul Friedländer, *Plato,* 3 vols. (Princeton, N.J.: Princeton University Press, 1969), 3: 397–403. Sparta was abstinent (*Laws* 637a–b), and where there is no wine, does this not mean a misperception of Dionysus and his entire significance if not a ban against him? If so, Möbius was abstinent for most of his adult life, and so was Bleuler—and Jung, too, for a time at Bleuler's Burghölzli. (On Jung's enjoyment of drink in Basel, see Albert Oeri, "Some Youthful Memories of C.G. Jung," *Spring: An Annual of Archetypal Psychology and Jungian Thought* [1970]).

ing life itself (zoe) as some commentators have said, then to misread his manifestations could seriously mislead the very processes of healing. Yet, until the ghost of Nietzsche be laid to rest, every Dionysian event in therapy will tend to be seen as a herald of Wotanic eruption. We will tend to protect ourselves and analysands in the manner of the movement to the self that is depicted in *Psychology and Alchemy,* which model, on closer look, may turn out to be a centering in flight from Dionysus.

The Second Dionysus

Nilsson and Guthrie [47] have said that Greek myths are described according to the personal bias of the writer and according to the spiritual horizons of a period. Dionysus, a most paradoxical figure, offers commentators upon him a variety of perspectives and attributes. Which of these we choose to make our starting-point for understanding the "Dionysian experience" reveals, according to Guthrie, the writer's essential concern as much as it reveals the god's essence.

For instance, Nietzsche stresses the ecstatic, excessive, barbarian, titanic, even criminal aspects; Harrison, who considers herself in this regard a disciple of Nietzsche (Preface to the second edition of *Themis*), takes the suffering, intoxicated Dionysus first, but identifies him with Bergson's instinctual life force; Kerényi seems to go also along this path, pointing again and again to the wine, the vegetative life and zoe; Nilsson lays stress upon the child; Rohde emphasized the connection with Hades, the mysteries and the cult of souls; Otto places the madness foremost but takes it as the expression of an inner antithesis: Dionysus, the god who holds life and death together; Grant considers him the "irresistible irrational" and integrates the tales and cult of him around this perspective; Dodds and Guthrie place freedom and joy in the foreground, forgetting oneself, one's station, one's differences; Jeanmaire combines joy with festivals, wine, and an agrarian cult of the people by means of an archaic tree or vegetation cult. One could also start with the god's non-heroic bisexuality, or with his *thiasos,* i.e., he does not appear alone, but is a god with a community.

---

47. Cf. "Dionysus and Bisexual Consciousness" in my *The Myth of Analysis* for references and quotations from Nilsson, Guthrie, and other authors mentioned in this paragraph.

Jung stresses dismemberment and draws attention to the dismembered Dionysus in the following additional passages so far not mentioned here: CW7: 113 (2nd. ed.); CW8: 162; CW11: 53, 387, 400; CW14: 365, 259n. In these passages, Dionysus emerges less contaminated with Wotan, though Nietzsche still hovers in the background as exemplary of dismemberment, for it was with the dismembered Zagreus-Dionysus that Nietzsche was identified, signing himself "Zagreus" in his later letters.[48] In CW7: 113 (2nd. ed.), Jung writes of the "divine punishment of being torn asunder like Zagreus," still with Nietzsche in view, "This was what Nietzsche experienced at the onset of his malady. Enantiodromia means being torn asunder into pairs of opposites."

But then dismemberment loses the background of Nietzsche and even of the rending by the opposites, and begins to take on a wider archetypal significance. Jung writes, "The classical world thought of this pneuma as Dionysus, particularly the suffering Dionysus Zagreus, whose divine substance is distributed throughout the whole of nature";[49] "...so his worshippers tore wild animals to pieces in order to reintegrate his dismembered spirit."[50] In Aion,[51] dismemberment is again placed against the background of the Neoplatonic Dionysus: "The divine powers imprisoned in bodies are nothing other then *Dionysus dispersed in matter.*" Thus, dismemberment becomes a way of discovering the *puer* spirit, for "Dionysus, youngest of the gods" belongs to the theme of the "renewal of the ageing god."[52]

The movement between the first and second view of dismemberment compares with crossing a psychic border between seeing the god from outside or from within his cosmos. In this respect, Dodds speaks of white and black Maenadism, and Kerényi writes, "The God sends his madness, the dark counter-image of the Dionysian, not to his devotees who give themselves to his miracle, but to his enemies who defend themselves against him."[53] Although misperceptions of the god through Wotan may

48. CW11: 142.

49. CW11: 378.

50. Ibid., 400.

51. CW9.2: 158n.

52. CW14: 379.

53. Karl Kerényi, *Griechische Miniaturen* (Zurich: Rhein-Verlag, 1957), 133 (my translation); for Dodds's references and a longer discussion of black and white Maenadism

well produce the darker side, there is no surety that upon entering his cosmos all shall be well. As Dionysus supposedly comes into civilized Greece from "borderlands" (Thrace, Asia-Minor, Crete, Egypt), so, as Kerényi says: "where Dionysus appears, there appears also the border."[54] The Dionysian experience thus refers to a borderline state in which the black and white aspects of dismemberment meet.

If we leave the "malady" of Nietzsche as our model for dismemberment, we may also leave the view of it as only rending by opposites and violent enantiodromia. Instead, we may understand the violence in a new light. If we take our clues from Jung's exploration of the theme in alchemy ("The visions of Zosimos," CW13), dismemberment refers to a psychological process that requires a *body metaphor.*[55] The process of division is presented as a body experience, even as a horrifying torture. If, however, dismemberment is ruled by the archetypal dominant of Dionysus, then the process, while beheading or dissolving the central control of the old king, may be at the same time activating the pneuma that is distributed throughout the materializations of our complexes. The background of the second Dionysus offers new insight into the rending pain of self-division, especially as a body experience.

Jung reminds us that Dionysus was called the divided one.[56] His dismemberment was evidence of his divisibility into parts. In each part he lived as the pneuma dispersed in matter. Bits of the Dionysian spirit are like sparks shining in the *terra foetida,*[57] or rotten stench of the decaying body as it dissociates into pieces. We experience this process in psychosomatic symptoms, in hysterical conversions, in specific sadomasochistic perversions, in cancer fantasies, in fears of ageing, in horror of pollution, or in disintegrative incoherent conditions that have a body focus. This experience has its other side. The dismemberment of central control is at the same time the resurrection of the natural light of archetypal consciousness distributed in each of the organs.

Jung describes this organ consciousness in a footnote on Joyce's "visceral thinking" in *Ulysses:* "an *abaissement du niveau mental* constellates what

---

and the "border" question, see "Dionysus Re-Imagined" in my *The Myth of Analysis.*
    54. Ibid.
    55. CW12: 530 (2nd. ed.); CW1: 89; CW14: 64.
    56. CW14: p. 259n.
    57. CW14: 64.

Wernicke calls the 'organ-representatives,' i.e., symbols representing the organs."[58] The context for this remark is the *leitmotif* of body parts—kidneys, genitals, heart, lungs, esophagus, etc.—in each of the chapters of *Ulysses.*[59]

From this perspective of dismemberment, our rending can be understood as the particular kind of renewal presented by Dionysus. This renewal describes itself by means of a body metaphor. The renewal that goes by way of dismemberment is not a reassembly of parts into another organization. It is not a movement from integration to disintegration to reintegration. Perhaps it is better to envision this renewal not as a process at all. Rather, the crucial experience would be the awareness of the parts *as parts* distinct from each other, dismembered, each with its own light, a state in which the body becomes conscious of itself as a composite of differences. The scintillae and fishes' eyes of which Jung speaks in regard to the multiple consciousness of the psyche[60] may be experienced as embedded in physical expressions. The distribution of Dionysus through matter may be compared with the distribution of consciousness through members, organs, and zones.

Freud, who began his construction of psychology on the base of hysteria, used this kind of Dionysian metaphor. The *zoe*, the child, and the bisexuality that are Dionysus reappear metaphorically in erogenous zones and in the polymorphous perverse child described by Freud. Adler, too, went in this direction when deriving character from organ inferiority. The structure of each individual's consciousness was intimately linked with the psychic representatives of particular organs. Ultimately, renewal (cure) for both Freud and Adler find an archetypal background in the second Dionysus of Jung. Conceptual fantasies such as "visceral thinking," "erogenous zones," and "organ inferiority" refer on another level to the psychoid Dionysus. Here, we make a distinction between *zoe*, or life force of the body, and the pneuma of that life force. By attributing a "god" to *zoe*, the life force is given psychic interiority and a specific kind of consciousness which might partly be characterized as an awareness of self-divisibility into many parts.

---

58. *CW* 15: 112 and note.

59. That each organ has a "psychic representative" is also mentioned in *CW* 12: 440 (2nd ed.).

60. *CW* 14: 42ff., esp. 64; *CW* 8: 388ff.

Finally, if we draw the implications fully, dismemberment becomes necessary for awakening the consciousness of the body. The second Dionysus in Jung's work gives to the first Nietzschean "Dionysian experience" another meaning than Wotanic eruption and disintegration. It means an initiation into the archetypal consciousness of the body. Through Dionysus, the body may be re-appreciated as a metaphorical field and not only in behavioral interaction with the world of other bodies. Dismemberment severs the only natural connections, the habitual ways we have "grown up" and "grown together." It disconnects the body's habits at the animal-vegetable level, releasing a subtler appreciation of the members and organs as *psychic representations*. Religions speak of the resurrection of the flesh and the construction of the subtle body.

This movement seems possible only when the dominant organization lets go its hold. The *abaissement du niveau mental* results in the activation of the psychic life of the organs. Or, perhaps, these events occur in reverse order: Dionysus constellates through the dissolution into parts, thereby bringing about what we subsequently call a lowering of the mental level. The ageing god we call "ego" loses his support in the body's organization as it dissociates. The Dionysian experience would then be essential for understanding what Jung meant with the fundamental dissociability of the psyche and its multiple consciousness. It also becomes clearer how this experience and that of the mandala tend to exclude each other, since the latter would integrate what the former would loosen.

Dionysus was called *Lysios*, the loosener. [61] The word is cognate with *lysis*, the last syllables of *analysis*. *Lysis* means loosening, setting free, deliverance, dissolution, collapse, breaking bonds and laws, and the final unraveling as of a plot in tragedy.

Returning now to *Psychology and Alchemy*, [62] we may conclude that the voice's declaration "Everything must be ruled by the light" may be understood in two ways. (Therapeutic considerations would not play a part in determining between the two ways, since Jung presents the material there not as a case but as empirical evidence for the centering process. [63] On the one hand, the light may mean changing conscious-

---

61. See "Lysios," in W. H. Roscher, *Ausführliches Lexikon der griechischen und römischen Mythologie* (Hildesheim: Olms, 1965), 2: 2212.

62. *CW* 12: 117f. (2nd ed.).

63. Ibid., 45.

ness through opposites, where the active intervention of the intellect, the symbols of the self and the mandala become the counterpoise to the Wotanic experience. As Jung's intention is to present precisely this kind of centering imagery, the light is understood in this way.

On the other hand, the light may mean the light of nature, and changing consciousness through sames where like works upon like. Then fragmentation would be imagined not from within the viewpoint of centering, but from within Dionysian consciousness itself working within dissolution. The dispersed pneuma of the second Dionysus that emerges through dissolution would be the light called for by the voice, implying the *lysis* of the Dionysian experience.

I suggest that if we miss the possibilities for light in experiences of dissolution, we then tend to emphasize, as a defensive compensation, centering and wholeness. So, it has seemed to me useful to work out this Dionysian background to the important idea of wholeness in Jungian thought.

꧁꧂

2

ATHENE, ANANKE, AND THE NECESSITY OF ABNORMAL PSYCHOLOGY

> *Not even a god can cope with Necessity.*
> —Plato, *Laws*, 818*b*

The "Infirmitas" of the Archetype

Fundamental to depth psychology and to the soul is hurt, affliction, disorder, peculiarity—"abnormal psychology" or "psychopathology." Depth psychology was called into existence as a treatment for abnormal psychology. Depth psychology was, and remains, a *logos* for the *pathos* of the psyche. By "psychopathology" I mean the category of psychic events publicly and/or privately declared abnormal and which cannot be altogether repressed, transformed, or accepted. These intolerable aspects show themselves paradigmatically in the symptom that Freud said is the starting point of depth psychology.[1] But I would like to extend our concept of psychopathology by introducing the term *pathologizing* by which I mean the psyche's autonomous ability to create illness, morbidity, disorder, abnormality, and suffering in any aspect of its behavior, and to experience and imagine life through this deformed and afflicted perspective.

In two long essays[2] on psychopathology I have attempted to refute the contemporary denials of it in various branches of therapy. The nominalism of psychiatry considers its terms contingent, without necessary

---

Presented at the Eranos Conference, August 1974, and published as "On the Necessity of Abnormal Psychology" in *Eranos Yearbook* 43 (1974). Reprinted, with revisions made in 2007 included here, in *Facing the Gods*, edited by James Hillman (Thompson, Conn.: Spring Publications, 2022 [1988]).

1. *NIL*, 78, par. 31.

2. "On Psychological Language," in my *The Myth of Analysis: Three Essays in Archetypal Psychology* (Evanston, Ill.: Northwestern University Press, 1972), and "Pathologizing," in my *Re-Visioning Psychology* (New York: Harper & Row, 1975).

relation to causes or to the souls of those exhibiting that to which the terms point. Political reformers and existentialists find the field itself fundamentally unnecessary, an accident of historical, social, or political institutions. Humanistic, transcendental, and Oriental therapies assume the primacy of spirit, self, health, so that psychopathology has only secondary illusory reality. Psychopathology is thus contingent, accidental, accessory: all deny the necessity of abnormality.

Medical and religious approaches interpret psychopathology as something wrong (sick or sinful). They either physicalize or metaphysicalize (moralize). They look for the necessity of abnormal psychology outside the psyche, either to a theory of physical disorder in general (disease) or to a religious doctrine concerning suffering. Neither start with psyche. Pathologizing is still not a necessity of the soul.

In contrast, we have tried to base pathologizing wholly within the psyche and to show its necessity for the psyche. We made this move by grounding pathologizing within the archetype. Then we showed that when we do start with psyche, as in alchemy, the art of memory, and mythology, we find pathologized events inherent to these psychological systems. Both Freud and Jung adhere to this third, psychological line in their thoughts about psychopathology. From the beginning they connected it with fantasy images and viewed it mythologically.

Starting with psyche means to take pathologizing to be a valid form of psychological expression, as an underived, metaphorical language, one of the ways the psyche legitimately and spontaneously presents itself. To understand this language, we place it within similar metaphorical contexts. An obscene, bizarre, or afflicted event or image in our psychic life needs to be examined, not in terms of norms derived from physical "nature" or from metaphysical "ideals," but in terms of the imagination where withered arms, blighted crops, monstrous dwarfs, and every sort of "distortion" belong and have significance in themselves, just as they are. To understand what an individual's abnormal psychology is saying, we may not turn to what is "normal." Our norms must be like the stuff we wish to understand, norms that are themselves pathologized.

Here we take our cue from Jung: "The gods have become diseases."[3] Jung is indicating that the formal cause of our complaints and abnormali-

---

3. CW 13: 54.

ties are mythical persons; our psychic illnesses are not *imaginary* but *imaginal* (Corbin). They are indeed fantasy illnesses, the suffering of fantasies, of mythical realities, the incarnation of archetypal events.

Following Jung along this path is the main work of archetypal therapy. We have looked at the myths and the implications for abnormal psychology—of Eros and Psyche, of Dionysus, of such figures as the *puer aeternus*, Saturn and *senex*, the child, Hades and the Underworld. In these different examples we saw that the pathological is inherent to the mythical. Our deepest intention has been to move psychopathology, the basis of our field, from a positivistic nineteenth-century system of mind and its disorders to a nonagnostic, mythopeic psychopathology of the archetype.

Essential to the move is the recognition of the gods as themselves pathologized, the "infirmities of the archetype." Without elaborating what is familiar to you, I think the main point is made if we recognize that Greek myths (and those of the Celts or the Hindus,[4] the Egyptians or the American Indians) require the odd, peculiar, extreme—the abnormal psychology of the gods.[5]

---

4. Cf. David Kingsley, "'Through the Looking Glass': Divine Madness in the Hindu Religious Tradition," *History of Religion* 13, no. 4 (1974): 270–305.

5. In stressing the pathologized aspect of the imaginal, I am aware of diverging here from the view of Henry Corbin who is the founder of the term "imaginal" and to whom my work is, and will forever remain, profoundly indebted. Corbin considers the imaginary of "the fantastic, the horrible, the monstrous, the macabre, the miserable, and the absurd" to reflect secularization of the imaginal: "In contrast, the art and imagination of Islamic culture in its traditional form are characterized by the hieratic, by seriousness, gravity, stylization, and significance" (Henry Corbin, "Mundus Imaginalis, or the Imaginary and the Imaginal," *Spring: An Annual of Archetypal Psychology and Jungian Thought* [1972]: 16). Clearly, pathologizings of the image do *not* belong to the *mundus imaginalis* as he has given us this word. But in the soul-making of actual psychotherapy, pathologizings are often the *via regia* into the imaginal. Here we follow Jung for whom there was no image that could not become the vehicle of active imagination and the movement of consciousness to mythic depths. In fact, the more irksome the image, the more likely it was a symbol mobilizing precisely those mythic depths. Just these perverse thoughts, obscene words, obsessive fears and memories are the *materia prima*. Each beginning is with "the macabre, the miserable, and the absurd." And we return to the *materia prima* with each new move of the psyche. The difference between Jung and Corbin can be resolved here if we practice Jung's technique with Corbin's vision, that is, active imagination is not for the sake of the doer

From this mythical point of view, each archetype has its pathologized themes, and each pathologized event has an archetypal perspective. The norms of myth give place for what cannot find place in academic psychology, medicine, and religion. Moreover, the pathologizing in a myth is *necessary* to the myth and cannot be excised without deforming the myth. For this very heuristic, therapeutic reason, archetypal psychology reverts to mythology.

The figures of myth—quarreling, cheating, sexually obsessed, revenging, vulnerable, killing, torn apart—show that the gods are not only perfections so that all normalities can fall only on humans. The mythemes in which the gods appear are replete with behavior that, from the secular standpoint, must be classified under criminal pathology, moral monstrosity, or personality disorders.

When we think mythologically about pathologizing, we could say, as some have, that the "world of the gods" is anthropomorphic, an imitative projection of ours, including our pathologies. But one could start as well from the other end, the *mundus imaginalis* of the archetypes (or gods), and say that our "secular world" is at the same time mythical, an imitative projection of theirs, including their pathologies. What the gods do in an imaginal realm of myth is reflected in our imagination as fantasy. Our fantasies reflect theirs, our behavior only mimetic to theirs. We can imagine nothing or perform nothing that is not already formally given by the archetypal imagination of the gods. If we assume that the necessary is that which occurs among the gods, i.e., that myths describe necessary patterns, then their pathologizings are necessary, and ours are necessary to the mimesis of theirs. Since their *infirmitas* is essential to their complete configuration, it follows that our individual completion requires our pathologizings.

If so, we are as much in harmony with the archetypal realm when afflicted as when in beatific states of transcendence. Man is as much in the image of the gods and goddesses when he is ludicrous, enraged, or tortured, as when he smiles. Since the gods themselves show *infirmitas,* one path of the *imitatio dei* is through infirmity. Furthermore, it is this *infirmitas* of the archetype that can be nurse to our wounds and

---

and *our* actions in the sensible world of literal realities, but for the sake of the images and to where they can take us—*their* realization.

extremities, providing a style, a justification, and a sense of significance for ours.

What I am asking you to entertain is the idea of the sickness in the archetype[6]—and this is not the same as the archetype of sickness. That latter approach to abnormality is that of a single scapegoat archetype, a morbid principle like thanatos, a sickness demon, a devil or shadow, who carries the evil[7] so that the others may remain supremely ideal. That approach enucleates the core of pathologizing intrinsic to each archetypal figure and necessary to that figure's way of being. Whereas our approach tries to understand pathologizing as an inherent component of every archetypal complexity, which has its own blind, destructive, and morbid possibility. Death is fundamental to each pattern of being, even if the gods do not die. They are *athnetos,* which implies that the *infirmitas* they present is also eternal. Each archetype has a way of leading into death, and thus has its own bottomless depth so causing our sicknesses to be fundamentally unfathomable.

To express this *infirmitas* of the archetype theologically we would say that Original Sin is accounted for by the sin in the Originals. Humans are made in the images of the gods, and our abnormalities image the original abnormalities of the gods that come before ours, making pos-

---

6. By "archetype" I can refer only to the phenomenal archetype, that which manifests itself in images. The noumenal archetype *per se* cannot by definition be presented so that nothing whatsoever can be posited of it. In fact, whatever one does say about the archetype *per se* is a conjecture already governed by an archetypal image. This means that the archetypal image precedes and determines the metaphysical hypothesis of a noumenal archetype. So, let us apply Occam's razor to Kant's *noumenon.* By stripping away this unnecessary theoretical encumbrance to Jung's notion of archetype we restore full value to the archetypal image. Cf. my "An Inquiry into Image," *Spring: An Annual of Archetypal Psychology and Jungian Thought* (1977): 70.

7. Our polytheistic psychology has no one Devil to whom all destructive processes belong: "The Greeks have no category of divinities generally recognized as essentially malignant, no real Devil or devils." (Arthur Darby Nock, "The Cult of Heroes," *Harvard Theological Review* 37 [1944]: 172). In this view the shadow is not a separated archetype, but is archetypal, i.e., an ontological distinction within the gods themselves, always with them, never cast down into the human world only. Each god contains shadow and casts it according with how he or she shapes a cosmos. Each god is a way in which we are shadowed.

sible ours. We can only do in time what gods do in eternity. Our infirmities will therefore have to have their ground in primordial infirmity, and their infirmities are enacted in our psychopathologies. If those concerned with the plight of religion would restore it to health and bring its god back to life, a first measure in this resuscitation would be to take back from the Devil all the pathologies heaped on his head. If God has died, it was because of his own good health; he had lost touch with the intrinsic *infirmitas* of the archetype.

Necessity

I have submitted that pathologized events participate in the archetype itself. They are a *via* to archetypal experience that cannot be experienced fully otherwise. This implies that pathologized events belong to the archetype necessarily. Consequently, they are necessary to our lives.

But what is Necessity? In search of answers to this question we shall be elaborating this main point: *Necessity in Greek mythical thought is spoken of and experienced in pathologized modes.* Pathologized experiences are often connected directly with Ananke (Necessity).[8] Let us look in more detail at this connection.

In his exhaustive monograph, Heinz Schreckenberg[9] reviews all the proposed etymologies and contexts of *ananke* and comes to the conclusion that the word in Homer is borrowed from a probable semitic root *chananke* based on three consonants, *hnk.* We can layout Schreckenberg's findings as follows:

Old Egypt.	*hnk*	narrow
Old Egypt.	*hnk*	throat
Old Egypt.	*enek*	surround, embrace, strangle
Coptic	*chalak*	ring
Akkadian	*hanaqu*	constrict, strangle; to wind tightly around the neck like the neckband of a slave
Syriac	*hnk*	chain, suffocation
Hebrew	*anāk*	chainformed necklace (Song of Songs 4:9; Proverbs 1:9)

---

8. E.g., Empedocles, fr. 115, where exile, wandering, and being ceaselessly buffeted by elemental forces result from Necessity.

9. H. Schreckenberg, *Ananke: Untersuchungen zur Geschichte des Wortgebrauchs* (Zetemata, 36) (Munich: Beck, 1961).

Chaldean	hanakin	fetters laid on the necks of prisoners
Arabic	hanaqa	strangle
Arabic	hannāka	necklace
Arabic	iznāk	the cord binding yoked oxen

His evidence[10] extends far further than this digest and it tallies with more usual etymologies of *ananke*, relating it with the German *eng* (narrow), with angina, *angst*, and anxiety, with *agchein* (Greek), to strangle, and with *agham* (Sanscrit), evil.[11] Even Plato's etymology (*Cratylus* 420c–d) imagines *ananke* by means of a metaphor of narrowing. "The idea," says Plato, "is taken from walking through a ravine which is impassable, and rugged, and overgrown, and impedes motion—and this is the derivation of the word necessary."

Schreckenberg places particular stress upon the yoke/collar/noose meanings of his etymology, leaving no doubt that, at core, necessity means a physically oppressive tie of servitude to an inescapable power.[12]

The Latin for *ananke* is *necessitas*. Here, too, we find the notion of a "close tie" or "close bond" such as the bond of kinship, blood relationship. *Necessitudines* are "persons with whom one is closely connected, relatives, connections, friends.[13] A *necessaria* is a female relative or friend. As well, this word refers to natural and moral ties between persons. This suggests that the family relationships and the ties we have in our personal worlds are ways in which we experience the force of necessity. Our attempts to

---

10 Ibid., 169–74.

11. Liddell and Scott, *A Greek-English Lexicon* (Oxford: Clarendon Press, 1964); Richard Broxton Onians, *The Origins of European Thought* (Cambridge: Cambridge University Press, 1954), 332.

12. Schreckenberg, 176, with photographic Appendix of prisoners and slaves with cords around their necks. The special emphasis, which Schreckenberg lays upon the yoke and slave's collar in his etymology, opens a perspective toward the perplexing question of slavery in the same antique cultures from where he draws his etymology. Following his line of thought joining servitude with necessity, slavery becomes *eo ipso* justified, even implied, by the word necessity itself. (The jailhouse in Athens and Thebes was called *anankaion*.) Slavery might then even have been experienced as an operation of Ananke, part of the way of all things, a founding principle of universal order. My point here is not to justify slavery, but to suggest that archetypal ideas, persons, and myths, such as Ananke, are determinants in social attitudes and structures.

13. Onians, 333n.; Lewis and Short, *A Latin Dictionary* (Oxford: Clarendon Press, 1894).

be free of personal binds are attempts at escaping from the tight circle of *ananke.* That patients in therapy complain that they suffocate in the family circle, or that they are strangled by their marriage partner, or fall victim to pathologizings in throat and neck all bespeak Necessity. From this perspective the family complex is a manifestation of Necessity, and servitude to kinship ties is a way of observing her demands.

Let us turn now to *ananke* in poetic, mythological, and philosophical contexts.

First, we must recognize the central place that this goddess Ananke held in the imagination of cosmology-makers. For Parmenides (frs. 8 and 10) Ananke governs Being; for the Atomists, too, though differently.[14] In so-called Pythagorean and Orphic thought Ananke was mated with a great serpent Chronos, forming a kind of binding coil around the universe (Onians, 332). Time and Necessity set limits to all the possibilities of our outward extension, of our worldly reaches. Together they form a syzygy, an archetypal pair, inherently related, so that where one is the other is too. When we are under the compulsion of Necessity, we experience it in terms of time, e.g., the chronic complaints, the repeated return of the same enclosing and fettering complexes, the anxiety occasioned by the shortness of our days, our daily duties, our "deadlines." To be free of time is to be free of necessity. To have free time constellates a fantasy of free-from-necessity. As the physical yoke of slavery is the concrete image within the idea of necessity, so the freedom from this yoke expresses itself in fantasies of free time and leisure as a paradisiacal happiness without pathology.

The dependency of all things upon the chaining limits of Necessity is expressed in another, milder, image in Orphic cosmology. The idea that Zeus rules the world through close collaboration with *Ananke* (Euripides, *Alcestis,* 978f.) is turned by Orphism into the image of Zeus and his wet nurse Adrasteia, another name for Ananke.[15] She is his wet nurse and, by suckling at the breast of Necessity, he draws his power and wisdom with that milk. In some contexts his nurse Adrasteia is his daughter, so that the bind is expressed in the close tie of kinship, of family obligation,

---

14. Schreckenberg, 114ff. For a discussion of *ananke* in Leucippos and Democritus.

15. Schreckenberg, 133; W.H. Roscher, *Ausführliches Lexikon der griechischen und römischen Mythologie* (Hildesheim: Olms, 1965), "Necessitas."

even of incestuous love. This Orphic image reveals the possibility of a loving and nourishing connection with Necessity. Here the relation with her power is imagined less as oppressive servitude than as dependency upon the milk of the daughter-mother soul.[16]

The image of Zeus and Adrasteia-Ananke presents the idea of *amor fati*, a paradoxical conjunction of what many philosophers conceived to be opposites (Empedocles, fr. 115: Charis and Ananke;[17] Agathon in *Symposium*, 195c). Macrobius (*Saturnalia*, 1.19.17) says that two of the four powers present at birth are Eros and Ananke, and they are paired. Eros is the kiss; and Ananke, the knot or tie. Later, and in some detail, we shall see the pair again opposed as Peitho and Bia (persuasion and force).[18]

The tragedians, however, had recourse to *ananke* when things were at their worst. Aeschylus's Prometheus says:

> Oh woe is me!
> I groan for the present sorrow,
> I groan for the sorrow to come, I groan
> questioning when there shall come a time
> when He shall ordain a limit to my sufferings.
> What am I saying? *I have known all before,*
> *all that shall be, and clearly known;* to me,
> nothing that hurts shall come with a new face.

---

16. Cf. "Of Milk" in *UE* 3: *Senex & Puer.*

17. On the relation of Love (Philotes) and Strife (Neikos) in Empedocles, see Denis O'Brien, *Empedocles' Cosmic Cycle* (Cambridge: Cambridge University Press, 1969), 104–27. Paul Friedländer, *Plato,* translated by Hans Meyerhoff (Princeton, N.J.: Princeton University Press, 1969), 3: 362 and note, makes clear the identity of Love with Aphrodite-Charis and Strife with Ananke. (That Necessity works through discord and strife, and that discord and strife are necessary, is also a psychological lesson we learn from these mythological relations.) Ultimately Aphrodite and Ananke become interchangeable: they can both create Eros and can both appear through Nemesis (revenge). We experience this identity particularly in the immovable fixations of love. Parmenides expressed this psychological experience in metaphysical language, W. K. C. Guthrie, *A History of Greek Philosophy* (Cambridge: Cambridge University Press, 1965), 2: 62; F. M. Cornford, *From Religion to Philosophy* (New York: Harper Torchbook, 1957), 222–23.

18. Bia and Ananke are interchangeable terms and figures (*Paulys Real-Encyclopaedie der classischen Altertumswissenschaft,* edited by Georg Wissowa [Stuttgart: J.B. Metzler], 3: 379–80). *Peitho* was another name for Aphrodite who was worshipped in that form (Roscher, "Peitho," 1796–1804).

> So must I bear, as lightly as I can,
> the destiny that fate has given me;
> for I know well against necessity,
> against its strength, no one can fight and win.[19]

Note the repetitiveness of this suffering: "nothing that hurts shall come with a new face." This is a quality of *ananke*-caused affliction. It is not shock and surprise at the unexpected but the chronic, repetitious complaint.

Prometheus Bound opens with Prometheus being tied and nailed at the limits of the world under the constraint of Necessity. It is as if at the very edges of existence, gone as far outward as possible, he meets the greater might and violence (Bia) of Necessity and there he is nailed. Only Necessity can limit the Promethean fantasy, and necessity is experienced by that fantasy as an anguish.

Again in Aeschylus (*The Persians*) when the Queen has been "struck down by disasters exceeding speech and question" (290) the word "necessity" comes to her lips. The idea that it is useless to speak against necessity appears also in Euripides (*Phoenician Maidens*). At the very end Oedipus says (1762f.): "Yet what boots it thus to wail? What profits vainly to lament? Whoso is but mortal must bear the necessity of heaven." Again this opposition between persuasive speech and implacable force.

Euripides (*Bacchae*, 89) uses the term *anagkaisi* for physical anguish. To be in pain, torment, suffering is to be in anguish, in straits (*Einengung*), in need or necessity. The archetypal sufferer, Sophocles's Philoctetes, whose wound cannot heal, cries out in pain, and the word the Chorus uses for this pain is *anangas, anangan* (206, 215). Being caught or forced by necessity is expressed concretely as *being in the hands* of another power (Schreckenberg, 45); e.g., when Apollo seizes baby Hermes, or Hercules grabs the snakes in his cradle, the physical pressure, the squeeze, is *ananke.*

But perhaps the most telling description of *ananke* is given by Euripides in his *Alcestis* (962ff.) when the Chorus says:

> I myself, in the transports
> of mystic verses, as in study
> of history and science, have found

---

19. Lines 96–104; translated by David Grene, *Aeschylus II* (Chicago: The University of Chicago Press, 1956), italics added.

nothing so strong as Compulsion [*Anagkas*],
nor any means to combat her,
not in the Thracian books set down
in verse by the school of Orpheus,
not in all the remedies Phoebus has given the heirs
of Asclepius to fight the many afflictions of man.
She alone is a goddess
without altar or image to pray
before. She heeds no sacrifice. [20]

Here Ananke is the Great Lady (*potnia*) of the Underworld, the invisible psychic principle that irreversibly draws all things to her, thereby pathologizing life. Only Hades is similarly spoken of as "without altar or image to pray before." [21] Orphic thought did make this straight-out identity of Ananke with the Underworld Queen, Persephone (Schreckenberg, 70n.). [22] Her name has been translated to mean "bringer of destruction," so that the process of pathologizing can be understood as a mode of moving the psyche (in this particular drama the soul image is presented in the figure, Alcestis) toward the underworld. That this movement from life to death is heroically stopped by Hercules also belongs to the theme explored in detail in *The Dream and the Underworld*.

May I draw your attention to the fact that in the *Alcestis* passage the language for dealing with *ananke* is that of therapy: remedies of Asclepius—and there are none. Nor are mysticism, orphicism, history, science, a match for her force. Is this because she has no image, no altar to pray before? Here it is suggested that not only is Necessity beyond the reach of speech, but further, that necessity is experienced when one is compelled and there is no image of what is occurring. It is as if there were a relation—even an inverse proportion—between images and drivenness: the more the image and altar, the less the blind necessity. The more the compulsion, the less we are able to sacrifice, to connect our personal compulsion with something divine.

---

20. Lines 962–75; translated by Richmond Lattimore, *Euripides* (Chicago: The University of Chicago Press, 1955). For textual comments on this passage, see Euripides, *Alcestis*, edited by A.M. Dale (Oxford: Clarendon Press, 1954), 119–21.

21. Cf. my *The Dream and the Underworld* (New York: Harper & Row, 1979), 27ff.

22. Roscher, "Necessitas," 71, reports that Ananke is associated with Persephone on two graves.

This inverse proportion is a signal idea in Jung's notion of the archetype. There is a red compulsive end and a blue imaginative one. As the
red is the body of the blue, the blue is the image of the red. Without
images, we are more blind for we have not been able to imagine the force
that drives us. With images, the *necessity appears inherent to the image itself.*
This shifts the compulsion from the red to the blue. We recognize that
compulsion is essential to the very nature of the image and that what
drives us are images.

The relationship between necessity and images can also be put this
way: Necessity seizes us through images. An image has its own inherent
necessity, so that the form an image takes "cannot be otherwise—whether
when we paint, move a line of verse, or when we dream. An image exists
in its specific epiphany and course of behavior (the compulsion of necessity that Jung calls "instinct").

Because the force of the image is inseparable from the image, it is
spoken of as unimaged. Necessity has no image because it works in each
and every image. We must not take this unimaged force literally and
metaphysically, as if archetypes were in themselves unimaged, unknow-
able, and transcendent to their appearances. The unimaged power of the
image is right in the image itself: the archetype is wholly immanent in
its image. This unimaged power gives an image its compelling effect and
the implacable law of its precise forming. This *inexorability of the image* is
none other than Necessity who, as the Alcestis passage says, is herself
"without image."

Thus fantasy is no carefree daydream, but the implacable carrier of
the necessities that drive us. Psychic reality is enslaved to imagination.
Imagination does not free us but captures us and yokes us to its myths;
we are workers for its Kings and Queens. We are tied in blood with
what Jung calls our "instinctual images." To insist, as Jung does, that
human reality is primarily psychic and that the image is the primordial
and immediate presentation of this reality requires a further recognition.
Reality is only so if it is necessary. To use the word "reality" implies an
ontological condition that cannot be otherwise. Therefore there must
be something unalterably necessary about images so that psychic reality, which first of all consists in images, cannot be mere after-images of
sense impressions. Images are primordial, archetypal, in themselves ultimate reals, the only direct reality that the psyche experiences. As such
they are the shaped presences of necessity.

Personally, experientially, this implies that when we search for what is implacably determining our lives and holding them in servitude, we must turn to the images of our fantasies within which necessity lies concealed. Furthermore, this implies that we must beware of being too "active" with our images, moving them around to redeem our problems. Then the practice of active imagination would become an attempt to dodge the necessity of the image and its claim upon the soul.

Even if Necessity is said to be unimaged, there does belong to this great goddess, who is at the same time a metaphysical principle, a cluster of particular metaphors which tell us how she works her ways. Since she refers to the binding, encircling limits,[23] we find that bonds and ties, the ring,[24] cord, noose, collar, knot, spindle, wreath, harness, and yoke[25] are ways of speaking of the rule of *ananke*. So, too, is the nail. The nail driven into a figure (like Prometheus, like Christ) or into the head of a figure—Etruscan, Norse, Latin—indicates the ineluctable claim of necessity.[26] No way out.[27] It must be.

We may pause to reflect here upon the wreath: for instance, the crown of laurels of the poet laureate, or the garland given the victor in a competition. This acknowledgement also implies a binding obligation, a necessity to be that for which one has been crowned.[28] The wreath is the yoke and collar of the brow. The singer must go on singing, once the laurel has been placed around his head. The acknowledgement, moreover, sets limits to the range and possibility of one's powers. Recognition binds one's soul to a specific destiny.

---

23. The subject of encircling limits in Homer and after has been treated exhaustively in Onians, "Peirata," 310–42. It is mainly in that chapter that we find Onians's discussion of *ananke*.

24. Cf. Schreckenberg, 144.

25. Cf. Aeschylus, *Agamemnon* 218.

26. Particularly a steel nail (Horace, *Odes* 1.35.17ff; 3.24.5ff., where it is Tyche (chance) who drives the nails into the scalp of her victims). Euripides, *Alcestis* 979, for a steel image in connection with Necessity.

27. Cf. Schreckenberg, 41, on the relation between Necessity and the "ausweglose Situation."

28. "In being crowned as a singer...he is bound with a particular fate, obligation as well as power." Onians, 407 n.1; 376: "Attention was paid to the head because it contained the *psyche*." Also, 444–51.

We have been concerned mainly with the *person* and *images* of Necessity. The *idea* of necessity receives further elaboration from philosophers. Philosophy has generally considered necessity in two different ways. Sometimes philosophers speak of it as lawless chance (like the Greek *tyche*), as a principle of randomness, blind, mechanical, statistical, pointless. Other times they take the converse position, relating necessity with the regular, predictable, and *gesetzmässig*. Arguments about necessity often lead into pitched philosophical battles between determinism versus free will, or physis versus spirit.

Philosophers define necessity succinctly: "nicht-anders-sein-können" or in the words of Thomas Aquinas "quod non potest non esse" (that which cannot not be). In Aristotle, necessity is brought into relation with "compulsion," just as at the opening of *Prometheus Bound* Necessity appears together with Bia (Force or Compulsion). This same pairing was observed at Corinth according to Pausanias (2.4.6), for in that city Ananke and Bia were honored together in a temple, access to which was forbidden. Again: no access to necessity.

Closed rigidity, inaccessibility, is precisely the feeling of Parmenides' idea of Ananke.[29] She holds his universe fast in permanence, immobility, and absoluteness, allowing no change. His immovable necessity repeats in a philosophical description the implacable *ananke* of the *Alcestis.*

When we read Parmenides psychologically, then the real events in our souls, those having true reality, are those that do not move. It is just in immobility, in the changeless fixations of our psychic cosmos, where we are bound and stuck, that necessity is operating.

Aristotle gives a few clear statements about necessity in his *Metaphysics* (1015a),[30] which have determined our thinking about it ever since. Aristotle says: "And necessity is held to be something that cannot be persuaded—and rightly, for it is contrary to the movement which accords with purpose and with reasoning." Further: "That which impedes and tends to hinder, contrary to purpose." Note here: "Contrary to purpose," which colors by definition our experience of necessary events as useless

---

29. Guthrie, 2: 35–37, 72–73.

30. I have used both translations: Hugh Tredennick (London: Heinemann, 1961) and W.D. Ross, *The Works of Aristotle,* 2nd ed. (Oxford: Clarendon Press, 1940).

and against our purposes. We usually experience our pathologizings as purposeless. We feel them to be hindrances, impediments without reason. Here we can see how well Aristotle's notion of necessity services the medical position that regards pathologizing as having no purpose, an irksome hindrance to be removed. The necessity is painful, says Aristotle, "for every necessary thing is ever irksome."[31]

We may read Aristotle, too, from an archetypal viewpoint. To us he is saying that the gods themselves, because they are necessary, are, forever plaguing us. Their irksomeness is inherent to their very necessity. They must be a bother. We must be in their service and feel their yoke. There is a Greek answer to Job: not a devil's trick or satanic force makes the divine plague our mortal life: pathologizing is given with the nature of the divine itself.

Another of Aristotle's formulations is also of special value. This is the idea that necessity works as an inexorable internal cause, as a virtue or inherent property of an event itself. "Necessity is that because of which a thing cannot be otherwise": it is that "without which" a thing cannot exist. He notes that necessity can operate as the function of the nature of a thing, rather than being only an external mechanical cause. Necessity belongs to the state or condition itself, to the very nature of an image, as we said above. An event is not only forced from without, but forced from within by its own image. As Guthrie puts this difference:

> To us, problems of causation in science are concerned with the ex-planation of sequences, chains of cause and effect linking together x and y and z. The Greek on the other hand investigated what he called "the nature of things," and asked himself "what is it in x that causes it to behave as it does?"[32]

Here Jung's archetypal theory and therapy is traditional and Greek. It asks: "What is it in the very nature of my disturbance and my affliction that is necessary, self-caused (caused by self)"? Other therapies look outside to external necessity—society, family, or other kinds of conditioning—searching to unravel necessity in the linkages between x and y and z. They ask the more technical question "how"; archetypal therapy asks

31. Lyperon = "irksome" (Ross); "disagreeable" (Tredennick); compare both with Empedocles (fr. 116) who calls Ananke "intolerable."

32. Guthrie, 2:417.

the more philosophical "what"—and eventually, the religious question "who," which god or goddess, which *daimon*, is internally at work in what is going on. Jungian therapy is therefore theophanic, in Corbin's sense. It asks the god in the disease to come to light.

It is, however, in Plato where we can find the most illuminating and explicit ideas concerning the relations between necessity and the troubles of the soul. In the *Timaeus*, Plato's cosmology or system of the universe, there are two main principles at work. The first is *nous*, the logos, or intellectual principle, reason, order, intelligibility, mind—or however else we wish to translate *nous*. The second principle is *ananke*, Necessity. The famous passage in the *Timaeus* (47e–48a) puts their relation as follows:

> Now our foregoing discourse has set forth the works wrought by the craftsmanship of Reason [*nous*]; but we must now set beside them the things that come about of Necessity [*ananke*]. For the generation of this universe was a mixed result of the combination of Necessity and Reason. Reason overruled Necessity by *persuading* [italics added] her to guide the greatest part of the things that become towards what is best; in that way and on that principle this universe was fashioned in the beginning by the victory of reasonable persuasion over Necessity. If, then, we are really to tell how it came into being on this principle, we must bring in also the Errant Cause. [33]

In this discussion, the term *archai*, first principles or starting points, occurs in various senses. Plato says that it is not fire or water or the four elements that are the true *archai*. There are two: Nous and Ananke, Reason and Necessity.

Here Necessity is characterized as the Errant Cause. Jowett translates *planoumenai aitia* as "variable cause"; Thomas Taylor, as "erratic cause;" and Plato's commentators use, for the operations of this principle, such words as: rambling, digressing, straying, irrational, irresponsible, deviating, misleading, deceiving, irregular, random. *Planos* can refer to the wanderings of the mind in madness and to the fits of a disease. Such is the way Plato speaks of *ananke*.

Necessity operates through deviations. We recognize it in the irrational, irresponsible, indirect. Or to turn it again: necessity appears in

---

33. Francis MacDonald Cornford, *Plato's Cosmology: The Timaeus of Plato* (London: Routledge, 1948), 160.

those aspects of the universe (and let us recall that the Platonic universe is wholly ensouled, always a psychic universe) that are errant. Moreover, necessity is particularly associated with that area of experience that is unable to be persuaded by or subjected to the rule of mind.

Grote called this Errant Cause "the indeterminate, the inconstant, the anomalous, that which can be neither understood nor predicted. It is Force, Movement, or Change, with the negative attribute of not being regular, or intelligible."[34] And Cornford explains: "The body of the universe...contains motions and active powers which are not instituted by the divine Reason and are perpetually producing undesirable results...these bodily motions and powers can only be attributed to an irrational element in the World-Soul."[35] Necessity resides as an internal cause in the soul and perpetually produces irksome results. These resulting irrationalities we call the deviations of abnormal psychology, and this creating activity I have called pathologizing. As Freud's "starting point," the symptom is conceived to be different from and foreign to the rational ego, so this "starting point" (archē) of Plato, the errant operation of ananke, is equally alien from the realm of reason. You may have noticed that I continue to call pathologizing a creating activity. Plato presents ananke in a similar manner. He assumes it to be an archū, a first principle not derivative of anything else. It is also a creating principle entering into the formation of the universe. And it is necessarily always there, not gradually overcome through the extension of the rule of reason. As the demiurge never wholly reduces chaos to order, so reason never wholly persuades necessity. Both are present as creating principles, always. "In the whole and in every part, Nous and Ananke cooperate; the world is a mixture resulting from this combination."[36] Or in our terms, the abnormal is mixed throughout every act of existence, for psychic life is based in the complex, and pathologizing never comes to an end.

Let me put my thesis still one more time, now through the voice of the great classicist E.R. Dodds:

> The inferior soul [in Plato's Laws] seems to stand to the good one
> in the same relation as Necessity to Mind in the Timaeus myth:

---

34. Quoted from Cornford, Plato's Cosmology, 172.
35. Ibid., 176.
36. Friedländer, Plato, 1: 205. Cornford, Plato's Cosmology, 203, makes the same point.

it is a sort of untrustworthy junior partner, liable to fits of unreasonable behavior, in which it produces "crazy and disorderly movements" (*Laws* 897d)—a phrase that recalls both the "scared and crazy movement" attributed to the souls of human infants elsewhere in the *Laws* (791a) and the "discordant and disorderly movement" of the mythical chaos in the *Timaeus* (30a). All these movements I take to be symbols, not of deliberate evil, but of irrationality, the element both in man and in the cosmos which is incompletely mastered by the rational will. [37]

This abnormal, scared, and crazy movement of the soul is not only necessary; it is Necessity itself.

When my eminent colleagues here at this Eranos Conference, Professors Sambursky, Hadot, Kirk, and Rowe, each of whose field is Greek thought, work over these same texts, they will read them in the light of their interests and persuasions. Plato is indeed speaking of their fields: cosmology, cosmogony, metaphysics, physics, philosophy in the widest sense. But Plato is also speaking of Soul[38] and therefore of psychology; so I beg indulgence to read these same passages with a psychological eye, attempting to draw insights for depth psychology and therapy of soul from what Plato says about errancy, chaos, and the necessity that is never brought fully into order. The psychological viewpoint sees Necessity and Chaos not only as *explanatory principles* in the realm of metaphysics; they are also mythic events taking place also and always in the soul, and thus they are fundamental *archai* of the human condition. To these root principles the *pathe* (or motions) of the soul can be linked. [39]

---

37. E.R. Dodds, "Plato and the Irrational," in his *The Ancient Concept of Progress* (Oxford: Clarendon Press, 1973), 116.

38. Cf. ibid., "[Plato] has projected into his conception of Nature that stubborn irrationality which he was more and more compelled to admit in man (*Tim.* 90c-d)."

39. In the *Timaeus* (48b, 52d) the four elements are spoken of as *pathē*. *Pathē* basically means a "passive state," and then secondarily, suffering, affliction. The elements are not themselves *archai*. Rather, they are modes of happening, ways of being moved, modified, affected. Cornford *Plato's Cosmology* (198n., 199) and Friedländer, *Plato* (3: 370–71) call them "qualities" of Chaos. They are the modes through which Necessity works. They are, so to speak, the elementary modes of being affected; they give four styles to the workings of the errant cause in our chaotic conditions. Or, in alchemical language, the four elements are modes of the *materia prima* and are experienced as four modes of our primal suffering. Empedocles's suffering that is ordained by Necessity is described (fr. 115) as his being buffeted from one element

Psychology has already recognized the faceless, nameless Chaos, this "scared and crazy movement" in the soul, as *anxiety*, and by naming it such, psychology has directly evoked the goddess Ananke, from whom the word anxiety derives. If anxiety truly belongs to Ananke, of course, it cannot be "mastered by the rational will." When anxiety floods us or attacks us, we can but receive it as a gap (*chaos*) in rational continuity. Hence, anxiety does not submit to analysis; it works its ways inescapably until its necessity is admitted. Why not, then, view experiences of anxiety as reflections in the depths of human being of the operations of Ananke? Psychology has tried to reduce her necessary movements to specific necessities: the drives of sexuality (Freud), the dread of death and non-being (Heidegger), original sin (Kierkegaard), or to physiological mechanisms. But no rational theory of it is possible. There is no reason for it but the necessity in it. The grounds of anxiety reside in necessity itself, as it is at this moment constellated, the necessity of this constellated image, the present *path*☐ of the soul where the soul is now scared by the necessity yoking it to its destiny.

The relation between Necessity and the human condition can be made yet more explicit if we turn to the very end of the *Republic*; Plato describes the Moirae (Fates).[40] Each soul receives its specific lot from Lachesis. Clotho then ratifies it, and by the spinning of Atropos, "the web of destiny is made irreversible." No way out. It cannot be otherwise.

---

to another; Plato sees the primal elements in their chaotic conditions as perpetually tossing (52*e*) and swaying ("perpetually in motion, coming to be in a certain place and again vanishing out of it," 52*a*). The four elements as *pathē* suggests an "elemental psychopathology" or a logos of the soul's suffering in terms of the elements. (Cf. T. S. Eliot's four modes of "death" in "Little Gidding" (*Four Quartets*). Bachelard's work presents the four elements as the fundaments of consciousness; as well they may be considered the basic qualities of pathologizing, enabling us to examine the phenomenology of images and behavior in terms of fire, air, water, and earth. This move is not meant to lead away from the concrete image into just one more fourfold system of abstraction, but rather to explore the therapeutic implications of the image, whether its possibilities belong more appropriately to fire, say, than to earth, air, or water. For the worst suffering is that of Empedocles who is tossed from element to element, belonging to none.

40. For a full and recent discussion of the Moirae (and also the other "fate goddesses"), see B. C. Dietrich, *Death, Fate and the Gods* (London: Athlone Press, 1967). On the one hand, Ananke rules the Erinys according to Orphic Hymn 69 (translated by Thomas Taylor); on the other, she is a later conceptualization of them (Dietrich, 98).

"And then," Plato goes on to say, "without a backward look it [the soul] passed beneath the throne of Necessity." Thus do souls enter the world. Each soul is born by passing under the chair of Ananke.[41] Despite the fact that Plato insists all through his works upon the affinity of the soul with *nous*, he presents Ananke in the Myth of Er as she who determines psychic life from the beginning.

As Ananke is located mythically in the middle of the universe and formally in the middle section of the *Timaeus* dialogue, so following Friedländer's suggestion, we may conceive of her locus in the human being not in the head, place of the noetic psyche, but lower down in the middle, a region of the "absolutely indefinite. Called by various names, the indefinite represents the power of unreason, chaos, and the anti-divine."[42] These central depths in Platonic physiology refer particularly to the liver.

One way of reading the wayward movements of the errant cause would be by studying livers (*Timaeus* 71a–72b) and entrails. The diviner, as Cornford points out, is the one who reads, not the rational, but the irrational and appetitive soul for insight into fate.[43] The practice of

41. For a rich discussion of "The Knees of the gods" and Ananke's spindle, see Onians, 303–9. The Myth of Er has provided a grounding image for Platonist fascination with astrology as a mode of psychology. The same Necessity governs the soul's movements as well as the motions of the stars. As souls pass beneath her seat, so on her lap turns the spindle ruling the planetary motions. What happens to soul and to Stars is on the same web. So one tries to puzzle out the compelling necessities of the soul by consulting the motions of the planets. As Paracelsus explained, a physician of pathologies cannot consider himself as such unless he has knowledge of the other half of the soul in the planetary bodies. But astrologers have taken this correspondence literally, rather than imaginally. For it is neither the actual stars nor the astrological planets that are the rulers of personality. Astrology is a *metaphorical* way of recognizing that the rulers of personality are archetypal powers who are beyond our personal reach and yet are involved necessarily in all our vicissitudes. These powers are mythical persons, gods, and their motions are not described in mathematics but in myths.

42. Friedländer, *Plato*, 3: 382.

43. Cornford, *Plato's Cosmology*, 289. The relation of psyche and internal organs (guts and liver) is a subject all for itself: cf. Ernst Bargheer, *Eingeweide: Lebens- und Seelenkräfte des Leibesinneren* (Berlin: Walter de Gruyter, 1931); Nikolaus Mani, *Die historischen Grundlagen der Leberforschung* (Basel/Stuttgart: Schwabe, 1959); Onians, 84–89; Esther Fischer-Homberger, "Zur Geschichte des Zusammenhangs zwischen Seele und Verdauung," *Schweizerische medizinische Wochenschrift* 103 (1973): 1433–41.

divining *literalizes* a "depth" psychology of "internal" necessity into actual liver and entrails by the art of hepatoscopy and haruspicy. Today seers similar to those of the *Timaeus*—analysts of the psyche—often fall into a similar magical literalism when trying to read the motions of the irrational and appetitive soul in a divinatory way, calling signals from dreams in regard to the future movements of fate.

Hellenistic magical methods that attempted to harness the power of Necessity were directed to this inner depth, especially the *phrenes,* air region or air soul.[44] The magic formula (derived from *ananke*) *hepanagkos* meant to put into a spell, to fix or bind, to compel the inner essence through magic power.[45] One tried to rule a person's fate and make a person one's slave by forcing a necessity upon the *phrenes.* It was believed that one of the ways necessity bound the soul was through the soul's being fettered to the body, and the place of this attachment was the *phrenes.* Therefore, by gaining control over the *phrenes* or air-soul of a person, one could govern the motions of his physical actions (behavior). Here again we see the notion of necessity as an Aristotelian internal cause, i.e., working internally within a thing and necessary to that thing, but now literalized into the physical interior of a person. Necessity is reduced to the literal flesh (cf. Schreckenberg, 61-64).

This literalism about the body supports philosophies of transcendence (Gnostic, Neoplatonist, and other redemptive religions of late antiquity: Schreckenberg, 157-64). A similar literalism affects today's redemptive religion—psychotherapy. Differences between *nous* and *ananke* become an opposition between mind and body. Freedom from necessity then becomes freedom from the physical body (or freedom of the physical body) where the soul is "bound" (cf. *Phaedo* 82e[46]—or Wilhelm Reich).

---

44. Schreckenberg, 133. The Eumenides (Erinys or Furies, divinities of Necessity, see below on Aeschylus and notes), affect man and drive him mad through the *phrenes* (*Eumenides* 2.301, 331, 344), which Lattimore consistently translates as "heart;" Thomson, as "bosom." On "phrenes" see Onians, 13–15, 23–43. His work shows that the term refers to an organ of consciousness and not only a physical place (lungs or diaphragm), hence I have used the term "air soul."

45. Schreckenberg, 133–64, examines the whole *Fragenkomplex,* cf. Martin P. Nilsson, *Opuscula Selecta* (Lund: Gleerup, 1960), 163–64.

46. When Porphyry in his life of Plotinus (chap. 2) gives answer, in an oracle from Apollo, to the question of where Plotinus's soul had gone after death, we can read: "The bonds of human necessity are now loosed from you." *Nota bene* the role of

The locus of this deep place can be the lungs (*phrenes*), liver, the "inmost marrow" (*Timaeus* 73b-d)—or the deep musculature of Rolfian therapy. The fantasy at work here is that Necessity rules from "deep inside," and the deeper one goes the more one discovers how rigidly determined, how enslaved one is inside the armor of the body.

As the redemptive ancient religions offered release from necessity through physical death, modern redemptive therapies use physical methods aiming at the same freedom. In both, ancient and modern, thinking in terms of physical positions is countered by thinking of metaphysical oppositions. This is the style of thought that operates within the transcendental denial of pathologizing (Hillman, *Re-Visioning Psychology*, 64–67). To be free of "hang-ups," and especially from the symptoms the flesh is heir to, is another way of hoping for freedom from Ananke who reaches us precisely through the enslaving servitudes of the irrational and appetitive soul and its errant ways. But not only...

Not only the literal flesh, which is neither irrational nor errant but an ancient animal full of grace, binds us; but rather the soul in which that flesh has its life. The image by which the flesh lives is the ultimate ruling necessity. We are in service to the body of imagination, the bodies of our images. And what fills our souls out and gives body to our images and experiences is the sense of necessity that is always, in all systems of psychic and religious discipline, associated with "body." Whenever necessity holds sway, it is blamed on body. So, if we hear these systems psychologically, they are also saying: when you flee Necessity you suffer in flesh, and worse, you lose the body of your imagination, literalizing the body of its imagery into clinical diseases and medical treatments.

When we think psychologically about the fantasy of the locus of Necessity in the deep body, then neither bodily death nor body-therapy are the issue, for both have taken "body" literally as flesh. Rather, the deeper we go, the more we come upon what "cannot be otherwise." The further we interiorize, the more our psychic necessities take on body as we become drawn into an attentive caring for (therapy) and imaginative understanding of the necessities that rule the soul through its psychic body, its images deep inside, the mythic depths inside its fantasies.

Apollo in his style if thought (*Phaedo*) and what I call the "Apollonic consciousness" of transcendent approaches to the problems of the psyche."

The difference between Nous and Ananke is presented as a tearing conflict in the soul of Orestes at the end of the *Oresteia* trilogy in the tragedy called the *Eumenides.* Orestes has sinned, but sinned at the command of a god, Apollo, who in turn represents Zeus. Orestes has committed an act of criminal psychopathology: matricide. In the language of the Empedocles fragment (115), he has "polluted his hands with blood," and is thus hounded by the Eumenides, another way of speaking of Ananke. They demand revenge, fulfillment of necessary laws. And they are the unknown causes of our hurts (*plegai*),[47] for

> All that concerneth mankind they dispense.
> Yet whenever a man falls foul of their wrath,
> He knoweth not whence his afflictions approach.[48]

They bring the collaring noose, which, as we have seen, is one of the specific attributes of Ananke. Orestes says (749): "This is the end for me. The noose [*agchone*] or else the light." Eumenides or Apollo, Ananke or Nous (Zeus).

The balloting over Orestes's fate is equal. Then Athene intervenes. There is a climactic argument back and forth between her and the Eumenides. But finally Athene persuades them and wins Orestes his life. The key word in her victory is persuasion, *peitho*, the word translated in our language as rhetoric. *Rhetoric persuades necessity.* The greatest trilogy of all mythical drama ends with the reconciliation of Zeus and Destiny, which as Cornford[49] says is another way of putting Plato's principles of Nous and Ananke, Reason and Compulsion, or what Herodotus calls Peitho (persuasive argument) and Bia (violent force).[50] (We have already

---

47. *Plegai* can also mean blows, strokes, hurts, afflictions. It is the source of our word "plague."

48. *The Oresteia of Aeschylus,* edited and translated by George Thomson (Cambridge: Cambridge University Press, 1938), 1:345 (lines 931–35).

49. Cf. Concord's brilliant "Epilogue" to *Plato's Cosmology* on the comparison between the *Timaeus* and the *Oresteia*; see also Thomson, 2:231.

50. "Peitho and Ananke sind terminologisch Gegensatzkomplemente." Schreckenberg, 102n.77. Their opposition is already in Empedocles, one between Ananke and the Charites (Roscher, "Peitho" [with Charis], 1796). An attribute, which the two goddess-figures have in common, is the *necklace.* Ananke's collar we saw above in Schreckenberg's etymological analysis; Peitho decorates Pandora with golden necklaces (Hesiod, *Works and Days* 75). Evidently, what one wears around one's throat has the implications of fate. Neckdress—from numbered dog tags to collar-

seen Bia [child of Styx]—as Ananke's partner in the temple at Corinth and as instrumental in the nailing of Prometheus.)

What has made this reconciliation possible? How has it come about? What does Athene do to heal the division between light and mind and reason on the one hand and the unknown causes of afflictions on the other? First, we know that Athene has an affinity with Necessity, because Athene has also invented *instruments of limitation and containment,* bringing the arts of pottery, of weaving, of measuring, of the bridle, yoke, and harness. In her is combined the very contradictions she must reconcile: the Nous of her father and the binding force of Ananke with whose collaboration (*Alcestis* 978) her father rules.

But the deeper clue to the entire resolution, and to this part of our investigation, is the term *peitho:* the persuasion of Athene, the winning speech, the charm of words. We must recall here that all along the tragedians and philosophers have insisted that Ananke is implacable, unable to be reached by persuasion, beyond the power of words. But Athene finds a way: "Persuasion guided the speech of my mouth," she says (971).

The content of Athene's words is that she offers the Erinys—the torturing furious forces of necessity who oppress Orestes—*a place* within the divine order. She offers a sanctuary, a cave, an altar ("new chambers," 1005) where these powers may reside and be honored and yet *remain alien:* or "resident aliens" as they are called (1012, 1019).[51] The unimaged nameless ones shall be imaged and named. Sacrifice is possible. Reconciliation occurs.

The reconciliation occurs between the divinities themselves when Orestes and his patron Apollo are offstage, having already exited 250

---

and-ties or golden chains and inset gems—particularizes destiny. The undressed throat is the unarticulated and inarticulate flesh without a specific sense of its own necessity. See further on jewelry and joints, Alfred J. Ziegler, "Rheumatics and Stoics," *Spring: An Annual of Archetypal Psychology and Jungian Thought* (1979): 19–28. For a full discussion of the pair Peitho-Ananke (as Bia), see Pedro Laín Entralgo, *The Therapy of the Word in Classical Antiquity,* translated by L. J. Rather and John M. Sharp (New Haven: Yale University Press, 1970), 64–90.

51. Cf. Thomson, 1: 68 for "resident aliens." Lattimore translates "guests of the land." The psychologically important point is that these figures are not fully integrated. They keep their specific identity. They remain "outsiders," guests, aliens, even if having received a place. *Placing*—neither repressing nor transforming (converting)—equals archetypal healing in this context.

lines before the final triumphal procession.[52] It is not Orestes, the suffering hero in the center, who brings about the healing.

Although the problem from which Orestes suffers involves his father and his mother, their sins and their murders, it is neither Orestes the person, nor the archetypal protagonist of the human ego that is finally the problem. It is a cosmic, universal agony in which he is caught. By returning to Greek myths we can see our personal agonies in this impersonal light.

This conclusion to the *Oresteia* has often been discussed as political and transcendental, as representing change in Athenian society, or in terms of conflicts between patriarchy and matriarchy, between Upperworld and Netherworld gods, between kinds of legalities, but I wish us to understand these matters psychologically. This tragedy bears upon the suffering of the riven soul, Orestes. It tells of the fundamental conflict between the reason within us and the powers of fate that cannot listen to that reason, that cannot be reached by understanding or moved from their compulsive course. This course is like our psychopathology which I defined earlier as that part of us which cannot be accepted, cannot be repressed, and cannot be transformed. Orestes is a figure of the soul torn between *archai*. He is both normal and abnormal psychology. Like Oedipus, Orestes is psychological man, a mythical case history.[53] But, unlike Oedipus, Orestes is relevant to the problem of *general* psychopathology rather than to a specific form of it. The *Oresteia* bears upon "the hurts of life without whence and why" (933), and ties them to necessity itself. Where the affliction of Oedipus refers eventually to a heroic ego, its blindness, mistakes, and repentance, Orestes suffers the cosmic conflict of the soul torn between gods, the necessary psychopathology of the universe.

There is a great deal to be said about the relations between words and force. This relation is at the very root of psychotherapy which is, in short, the discipline of this relation, since much of its work tries to move compulsive actions into words. Freud first called psychotherapy the talk-

52. Cf. Philip Wheelwright, *The Burning Fountain: A Study in the Language of Symbolism* (Bloomington: Indiana University Press, 1968), 238.

53. The place of Orestes in modern consciousness has already been superbly exposed by David L. Miller in his "Orestes: Myth and Dream as Catharsis," in *Myths, Dreams, and Religions,* edited by Joseph Campbell (New York: Dutton, 1970), 26–47.

ing cure, recognizing it to be a work of *peitho,* an art of persuasion or rhetoric. An analysis repeats the struggles in the soul of Orestes between reason and compulsion, and it repeats the speech of Athene, who persuades to reconciliation by finding place and giving image to the driving necessities. In the mouth of Athene speech becomes a curative *hymn,*[54] a word which etymologically means "spun" or "woven" words (see below on Athene and weaving).

The relation between word and force is also reflected in society, suggesting that the rule of coercive violence increases when our art of convincing words declines. *Peitho* takes on an overwhelming importance both in the healing of the soul and the healing of society. Our engagement at Eranos—a spoken meeting, a ritual of speech—belongs also to the devotion and cult of *peitho.* For here, too, we try to find persuasive, convincing words that can touch and move the ununderstood, unimaged forces of the spirit. The task of formulation cannot be overestimated.

Why are words so important in a culture, and why has the art of persuasion, Athene's *peitho,* so fallen into disuse in ours? The conclusion to the *Oresteia* answers the first question: words are able to persuade the darkest elements to take part and have place. We must speak and let them speak. The answer to the second question refers to the profound determining importance of psychological and spiritual reality.

If ultimate reals are objects, things, material events—dead things out there as Descartes would have it and materialism insists—then speech has no effect. *Flatus voci*—empty words, a waste of breath. Actions speak louder; Bia, not Peitho. Then language must become simplified, an operational tool, part of the positivist's and materialist's kit for clear directions in handbooks, words that fit computing instruments to move and shape objects out there.

If, however, reality is psychological and spiritual, by which I mean ideational, religious, imaginal, fantastic—as it is especially in psychotherapy and as it was in the Greek world view—then affecting reality requires instruments for moving ideas, beliefs, feelings, images, and fantasies. Then rhetoric, persuasion, holds major importance. Through words we can alter reality; we can bring into being and remove from being; we can

---

54. *The Homeric Hymns,* translated by Charles Boer (Chicago: The Swallow Press, 1970), 137–38. Cf. concluding passage of "Hymn to Pythian Apollo," 161ff.

shape and change the very structure and essence of what is real. The art of speech becomes the primary mode of moving reality.

The relation of words and healing has been beautifully developed by Pedro Laín Entralgo, the Spanish medical historian: "Words, vigorous and persuasive words: they are the key to interhuman relations."[55] He paraphrases what Ulysses says in the *Philoctetes* (line 99) of Sophocles, a phrase that is an epigram for psychotherapy: "In the life of men it is the tongue and not the act that governs all."[56]

My words now are an attempt to remind us of something Professor Izutsu wrote nearly twenty years ago: that language is primarily a magical power that resides "in its very semantic constitution" and determines the organization of grammar, syntax, and meaning; that it is the voice which actualizes the "sacred breath" into words; and that language can heal because it is *eo ipso* and *a priori* sacred.[57] Speech exposes the inmost nature of man, said Sophocles (*Oedipus at Colonus* 1188). The goddess Peitho—who can and does alter necessity—"has no other temple than the word," said Euripides.[58] If so, then right speech is also one way of restoring "the Temple." Rhetoric, as I conceive it, is a *devotio*, an attempt to return the word to the gods and to give appropriate form to the divine magic, the sacred breath in language. Little wonder that speaking at Eranos so often produces that pathologizing phenomenon the French call *le trac* (stage fright).

Free speech is therefore a psychological fundament, a requirement of soul that finds freedom within necessity through language. Speech arises from the same inmost depths where necessity holds the soul in bondage, creating our pathologizings. Speech expresses the air-soul of the *phrenes*. Human speech, especially in psychotherapy, is never wholly the logos of Nous. It is always also wayward, spontaneous, digressing like the Errant Cause.[59]

---

55. Laín Entralgo, *The Therapy of the Word*, 68.

56. Ibid. There is an irony here, however, since in that play Ulysses is shown as a man of action whose words are most deceitful. Moreover, he is unable to convince Philoctetes, even more a man of action; only Hercules can.

57. Toshihiko Izutsu, *Language and Meaning: Studies in the Magical Function of Speech* (Tokyo: The Keio Institute of Philological Studies, 1956), 103, 26.

58. These two quotations are discussed by Laín Entralgo in *The Therapy of the Word*, 66–67.

59. Izutsu, 13: "As there can be no magical use of language without at least a mini-

Therapy through the word cannot end Ananke's archaic and furious dominion, nor does it intend to, for then we would lose the connection of the archetypes with our physical experience and our mortality. Nor is our aim to foreclose her claims as resident alien in the soul. But we can give her modes of expression, ways to image herself in words, persuading her from her implacable silence[60]—an archetypal therapy, a therapy of the archetype itself.

The Fantasy of Normalcy

The movement of our line of thinking leads now to this formulation: if pathologizing is necessary and is the expression and experience of Necessity itself, then this errant, disordering activity must be a "norm" of the soul, much as Plato imagined it. If the archetypes themselves are internally limited to and by their images, so that they, too, show pathologies (the *infirmitas* of the archetype), then pathologizing is woven throughout all psychological existence, and whatever we call "normal" must include it. All structures of consciousness, all conditions of existence as archetypal perspectives, including those called healthy, whole, realized, or normal, are also pathologized.

Let me press this further: rather than trying to understand the necessity of psychopathology and what place pathologizing has in the soul, we now would turn to understanding normalcy and what place normalizing has in the soul. We would turn to normalcy not as it literally presents itself in its own terms as "normal," but as a specific archetypal perspective with its own style of pathologizing.

By this I do not mean that everyone is sick—the therapeutic fallacy, or that normalcy is sickness—the Laingian variation of that fallacy. Rather I

---

mum of logicality, so in ordinary descriptive use of language—or even in scientific discourse—the actual words employed cannot in the nature of the case be entirely free from illogicality. In natural language there is always something that stubbornly resists a thoroughgoing logical analysis."

60. It is not only that Ananke and Bia cannot hear (deaf) and carry the usual epithet "blind"); but, like Death, Necessity works in silence, does not speak. Empedocles, according to Plutarch, contrasted musical Persuasion with nonmusical and silent Necessity; cf. Entralgo, 90.

am trying to circumvent the dualistic model of normal-abnormal by suggesting that each archetypal structure imagines a cosmos which includes its pattern of pathologized events. Furthermore, in what follows I shall be trying to expose the normalcy fantasy itself as an inherent necessity within one specific archetypal perspective.

"Norm" and "normal" derive from the Latin word *norma,* meaning a carpenter's square. *Norma* is a technical, instrumental term for a right angle; it belongs to applied geometry. *Normalis* means "made according to the square"; *normaliter* means "in a straight line, directly." The sixteenth- and seventeenth-century meaning of "normal" was: rectangular, perpendicular, standing at a right angle. But the word in our present sense betrays distinctly nineteenth-century usages: normal as regular (1828); normal school for teacher training (1834); normal as average in physics (1859); normalize (1865); normative (1880); and normal as usual (1890).

This last definition contains two distinct meanings that fuse with each other:

1) Normal in the *statistical* sense, i.e., what is usual, common, frequent, regular, hence predictable or expected. This sense can be demonstrated graphically as that which falls in the middle region of a Gaussian curve, hence mean, middle, average, centered. Abnormal, in this same quantitative approach, refers to that which is unusual, extreme, exceptional, deviate, out-of-line, outstanding, rare, odd, anomalous. The statistical sense is not meant to imply any values other than quantitative. Unusual means simply infrequent.

2) Normal in the *ideal* sense, i.e., what most or best approximates an ideal standard, a pre-established image or *Vorbild.* This standard can be given by theology (*imitatio Christi*); by philosophy (Stoic man, Nietzschean man); by law (the citizen); by medicine (resilient adaptation); by culture and society (conformity with canons). For the sake of exposition we can call this second kind of normalcy qualitative. It does imply value judgments, since nearness to the ideal is normal in a laudatory sense, and remoteness from it is abnormal in a pejorative sense.

The two usages of normal—statistical and ideal—may be quite distinct. For instance we may suffer from a psychosomatic duodenal ulcer. This is frequent in men of certain sorts doing certain things. As frequent, it is statistically normal, even if ideally it is abnormal. Or, we may have the highest intelligence quotient in a community of likes (age, sex, economic level, ethnic group, etc.) and thus approximate most closely the ideal norm, even if this high intelligence be statistically abnormal.

Generally, however, the two kinds of norms merge in our minds. There may be several reasons for this. First, even the bony language of statistics carries metaphorical connotations. When we say *mean, middle, average or extreme, exceptional, deviate,* we are denoting statistical frequencies but also connoting qualitative valuations deeply embedded in language. Second, the populist, egalitarian, sociological vision of the world that dominates our value systems wants the merger of the two norms, of quantitative and ideal. Under the Reign of Quantity, as René Guénon has called our age, *ordinary, regular, balanced, centered, predictable* have become ideal norms and have set the standards for the soul. "Abnormal" is both a statistical definition and a moral condemnation. What is odd becomes wrong; what is unusual and irregular becomes reprehensible. Third, the psyche *sui generis* envisions ideal norms or ideal types, the "universali fantastici" or poetic metaphors of Vico. We seem unable to exist without mythic persons who present ideal standards. But today our shrines and altars are empty so that in the vacant niches appear the secular commonalities, frequencies, and averages ennobled into ideal norms by the psyche's mythologizing. We witness the Reign of Quantity in the reign of the common man of common sense, the infiltration of statistical normalcy into ideal norms.

The quantitative approach represents the point of view of physis toward psyche, of matter toward soul, and therefore it enters psychology from the science of material nature. In fact, one of the dictionary meanings of normal is "natural." The method in psychology which uses the regularities of nature (physis) as ideal norms we may call "Aristotelian." This method implicates us in psychology's *naturalistic fallacy,*[61] i.e., judging psychic events by comparing them with similar events in nature. When physical, literal nature becomes the norm, the psyche is being viewed usually from the perspective of the mother archetype and her hero.[62]

The Aristotelian approach derives from defining the psyche in terms of the natural life of the body;[63] whereas we have been working out a

---

61. Re-Visioning Psychology, 85–87.
62. Cf. "The Great Mother, Her Son, and the Puer," in UE 3: Senex & Puer.
63. Aristotle, De anima 412–13; 415b10.

psychology that is more Platonic. Its examination of soul is related primarily with death, with what is below and deeper than natural life and its viewpoint. The difference between the Aristotelian and the Platonic can also be put as one between the medical and the mythical in regard to pathologizings. Norms for the soul that speak of adaptation, life-enhancement, balance, or golden mean are "Aristotelian" or medical;[64] they remain within the natural perspective and fail to appreciate the necessity of pathologizing for myth and the necessity of death-boundedness for soul.

Although Plato praised the middle path, he also encouraged steps away from it, as in the *Symposium* and the *Phaedrus* where erotic intensity and various styles of extreme mania are presented as favored ways of soul. Furthermore, in the *Phaedo* (81–82), Plato speaks of *andras metrious*, ordinary decent citizens, who in their reincarnation are compared with bees and ants, wholly collective souls happily bound to the lines of nature, predictable, communal, undeviating. The very word *metrios* (the middle class praised in Aristotle's *Politics*) refers to *metron*, the rule, standard, norm, measure.

The Platonic approach is carried further by Marsilio Ficino in his translation and commentary of the *Symposium*.[65] This work was one of the most influential treatises of the Renaissance. It is an esoteric, ecstatic psychology book whose intention is to lead the soul to love. For Ficino (*Commentary on Plato's Symposium*, 4.8), the middle path that neither ascends nor descends is the position of practical men of action, whose concern is with morality and whose position is that of observer. Such men "remain in the pleasures only of seeing and social relations." The middle path avoids both the descent into voluptuous touching and ascent into contemplative abstraction.

---

64. See W.A. Scott, "Conceptions of Normalcy," in *Handbook of Personality Theory and Research*, edited by Edgar F. Borgatta and William W. Lambert (New York: Rand McNally, 1968), for a collection of such norms where normality equals mental health, adjustment, happiness, productivity, social integration, minimum of conflict and destruction, etc.

65. Marsilio Ficino, *Commentary on Plato's Symposium on Love*, translated and edited by Sears Jayne (Thompson, Conn.: Spring Publications, 2023 [1985]).

Some Platonists[66] held this middle path in less regard than the other two, since the voluptuous movement into animal generation was a model for the experiences of the upward exaltation—*les extrèmes se touchent.* Ficino's characterization of the middle path implies a profound critique of the realm of perception, action, and social relations. Only to observe, to ask the moral question of events, to turn the movements of the soul into practical actions, all belong to the horizontal middle way, which is a defense against the daemonic power of love that draws one vertically down or up. The middle path of social-moral-practical man is the *defense of normality* against the compelling involvement of the other two ways.

The great passions, truths, and images are not normal middles, not averages. Tongue-tied Moses who kills, has horns and a black desert wife; Christ turning miracles, lacerated on the Cross; ecstatic Mohammed; Hercules and the heroes, even Ulysses; and the extraordinary awesome goddesses—all these are unpredictable extremes that bespeak the soul *in extremis.* And these mythic figures show *infirmitas* possessions, errors, wounds, pathologizings. In Vico's terms, metaphorical truth is more than life, other than life, even while it presents the ideal standards for life. The very ideality is partly expressed through pathologized enormities.

I am not pleading for a baroque Romanticism or Gothic horror, a new cult of the freakish to shock the bourgeois. Such is merely the other side of normalcy. Rather I wish us to remember Plato's *Timaeus:* reason alone does not rule the world or set the rules. Turning to the middle ground for norms, norms without enormity, refuses the errant cause of Ananke.[67] Such norms are delusions, false beliefs, that do not take into

---

66. Cf. Edgar Wind, *Pagan Mysteries in the Renaissance* (Harmondsworth: Penguin, 1967), 50ff., 68ff., 273f., for a discussion of Neoplatonism and Voluptas with references to Plotinus, Ficino, and Lorenzo Valla.

67. It is worth recalling here that Nous uses geometry for ordering the unformed into four fundamental shapes. As Cornford says (*Plato's Cosmology,* 210): "Thus the operation of Reason is carried, so far as may be, into the dark domain of the irrational powers." *Norma,* we remember, is originally a term from geometry. Where mathematics makes order out of the unordered, it is also a move "out of" the unordered, a move away from the dark domain of irrational powers and the necessities of pathologizing. Psychological books that emphasize geometrical descriptions of the psyche (Jung's *Aion,* for instance; or Marie-Louise von Franz's *Time and Number,* also belong among the transcendental denials of pathologizing and as such are less psychological than spiritual, less representative of imaginal soul realities, which are always pathologized,

account the full nature of things. Norms without pathologizings in their images perform a normalizing upon our psychological vision, acting as repressive idealizations that make us lose touch with our individual abnormalities. The normalcy fantasy becomes itself a distortion of the way things actually are.

To put it in the language of academic psychology: the nomothetic must include the idiopathic within its formulations as an inherent part of its general statements and laws, else our vision of soul, too, becomes normalized, indistinguishable from bees and ants: social, practical, natural; 1984. Then we are defended against the archetypes in our lives and against the powerful images of our culture that can no longer reach us, or only do so through the middle path of perceptual observations, archetypes as allegories of moral practical action or as aesthetic illustrations without persuasiveness. Then we have modeled ourselves upon norms without archetypal dimensions, man the measurer of all things, the observer outside, even outside his own suffering, treating it also from outside, observationally, objectively, living a life without any inherent sense of necessity.

Athene

Now this middle position, too, must be archetypally influenced. To call it a defensive delusion is not enough; it too must reflect a god since there are gods in our diseases.

Here we return to Athene who performed the great reconciliation between Zeus and the Furies, Nous and Ananke. I have already pointed out that Athene shares limiting, harnessing attributes with Ananke. Besides, she has a Persephone aspect;[68] a horse aspect[69] like the Erinys; she wears on her breast the Gorgo, that terrifying image of irrationality; her animal, the owl,[70] is her "wisdom," but it is also a bird of doom,

---

than of an abstract metaphysical reality that presents itself in "pure" forms.

68. On Persephone-Athene, see Karl Kerényi, *Athene: Virgin and Mother in Greek Religion*, translated by Murray Stein (Woodstock, Conn.: Spring Publications, 1978), 49–50, and the translator's excellent postscript.

69. On the horse (Athene), see ibid., 15, 38, 69–72 (Gorgo, Mare); Marcel Detienne, "Athene and the Mastery of the Horse," *History of Religions* 11, no. 2 (1971): 161–84; on the horse (Erinys), see Dietrich, *Death, Fate and the Gods*, 137ff.

70. On the owl (Athene), see Kerényi, *Athene*, 37, 48, 50, 104 n.312; Edward A. Armstrong, *The Folklore of Birds* (London: Collins, 1958), 113–24; on Moirae as flying gray

a screeching night-creature that can be situated among the Harpies, Sirens, Keres, Moirae-winged images of fateful necessities.

However, and in contrast, Athene is the head-sprung daughter of Zeus, the very epiphany of his Nous, his introjected Metis (Athene's mother). Metis ("wise counsel") stems from the same indogermanic root MĒ as *metron*, measure, rule, standard.[71] It is particularly in the realm of the city that Athene Polias[72] upholds the norms of the cultural canons. One of her later epithets was Pronoia, *providentia*, foresight, for her structure of consciousness can espy predictabilities, prepare for them, and thus normalize the unexpected. Athene, as Hygieia,[73] shows the same foresighted preparedness in the realm of health. Do we not appeal to her still today under the conceptual guise of "mental hygiene" and the community mental health centers organized by the state? Athene's name itself, according to Kerényi, refers to a containing receptacle "a kind of vessel, a dish, beaker, or pan";[74] she was the protective divinity of the potter; and the clay bowl was a primary votive offering in the Athene cult.[75] Normalizing occurs also through having a receptive openness and contained inner space for whatever comes.

The Roman Athene, Minerva[76] (whose name derives from *memini, mens,* mind) had under her protection all craft guilds, school teachers ("normal school"!), and the medical profession groups whose task is exercising governance over the Errant Cause through the wise counsel of practical intellect.[77]

---

night-daemons, Dietrich, 71 (also on Keres, 240–48); John Pollard, *Seers, Shrines and Sirens* (London: Allen & Unwin, 1965), 140.

71. Walter W. Skeat, *An Etymological Dictionary of the English Language* (Oxford: Clarendon Press, 1882).

72. On the city (Athene), see Kerényi, *Athene,* 33, 38, 45, 50, 78; R.F. Willetts, *Cretan Cults and Festivals* (London: Routledge, 1962), 278, discusses the movement of Athene from earliest Minoan-Mycenaen household and palace protectress to goddess of the *polis.*

73. Roscher, "Hygieia," 1/2: 2772.

74. Kerényi, *Athene,* 45.

75. Ibid., 46.

76. Roscher, "Minerva," 2/2: 2986–991. Like Athene Ergane (Worker), Minerva was the patroness of artisans, among whom numbered physicians, and also school teachers who were paid their annual honorarium on the day of the Minerva festival.

77. "The word *metis* always signifies *practical* understanding." Walter Friedrich Otto, *The Homeric Gods: The Spiritual Significance of Greek Religion,* translated by Moses

As giver of bridle and yoke and "the science of numbers,"[78] Athene presents the persuasive necessity of reason, the mathematical and logical necessities where, as Aristotle (*Metaphysics* 1015a-b) says, "a conclusion cannot be otherwise" for it follows necessarily from first premises in the deductive processes. Thinking is yoked and bridled by the logics of reason. Athene brings Zeus and Ananke together because *in her very person reason and necessity are combined.* Athene-Minerva moves Ananke from the violence of Bia to the force of mind of which her convincing speech (*peitho*) is example. Athene is necessity moved from otherworld to this world, from blindness to bright-eyedness (*glaukopis*), from spinning to weaving, from impenetrable erratic compulsion to the practical intellect's foresighted protective measures in regard to necessity, which measures themselves become another kind of necessity.

This psychological process I would define as normalization and I would consider Athene to be the archetypal person within the fantasy of normality. When psychology speaks in terms of norms, when it attempts to normalize, when it represents the point of view of the cultural canon and gives wise counsel from the practical understanding—protective, hygienic, politic, sensible—then psychology is enacting Athene.

Moreover, we can bring support for our having called the normative perspective "maternal." Unlike Hera and Artemis who were *not* addressed in Greek cult with the term Mother, Athene was called *Meter.* This virgin without offspring was nonetheless a mother—however, she was never depicted holding a child.[79] Here we have occasion to discriminate with more precision the term "mother" used sweepingly in depth psychology.[80] The mothering of Athenian consciousness is institutional, a mothering of nonreligious, secular brotherhoods (*phratriai*).

Hadas (New York: Pantheon, 1954), 54; cf. Kerényi, *Athene* on Metis-Athene, 21–23, 32, 36f., 44, 67f., 109, 111.

78. Robert Graves, *The Greek Myths* (Harmondsworth: Penguin, 1960), 1:96.

79. William Henry Denham Rouse, *Greek Votive Offerings* (Cambridge: Cambridge University Press, 1902), 257n.2; Kerényi, *Athene,* 24, 32f.

80. It is insufficient to call Great Mother, or the Mother archetype, every female image—Luna, Demeter, Hera, Isis, Artemis, Cybele, Aphrodite, etc.—as does E. Neumann in his work on this subject. He only amalgamates what is beautifully precise, and subtly differentiated in the particular persons and images. For one attempt at differentiating mothering from nursing, see my "Abandoning the Child," elsewhere in the volume.

To find Mother Athene we must turn to the conventions of like-minded men, the nomothetic standards of science, business, trades, professions, and government and their unavoidable norms of inclusion and exclusion.[81] When the soul is examined from an institutional standpoint or approached with conventional thinking and feeling, the perspective operating is that of Athene.

Elsewhere I suggested that Plato's dialogues can be examined archetypally in terms of the gods[82] and the variances within his philosophy can be understood as appropriate to the polytheism of his consciousness. The dialogue that appears to be especially the "child of Athene" is the *Statesman.*

There we find that the particular craft with which statesmanship is compared is the art of combining, and the images for this art are those of Athene: measuring and weaving (*Statesman* 283–87).[83] Athene's handwork is the paradigm used by Plato for the craft of politics. We have already seen Athene's ability to combine or to weave the revengeful, implacable forces into the structure of the Acropolis by that remarkable combinatory term "resident aliens" which is, after all, a resolution of the "Orestes problem" by means of a political metaphor. Plato says that Athene (together with Hephaestus) governs the crafts for the "daily needs of life" (*Laws* 11.920e)—as if to say that the maintenance of daily, practical life of the community is her main concern. Inclusion of the

---

81. On Athene and the *Phratria*, see Kerényi, *Athene,* 27, 79, 106. Martin P. Nilsson, "Appendix II: The Phratries," in his *Cults, Myths, Oracles and Politics in Ancient Greece* (New York: Cooper Square, 1972), 170: "The phratries obtained such gods common to them all, as maintained the social and civic order, Zeus and Athena. The phratries give an example of the diluting and secularizing of religion when the State lays its dead hand upon it." Admission was through voting: standards of inclusion and exclusion.

82. This method is indicated in Plato himself (*Phaedrus* 252–53) who describes styles of loving in terms of "followers" of the different gods. In the dialogues themselves we see imagery and ideas—and pathologizing—appropriate to Apollo in the *Phaedo;* we see Pan in the *Phaedrus;* Dionysus in the *Symposium;* Hermes in the *Cratylus;* Zeus and Athene in the *Laws.* According to Wind, *Pagan Mysteries in the Renaissance,* 103, "Athena and Eros were worshipped jointly on the grounds of the Academy." It is from these two sides, "Athenian" and "Erotic," that Platonic commentators have attempted to grasp Plato's Socrates—or have been grasped by those gods through him.

83. Cf. Friedländer, *Plato,* 3: 289; Roscher, "Athene," 1/1: 681f.

excessive and abnormal by weaving it in is the art of political consciousness. Such weaving, as Plato takes great metaphorical pains to establish, is not patching quilts, tacking boards, stitching leather, darning holes. It is not repairing. It is not collage. It is not bricolage, haphazard, without inner necessity. Rather, Athene's art is the systematic plaiting of strands together; and as her own person is a combination of Reason and Necessity, her art of combination produces a whole fabric (*Statesman* 283b). All strands find place in and contribute to the gestalt—as do the Erinys. The old Furies brought in, nothing left out, no extremities hanging over the edges: integration as ideal norm.

It is in this integrative sense that we can understand the importance of Minerva in Bruno's art of memory.[84] Minerva makes possible the very art itself; her ladder connects all things by means of gradations of images. Or, as we have seen in the *Eumenides*, it is Athene (Minerva) who makes space within. She is the inner space-making function of mind, the goddess who grants *topos*, judging where each event belongs in relation with all other events. She is mind as a containing receptacle which normalizes through interior organization.

However, this structure of consciousness can turn norms into weapons. We see this in the *Iliad* (21.399ff.). Athene takes up a boundary stone (that which sets limits) and hurls it at Ares, striking him in the neck (place of necessity). He is flattened by her force, "subjugated" to her limits.

It becomes more apparent why those gods who are strongly contrasted with Athene are "irrational": Ares and Aphrodite (in the *Iliad*); Poseidon (in the *Odyssey*); Dionysus (whose drunkenness can be cured with an owl's egg,[85] and who calls Minyas's daughters away from their weavings); Pan (no goat was allowed on the Acropolis and its spittle was poison for her olive tree.)[86] The dynamic emotionalities, rages, posses-

---

84. Cf. Yates, *Art of Memory,* 290, and his *Giordano Bruno and the Hermetic Tradition* (London: Routledge, 1964), 312, where Bruno confesses himself a child of Minerva. ("Her have I loved and sought from my youth, and desired for my spouse, and have become a lover of her form.") The relation between Minerva and images of the mind may help us to understand (beyond the evident artisan or handcraft meaning) the fact that it was to Athene that sacrifice was made by burnishers at Olympia before polishing the image (Rouse, *Greek Votive Offerings,* 59 n.20).

85. In another tale, the sober owl drives off bees from the entrance to a wine cellar (Hyginus, *Fabulae,* 136).

86. Kerényi, *Athene,* 97. The relation between Athene and goat is treated at length by Kerényi on 96ff.

sions, moist hysterics, depressions, and wild nature outside the *polis* do not belong within the cosmos of Athene's normalization. They cannot be held in her wide, but uncracked bowl.

These syzygies continue to work in our perspectives. It is difficult to imagine the nature of Athenian consciousness without ourselves falling into one or another of these affect-laden stances with which she is in an opposition.

A second metaphor from the *Statesman* also refers to the weaving in of Ananke within the body politic—and of course the body politic is also an image, a way of speaking about the constitution of the soul. This time the metaphor concerns the social hierarchy from slaves to kings (*Statesman* 287–91) which are combined by the art of statecraft. From what we have already seen, we know that "slaves" refer to *ananke,* and that within the soul the slaves are the compelled and the compulsive.

Following a proposal I have made elsewhere ("An Essay on Pan") that ideas and behaviors (including pathologized behaviors) are always the enactment of mythical fantasies, it would now be appropriate to develop the relations further between the mythical imageries of Athene and the ideas of norms, and then to link these images and ideas with behavioral pathologies. In other words we are obliged to recognize the *pathologizing of Athene.* In the same way that ascension belongs to the *puer* archetype, constriction to Saturn, will power to the Hero, growth to Magna Mater and her Child, so normalizing belongs to Athenian consciousness. (This is so the case that we still today call "Athenian" the normative ideals of "nothing to excess" and the doctrine of the Golden Mean.) And in the same way that these other ideational attitudes—ascension, constriction, will power, growth—provide background support for a manner of pathologizing, so normalizing too is a manner of pathologizing containing its own archetypal justification.

Athenian justification takes place by means of the appeal to objective norms. To feel that norms are objective and to think that objective norms *are,* independent of structures of consciousness and the archetypal persons governing them, reveal that we are standing in Athene's temple. The interweaving of normative and objective thinking is precisely the blind spot in Athenian consciousness. Here it cannot see through itself and into the archetypal fantasy it is enacting. This consciousness experiences norms as objective and the objective as normal, and from the objective we must derive our norms. Athenian consciousness turns outside to objective "others" (*polis*) for validating the necessity of its perspective.

This consciousness remains eternally bound to its "father," Zeus, giving it a certainty of judgment and a conviction of objectivity; it maintains an impersonal and selfless concern for "the good of the whole." This whole, however, by being objectified (rather than individualized) becomes abstracted into an idealized norm. The subtle infusion of the abstract into the practical has the advantage—and disadvantage—of removing actual practical concerns into principled standards and objectives. It becomes hard to distinguish between the virtue and the tyranny of judgment in Athenian consciousness.

That there is abnormalcy in normalizing, that the watchword of integrated normality is the very place of Athene's style of psychopathology, is most vividly imaged in her function of protectress of the "city," where the preparedness of her *pronoia* is also the military defensiveness of paranoia. She is patroness of weapons and is herself "an armed goddess with body almost wholly covered by a shield."[87] The structure of consciousness keeping us rational, practical, and *en garde* for the daily needs of life is the very same structure that keeps us encased in our body armor, the defensive postures that are archetypally necessary to civilized normality.

This protectively practical structure is so close to our habitual ego defenses that it is especially difficult to recognize. Otto reminds us of Athene's closeness to action, her readiness and immediacy. He speaks of her as the intelligence that guides us in the midst of the operations of life, much like Piaget who defines intelligence as an ego activity that solves problems through operational combinations. This is an archetype that does *not* reveal itself in affects. She has neither the savagery of battle nor the distance of contemplation (says Otto); she is therefore not discernible through affective seizures or spiritual highs. She is "ever near,"[88] and because she is so close we do not see her.

To locate Athene psychologically we must go close to what we call the ego (and Athene was counselor of many heroes).[89] Athene acts as

---

87. Otto, *Homeric Gods*, 43, referring to her earliest epiphany in Mycenaean art.
88. Ibid., 60.
89. Most important of all, Ulysses; cf. W.B. Stamford, "The Favorite of Athene" in his *The Ulysses Theme: A Study in the Adaptability of a Traditional Hero* (Thompson,

self-restraining voice or insight within our reflections. She is the internal Mentor—and it is as mentor-bird that she appears so often in the *Odyssey*.[90] When one takes counsel with oneself, the act is itself Athenian, and so the counsel that emerges reflects her norms. She is the reflection awake in the night, like the owl and the sudden call, like her trumpet that makes one hear despite one's inner deafness. When we speak of reflection in psychology or call up inner figures of the imagination to reflect our concerns, we need to remember that reflection has many styles. Athene's counsel presents the norms of this world, and its necessities, in close cooperation with the ego's interests. This is not a reflection that is nymphic and fantasyful, pueric and inspirational, Saturnian and abstracted, Apollonic and clarified, not a musing reflection, nor one that is erotic, speculative, or Hermetic.

The upshot of what we have been working out here can be summed up as follows: 1) the normative is only one archetypal perspective toward psychological events as Athene is only one of twelve Olympians—and there are further perspectives, particularly of the Underworld, that are not Olympian. 2) Norms having objective validity are "absolute," "normal," and "objective" only for Athenian consciousness for which such fantasies are archetypally necessary. 3) The normative approach to the psyche is inherent to a *Weltanschauung* that feels its primary obeisance to "outside" images, or what we today refer to as "conscious" psychology (statistical, social, practical, preventative, hygienic, communal); or "outside" as above, the high objective truths of Zeus. 4) The normative approach experiences Necessity as it is translated by Athene, i.e., necessity presses upon us as demands to comply with images that are *représentations collectives,* coming from *res publica,* from normative standards that are rationally demonstrable, rather than from images of the imaginal. Pathologizing becomes *eo ipso* abnormal. We conceive ourselves as social, economic, natural, or political beings rather than as imaginative beings.

Conn.: Spring Publications, 2022 [1992]), 24–42, where the operations of Athenian intelligence are analytically exposed. Other heroes aided by Athene are Achilles, Diomedes, Jason, Cadmus, Bellerophon, Perseus.

90. Willetts, *Cretan Cults,* 314.

We formulate our necessities in terms of "outside" needs; our actions are guided by what is rational, politic, hygienic, foresighted, precautionary. 5) Imagination itself receives an inspired and prophetic interpretation from Athenian consciousness. Its fallen forms will be either denounced as unprincipled and impractical or ennobled with foreshadowings and implications; but they will not be permitted the independence of their deformity—for each and every event must fit, be fitting, and fit in. 6) To be normal in any society is to enact a particular style of that society's fantasy. The appeal to normality conceals a defense against other archetypal enactments which then must perforce be judged "abnormal." 7) From this standpoint there must be abnormality against which this style of consciousness defends itself and integrates by normalizing. Thus we have arrived at "the necessity of abnormal psychology." Also we have exhibited our main concern in this paper: before psychotherapy is in a position to do anything at all in regard to psychological abnormality, it is obliged first to recognize the archetypal dominant in the style that casts a world into norms, normalizing, and normality, i.e., the archetypal person of Athene.

The image of Athene, helmeted in full armor, returns us to our opening reference to Freud. The little symptom so alien to the normative view of the ego is the chink in the structure cracking all normative images of how we should be—all denials of pathologizing made impossible by the persistent backaches, the indigestion, the bad moods and hounding ideas. The fatal flaw is indeed Fate, Necessity, reaching our soul through her daughters, despite all shields of prudence that would take arms against it. Through the power of the image, expressing itself as a symptom and presenting the erratic claims of Necessity, we discover a psychological vision of human being for whom neither naturalism nor spiritualism nor normalism applies. Natural man who is at one with harmonious development, spiritual man at one with transcendent perfection, and normal man at one with practical and social adaptation are transformed by being deformed into psychological man or woman who is at one with soul.

~―∦―~

3

THE INSIDE OF STRATEGIES:
ATHENE

Inside our plans and projects lie motivations. Inside our ideas and methods of thinking are patterns that shape their logics. It is as if the laws of logic, and language itself, submit to the rhetorics of imagination. Theories of Lévi-Strauss in anthropology and Noam Chomsky in linguistics, in quite different ways, also rely upon notions of deep formative structures affecting, if not determining, the manner in which conscious thought and action proceeds. The notion that there is an "inside" to actions has been fundamental to depth psychology since its inception with Freud more than one hundred years ago. An "unconscious" aspect of the human mind is the name that this inside received, by now having become all too familiar and also too generalized. We speak cavalierly of "the unconscious," of unconscious motivations, unconscious complexes inside the mind, therewith concealing from our awareness that indeed this territory of motivating patterns, because it has been named "unconscious," was not truly inside, not truly unconscious, but rather quite "known" simply by the fact that it could be named "unconscious."

Jung and archetypal psychology addressed the vague generalization of the inside by differentiating the patterns and motivations in terms of a variety of complexes, styles, images, rhetorics—thereby allowing them to be imagined further. And, they must be *imagined* since this inside does not appear, except inferentially. We do not see the complexes, this inside, as such; it appears only in symptoms and other phenomena of behavior. The inside is truly inside and, therefore, outside human grasp. As Jung said, the unconscious is a *Grenzbegriff*, a bordering concept that puts limits to all epistemologies of human knowing. Whatever this unconscious has or does remains inside itself, over the border on the other side.

Presented at the Milanesiana Festival, Milan, Italy, July 2005.

I have burdened you with this abstract introduction in order to make clear at the beginning that we do not know what lies inside strategies, strategies of whatever kind. About them we can only imagine. Whatever follows now will be in the terrain of imagination; I shall be trying to "go inside" by means of imagining the dominant configurations that shape human acts and thoughts, styles and desires.

I am imagining these figures as the forming influences giving a deeper archetypal validity and credence to those figures hypothesized by psychoanalysis—mother and father imagos, anal and oral complexes, shadow, animus and anima, and so forth. These abstractions, even at best when they are personified, are without genealogies, mythologies, and elaborated symbolic particularities that give to human experience the feeling that they are agencies of determining power, or as Thales said, at the beginning of Western philosophy, that "all things are full of gods."

So our question now becomes which specific figures lie inside human strategies for the "successful achievement of desired ends"—for such is a concise definition of strategy. A strategy is the thoughtful planning required to reap advantage whether in urban planning, economic investment, corporate mission, national policy, or military engagement.

The word itself gives a clue. "Strategy" derives directly from the Greek term for a military commander and a chief magistrate, what today might be the CEO of a corporation or President of a major institution. It is a word psychologically located in the context of civilization, born within a city. Strategies are necessary for civilized order, making possible the implementation of the societal compact. Otherwise, we would find ourselves in Hobbesian world of "all against all" and life, as he said, "brutish, nasty, and short."

The civilized city, the *polis*—and its cognates *poly, plus, pleroma, palude*—means a flowing, a throng of the *hoi polloi*, a polymorphous multitude moving through the piazzas, streets, and alleys. Strategies bring the potential chaos into a successfully functioning order.

As the city rises as a structure from the morass of the *polis*, so the model city of the Western imagination, Athens, attributes its origin to its great goddess, Athene, one among the plethora of Greek personified powers.

Athene has been summed up as a "protectress of the civic order" and it is she who is "at the heart of the Western civilization's myth of progress."[1]

---

1. Ann Shearer, *Athene: Image and Energy* (London: Viking, 1996), 21, 28.

She guided the city's magistrates and the city's generals with gray-eyed sober counseling. Military science and political science, the wide view together with the immediate insight, as well as the brilliant confluence of theoretical science and applied technology—all this Western civilization owes to her. She was called a fortress, and representations of Athene show her dressed in defensive armor, shielded, helmeted, and weaponed, sometimes with a small figure of Nike, victory, on her shoulder. "Nous kai daimonia"—mind and intelligent reasoning—these qualities attributed to her make strategy possible. Moreover, Athene was a contriver, an inventor of devices or what now might be considered tactical maneuvers, the skills for resolving knotted problems, best exemplified concretely in her cult of wool weaving, which translates into the political craft of weaving a fabric of the many contending factions of an organization.

I hardly need to recall to you with your rich classical heritage that Ulysses—that most wily and civilized of heroes—was Athene's favorite. She even explains to him why! Ulysses is *epetes, anchinoos,* and *echephron.* The first two terms appear extremely rarely; in fact, all three are beyond my scholarly capacity. Nonetheless, they are said to refer to a gently civilized restraint, a skillful accuracy in perceptual judgment, and self-mastery over impulsive action. These qualities characterize the inner stuff of the strategic mind.

Let us say, Athene's mode of control proceeded strategically, not merely by discipline or coercion. For instance, for a city to progress, its youth must be harnessed. Athene presided over the *phratria*—the clubs, fraternities, or guilds—that wove together young men with civic feeling. Young women, too, were integrated into the public order through the institution of marriage. Parents took their daughters to the Athenian acropolis before marriage to bring them under the tutelage of Athene. Athene's Roman form, Minerva, was patroness of teachers whose charge it was to care for the development of the civilizing mind and its ideals.

Whether by forming young men into fellowships, young women through household and marriage, or by schooling, each was a strategy for protecting civic life.

Athene did not rule alone—there were twelve Olympians and others beside. She had particular troubles with Dionysus, Poseidon, Ares, and the lovely Aphrodite.

Conflict with Poseidon lies at the source of Athens itself, for the tales say that both a sprig of an olive tree and a spring of seawater appeared miraculously out of the ground. The people voted to decide which gift founded Athens, what was its deepest "nature." By one vote only, the people decided for the olive so necessary to civilization, the oil for cooking, for lighting and healing; yet barely preferable over the wild sea surges, unpredictable floodings and luring deeps of Poseidon. Poseidon and Athene were also in conflict over the gift of the horse: the animal "belonged" to Poseidon, but the controlling bridle was given by Athene. The entire *Odyssey* of Homer can be read as a struggle between Poseidon and Athene over the fate of Ulysses.

The difference with Ares, like that with Poseidon, turns on the distinction between eruptive immediacy and distanced reflection. Though Athene too wants victory, she conquers through thoughtful judgment rather than with strength and fury alone. Dionysus with his dancing crowd of followers, the inconstant ebb and flow of his vitality, his wine, and the underworld cult in relation to the mysteries of the soul and death, as well as the tragic sense of life, was indeed an alien world view to that of Athene. Where she was a victor, he was often a victim; he soft and half naked; she armored from head to toe. His associated animal, the goat, was forbidden on Athene's grounds.

As for differences with Aphrodite, where would one begin! Already enmity was set up by Paris's unfortunate choice—not the choice he made for the goddess of love, beauty, and sexual delight but the folly of choosing at all among the gods! Just one look at the images of these two powers exaggerates the differences: the one with a horrible Gorgon on her breastplate staring you in the face, paralyzing; the other poised half-naked at her bath, a suggestive come-on; one with the dreaded owl, the other with doves and roses; one called the virgin, the other, promiscuity.

If there is one particular quality shared by these four, it must be named "surprise," which means an unexpected seizure or seized by the sudden, like a *coup de foudre* of Aphrodite or the Dionysian *entheos*, which calls the daughters of Minyas away from their civilized tasks (wool work!) to dance wildly in the hills. A military commander may use surprise as a stratagem and gather intelligence to protect his position from surprise by the enemy, nonetheless surprise cannot be brought under the aegis of reason anymore than other gods can submit to Athene's rule. "The unexpected always happens," as the old English proverb says.

Since other forces are also at work, are there strategies appropriate to them? In ancient Greece, oracles of Delphi and Dodona, for instance, offered possible means of avoiding surprises. Soothsayers, dream inter-preters, astrologers and experts in the examination of natural signs such as the flight of birds, the dissected liver, the entrails of sacrificed animals were each strategies in the wider sense, methods for discovering "the successful achievement of desired ends." The question remains: can the arbitrary spontaneity of Tyche (Luck) who became Lady Fortuna in the Renaissance be managed by any strategy at all? Whether we use magical means or ones more Athenian (predictions based on statistical probabili-ties), each individual event is essentially anomalous, and so surprise is potentially always present. As Heraclitus said, the nature of things loves to hide.

We are arriving quickly at the end—an end in which I reveal my own strategy. I hope I will have achieved my desired goal by means of this contrast between Athene and the four instances of difference with her mode of operation. This strategy of mine has intended to show that any human civilization cannot be ruled by one principle alone, even the wisest and most intelligent. Moreover, the word "strategy," which so accurately embodies Athene's style, does not apply to the inspiration and passion fostered by Ares, Dionysus, Poseidon, and Aphrodite. Their urges and rages, their inspirations are sudden, without forethought. They show no self-restraint, mastery over impulses, accuracy of judg-ment. Can we speak of "strategy" at all in regard to their modes of opera-tion? Perhaps the term belongs exclusively to Athene, and, therefore, as a single vision of accomplishment—accomplishment through planning and prudence—strategy offers no protection to surprise.

Owing to the monocular vision of any single god or goddess, strategy is a self-limiting idea. Not because this or that strategy is faulty, but because any single perspective is fundamentally flawed. Even Athenian science bears this flaw. As Paul Feyerabend writes, "...reason cannot be universal and unreason cannot be excluded. This feature of science calls for an anarchistic epistemology."[2] So even in the realms where Athene and rational strategy are most called upon—corporate governance, national administration, planner's think tanks, and most markedly the war in Iraq—there are obvious and tragic strategic failures because too many other dominants have been left out of the calculations. But even

2. Paul Feyerabend, *Against Method: Outline of an Anarchistic Theory of Knowledge* (Lon-don: New Left Books, 1975).

more: these other styles, methods and motivations are anathema to the very idea of a strategy.

In brief: once we have got "inside" the idea of strategy, we are able to imagine its essential limitation, and like the city of Athens itself, a strategy must come to a fall. The human soul allows no invincible fortress, no matter how intelligently conceived, to withstand the surprising forces of unpredictable events.

4

ABANDONING THE CHILD

Subjectivity

The position of the psychologist at these meetings has its special difficulties, and I would like to start by mentioning them—perhaps as a rhetorical device to gain your sympathy, perhaps as an appropriate subjective prelude to any psychological statement, perhaps to impart something of the nature of psychology, and of my theme, the child. Whereas colleagues who come to this podium must meet the difficulty of making their special knowledge generally understandable, the psychologist begins the other way around. We begin with the general, that which we all share, the all-too-human soul, hoping to make this common event specifically relevant to each individual. So it shall be less a matter of having something new to tell, than of bringing the familiar home, of making the objective subjective.

Owing to this different focus, psychotherapy also has a different purpose than that of the other disciplines. (I use the terms psychotherapy and psychology interchangeably, for a psychology that is not a depth psychology is inevitably superficial and off the mark, and a depth psychology is inevitably a psychotherapy because of its effects upon the unconscious grounds of the psyche.) Because psychotherapy's subject matter is indeed "subject matter," the soul, our field seems to have an obligation to the same soul from which it extracts its ideas. It tries to remain always in relationship with its subject matter, but not merely in the empirical manner of good scientific method, paying respect to facts. Rather, it must pay back its ideas to the soul, feed it, be of value to the soul, rather than merely using the psyche to make psychology. Depth

Delivered at the Eranos Conference, August 1971, and first published in *Eranos Yearbook* 40 (1971).

psychology may use the soul as its empirical object but this object is at the same time a person, a subject. Since this soul has its locus in each of us, the focus of depth psychology and the purpose of its psychological ideas will be to touch something subjective. The field moves only when its subject matter is moved. "For," as Freud wrote, "a psychoanalysis is not an impartial scientific investigation, but a therapeutic measure. Its essence is not to prove anything, but merely to alter something." ("Analysis of a Phobia in a Five-Year-Old Boy" [1909], CP3: 246). Depth psychology begins and continues as a therapy, whose essence is to affect the human soul.

It has long seemed to me necessary that a psychological lecture participate in the work of psychotherapy. A lecture too aims at altering something, otherwise it is not truly psychological (in the sense I am using that term), but only about psychology. If psychotherapy is to move out of the consulting room and into life more generally, then one of the places for general psychotherapy is in the psychological lecture.

This kind of lecture shall have to discover the style suiting its purpose, a style not yet worked out, where subjectivity is paramount, and yet where subject talking to subject is not conceived by older models of altering something, e.g., preaching, personal confessing, or polemical debate, because psychological alteration means affecting subjectivity in depth through the constellation of symbolic and emotional reality. By aiming at the constellation of "subject matter," I shall not be proving something, demonstrating, explaining, or even informing. And the way of proceeding, too, will have to be discovered, since we are used to a lecture on a linear model that marshals evidence and arrives somewhere with a result, ending in a point. But we shall today be entertaining a theme, rather than answering a problem, hoping our method to move us through a series of reflections on the same subject, like a string of watercolors, evoking insights, perspectives, emphasizing metaphorical speech, aiming to suggest and open, and where the aim is not a conclusion, not to close the subject, but to open it further.

Thus in yet another way psychology differs from the other disciplines represented here: it depends so much upon the psychologist. Other fields do have a more or less objective area under observation and the field does more or less show historical advancement in problem-solving. Does psychology move forward in the same way, and is it meant to? Do we or should we have more awareness of psyche today? Has the effect of depth psychology upon the psyche resulted in your soul or mine being more conscious, more loving, more harmonious than was the soul of others a century ago before Freud, or two centuries ago before Rousseau, Pinel, and Herbart? And here I am raising less the Kantian question of ethical progress than a psychological question about the relationship between psychology, psychologist, and psyche. In what other discipline are the three so inherently necessary for the movement of any one of them? The psyche requires an adequate psychology to reflect itself, just as psychology depends upon the psyche of the psychologist who in turn exemplifies his psychology. The closer psychology reflects its subject matter, the psyche, the more it merges, as Jung said so often, with the psychologist himself, and becomes like music or painting always a subjective statement.

This is uncomfortable and embarrassing, and well might it be, for embarrassment is a corrective to psychology's pretentiousness. The psyche's subtlety and depth—did not Heraclitus warn of this—will far outreach any psychology which is always bound by its subjective limitations. It is better, despite the embarrassment, to bring up the subjectivity of psychology, than to cover it over with that fantasy of objectivity so infecting our field. So we shall not pretend that the analyst is objective (Freud behind the couch; Jung with his amplificational knowledge), nor shall we entertain this afternoon notions of an objective psyche, an objective level of dreams and objective meaning of psychic events that can be impartially investigated by the psychologist engaged in scientific or scholarly work on objective material: cases, dreams, syndromes, associations. None of this material exists independent of persons and the psyche of the investigator. This so-called objective material is the most subjective stuff of life: it concerns what people remember, how they fantasy, where they love. It is the report of wounds and where life went wrong: it is the scrutiny of secrets and the confession of prayers.

Just here our theme begins: abandoning the child. For the intense subjectivity of psychology, the discomforting embarrassment we feel with its inadequacy vis-à-vis our older brother disciplines, and its extraordinary bigger-than-big inflation, despite the continual rebirth of its problems in which there is no maturing and no advancement so that everything has to be done again anew by each of us entering psychology—this all reflects the archetype of the child. To cast psychology in an objective form, to consider it positivistically, a progress, equal to its tasks, to see psychology's strength and not its weakness (and pretension and omnipotence fantasy to understand all and everything) is to cast out the child.

What is the Child?

What is this "child"? That is surely the first question. What-ever we say about children and childhood is not altogether really about children and childhood. We need but consult the history of painting to see how peculiar are the images of children, particularly when comparing them in their distortions with contemporary exactitude in depicting landscapes and still lives or the portraits of adults. We need but consult the history of family life, education, and economics to realize that children and childhood as we use the terms today are a late invention. What is this peculiar realm we call "childhood," and what are we doing by establishing a special world with children's rooms and children's toys, children's clothes, and children's books, music, language, caretakers, doctors, of playing children so segregated from the actual lives of working men and women? Clearly, some realm of the psyche called 'childhood' is being personified by the child and carried by the child for the adult. How curiously similar this *Daseinsbereich* is to the realm of the madhouse some centuries ago and even today, when the madman was considered a child, the ward of the state or under the parental eye of the doctor who cared for his "children," the insane, like his family. Again, how extraordinary this confusion of the child with the insane, of childhood with insanity ("Madness is childhood"—Foucault [1965], 252).

The confusion between real child and his childhood and the fantasy child that obfuscates perception of child and childhood is classical to the history of depth psychology. You may remember that Freud at first believed that repressed memories causing neuroses were forgotten emotions and distorted scenes from actual childhood. Later he abandoned this child, realizing that a fantasy factor had placed in childhood events that had never actually happened; a fantasy child was at work and not an actual occurrence in the life of the person. He was obliged then to separate child of fact from that of fantasy, outer child events from inner childhood. Nevertheless, he stuck to his belief that the job of therapy was the analysis of childhood. A statement of 1919 is typical: "Strictly considered...analytic work deserves to be recognized as genuine psychoanalysis only when it has succeeded in removing the amnesia which conceals from the adult his knowledge of his childhood from its beginning (that is, from about the second to the fifth year)...The emphasis which is laid here upon the importance of the earliest experience does not imply any underestimation of the influences of later ones. But the later impressions of life speak loudly enough through the mouth of the patient, while it is the physician who has to raise his voice on behalf of the claims of childhood" ("A child is being beaten," CP2:77).

What childhood did Freud mean? Actual children, as I pointed out here two years ago, were never analyzed by Freud. He did not analyze children. Was the childhood the analyst had to recapture actual childhood? Here, Freud himself remains ambiguous, for the actual small young human we call "child" merges in Freud with a Rousseauian, even Orphic-Neoplatonic child who is "psychologically a different thing than an adult" (NIL, 190). ("Childhood has its own ways of seeing, thinking and feeling; nothing is more foolish than to try to substitute our ways." Rousseau, Emile II.) The difference lies in the child's special way of reminiscing: "a child catches hold on...phylogenetic experience where his own experience fails him. He fills in the gaps in individual truth with prehistorical truth; he replaces occurrences in his own life by occurrences in the life of his ancestors. I fully agree with Jung in recognizing the existence of this phylogenetic inheritance" ("From the History of an Infantile Neurosis" [1918], CP3:577–78.)

The actual child was thus himself not altogether actual because his experiences consisted in the confabulations of "prehistoric" occurrences, i.e., nontemporal, mythical, archetypal. And childhood thus refers in Freud partly to a state of reminiscence, like the Platonic or Augustinian memoria, an imaginal realm that provides the actual child with "its own ways of seeing, thinking, and feeling" (Rousseau). This realm, this mode of imaginal existence is to be found, according to popular and depth psychology, in primitive, savage, madman, artist, genius, and the archeological past; the childhood of persons becomes merged with the childhood of peoples. But the child and the childhood are not actual. These are terms for a mode of existence and perception and emotion we still today insist belongs to actual children, so that we construct a world for them following our need to place this fantasy somewhere in actuality. What children are in themselves, "unadulterated" by our need for carriers of the imaginal realm, "beginnings," (i.e., "primitivity," "creation"), and the archetype of the child, we do not know. We cannot know until we have understood more of the working of the fantasy child, the archetypal child in the subjective psyche.

Freud gave to the child image and to the fantasy of childhood a group of startling attributes you may remember: child had no super-ego (conscience) like the adult; no free associations like the adult, but confabulated reminiscences. The child's parents and problems were external, rather than internal as with the adult, so that the child had no symbolically transferred psychic life (NIL, 190). How close to the mental life of "madness," of artist, and how close to what we call "primitive"–this absence of personal conscience, this mixture of behavior and ritual, of memory and myth.

But more startling than the attributes Freud enunciated are those we may draw from his ideas. First, Freud gave the child primacy: nothing was more important in our lives than those early years and that style of thought and emotion of imaginal existence called "childhood." Second, Freud gave the child body: it had passions, sexual desires, lusts to kill; it feared, sacrificed, rejected; it hated and longed and it was composed of erogenous zones, preoccupied with feces, genitals, and deserved the name polymorphous perverse. Third, Freud gave the child pathology: it lived in our repressions and fixations; it was at the bottom of our psychic disorders; it was our suffering.

These are startling attributes indeed if they be compared with the child of Dickens, for Dorrit and Nell, Oliver and David had little passion and little body, and no sexuality at all, especially in view of little Hans and little Anna and other children of psychoanalytic literature. Perversity, when it entered in Dickens at all, came from adults, from industry, education and society; pathology was in deathbed scenes that claimed children back to paradise. Against Dickens we can see Freud's vision most sharply, even if in both the child as fact and the child as image were still not disentangled.

Jung's essay on "The Psychology of the Child Archetype" in 1940 moved the matter much further; actual child is abandoned and with it the fantasy of empiricism, the notion that our apperception of the factor in our subjectivity results from empirical observation of actual child-hood. Jung writes:

> It may not be superfluous to point out that lay prejudice is always inclined to identify the child motif with the concrete experience "child," as though the real child were the cause and pre-condition of the existence of the child motif. In psychological reality, how-ever, the empirical idea "child" is only the means...by which to express a psychic fact that cannot be formulated more exactly. Hence by the same token the mythological idea of the child is emphatically not a copy of the empirical child...not—and this is the point—a human child. (CW9.1, p. 161n.)

What accuracy can our studies of the human child have so long as we have not recognized enough the archetypal child in our subjectivity affecting our vision? So let us leave the child and childhood to one side and pursue what Jung calls the "child motif" and the "childhood aspect of the collective psyche."

Our question now becomes, what is the child motif that projects so vividly and draws such fantasies onto itself? Jung answers:

> The "child" is all that is abandoned and exposed and at the same time divinely powerful; the insignificant, dubious beginning and the triumphal end. The "eternal child" in man is an indescribable experience, an incongruity, a handicap, and a divine prerogative; an imponderable that determines the ultimate worth or worth-lessness of a personality. (CW9.1: 300)

Jung elaborates these general and special features: futurity, divine heroic invincibility, hermaphroditism, beginning and end, and the motif of abandonment from which my theme is drawn. Jung's elabo-rations of 1940 should be taken as an addition to those in his previ-ous works where the child motif is related to archaic mythical thinking and the mother archetype (CW5, passim) and to paradisiacal blissful-ness (CW6: 422f.). Some of the aspects Jung discusses Freud had already described in his language-style. The idea of the creative child occurs in Freud's equation child=penis, and the rejected child in his equation child=feces. "'Feces,' 'child,' and 'penis' thus form a unity, an uncon-scious concept (sit venia verbo)—the concept, namely of a little thing that can become separated from one's body" ("From the history of an infan-tile neurosis" [1918], CP3: 562f.).

To these features I would add two others from our Western tradition, the first specifically Christian, the second specifically Classical. In the Christian tradition (Légasse) "child" refers also to the simple, the naive, the poor and the common—the orphan—of society and of the psyche, as it did in the language of the Gospels, where child meant outcast, the precondition for salvation, and was later placed in association with the feelings of the heart opposed to the learning of the mind. In the Classical tradition, the child appears in those configurations of masculine psychology represented specifically by Zeus, Hermes, and Dionysus, their imagery, mythemes, and cults. The child motif there may be kept distinct from the child-and-mother motifs and also the child-hero motifs that have a distinctly different psychological import.

Our theme follows Jung literally when he says: "The child motif represents something not only that existed in the distant past but something that exists now...not just a vestige but a system functioning in the present whose purpose is to compensate or correct, in a meaningful manner, the inevitable one-sidedness and extravagances of the conscious mind" (CW9.1: 276). If, according to Freud, the essence of the psychoanalytic method is to alter something, and if the child, according to Jung, is that which acts as psychological corrector, our reflections this afternoon require that we bring the child back from his abandonment even while we speak of him. Then the general theme may become specifically focussed in the private subjectivity of each and may act to alter the one-sidedness of consciousness in regard to the child.

Abandonment in Dreams

We find the abandoned child first of all in dreams, where we ourselves, or a child of ours, or one unknown, is neglected, forgotten, crying, in danger or need, and the like. The child makes its presence known through dreams; although abandoned, we can still hear it, feel its call.

In modern dreams we find the child endangered by: drowning, animals, road traffic, being left behind in a car trunk (the "chest" motif), or a pram or supermarket cart (the "basket" motif); kidnappers, robbers, members of the family, incompetents; illness, crippling, secret infections, mental retardation, and brain damage (the idiot child); or a wider, less specific catastrophe such as war, flood, or fire. Sometimes, one wakens in the night with the sensation of having heard a child crying.

Usually the dreamer's response to the motif of abandonment is acute worry, a guilty responsibility: "I should not have let it happen; I must do something to protect the child; I am a bad parent." If it is an infant in the dream, we believe we must keep the sense of this "child" with us all the time, feed it every three hours with thoughtful attention, carry it on our backs like a papoose. We tend to take the child as a moral lesson.

But guilt puts the burden of altering something (Freud) and correcting something (Jung) altogether upon the ego as doer. After all, the dreamer is not only in charge of the child; he also is the child. Consequently, the emotions of worry, guilt, and responsibility, morally virtuous as they may be and even partly corrective of neglect, may also prevent other emotions of fright, loss, and helplessness. Sometimes the more we worry over the child the less the child really reaches us. So, as long as we take up any dream mainly from the position of the responsible ego, by reacting to it with guilt and the energetics of seeing matters straight, improving by doing, by changing attitudes, extracting from dreams moral lessons for the ethically responsible ego, we reinforce that ego. We thereby emphasize the parent-child cleavage: the ego becomes the responsible parent, which only further removes us from the emotions of the child.

Crucial in all dream integration—integration, not interpretation, for we are speaking now of integrity with the dream, standing with it and in it, befriending it in all its parts, participating in its whole story—is the emotional experience of all its parts. Gestalt therapy attempts to drive this home by demanding that the dreamer feel himself into all the parts: the distraught parent, but also the wild dogs, the flooding river, the secret infection, and the exposed child. It is as important to collapse with the child's crying, and to hate savagely the childish, as it is to go home from the analytical hour resolved to take better care of the new and tender parts that need help to grow.

As interpretation and ego responsibility may strengthen the parent at the expense of the child, so too may amplification not reach the child who is abandoned. An amplification of the child in the river, wandering lost in the forest, or attempting a task beyond his strength, in terms of fairy tales and myths and initiation rites may stain the motif accurately so that we see certain aspects clearly—mainly heroic new consciousness emerging—but the staining technique of amplification to bring out the objective meaning may also obliterate the subjective reality of dereliction. Amplification often takes us away from the misery by placing it on a general level. For many psychic events this extension of awareness through amplification is just what is needed, but for precisely this motif it would seem contra-indicated because the forsaken child can best be refound by moving closer to subjective misery and noting its precise locus.

Both responsibility and amplification are insufficient methods for this motif. As activities of the reasoned, mature person they distance us yet further from the child.

Abandonment in Marriage

Because every home established, every nest, niche of habit offers the abandoned child a sanctuary, marriage unavoidably evokes the child. Sometimes an early marriage is obviously intended to find a basket for the child that was inacceptable in the parental house. The pattern may continue long afterwards: husband and wife in tacit agreement taking such care of the abandoned child left from their parental homes that they cannot find the child appropriate to themselves.

Being at home, coming home, heading for home—these are emotions which refer to the child's needs. They indicate abandonment. These emotions transform the actual home, its walls and roof, into a picture-book fantasy with psychic walls and psychic roof in which we place our vulnerability and in which we may be safely exposed to the polymorphous perverse fragmentation of our demands. At home, we are not only mother who embraces and father who captains, but also a little child. What is rejected everywhere else must be allowed here at home.

This reality, which some psychotherapists have called "the inner child of the past" and others "neurotic interaction in marriage" is as important in the fantasies which are enacted in a marriage as are the various patterns of the conjunction described by Jung. What prevents the aspirations of the conjunction are the fierce incest demands of the child, whose desires for union are of another order than the marriage *quaternio* (*CW* 14 and 16, *passim*) and whose image of "contained" and "container" (*CW* 17: 331, *et. seq.*) is wholly in terms of his anxious dereliction. Where else can he go? This is his home too, and more important to him than wife and husband are mother and father, nursing and protection, omnipotence and idealizations.

A purpose of marriage has been defined in terms of procreating and caring for children. But there is also the archetypal child who is constellated by marriage and whose need for care would wreck the actual marriage by insisting that it rehearse archetypal patterns that are pre-marital (uninitiated, infantile, incestuous). Then there occur those struggles between the actual children and the psychic child of the parents as to whom will be abandoned. Then divorce threatens not only the actual children but the abandoned child of the parents that found containment in marriage.

The concentration of abandonment in marriage because there is no other home for it makes marriage the principal scene for enacting the child archetype (not the *conjunctio*). In marriage we find the idealizations of the child: marriage as alpha and omega of life, hermaphroditism lived as "role-sharing," futurity lived as the planning of hopes and fears, and defensive vulnerability. The couple's attempts to contain the child (not each other) produces a familiar pattern alternating between emotionalism and none at all, marriage stiffened into a social norm. Lost in the oscillation is the imagination which the child can bring. Imagination is blown off in affects or concretizes into plans and habits that keep the child cribbed. If we may speak of a "marriage therapy" then it would be based, not on the "neurotic interaction" of the couple, but on the child as central factor in marriage, and the child's imagination, i.e., the cultivation of the imaginal psyche, the peculiar fantasy life that plays between your child and mine.

Baptizing the Child

Usually we feel something fundamentally wrong in regard to the child, which wrong we then place into or onto the child. Societies have to do something with children in order to make right this wrong. We do not take children as they are given; they must be removed out of childhood. We initiate, educate, circumcise, inoculate, baptize. And if, in the romantic manner, we idealize the child—and idealizations are always a sign of distance—calling the child a *speculum naturae*, we do not altogether trust this nature. Even the child Immanuel (Isaiah 7:14–16) has first to eat butter and honey before he can distinguish between good and evil. The child *per se* makes us uneasy, ambivalent; we are anxious about the human propensities concentrated by the child symbol. It evokes too much of what has been left out or is unknown, becoming easily associated with primitive, mad, and mystical. When one looks at the early controversies over infant baptism, one wonders just what psychological content was so exercising these excellent Patristic minds. Their energy spent on the child is comparable to that of ours spent on childhood in modern psychology.

At first, though, they (Tertullian, Cyprian) did not urge early baptism, and Gregory of Nazianzus preferred some degree of mind, about the age of three, before baptism. But Augustine was adamant. Because man was born in original sin, he brought it with him into the world, as Augustine himself had done from his pagan past. Only baptism could wash this from the child. Augustine was clear about the child's need of salvation, quoting Job 14:4-5: "None is pure from sin, not even the infant whose life is but a day upon earth" (*Confessions* I: vii [11]). And what is innocent? "The weakness of infant limbs is innocent, not the infant's soul [*animus*]" (ibid.). How Freudian: the child cannot perform with its still too young faculties those latent perversities that are in the soul. The soul carried not mere general sin, but the specific sin of pre-Christian, un-Christian impulses of polytheistic paganism which Freud was later to discover and baptize "polymorphously perverse," and which Jung was later more comprehensively to describe as the archetypes. Baptism could redeem the soul from childhood, from that imaginal world of a multitude of archetypal forms, gods and goddesses, their cults and the unchristian practices they substantiated.

Inasmuch as the child is not a vestige but a system functioning now, and inasmuch as a sacrament is not a vestige of a one-time historical happening, but continues now, then the baptism of the child is always going on. We are continually baptizing the child, lustrating the psyche's "childhood," its "beginnings," its reminiscing, with the apotropaic rites of our Augustinian culture, cleansing the soul of its polytheistic imaginal possibility that is carried emblematically by the child, thereby taking the child of the psyche a "prisoner for Christ" (Gregory of Nazianzus, "In Praise of Basil"), much as the early church replaced the infants of the hero cults and pagan pantheon with the Jesus child.

This christening goes on whenever we connect to the child motifs in our dreams and feelings using only Christian models. Then we regard the polymorphic potential of our inherent polytheism as fundamentally in need of updating by transformation into unity. Thus we prevent the child from performing its function of that which alters. We correct it, rather than let it correct us.

Regression, Repression

Baptism served two functions for which we have modern names: it prevented regression and it offered repression. Our most immediate experience of the child today is through these experiences.

What depth psychology has come to call regression is nothing other than a return to the child. Since this is so, we might inquire more fundamentally into psychology's notion of maturity that has regression as its counterpart and into psychology's idea of development that requires the child to be abandoned. Regression is the unavoidable shadow of linear styles of thinking. A developmental model will be plagued by its counter-movement, atavism, and reversion will be seen, not as a return through likeness to imaginal reality along Neoplatonic lines (Proclus, Plotinus), but as a regression to a worse condition. Psychology presents "going back" as "going down," a devolution to prior and inferior patterns. Maturity and regression become incompatible. For regression we lose respect, forgetting the need of living things to "go back to beginnings."

Regression is made tolerable in theory today only in terms of a "regression in the service of the ego" (Kris [1952]). Even in Jung, regression is mainly compensatory, a *reculer pour mieux sauter.* In Maslow, Erikson, Piaget, Gesell, as well as in Freudian ego psychology, if we do not advance along certain well-researched paths from stage to stage we become fixated in "childhood" and show regressed behavior, styles called puerile and infantile. Behind every forward step into "reality" there is the threatening shadow of the child—hedonistic or mystical, depending upon how we regard the reversion to primordiality. This child we propitiate with sentimentality, superstition, and kitsch, with indulgent holidays and treats, and with psychotherapy which partly owes its existence and earns its living from the regressive pull of the child.

Our model of maturity tends to make regression attractive. At a distance we idealize the angelic state of childhood and its creativity. By abandoning the child we place it in arcadia, borne by the sea, cradled, rocking softly at water level among reeds and rushes, nourished by nymphs who delight in its whims, shepherds, kindly old caretakers who welcome the childish, the regressed. Then of course the counter-movement sets in again; the hero constellates; from the abandoned child the great leap forward, the draining of the Zuider Zee with which Freud compared the work of psychoanalysis (NIL, 106).

Because the major content of repression is the child, the contemporary revolution on behalf of the repressed—black or poor, feminine or natural or undeveloped—becomes unavoidably the revolution of the child. The formulations become immature, a touch pathetic, the behavior regressed, and the ambition invincible and vulnerable at the same time. Hermaphroditism of the archetype also plays its role in the revolution, as does that peculiar mixture of beginning and end: hope exemplified in apocalyptic destruction. Our theme thus touches upon psychology's relation to the times and its struggle with the child, all of which suggests that it might be profitable to reflect the statements of Marcuse, Laing, and Brown concerning the contemporary revolution of the repressed in the light of archetypal psychology, i.e., as expressions of the cult of the child.

Evoking the Child

We are familiar with situations that call the child back from where we have left it. Going backwards into familiar places, sounds, smells; each *abaissement du niveau mental*, new conditions that constellate thrill and the fantasy of complete newness, that one can make of something whatever one wishes; also, sudden falls into love, into illness, into depression. The child is also evoked by unfamiliarity where imagination is asked for and we respond instead with stubborn petulance, inadequacy, tears.

But the regressed condition that no one wants can also be directly prompted in psychotherapy. For here is a haven, to creep out of hiding; here one may show one's unwanted, unlovable, ugly concealments, and one's huge hopes. These feelings have all been given appropriate psychological names: infantile desires, self-destructive fantasies, omnipotence cravings, archaic impulses. But in deriding these names we ought not to forget—and we are each therapists of the psyche since it is a devotion that cannot belong to a profession only—that always these childish pathological conditions contain futurity. The very way forward through the condition so unwanted, ugly, and preposterously expectant lies just in the conditions themselves. The pathology is also the futurity. In it the insights lie; from it the movement comes.

By recognizing a basic cry we may evoke this child in the pathology; it is as if there were a basic cry in persons that gives direct voice to the abandoned content. For some persons it is: "Help, please help me"; others say, "take me, just as I am, take me, all of me without choice among my traits, no judgement, no questions asked"; or "take me, without my having to do something, to be someone." Another cry may be "hold me," or "don't go away; never leave me alone." We may also hear the content saying simply, "Love me." Or we can hear, "teach me, show me what to do, tell me how." Or, "carry me, keep me." Or the cry from the bottom may say, "Let me alone, all alone; just let me be."

Generally the basic cry speaks in the receptive voice of the infant, where the subject is an object, a "me" in the hands of others, incapable of action yet poignantly enunciating its knowledge of its subjectivity, knowing how it wishes to be handled. Its subjectivity is in the crying by means of which it organizes its existence. So, as well, we hear in it the basic cry a person addresses to his environment, turning his entourage into helpers, or lovers, or constant companions (a *thiasos*) who will nurse, dance attendance, or teach, or accept all blindly, who will never let him alone, or the reverse, from whom he flees in continual rejection. And the cry says how a person is unable to meet his needs himself, unable to help himself, or let himself alone.

It is worth insisting here that the cry is never cured. By giving voice to the abandoned child it is always there, and must be there as an archetypal necessity. We know well enough that some things we never learn, cannot help, fall back to and cry from again and again. These inaccessible places where we are always exposed and afraid, where we cannot learn, cannot love, and cannot help by transforming, repressing or accepting are the wildernesses, the caves where the abandoned child lies hidden. That we go on regressing to these places states something fundamental about human nature: we touch upon an incurable psychopathy again and again through the course of life yet which apparently does go through many changes before and after contact with the unchanging child.

Here we strike upon the psychological relationship between what philosophy calls becoming and being, or the changing and the changeless, the different and the same, and what psychology calls growth on the one hand and on the other psychopathy: that which cannot by definition reverse or alter but remains as a more or less constant lacuna of char-

acter throughout life. In the language of our theme we have the vulnerability of the abandoned child, and this same child's evolving futurity.

In this conundrum we usually pick up one side or the other, feeling
ourselves different, changing, evolving, only to be smashed back by the
shattering recurrence of a basic cry, which in turn leads to the belief of
being hopelessly stuck, nothing moving, just the same as always. The
history of psychotherapy has also been driven back and forth by this
apparent dilemma. At times degeneration theory (inheritance and constitution, or an idea of predestination) declare character is fate and that
we can but move within predetermined patterns. At other times, such as
today in American humanistic developmental psychology, the category
of growth through transformation covers all psychic events.

Neither position is adequate. Like the metaphorical child of Plato's
Sophist (249*d*) who, when asked to choose, opts for "both," the abandoned child is both that which never grows remaining as permanent as
psychopathy and also that futurity springing from vulnerability itself.
The complex remains, and the lacunae; that which becomes different
are our connections with these places and our reflections through them.
It is as if to change we must keep in touch with the changeless, which
also implies taking change for what it is, rather than in terms of development. Evolution tends to become a "means of disowning the past" (T.S.
Eliot); what we want to change we wish to be rid of. A subtle psychological perception is required to distinguish in our natures the changeable
from the changeless, and to see the two as intimately connected so as
not to search in the wrong place for growth and the wrong place for stability, or to presume that change leaves stability behind and that stability
is never vulnerable.

The Return of the Child

If the child is repressed in the amnesia of "the second to the fifth year,"
as Freud wrote, then it is the little child who shall return. Abandonment does not succeed; the murderer's hand fails; fishermen, shepherds,
maids appear; the child becomes a foundling to come back and carry
the day.

It is not merely that the childish returns in the leftovers of childhood,
but everything that emerges from unconsciousness comes back too
young. Everything begins in youthful folly because the doors to the cel-

lars and gardens of the mind are barred not only by a censor, a flaming sword, or a Cerberus, but by a little boy or girl who magically transforms everything passing over the threshold into its own condition.

Thus, as Freud saw, the world of the unconscious is the world of childhood, not actual childhood or the childhood of the human race, but a condition governed by the archetype of the child; thus, as Jung saw, this archetype is herald, the prefiguration of every change that we go through in depth. Everything comes back too young, implying that the adequate connection with the unconscious will have to show inadequacy. We are not able, still dependent on that child, its whims, its atmosphere of specialness, still needing our hurts, the way it touches our eros, making us each at moments into pedophiles, child lovers.

Moreover, all the other faces of the repressed, the personally forgotten and the primordially unknown, will return in a childlike style. Besides the revolution, all those other things ostracized from the agora of daily life—art, insanity, passion, despair, vision—will come in with this peculiar childishness which at times we ennoble as the childlikeness of the creative.

The childishness that returns as the personal shadow deserves better treatment than merely the Freudian one. Jung indicated that the treatment of childishness, of psychopathology, at the archetypal level is to "dream the myth onwards" (CW9.1: 271), to let its prospective nature speak. By allowing the child to be the corrector, it performs one of its archetypal functions: futurity. What comes back points forward; it returns as the repressed and at the same time comes back in order to fulfill a Biblical cure for psychopathology: "and a little child shall lead them" (Isaiah 11: 6).

Consequently, the cue to the future is given by the repressed, the child and what he brings with him, and the way forward is indeed the way back. But it is immensely difficult to discriminate among the emotions that come with the child, mainly because he does not return alone.

It is as if the little girl abandoned returns with a protector, a newfound father, a strong male figure of muscular will, of arguments and cunning, and his outrage, his blind striking-out mingles with her pained tantrums, his sullen melancholy becomes indistinguishable from her withdrawn pouting. Though they coalesce, child and guardian also struggle for separation. In face and gesture there are alternating movements, an alternating look in the eye, appeal for help, resistance to it, bitterness of tears coming grudgingly, fought off, clenched, and then abandoned cataclysmic sobbing. Sometimes the little girl returns as a gamin of the streets, dirty, or a tomboy of the fields, earthy, half-male, hardened from the long neglect and the tutorials of the animus, a girl-child almost wolf-child, all thumbs and elbows, returning yet saying "let me alone."

With the little boy a similar pattern occurs for it is equally difficult to distinguish him from the milkmaids and nymphs and sisters who have succored him during the repression. The softness and vanity and demands which he brings with him, passivity and vulnerability, the reclusive nursing of himself, hardly differ from what psychology has called anima states.

With the child's return comes childhood, both kinds: actual with its memories and imaginal with its reminiscences. We have come to call this memorial factor with its two kinds of remembrances "the unconscious," personal and collective. But this term, "the unconscious," only adds to the burden of differentiating the complexity of psychic life. It might be more beneficial to separate the child (as the reminiscent factor which returns a person to the primordially repressed of non-actual substructures) from a category so indefinite as the unconscious. Then we would be in a better position to free 'childhood' as an imaginal mode of perceiving and feeling from its identification with actual childhood which usually had less freedom and joy, less fantasy and magic and amorality than we sentimentally attribute to it. Our cult of childhood is a sentimental disguise for true homage to the imaginal. Could childhood be called by its true name —the realm of archetypal reminiscence—then we would not have to become unconscious to find the mythical. We have psychologically confused the coming up of events from the unconscious with the coming back of reminiscence.

Psychology has taken the repressed child to be an axiomatic metaphor of psychic structure. Psychology assumes the repressed is less developed than the repressor, that consciousness is topographically, historically, and morally superior to the unconscious, characterized by primitive, amoral, and infantile impulses. Our notion of consciousness inherently necessitates repression of the child. This constellates our main fear: the return of the inferiority, the child, who also means the return of the realm of archetypal reminiscence. Archetypal fantasy is the most threatening activity of the human soul as we now conceive it, for our Western rational tradition has placed this activity in the ontologically inferior, the primitive amoral realm of actual childhood (cf. Bundy [1927]).

The shadow that we fear most and repress primordially, i.e., the kind of fantasy reminiscence that we name madness, is brought with the child. The fear of yielding control to it governs our profound amnesia. And so we have forgotten an evident psychological truth: anxiety reveals the deepest shadow. Rather than see the child in the shadow, recent psychology has been concentrating upon the shadows of aggression and of moral evil. But aggression can be enjoyable, and moral evil attractive. They are not fearful, shameful to the same degree as the child. Jungian focus upon the devil and the dark side of the god image has covered over our anxiousness, so that we have neglected the dark side of the Bambino, the other *infans noster* who was the first shadow found in the anxieties of classical analysis. The ruling power, contaminating the imaginal with the impulsive, is a monster child whom we have been abandoning for centuries.

So when the cry "l'imagination au pouvoir" goes up we should not feel deceived that a monster has been released, that the revolution becomes puerile nonsense, obscene, scatological, polymorphously perverse. The imagination to power is the child to power, because Western consciousness with its one-sided extravagances of will and reason at the expense of *memoria* has abandoned the *mundus imaginalis* to children.

The Fantasy of Independence

Child," writes Jung in his essay on this archetype, "means something evolving towards independence." In a phrase Jung catches the dilemma, for the child returns not only in the regression, bringing one into the imaginal world of childhood, but also in a striving out of childhood for independence. Abandonment, as Jung pointed out and Neumann elaborated, is the precondition for the independence and invincibility of the child-becoming-hero.

"Child means something evolving towards independence. This it cannot do," continues Jung, "without detaching itself from its origins: abandonment is therefore a necessary condition, not just a concomitant symptom" (CW 9.1: 287). The child is abandoned in order to reveal its independence. Out of feelings of isolation and rejection arises a fantasy of independence.

There is a similarity of metaphor, as others have observed, between Aristotle's entelechy, Leibniz's monad, and Jung's self of which the child is a primary image (CW9.1: 270, 278). Entelechy, monad, and self coincide in this fantasy of independence: self-substantial entelechy on the course of its actualization and the self-same windowless monad unique to itself different from all others are both recapitulated in Jung's self of individuation unfolding through the tensions of opposites, like a tree. Jung writes: "If a mandala may be described as a symbol of the self seen in cross section, then the tree would represent a profile view of it: the self depicted as a process of growth" (CW13: 304).

The tree is a cherished symbol in depth psychology—the tree test, the analysis of tree-images in clinical paintings and drawings, and the examination of the tree in art in order to grasp the personality of the painter. The tree suits our notion of personality growth, and indeed appears as a spontaneous metaphor for the imperceptible expansion from seed to fullness, in which history can be read, the dry years and wet ones, the blows and diseases, and the same metaphor provides for ancestral roots, vertical movement stretched between heaven and earth, branches, fruits in season, pruning. And we need these metaphors to place our lives and to place the feelings that something besides myself carries my life in a natural process and is uniquely mine, my tree of life.

At the same time, it is the task of psychology to point out what else these metaphors are saying so that consciousness does not become imprisoned in its own favorite images. One job of psychology is to bring archetypal reflection to its own systems, ideas, imagery, so that it, unlike the other disciplines, can apply itself to itself, aware of what shadows appear within its statements.

In regard to the tree, its style of independence may so dominate our awareness that we lose sight that we are being carried by it, for we are not trees but men, not vegetables but animals, not planted and rooted but roaming, not cyclic only in our rhythms but multiphasic with many processes taking place simultaneously, at different rhythms and in different directions and not necessarily following one overall entelechy. If, on the one hand, the tree fantasy states an independence of the self from the ego, the fantasy just as well states the independence of the self from other selves. It emphasizes separation, so that we forget that individuation and independent separateness are neither synonymous, nor necessarily involved.

The fantasy of independence comes out again in Jung's "Seven Sermons to the Dead" (1916), where the speaker in Sermon IV tells of two god-devils: the Burning One and the Growing One. The first is Eros, the second, the Tree of Life; the first "bindeth twain together, the second filleth space with bodily forms, growing with "slow and constant increase." "In their divinity," says the speaker, "stand life and love opposed."

Life and love are opposed when life is represented by the tree (CW 13: 459) that grows alone; its habitat, as Jung writes (CW 13: 406), is a mountain or an island, or it grows directly out of the sea water, upon a rock, or extends from a human body part, head or belly (CW 12, figs. 131, 135). Clinical drawings of the tree show the same independence as the alchemical imagery described by Jung. Evidently the slow and constant increase of the tree, representing personality in its individuation process (CW 13: 350), individualized already *in nuce* by its particular "nature," stalwart, memorable, alone, is a process of independence. Tree is the child in which abandonment has become the seed set apart.

Note that this tree does not appear in a community, as a member of a grove, one in an allée or orchard, a part of a forest. We do not see the forest for the tree, and, unless the trees like Philemon and Baucis are joined by their "vegetable love" and united by miraculous intervention, the tree in its independence shows a growth where life and love are opposed. That we may encourage our growth on an island or mountain, producing individuation from heads or bellies, or directly from the psychoid sea of our emotionality through concentration upon the subjective factor may occur, but then at the expense of the other god-devil Eros, who becomes the Burning One, feverish to connect that which is isolated and which must be isolated by the very metaphor that does not have the interdependence of connection inherent to its fantasy. Child and tree associate in mythologems that bring the two together: the child in the tree, born of a tree, hidden there, or carried to its death by the tree; by giving the tree a maternal meaning, matters have been left at that. But we may also regard them as a pair of radical extremes: solitary independence and symbiotic dependency, two fantasies and qualities of emotion that bespeak each other and call each other up. Though child may be abandoned, it is never alone; child does not represent a solitary self, but a psychic condition in need and cared for by animals, nurses, foster parents. It may grow, as Jung says, towards independence, and thus be latently heroic, as the tree, a singleton predetermined in seed, but its essence is dependent. Fundamental to the tree is that it is rooted to its fate and grows from it, and one way only—the tree never regresses; but the child is regression; it can do nothing alone; it must be sheltered, watered, kept. Thus when we are in the fantasy of independence we are also secretly in the fantasy of dependency, which projects independence as goal, that towards which we are evolving. Furthermore, when we are in the fantasy of independence, dependency seems incommensurable, a contradictory opposite, that which must be left behind; so the child will continually be abandoned that, in turn, constellates an ever-stronger Burning One and an ever more compulsive dependency upon Eros. To be free of this cycle would mean to abandon the tree of independence as our model of self in order to imagine dependency by means of other metaphors. For instance, independence could mean widening the areas of dependency, sensitivity towards one's needs for help and following, for a forest of comrades in symbiotic participation, for interchange and cross-fertilization, where life and love are not necessarily opposed.

The Fantasy of Growth

If any single notion now conjoins the disparate schools of therapeutic psychology, it is the fantasy of growth. Carl Rogers in a chapter describing "A Therapist's View of the Good Life" uses these phrases: "An increasing openness to experience," "increasing trust in his organism," "a process of functioning more fully," "greater richness of life." Erik Erikson in a chapter called "Growth and Crises of the Healthy Personality" describes psychic health in similar language: "an increased sense of inner unity, with an increase of good judgement, and an increase in the capacity to do well."

Karen Horney, in her book *Neurosis and Human Growth: The Struggle Toward Self-Realization*, speaks of the work of psychotherapy as giving "the constructive forces of the real self a chance to grow." The wholeheartedness of psychic health is built upon her "morality of evolution," a belief "that inherent in man are evolutionary constructive forces, which urge him to realize his given potentialities."

These are but three pointed examples. The growth fantasy is easy, appealing to the child: whatever is may become something else, transformed through a "natural" process of increase and in accordance with the "natural" development of inborn basic patterns. The personality is not conceived in original sin but in goodness, not in *privatio boni* requiring baptism but in *a priori* health and wholeness. We need but conform with the ground plan of our individual being and grow from there. Disease, perversion, insanity, evil—these are secondary accrued phenomena, lacunae, or fixations in the growth process which is primary. Jung's cautionary realism about the shadow in all psychic events, including wholeness, and Freud's pessimism reflected by his thanatos hypothesis have been crushed under the juggernaut of therapeutic enthusiasm which is but the recrudescence of messianic hope that no longer finds place in religion. Psychology does not notice that its constructs and interpretations have become dogmatic expressions of a fantasy, so that psychology no longer can reflect the actual psyche in conditions that bespeak neither hoping nor growing and are neither natural nor whole.

Astoundingly, psychology turns to the child in order to understand the adult, blaming adults for not enough of the child or for too many remnants of the child still left in adulthood. *The thinking of psychotherapy and of psychology of personality has been captured by the child archetype and its growth fantasy.* Psychological thought is deliberately childish. It continues the fantasy of creative expansion, widening, enlarging, so essential to the Romantic temperament according to Georges Poulet. This fantasy is hard to reconcile with that feeling of decline in our civilization and our subjective experiences of narrowing specialization, limitation, and decay. Psychology's growth fantasy seems a curious leftover of the early twentieth century's colonial, industrial, and economic fascination with increase: the bigger the better.

Little wonder that at a certain moment in our lives we feel we have done with psychology, that we feel unable to abide one more psychological explanation, for it is all too simple, too naive, too optimistic. At a certain moment we hear the child speaking through our psychological words, and this one archetypal perspective is inadequate for the complexity of our souls. Moreover, the childishness is not itself provided for by a fantasy of growth that abandons the child in an unsophisticated notion of growing.

Growth, like evolution and development, or like any of the pregnant terms with which psychology operates—unconscious, soul, self—is a symbolic, emotionally charged word, evocative rather than descriptive, generally hortatory rather than particularly precise. We have confused the general category of motion with one of its varieties, growth, so that all movements and changes become witness to growth. We call adaptation "growth," and even suffering and loss part of "growing." We are urged, nay expected, to "keep growing" in one way or another right into the coffin.

In this one idea of psychology various notions converge: 1) increase in size (or expansion); 2) evolution in form and function (or differentiation); 3) moral progress (or improvement); 4) conjunctions of parts (or synthesis); 5) stages in temporal succession (or maturation); and 6) negentropic self-generation (or spontaneity). These last two need further clarification, in that the process of maturation from stage to stage occurs, according to the growth fantasy, both rationally and spontaneously—not randomly—following the essential goodness of the child. Growth represents this goodness, manifests its activity being realized, and this goodness is part of the child's "instinct," "creative nature," "heart," not part of its intellect or "head," which is later and learned and not so deep.

These interlocking notions form part of what George Boas in his masterly, critical essay has explored as *The Cult of Childhood,* a title which means nothing less than obeisance to the child archetype in our modern Western culture. There is still more to it: added to the six components which I have tried to separate within the growth fantasy, there is also an underlying idea that growth equals health. To stop growing is to be fixated, stuck, neurotic. Moreover, decay, which certainly belongs to less naive models of growth, is apparently forgotten by psychology. What appears here as my simplification merely mirrors the simplifications in psychological theories.

But the idea of growth could be separated from the child's version of it and then it might be less simplified. Psychology could adopt a more sophisticated analysis of growth in terms of change of form as discussed by L. L. Whyte and as presented by Adolf Portmann in many subtle discussions of it here at Eranos. Then we might imagine growth less as increase and linear development, and more as changes in patterns of significance and imagery. The precision of this imagery arises in response to the empty non-formed aspects of the psyche. Its lacuna and voids (*increatum*) provide the "negative" background—much as empty areas in leaf patterns provide the characteristics in emerging leaf shapes in Goethian morphology. Psychological significance "grows" out of the negative, meaningless areas of our suffering. Significance occurs in relation with psychopathy; we find significance when the absurd and insignificant nonsense of our complexes take on changed shape. The changes are formal. Wholeness then would imply less the integration of parts into a unity as in the naive growth fantasy, but more the discrimination of patterns and the freedom of their changes.

We must be clear not to blame biology for the naive growth metaphor. Its origins precede its appearance in biology. Notions such as the "childhood of the race," evolution, and recapitulation by ontogeny of phylogeny indicate that this archetypal fantasy probably played its part in the formation of basic ideas of nineteenth-century biology, anthropology, and linguistics. (Much work needs to be done in order to uncover the archetypal patterns in the formation of these ideas.) In psychology many images of growth are of course taken from the naturalist's language: Froebel, speaking of children's education, conjures up flowers blooming, ducks taking to water, chickens scratching at an appointed stage. Erikson understands psychological growth through models of the "growth of organism" from a "ground plan." Gesell compares growth of the mind to that of plants; Koffka entitled his major work in Gestalt psychology (that so stresses wholeness) *The Growth of the Mind.* Piaget finds intelligence can best be accounted for by means of a developmental metaphor. Intelligence follows inherent maturational laws, producing progressively more stable states of adaptation. We move through smaller stages and larger periods, each stage and period providing foundation for the next.

Within and below lies "nature," the governing determinant of growth. To put the fantasy in the language of archetypal psychology: the archetypes of child as growth and its mother, nature, rule psychology's main view of the human being. The idea of nature further mystifies the imprecision, for it is an idea so rich, so varied, so symbolic that over sixty different conceptual connotations have been distinguished. It would be worth a full Eranos conference, perhaps several, on this complex subject of health, nature, and growth; fortunately our part is only a few reflections on the fantasy in relation to the child.

As Jung and Freud point out in different ways, discussion of the child always involves us with ideas of growth, and the actual child most vividly presents a pattern where all the notions—expansion, differentiation, improvement, maturation and spontaneity—coincide. The child gets bigger and better and more able "naturally." But neglected in these observations which have been elaborated into precise norms for the ages of childhood by Erikson, Koffka, Maslow, Piaget, and Gesell is the static child. For the child archetype does not grow but remains an inhabitant of childhood, a state of being, and the archetypal child personifies a component that is not meant to grow but to remain as it is as child, at the threshold, intact, an image of certain fundamental realities that necessarily require the child metaphor and which cannot be presented in another manner. Child Zeus and Child Dionysus and Child Hermes do not grow, as do Theseus and Moses for instance. The child is one of the faces—not stages—of the god, one of his ways of being, of revealing his nature. There is no question of moral improvement, of increase, or of differentiation through developmental process in these child images of these gods unless we use man and his childhood as the measure for archetypal events. Although these gods fulfill some of the patterns of abandonment, they do not leave behind dependency in order to become "mature" gods. The face of the child is eternally theirs, and if we are created in the image of the divine, so a face of the child in us is static, eternal, not able to grow. Perhaps I speak now of men, and the image in which they are made since curiously we do not have comparable images of a Child Athene, a Child Aphrodite, a Child Hera or Demeter.

By giving more favor to this idea of the child that is not meant to grow, we might imagine the child's abandonment and need for rescue as a continuous state, a static necessity that does not evolve towards independence, does not evolve at all, but remains as a requirement of the fulfilled and matured person.

Picasso speaks to our point: "Change does not mean development." "When I hear how people talk of the development of the artist, it seems to me as if they were seeing the artist between two opposed mirrors which were endlessly reflecting his mirror image, and as if they saw the series of images in one mirror as his past and the images in the other mirror as his future, while he himself supposedly stood for his present. They do not realize that all are the same images but on different levels." "I am astounded over the way people let the word development be misused. I don't develop; I am."

And finally, concerning abandonment, Picasso says, "Nothing can come about without loneliness. I have created a loneliness for myself that no one can imagine."

The Fantasy of Origins

The repressed child returns too in the fantasy of origins, a fantasy which seems to affect particularly those whose disciplines require a purgation of subjectivity for the sake of an objective rationality. Scientific scholarship shows much concern with beginnings, with *Ursprungsgeschichte, Urtext,* and *Urwort–Quellenforschung.* The search is for origins in roots, elements, sources. In psychology the fantasy of origins occurs elaborately in Freud's "primal horde" and primal scene and Rank's "birth trauma" to mention but two of the most obviously imaginary. But contemporary psychiatry's insistence that neurotic disturbances originate fundamentally in the deprivation during early years of maternal care (Bowlby) is, despite the objective nature of the supporting research and the unimaginative language in which it is presented, also an origin fantasy about babies, breasts, and what a mother should be.

There will always be an unease when one deals—as do the scholarly, investigative disciplines (*Geisteswissenschaften*)—with the depths of human nature, because these depths remain always open questions. The *a priori* of law, language, religion, and society are difficult to discover not merely because they are "buried in the past." Because these fields display the human spirit, they remain enigmatic in principle, and their riddles give rise to philosophical wonder—and to psychological anxiety. By believing that we can trace the phenomena of these disciplines to a source does not so much solve the problem as it does settle an anxiety. That the ultimate source is in the subjective factor, in the enigma of the human spirit, is disguised by the fantasy of objective origins.

Reductionism of the later to the earlier and of the complex to the simple not only presupposes a growth or evolution fantasy, but this mental process of reductionism seems to become less and less exigent as it nears its goal: an explanation in terms of origins. Reductionism is so easily satisfied. Its content with naive explanations for highly complex problems, for instance, its unsophisticated idea of causality, indicate that a subjective factor is influencing the objective rationality of the hypothesis. We should not let pass unobserved this psychological curiosity. The sophistication, and even intelligence, of scholars give way as they move from the immediate complexity of a problem at hand to an account of its remote origins. Their fantasy shows that, in their search for beginnings, they become guided by the child archetype. They seem to lose sight as they move from known to unknown, their evidence ever slimmer, that a hypothesis is truly hypothetical, a supposing, a conjecturing about an unknown lying behind the known, and that they have moved from one level of discussion to another where fantasy plays a more distinct role. So they become like the child described in Plato (*Republic* 378d) who "cannot judge what is allegorical and what is literal."

Research comes to a stop when it has formulated a fantasy of beginnings into a hypothesis of origins, when an allegory can be presented as a literal reality. Since the dominant of beginnings governs the research, the real origin searched for is the child archetype and the real prompter of the endeavour is the lost child. Under the influence of this archetype the research, psychologically, is itself an allegory: the search for an imaginary childhood, whether of language, of mankind, of neurosis, supposedly buried in a prior condition, whether in primitives, myths, archaeological digs, subconscious mental structures, root syllables.

Because these origins are imaginary we could also say that the origins lie in the imaginal, implying that the beginnings of every deep human question formulated into an academic, scholarly discipline lie in the *mundus imaginalis.* This provides the archetypal background or *causa formalis* of the matter under investigation. Hence, investigation is satisfied only when it reaches an extensively fantastic reconstruction of beginnings whether in the prehistory of the individual or of a field. When the imaginal is reached, the archetypal urge in the research is satisfied. The anxiety is quelled. The child, as it were, has come home.

The Fantasy of Creativity

The topic of this conference, creativity, also belongs partly among the fantasies constellated around the child archetype. There are many notions of creativity, and I have already examined them and grouped them in *The Myth of Analysis,* which spares us now from more than merely noting in passing the relevance of this theme.

In the literature of psychology one of the notions of creativity—originality, imagination, eros, novelty, play, spontaneity, naiveté—expresses the child. George Boas has gathered quotations mainly from critics and painters in which the creative vision and the vision of the child are identified. When we identify the creative with this set of connotations we have taken our perspective from the child archetype. Consequently, when we speak of the unconscious as the "creative unconscious," we are seeing it mainly in its guise of the child and our simplifications of its processes are childish. The cult of childhood continues in the awe with which we hold "creativity," the attention we pay the "creative man" and the "creative impulse." We should not be surprised that psychology's research into creativity frequently yields silly results, especially noticeable when play is given a disproportionate place, as if imagination were not a discipline or art, not a work. The last ideas of Winnicott are case in point. His prolonged devotion to the psychiatry of children resulted in a theory of play which extends the word to a metapsychology of creativity, the archetypal background to which is the child.

Concentration upon the child aspect of creativity makes us miss its other faces: the destruction and aggression of the shadow, the work of the ego, the renewing periodicity of the mother, the moodiness of the *anima,* and the ordering limits and inevitable failure given by the *senex*— all of which too enter psychological descriptions of creativity and which have their part in the formation of any oeuvre.

The Fantasy of Futurity

There is yet a fifth fantasy belonging to the child. This fantasy, too, seizes us from behind when the child is not held in consciousness. The child archetype speaks also in the language of goals. One of its essentials is futurity.

A goal, from the psychological point of view, is a final cause in Aristotle's sense of "that for the sake of which." Inasmuch as a final cause enters every complex as one of its four grounds, the child is never absent; we feel him in our hoping. But then he gets abandoned by throwing himself forward into goal fantasies, hopes literalized. Each complex projects a teleology about itself: how it will evolve, what purpose it has, how it can be resolved or brought to an end.

Therapeutic psychology too has a *telos* and speaks of goals which language it assumes it has taken "empirically" from the psyche. Thus it speaks of the synthesis of personality, individuation, conjunction of the opposites, self. It has as well an elaborated goal imagery—*lapis, mandala, tree, child*—which again is the result of "clinical findings." But the spontaneous imagery of completion and its literalization into goals are better kept distinct. Otherwise we place the *telos* inherent within the complex outside, at the end of the line. Then we move the *telos* from an internal component to an external image; then we take it literally, placing futurity in the future, a mistake as naive as taking the efficient cause literally and placing it in the past.

Predictions about the future of a complex and reduction to its past are both fantasies within it. Efficient cause and final cause are movements within every psychic complexity giving belief that the troubling question at hand has come from somewhere and is going somewhere, reflecting a genealogy myth and an eschatology myth. But psychologically, past and future function now so that a goal is a dynamism now at work in a complex. To separate out the *telos* is to separate way and goal. We could hardly cripple the movement of a complex more than by speaking literally of its goal, which aborts it of its teleological impulse, robs it of its child. The more we fix on the goals, like wholeness and self and individuation, the less likely it is that they are actually working. The more literal is our description, the more we are possessed by the fantasy of futurity, enacting the child even though disguised in the wisdom-language of highest and last things.

Mothering and Nursing

When the child returns through mimesis and we return to its condition, enacting childish behavior and experiencing childish emotions, there also returns the problem of "how to deal with it."

Here we shall note an essential contrast between mothering and nursing. In their early discoveries, Freudian and Jungian psychologies both were dominated by parental archetypes, especially the mother, so that behavior and imagery were mainly interpreted through this maternal perspective: the oedipal mother, the positive and negative mother, the castrating and devouring mother, the battle with the mother and the incestuous return.

The unconscious and the realm of "The Mothers" were often an identity. Through this one archetypal hermeneutic, female figures and receptive passive objects were indiscriminately made into mother symbols. What was not mother! Mountains, trees, oceans, animals, the body and time cycles, receptacles and containers, wisdom and love, cities and fields, witches and death—and a great deal more lost specificity during this period of psychology so devoted to the Great Mother and her son, the Hero. Jung took us a step forward by elaborating other archetypal feminine forms, e.g., the *anima,* and I have tried to continue in Jung's direction by remembering that breasts, and even milk, do not belong only to mothers, that other divine figures besides Maria, Demeter, and Kybele have equally important things to say to the psyche and that the women attendant on Dionysus were not turned into mothers but nurses. Like those frescoes of the madonna Church which conceals a congregation under her billowed blue skirts, the Great Mother has hidden a pantheon of other feminine modes for enacting life (cf. Malamud [1971]).

Mother and nurse are separated in the abandoned child motif. In myth they are two distinct figures. Similarly, in our reactions to the abandoned child's return—sudden spontaneous affects of the heart, weakness and longing, narcissistic demands and complaints, playfulness, fantasies of conquest, invincibility, specialness—we too might distinguish the taking up the child by the nurse and by the mother.

For the mothering attitude, it is always a matter of life and death; we are obsessed with how things will turn out; we ask what happened and what will happen. The mother makes things "great," exaggerates, enthuses, infuses the power of life and death into each detail, because the mother's relation to the child is personal, not personal as related and particular, but *archetypally personal* in the sense that the child's fate is delivered through the personal matrix of her fate, becoming fate in general which she then is called. The mother archetype gives the personalistic illusion to fate. Whatever she has to do with takes on overwhelming personal importance that actually is general and altogether impersonal: the desires and loathing of the mother-son relation so intimately personal become suprapersonal enormities, just as the experiences of despair, renewal, continuity, and mystery of the mother-daughter relation that seem so fatefully personal become impersonal eternal events.

The growth she furthers is all-out and passionate, the death overwhelming, *mater dolorosa,* for the mother is always too much: goodness and support, concern for weakness, or interest in ambition. Her toomuchness makes the child into hero and rebel, into princess and prostitute, for her passion converts our hurt derelict conditions into archetypal importance.

As Jung spontaneously remarks in that famous passage in his essay on the mother archetype (CW 9.1: 172): "Mother is mother-love, my experience and my secret." Although the mother experience is archetypal, "strange like nature," "cruel like fate," yet it is so acutely personal that, as Jung observes, we tend to "load that enormous burden of meaning, responsibility, duty, heaven and hell, on to the shoulders of one frail and fallible human being... who was our mother" (ibid.). "This figure of the personal mother looms so large in all personalistic psychologies that, as we know, they never got beyond it..." (159). In other words, the mother archetype itself is responsible for personalistic psychology and for loading the burdens of the archetypal upon personal figures, personal relations, and personal solutions, and for taking oneself so personally, one's problems and fate always as "mine." Consequently, the mother-complex does show in the too-much and too-little of personal life, flight into impersonal distance coupled with personal fascination and intensity.

Here mother and nurse divide even though, as Jung points out, the term "mother complex" having been borrowed from psychopathology always has associated ideas of injury and illness, and so intrudes into the domain of the nurse. And though Mary seems to be both (Jesus not having had a distinct nurse figure in his abandoned moments), so that our Western consciousness still has difficulty separating the two psychological attitudes, the division is necessary. The nurse is not personally connected with the child; it is not hers, nor is her history carried forward into the child; its life and death is not hers; her love for it is not incest and taboo. The constellation is not personal in the same way, so we should not assume that the nurse is a foster-parent, a substitute or "second" mother. Nor should we reduce these archetypal distinctions to psychodynamic notions of a "good" and "bad" breast, which ultimately return the configuration of the nurse to that of the mother.

The nurse is a figure in her own right which connects to the plight of abandonment in a different way. Primarily, the injury, illness, and exposure is met with the nursing instinct, binding up, repairing, protection, the aims of which do not go beyond these matter-of-fact needs; in the acts there is no fateful projection, no dream of what has happened and what will happen. There is care with little hoping.

The nursing attitude would allow the child to remain abandoned for that is where the nurse appears. She nourishes it in its weakness or nourishes the weakness, The mothering attitude expects something—growth, a personal fate to emerge, specialness. Caring and hoping flow as one. But the nurse is obliged to accept the child as it is, and, since this attitude can only appear out of a wound, in connection with woundedness, for nursing to be constellated there must first be dereliction. Thus, the converse also occurs: the nurse can make us feel injured and abandoned. It seems that neither mothering nor nursing alone is enough. The child needs both, as we need a personal and impersonal relation to fate.

I believe we might look at "hypochondria," complaints, and the narcissistic appeal for help as a peculiar constellation occasioned through the imaginal world, less a mother-complex than attempts to constellate the nurse. The hopeless fits of Picasso in bed in the mornings unable to draw, unable to paint; the bottles of pills and packages of powders of Stravinsky on every nearby table and shelf; Coleridge unable; Carlyle's stomach, he and his wife alternatingly nursing each other; Voltaire "dying" for forty years; Michelangelo and Dürer complaining; Scott Fitzgerald meeting Hemingway to talk about health; Proust in bed; Rossini in bed; Darwin in bed... here is the child and the nurse, a combination not yet examined adequately by psychology in its attempts to get at the constellations of creativity and genius, nor in its attempts to understand the psychopathology of hypochondria and neurasthenia, nor in its analyses of families and the battle between its members as to who will be ill and who the nurse.

The Dead Child

A motif tangent to our theme but separable is the dead child. The motif occurs in dreams, sometimes as an unborn child that never came into the world; as well, the dead child worries our lives in various ways: the fear of a child dying, overprotectiveness towards children and its reverse child-cruelty, and the question of abortion. This last is usually discussed in the language of expediencies—population control, moral sin, and legal wrong about the taking of life, women's rights. However, the return of the abortion theme in dreams and its power in the emotions attest to an internal importance deserving psychological attention.

Abortion echoes the older practise of child exposure (*apothesis*), abandoning the unwanted child to its death. As an interior drama the aborted child is the miscarriage of the archetypal qualities we have presented: hope for the future, the sense of conquest, the new start and fulfilled end. The dead child is our lost hope and failed spark, our creative disappointment and stricken imagination that can point no way forward, spontaneity, openness, movement gone. No wonder that grief and mourning may continue many years after an actual abortion since the abortion theme expresses the psychic condition of dead childhood.

The mother wishes to make the child last forever in the realm of making, doing, loving—Demeter with Persephone and Demophon is case in point. But its death evidences her limits. It has a fate separate from her, showing again that the child component is separable from the mother. If we remain within the perspective of the mother, then the dead child yields only lamentation, and we overlook whatever else this archetypal theme might be indicating.

For the dead child is also the child belonging to death, alluding not only to the death of life but the life of death (cf. Riklin [1970]). Then, death does not mean end as finish of life, but end as purpose of life, signifying the invisible, only psychic existence of Hades whose place is "below" and "beyond" life and whose time is "after" life with its visibility, its making and doing and loving. The child aborted then signifies life aborted, for the sake of Hades.

The dead child may also be an image for the soul's child, performing the role of psychopompos, which, like the image and emotion of a classical funerary stele, leads the psyche to reflections about all that belongs to the child archetype but from a wholly psychic viewpoint. The dead child then makes possible an interiorization of the futurity and growth fantasies, and independence reverses its meaning to express independence from the values of life. Death itself then is no longer viewed through the eyes of life, but, in being led by the dead child, one may regard death in its own terms as a specifically psychic condition, i.e., the condition where there is nothing else but psyche. Although this motif has been saccharinely sentimentalized—walk but through a Victorian graveyard for its statuary of dead angelic children as emissaries of the beyond—the psychic content concretized in the marble is nonetheless valid. This image uniquely unites Eros and Thanatos whose conjunction, although understood in Neoplatonism (Wind [1967]), was conceptually riven by Freud's rationalism. The dead child may offer healing to what the mind has torn apart and placed in opposition.

Childishness—Childlikeness

The deepest dilemma concerning the return of the child is that conundrum inherent to any archetype, its supposedly good and bad sides, the digestible and indigestible portions, according to whatever model of integration we are serving. In the case of the child these poles become childishness and childlikeness. On the one hand, one works to become mature, to put all childish things away, to develop out of infantalisms and *avidya* of ignorance. On the other hand, one is to become a child, for only into the child enters the kingdom of heaven, and the child should lead the psyche and be its "end." How does one then reconcile the two contradictory instructions: to overcome the child and to become the child?

The poles appear already in Plato for the child of the *Meno* is not the same as the child of the *Lysis,* the *Republic,* and the *Laws.* And the poles appear in Paul (1 Corinthians 14:20) who appeals for childlikeness of heart but will not have childishness of mind. Or, as Augustine put the dilemma: "For childhood is set before us to imitate humility, and childhood is set before us to beware of foolishness" (*Enarrationes in Psalmos* XLVII.1). The division in the archetype also appears in what Philippe Aries calls "the two concepts of childhood," on the one hand the indulgent coddling provided by the family, on the other, the rational disciplining provided by society, church, and education. The division finally appears in education theory today, between the tender-minded who take their lead from Rousseau, Froebel and the Romantics and their vision from "childlikeness," and the tough-minded who follow a pattern more Classical, more Medieval, seeing in the child a miniature adult whose waxlike impressionable "childishness" requires moulding by *Bildung.*

Jung suggests a choice between the opposites and an end to the ambi-valence inherent in any archetypal pattern. He offers childhood recaptured without its childishness. The solution he suggests is that by sacrificing childishness, one creates a new childlikeness. Innocence, play, and spontaneity are regained by giving up ignorance, games, and unruliness. We move from the false to the true freedom; only a childishness abandoned can be refound as childlikeness; clinging to silliness never makes the wise and holy fool. Surely this suggestion I have elaborated from Jung (*CW*11:742) seems right, for what place is there in the reborn man of individuation for childish petulance and incapacity, foibles and single-minded desires, and for the magical wishful hopes so subjective and so unconditioned by past experience? What else is consciousness but putting away all childish things?

Nevertheless, the distinction between the child and his childishness is difficult to maintain. In actuality is separation possible; can we choose one pole? Is not the child this very complex of opposites whose psychic impact derives precisely from the tension of its "good" and "bad," its static and changing, sides? Extract the childishness from the child and we are left not with an angel (which are anyway demons of might and terror), but with an idealized image of how one thinks one ought to be, the innocence of repression, again constellating an abandoned child who willy-nilly must return. We cannot advance psychology, or the psyche in the throes of its complexes, one jot by attempting to separate out even through sacrifice or for the sake of eschatology the pathological elements.

Perhaps this is what to become as a child now means psychologically. It means what it says: the state as a whole with its pathological childishness, to think as a child and to speak as a child, still babes in wisdom of perfected praise (Psalm 8:2; Matthew 21:16) whose reminiscences do indeed transcend experience.

Without the shadow of childishness how do we enter truly the consciousness of the child? Is there a way to innocence and humility other than through ignorance and humiliation, by being made simple, small, fearing. To be led by the little child then psychologically implies to be led not only by one's spontaneous surprise and frank wonder where something is new and we are innocent, but also by one's childishness: by the sense of loneliness and abandonment and vulnerability, by the idealizations of Greatness upon outer authorities and the inner powers of our complexes who give us parentage, by the intoxications of magical invincibility, by the peculiar sexuality that is both hermaphroditic and incapable of being actualized, and by the unadapted pitiless feelings, the child's cruelty, the short memory, stupidity, which too form the stuff of innocence.

Especially Freud's discoveries concerning the child need to be recollected in relation with the idea of rebirth that is so representative of the child archetype. Because the resurrection of the whole man includes the body, its sinful, weak, lustful members (Romans 6:12–13), we cannot neglect the child in the body Freud reaffirmed. If we are anywhere most the victim of childishness, or more at war with it, it is in the body, treated as an enemy, as an inferior to be disciplined or indulgently coddled. Yet, if the child—even Freud's—is at least partly a reminiscing imaginal factor, then the body impulses we associate with the child also must at least partly refer to an imaginal body. Then even our polymorphous perversions and our longings of childishness would provide entry to the childlikeness of resurrection, where the work of rebirth would proceed through infantile sexuality, a discipline of perversion. We could no longer insist upon distinction between childlike and childish.

But must so much be given over to this one archetype so that it personifies not only body and the concrete mode of direct experience but almost all of our subjectivity as well? Must the child carry our bodily delights and our imaginal reminiscing, our wholeness and our creative liberation, our play and our eros, our past and our future? If we give all these aspects of existence to the child, then of course these areas of experience become childish. Then eros is loaded with childish longings, the body a childish complaint, the revolution a childish enactment, imagination a childish fantasy and concrete play an inferior activity. Then too we can never be satisfied with any of these areas as they are; they must be "developed"—our fantasy by means of active imagination or art therapy, and our bodies, our eros, our fun, and the revolution too, must go through a process of becoming more conscious, more "mature," to lose "primitivity."

Even childhood does not have to remain a province of the child. For childhood is mainly a word we use to cover these modes of experience and perception, imaginal modes, which we abandon every moment for the sake of more adult behavior, that is, more conceptual and more willed. If we abandon "childhood" as a cover for what is most valuable to human life, then the dilemma of childish and childlike may be resolved. Because we do not need to be fresh, naive, and simple "to become as a child," we could abandon the idealization of play as the path to the imaginal. We would no longer believe that we must be innocent to be new, simple to be whole. The restoration of the childish shadow to the ideal of childlikeness would return to wholeness its affliction and weakness, and to the imaginal both its psychopathological distortions and the hard work of actualization.

Bearing the Child

Because abandoning the child is a mythological motif, it stands as a permanent psychological reality, not to be cured but to be enacted. But how? Mythology may give theme and pattern, but depth psychology with its practical aim "to alter something" leaves to the subject the manner of enactment. We have no simple answer, and what has gone before has deliberately complicated a rather uncomplicated motif. Thomas Mann wrote that only the exhaustive is truly interesting; in psychology, only the complicated is truly representative.

The pattern we have been exposing shows a vicious circle. Abandoning of the child in order to become mature and then abandonment to the child when it returns. Either we repress or we coddle this face of our subjectivity. In both cases the child is unbearable: first we cannot support it at all, then we give way to it altogether. We seem to follow a pattern contained in the word "abandon" itself, as it is contained in the alternate and opposite meanings of "losing" and of "releasing." On the one hand we free ourselves of a condition by letting it go from us, and on the other hand, we free ourselves by letting go to it.

One of the ways we abandon ourselves to the child has been in the form of fantasies, called ideas, by means of which the child in sublimated form captures our consciousness. It is a psychological axiom that the more we move away from the repressed child the more vulnerable we are to possession of this abandoned part (CW 9.1: 277). The more unbearable we find the childish emotionalisms in our subjectivity, the more are we prey to childlike simplifications in our ideas that attempt to reflect objectivity, maturity, and responsible unemotionality. Then the child dominates our theory-forming with naive concepts of psyche and therapy, of growth and wholeness, of revolution and freedom, of love and genius. Then we choose, or are chosen by, sentimental philosophies of feeling that deny value to intellect—only connect, relate, believe, encounter—for the child represents the good, innocent heart. And this child is the primary anti-intellectual, who knows without learning things that are hidden from the learned but revealed unto babes (Luke 10: 21–22).

Indirectly we have also been examining the way in which we constellate this mythical motif in our individual subjectivities. The relation between psyche and myth goes in two directions; the mythemes govern the soul, but at the same time as it lives they are drawn into enactment. Of these enactments, the heroic model of consciousness always refers back to the child for its origins. We can never perform the ego's tasks, coping, struggling, advancing into light and knowledge, without also regressing to the child. The concept of ego so permeated by hero mythemes is based also upon the abandoned child as its precondition. (CW9.1: 281–84; Neumann, 45). The child returns hidden in the hero's boots, to swagger and control its naively literal notion of reality.

Because myths are always true, they are always happening; we abandon the child daily in our attitudes and acts. Whatever we do not acknowledge as having begotten, whatever we disown, to whatever we refuse historical lineage becomes one more orphan. The orphan has no history, everything lies ahead, complete futurity. History provides parentage to psychic events, giving them background in race, culture, tradition. When we refuse the historical aspect in our complexes, how history reaches us through our complexes—for it is in them that my race, my ancestors, and my historical culture affect me most closely—then we create orphans: we abandon our complexes to the power of the child archetype. They go to the orphanage, the breeding ground of renegade psychopathy.

Thus, as a psychologist I must refuse the attack upon history now coming from two sides: from the mystics of religion who would make way for spiritual rebirth by breaking through the historical, and from the heralds of political change who would start anew, the past "a bucket of ashes" (Carl Sandburg). The cults of immediacy, of relevance, of transcendence, of revolution, whether in mind expansion or in social liberation are the cult of childhood in a new form (but read Marcuse!), negating the historical roots of the complexes turning them into orphans with nothing behind them. Then history, as to Oedipus, comes out of a void. Oedipus's delusion about his history was material to his tragedy.

It may seem odd for an American psychologist speaking to European intellectuals to stress history, since for Europe, as Joyce said, "History is a nightmare from which I am trying to awaken." Yet psychological reality is only partly separable from historical reality. Our subjectivity is complicated throughout with our Western history, and we can never awaken from it unless we recognize it in our complexes. If psychotherapy conceives its task in altering and in correcting "the one-sided extravagances of consciousness," then psychotherapy is an attempt also to re-vision history and its work in the complexes. Change in psyche is change in history, and that is why psychic change is so difficult, for it means moving history. Yet nothing moves in ourselves or in the world if history be not borne. A revolution that neglects taking history with it will change nothing; it will leave the psyche untouched, and thus become a new repression.

The child archetype, because of its ahistorical and prehistorical tendencies, by moulding consciousness after itself would have us lose history, producing a generation of abandoned children who see all things in their beginnings and ends, an existence of omnipotent hope and catastrophic dread. The obsession with this archetype also has its other side, the parental other pole to the child, which gives us a burdening sense of parentage, of worldwide responsibility, the parental inflation compensatory to the child. Then we become all *Sorge* amidst the existential *Geworfenheit.*

History gives a sense for what is authentic; it limits the possible. Without this historical sense everything is new and anything can happen. Any delusional course of salvation lies open—and the confusion in subjectivity about "how to be" and what the soul wants is matched with a myriad of liberation programs, including the turn Eastwards as a way out of Western History. Psychology itself tends to be just one more "trip," owing to the child's influence. But Jung's psychology is altogether a reflection of the historical psyche and is not a program for its transcendence. Jung's vision of a complex polyvalent wholeness, pregnant with innumerable possibilities and individually different, is too precious, too fertile to become but another delusional omnipotence fantasy with goals of stalwart independence achieved through naive growth to oneness, where becoming self and becoming god conflate.

Surely psychology can be more critical and less childlike in its use of "wholeness" and "self"; surely psychology can abandon in its theory its fantasies of growth, creativity, independence, and futurity, so that change might be left as change and its kinds more accurately noted—not always newness and development—and the unchanging may be viewed less sadly. Then individuation may be separated from development so as to reflect more precisely the actualities of experience. Is not psychology's task to reflect the psyche as it is rather than to structure it with a hermeneutic system or inculcate through therapy a psychological dogma?

Reflecting the psyche as it is has been the concern of this essay. And I do mean "essay"—an attempt to articulate and thereby constellate that level of archetypal subjectivity which is the child. But our attempt must inevitably fail in order to correspond with the subject itself. Our inadequacy reflects its helplessness. So we may not expect that what the psyche says through the word "childhood" can be translated into the mature and intellectual speech of science or scholarship. Psychology, it seems to me, has too long laboured in this mistake. Our essay rather follows some lines from T. S. Eliot (*Four Quartets*, "East Coker," V): "Every attempt/Is a wholly new start, and a different kind of failure…And so each venture/Is a new beginning, a raid on the inarticulate." In this way, the failure and the venture belong together. They are each part of instigating the new start in regard to the child by stimulating our imagination about archetypal childhood.

The dominance of the child archetype in our psychological thinking, besides softening our intellect, has deprived the adult of his imagination. This "inferior" activity has been relegated to childhood, like so much else unreal, autoerotic, and primitive. The adult must go back to childhood to re-find imagination—feeling it unreal, autoerotic, primitive—for lost childhood has meant lost imaginal power, amnesia as lost *memoria*, an abandoned capacity for reminiscence in the Neoplatonic sense. Thus "adult" and "mature" have come to signify demythologized existence whose underlying mythemes return to possess the adult and his psychology in the sentimental and simplified ways we have suggested. We might condense this psychological process into a formula: The less the child is borne as an emotional vulnerability and imaginal reality, the more we shall be abandoned to it in our rationalized fantasies.

Preferable to the division into child and adult and the consequent patterns of abandonment we have been sketching, would be a psychology less given over to the child, its woes and romanticism. We might then have a psychology descriptive of man, an aspect of whom is perennially child, carrying his incurable weakness and nurse to it, enacting the child neither by development nor by abandonment, but bearing the child, the child contained. Our subjective experience might then be mirrored by a psychology both more exact in its description and more sophisticatedly classical, where the child is contained within the man who carries in his face and mien the shame of the childish, its unchanging psycho-pathology—untranscended, untransformed—and the invincible high hopes together with the vulnerability of these hopes, who bears his abandonment in dignity, and whose freedom comes from the imaginal redeemed from the amnesia of childhood.

References

Ariès, Philippe. *Centuries of Childhood: A Social History of Family Life*, translated by Robert Baldick (New York: Vintage Books, 1962)

Boas, George. *The Cult of Childhood* (Dallas: Spring Publications, 1990)

Bowlby, John. *Child Care and the Growth of Love* (Harmondsworth: Penguin, 1990)

Bundy, M.W. "The Theory of Imagination in Classical and Mediaeval Thought," *Illinois Studies in Language and Literature* 12, nos. 2–3 (1927)

Collins, Philip. *Dickens and Education* (London: Macmillan, 1963), chap 8: "The Rights of Childhood"

Delcourt, Marie. *Stérilités mystérieuses et naissances maléfiques dans l'Antiquité classique* (Paris: Librairie E. Droz, 1938)

Eliot, T.S. "East Coker" and "The Dry Salvages," in *Four Quartets* (London: Faber and Faber, 1944)

Erikson, Erik H. *Childhood and Society* (New York: Norton, 1950)

—. "Human Strength and the Cycle of Generations," in *Insight and Responsibility* (New York: W.W. Norton, 1964)

—. "Growth and Crises of the Healthy Personality," in *Identity and the Life Cycle* (New York: International Universities Press, 1959)

Deardon, R.F. *The Philosophy of Primary Education: An Introduction* (London: Routledge, 1968), ch. 3: "Growth"

Foucault, Michel. *Madness and Civilization: A History of Insanity in the Age of Reason*, translated by Richard Howard (New York: Pantheon, 1965)

Gesell, Arnolf, Frances L. Ilg and Louise B. Ames, *Youth: The Years from Ten to Sixteen* (New York: Harper & Row, 1956)

Horney, Karen. *Neurosis and Human Growth: The Struggle toward Self-Realization* (New York: W.W. Norton, 1950).

Isaacs, Susan. *The Nursery Years: The Mind of the Child From Birth to Six Years* (New York: Schocken Books, 1968), chap 4: "The Norms of Development"

Koffka, Kurt. *The Growth of the Mind: An Introduction to Child-Psychology*, translated by Robert Morris Ogden (New York: Harcourt, Brace & Company, 1925)

Kris, Ernst. *Psychoanalytic Explorations in Art* (New York: International Universities Press, 1952)

Laistner, M.L.W. *Christianity and Pagan Culture in the Later Roman Empire* (Ithaca, N.Y.: Cornell University Press, 1951)

Légasse, Simon. *Jésus et l'enfant: 'Enfants,' 'petits' et 'simples' dans la tradition synop-tique* (Paris: J. Gabalda, 1969)

Malamud, René. "The Amazon Problem," *Spring: An Annual of Archetypal Psychology and Jungian Thought* (1971): 1–21

Marcuse, Herbert. *An Essay on Liberation* (Boston: Beacon Press, 1969).

Neumann, Erich. *The Origins and History of Consciousness* (London: Rout-ledge, 1954)

Picasso, Pablo. *Worte des Malers Pablo Picasso,* edited by J. Haase (Zurich: Sanssouci, 1970)

Poulet, Georges. *The Metamorphosis of the Circle,* translated by Carley Daw-son and Elliott Coleman (Baltimore: Johns Hopkins University Press, 1966), chap. 6: "Romanticism"

Riklin, Franz. "The Crisis of Middle Life," *Spring: An Annual of Archetypal Psychology and Jungian Thought* (1970): 6–14

Rogers, Carl R. *On Becoming a Person: A Therapist's View of Psychotherapy* (Wilmington, Mass.: Hougthon Mifflin, 1961), chap. 9

Stein, Robert. *Incest and Human Love: The Betrayal of the Soul in Psychotherapy* (Woodstock, Conn.: Spring Publications, 1984), Part 2: "Incest"

Stoffer, Hellmut. *Die Bedeutung der Kindlichkeit in der modernen Welt* (Munich and Basel: Reinhardt, 1964)

Whyte, Lancelot Law, ed., *Aspects of Form* (Bloomington: Indiana Univer-sity Press, 1961)

—. *Accent on Form: An Anticipation of the Science of Tomorrow* (New York: Harper & Brothers, 1954)

Wind, Edgar. *Pagan Mysteries in the Renaissance* (New York: W.W. Norton, 1969), chap 10: "Amor as a God of Death"

Winnicott, D.W. *Playing and Reality* (London: Tavistock, 1971)

5

WARS, ARMS, RAMS, MARS

You will recall, if you saw the film *Patton*, the scene in which the American general, who commanded the Third Army in the 1944–45 drive across France into Germany, walks the field after a battle: churned earth, burnt tanks, dead men. The General takes up a dying officer, kisses him, surveys the havoc, and says: "I love it. God help me, I do love it so. I love it more than my life."

This scene gives focus to my theme—the love of war, the love in war and for war that is more than "my" life, a love that calls up a god, that is helped by a god and on a battlefield, a devastated piece of earth that is made sacred by that devastation.

I believe we can never speak sensibly of peace or disarmament unless we enter into this love of war. Unless we enter into the martial state of soul, we cannot comprehend its pull. This special state must be ritualistically entered. We must be "inducted," and war must be "declared"—as one is declared insane, declared married or bankrupt. So we shall try now to "go to war" and this because it is a principle of psychological method that any phenomenon to be understood must be emphatically imagined. To know war we must enter its love. No psychic phenomenon can be truly dislodged from its fixity unless we first move the imagination into its heart.

War is a psychological task, which Freud recognized and addressed in several papers. It is especially a psychological task because philoso-

Presented at the conference "Facing Apocalypse," initiated by Robert Bosnak, Salve Regina College, Newport, Rhode Island, June 1983, and published together with papers by Norman O. Brown, Danilo Dolci, Wolfgang Giegerich, Denise Levertov, Robert J. Lifton, Joanna Macy, David L. Miller, Mike Perlman, and Mary Watkins in *Facing Apocalypse*, edited by Valerie Andrews, Robert Bosnak, Karen Walter Goodwin (Thompson, Conn.: Spring Publications, 2021 [1987]).

phy and theology have failed its overriding importance. War has been set aside as history, where it then becomes a subchapter called military history. Or war has been placed outside the mainstream of thought into think tanks. So we need to lift this general repression, attempting to bring to war an imagination that respects its primordial significance.

My method of heading right in, of penetrating rather than circumambulating or reflecting, is itself martial. We shall be invoking the god of the topic by this approach to the topic.

✿

During the 5,600 years of written history, there have been at least 14,600 recorded wars. Two or three wars each year of human history. Since Edward Creasy's *Fifteen Decisive Battles* (1851), we have been taught that the turning points of Western civilization occur in such battles as Salamis and Marathon, Carthage, Tours, Lepanto, Constantinople, Waterloo, Midway, Stalingrad... The ultimate determination of historical fate, we have been taught, depends upon battle, whose outcome in turn depends upon an invisible genius in a leader or hero through whom a transcendent spirit is manifested. The battle and its personified epitome become salvational representations in secular history. The statues in our parks, the names of our grand avenues, and the holidays we celebrate commemorate the salvational aspect of battle.

Neglected in Creasy's decisive battles are the thousands of indecisive ones, fought with equal heroism, yet which ended inconclusively or yielded no victory for the ultimate victor of the war; nor did these battles produce commemorative epic, statue, or celebration. Unsung heroes; died in vain; lost cause. The ferocity of battle may have little to do with its outcome, the outcome little to do with the outcome of the war. Verdun in the Great War of 1914–18 is such an example: a million casualties and nothing decisive. The significance of a battle is not given by the war, but by the battle itself.

Besides the actual battles and their monuments, the monumental epics that lie in the roots of our Western languages are, to a large proportion, "war books": the *Mahabharata* and its *Bhagavad Gita*, the *Iliad*, the *Aeneid*, the Celtic *Lebor Gabala*, and the Norse *Edda*. Our Bible is a long account of battles, of wars and captains of wars. Jahweh presents himself in the speeches of a war god and his prophets and kings are his warriors.[1] Even the New Testament is so arranged that its final culminating chapter, Revelation, functions as its recapitulative coda in which the Great Armageddon of the Apocalypse is its crisis.

In our most elevated works of thought—Hindu and Platonic philosophy—a warrior class is imagined as necessary to the wellbeing of humankind. This class finds its counterpart within human nature, in the heart, as virtues of courage, nobility, honor, loyalty, steadfastness of principle, comradely love, so that war is given location not only in a class of persons but in a level of human personality organically necessary to the justice of the whole.

Have I carried my first point that battles and the martial are not merely irrational relapses into archaic pre-civilization? The martial cannot be derived merely from the territorial imperative of our animal inheritance: "This is my realm, my feeding and breeding space; get out or I'll kill you." Nor do wars arise simply from industrial capitalism and its economic distress, the mystiques of tribes and nationalism, the just preservation of a state, masculine machoism, sociological indoctrinations or psychological paranoia and aggression. (Paranoia and aggression, if explanatory principles, themselves require explanations.) No, wars are not only man-made; they bear witness also to something essentially human that transcends the human, invoking powers more than the human can fully grasp. Not only do gods battle among themselves and against other foreign gods, they sanctify human wars, and they participate in those wars by divine intervention, as when soldiers hear divine voices and see divine visions in the midst of battle.

Because of this transcendent infiltration, wars are so difficult to control and understand. What takes place in battle is always to some degree mysterious, and therefore unpredictable, never altogether in human hands. Wars "break out." Once commanders sought signs in the heavens, from birds. Today, we fantasize the origin of war in a computer accident. *Fortuna*—despite meticulous battle plans and rehearsals, the battle experience is a melee of surprises.

---

1. Millard C. Lind, *Yahweh is a Warrior: The Theology of Warfare in Ancient Israel* (Scottsdale, Penn.: Herald Press, 1980).

We therefore require an account of war that allows for its transcendent moment, an account that roots itself in *archai*—the Greek word for "first principle"—*archē*, not merely as archaic, a term of historical explanation, but as archetypal, evoking the transhistorical background, that divine epiphanic moment in war.[2]

This archetypal approach holds that ever-recurring, ubiquitous, highly ritualized and passionate events are governed by fundamental psychic patterning factors. These factors are given with the world as modes of its psychological nature, much as patterns of atomic behavior are given with the physical nature of the world and patterns of instinctual behavior are given with the world's biological nature.

I want now for us to enter more closely into the epiphany of this archetypal principle, this god, Mars. Here is a reading from Ernst Jünger's diary, recording the start of the last German offensive in 1918:

> The great moment had come. The curtain of fire lifted from the front trenches. We stood up—we moved in step, irresistibly toward the enemy lines. I was boiling with a mad rage, which had taken hold of me and all others in an incomprehensible fashion. The overwhelming wish to kill gave wings to my feet. The monstrous desire for annihilation, which hovered over the battlefield, thickened the brains of the men in a red fog. We called each other in sobs and stammered disconnected sentences. A neutral observer might perhaps have believed we were seized by an excess of happiness.[3]

A scholar of Japanese culture, Donald Keene, has collected tanka and hundreds of other writings expressing the feelings of major Japanese authors (including liberals, leftists, and Christians) during the 1941-45 war. I shall quote only passages referring to Pearl Harbor. Nagayo Yoshio,

---

2. Compare Patton (*The Secret of Victory*, 1926): "...despite the impossibility of physically detecting the soul, its existence is proven by its tangible reflection in acts and thoughts. So with war, beyond its physical aspect of armed hosts there hovers an impalpable something which dominates the material...to understand this 'something' we must seek it in a manner analogous to our search for the soul."

3. Quoted in J. Glenn Gray, *The Warriors: Reflections on Men in Battle* (New York: Harper & Row, 1970), 52.

author of *The Bronze Christ*, on hearing of the declaration of war with the United States, wrote: "I never thought that in this lifetime I should ever know such a happy, thrilling, auspicious experience." The novelist and critic Ito Sei on the same occasion said: "I felt as if in one stroke I had become a new man, from the depths of my being." Honda Akira, scholar of English literature, wrote: "I have felt the sense of a clearing. Now the word 'holy war' is obvious...a new courage has welled up and everything has become easier to do."[4]

Glenn Gray writes in the most sensitive account of war experience that I know, *The Warriors*:

> Veterans who are honest with themselves will admit the experience in battle has been a high point in their lives. Despite the horror, the weariness, the grime, and the hatred, participation with others in the chances of battle had its unforgettable side. For anyone who has not experienced it himself, the feeling is hard to comprehend and for the participant hard to explain to anyone else—that curious combination of earnestness and lightheartedness so often noted of men in battle.[5]

These positive experiences are puzzling. It is the positive experience that we must reckon with because the savagery and confusion, the exhaustion and desertion correspond with what is objectively taking place. Those responses do not need explanations. But how mystifying the lightheartedness in killing, the joy of going into battle, and that infantrymen with bayonets fixed, snipers in ambush, torpedo men in destroyers report no particular hatred, little heroic ambition, unconcern for victory, or even passion for their cause for which they stand exposed and may even volunteer to die. Instead, they sometimes report altered states of perception, intensified vitality, a new awareness of the earth's beauty and nearness of divinity—their little plot, their meager, grimy life suddenly transcendently sweet. "It is well that war is so terrible," said Robert E. Lee, "we would grow too fond of it."

And, beyond all else is the group bonding to the platoon, the crew, a buddy.[6] Love in war. Thomas Aquinas notes that comrades in arms

---

4. Quoted by Donald Keene, "Japanese Writers and the Greater East Asia War," in *Landscapes and Portraits* (Tokyo: Kodansha, 1971).

5. Gray, 44.

6. Careful sociological research into the motivation of the American soldier (in

display a specific form of friendship. This battle-love is complex, gentle, altruistic, and fierce. It cannot be reduced merely to modern psychologisms: boosting masculinity with macho codes of honor, peer pressure that successfully represses cowardice, the discovery and release under the duress of battle of repressed homosexual emotion. Moreover, so strong and so transcending the aims of war itself is this love that a soldier, in fidelity to his buddies, may more easily shoot down his own officer than an enemy in the opposite trench.

To illustrate this love in war, I shall condense from S.L.A. Marshall an incident from his account of the desperate American retreat from the Yalu after the failed invasion of North Korea. There was a tight ravine under enemy fire through which funnel the only escape route lay.

> From end to end this sanctuary was already filled with bodies, the living and the dead, wounded men who could no longer move, the exhausted...the able-bodied driven to earth by fire. It was a sump pit of all who had become detached from their vehicles and abandoned to each other...200 men in the ditch so that their bodies overlapped. Americans, Turks, ROKs...Yet there was cooperative motion and human response. Men who were still partly mobile crawled forward along the chain of bodies...As they moved, those who were down and hurt cried: "Water! Water!"...Long since, nearly all canteens were dry. But the able-bodied checked long enough to do what bandaging they could...some stripped to the waist in the bitter cold and tore up their undershirts for dressings. Others stopped their crawl long enough to give their last drop of water...the wounded who were bound to the ditch tried to assist the able-bodied seeking to get out. Witnesses saw more of the decency of men than ever had been expected.[7]

Love and war have traditionally been coupled in the figures of Venus and Mars, Aphrodite and Ares. This usual allegory is expressed in usual

---

World War II) shows that the factors which helped the combatman most "when the going was tough" (as the quotation was phrased) were *not* hatred for the enemy or thoughts of home or the cause for which he was fighting. The emotions that did appear under battle duress—that is, when Mars was acutely constellated—were prayer and group fidelity. Piety and the love of fellows are what the god brings. (Samuel A. Stouffer, et. al., *The American Soldier: Combat and its Aftermath*, 4 vols. (Princeton, N.J.: Princeton University Press, 1949), 2: 165–86.

7. S.L.A. Marshall, *The River and the Gauntlet* (New York: Morrow, 1953), 300–301.

slogans—make love not war, all's fair in love and war—and in usual oscillating behaviors—rest, recreation and rehabilitation in the whorehouse behind the lines, then return to the all-male barracks. Instead of these couplings, which actually separate Mars and Venus into alternatives, there is a Venusian experience within Mars itself. It occurs in the sensate love of life in the midst of battle, in the care for concrete details built into all martial regulations, in the sprucing, prancing, and dandying of the cavaliers (now called "boys") on leave. Are they sons of Mars or of Venus?

In fact, we need to look again at the aesthetic aspect of Mars. Also there a love lies hidden. From the civilian sidelines, military rites and rhetoric seem kitsch and pomposity. But look instead at this language, these procedures as the sensitization by ritual of the physical imagination. Consider how many different kinds of blades, edges, points, metals, and temperings are fashioned on the variety of knives, swords, spears, sabers, battle-axes, rapiers, daggers, lances, pikes, halberds that have been lovingly honed with the idea for killing. Look at the rewards for killing: Iron Cross, Victoria Cross, Medal of Honor, Croix de Guerre; the accoutrements: bamboo baton, swagger stick, epaulets, decorated sleeves, ivory-handled pistols. The music: reveille and taps, drums and pipes, fifes and drums, trumpets, bugles, the marching songs and marching bands, brass, braid, stripes. The military tailors: Wellington boots, Eisenhower jackets, Sam Brown belts, green berets, red coats, "whites."[8] Forms, ranks, promotions. Flags, banners, trooping to the colors. The military mess—its postures, toasts. The manners: salutes, drills, commands. Martial rituals of the feet—turns, steps, paces, warriors' dances. Of the eyes—eyes front! Of the hands, the neck, the voice, ramrod backbone, abdomen—"Suck in that gut, soldier." The names: Hussars, Dragoons, Rangers, Lancers, Coldstream Guards, and nicknames: bluejacket, leatherneck, doughboy. The great walls and bastions of severe beauty built by Brunelleschi, Leonardo, Michelangelo, Buontalenti. The decorated horse, notches in the rifle stock, the painted emblems on metal equipment, letters from the front, poems. Spit and polish and pent

---

8. "Tomorrow I shall have my new battle jacket. If I'm to fight I like to be well dressed" (attributed to General Patton, in Charles M. Province, *The Unknown Patton* [New York: Hippocrene, 1983], 180.

emotion. Neatsfoot oil, gunsmith, sword smith; the Shield of Achilles on which is engraved the whole world.

Our American consciousness has extreme difficulty with Mars.[9] Our founding documents and legends portray the inherent nonmartial bias of our civilian democracy. You can see this in the second, third, and fourth constitutional amendments which severely restrict military power in the civilian domain. You can see this in the stories of the Massachusetts Minutemen versus European mercenaries and redcoats, and in the Green Mountain boys and the soldiers of the Swamp Fox—civilians all. And you can see it in the casual, individualistic Texans at San Jacinto versus the Mexican officers trained in the European mold.

Compared with our background in Europe, Americans are idealistic: war has no place. It should not be. War is not glorious, triumphal, creative as to a warrior class in Europe from Rome and the Normans through the Crusades even to the Battle of Britain. We may be a violent people but not a warlike people—and our hatred of war makes us use violence against even war itself. Wanting to put a stop to it was a major cause of the Los Alamos project and Truman's decision to bomb Hiroshima *and* Nagasaki, a bomb to "save lives," a bomb to end bombs, like the idea of a war to end all wars. "The object of war," it says on General Sherman's statue in Washington, "is a more perfect peace." Our so-called doublespeak about armaments as "peacekeepers" reflects truly how we think. War is bad, exterminate war and keep peace violently: punitive expeditions, pre-emptive strikes, send in the Marines. More firepower means surer peace. We enact the blind god's blindness (Mars Caecus, as the Romans called him, and Mars *insanus, furibundus, omnipotens*), like Grant's and Lee's men in the Wilderness, like the bombing of Dresden, overkill as a way to end war.

Gun control is a further case in point. It raises profound perplexities in a civilian society. The right to bear arms is constitutional, and our nation and its territorial history (for better or for worse) have depended on a citizen-militia's familiarity with weapons. But that was when the rifle and the Bible (together with wife and dog) went alone into the

---

9. Cf. Thomas J. Pressly, "Civil-Military Relations in the United States Civil War (1861–1865)," in *War: A Historical, Political, and Social Study,* edited by L. L. Farrar, Jr. (Santa Barbara: ABC-Clio Press, 1978), 117–22; O. A. Pease, "The American Experience with War," in ibid., 197–203.

wilderness. The gun was backed by a god; when it stood in the corner of the household, pointing upward like the Roman spear that *was* Mars, the remembrance of the god was there, and the awe and even some ceremony. With the neglect of Mars, we are left only the ego and the guns that we try to control with civilian secular laws.

If in the arms is the god, then arms control requires at least partly, if not ultimately, a religious approach. The statement by the Catholic Bishops is a harbinger of that recognition. We worry about nuclear accident, but what we call "accident" is the autonomy of the inhuman. Arms, as instruments of death, are sacred objects that remind mortals that we are not *athnetos*, immortal. The fact that arms control negotiations take on more and more ritualistic postures rather than negotiating positions also indicates the transcendent power of the arms over those who would bring them under control. Military expenditures, of course, "overrun" and handguns "get out of hand." I do not believe arms control can come about until the essential nature of arms is first recognized.

Our immigrant dream of escape from conscription into the deadly games of Mars on the European battlefields cannot fit Mars into the American utopia. Hence that paradox for Americans of a peacetime draft and the violence that conscription can occasion. This clash of archetypal perspectives—civil and military—appears sharply in Sicily in 1943 when General Patton slapped two conscripted soldiers who were in the hospital for anxiety states.[10] To the appalled general (a son of Mars), they were malingerers, cowards without love for their fellows. To the appalled American nation of civilians, Patton was the coward, slapping the defenseless sick, without love of his fellows.

By the way, our customary language betrays a bias in favor of the civil simply by calling it civil. Were we speaking from the military perspective, "civil" would be called "merchant," for these were the traditional class terms in many societies, including India and Japan, and in the Platonic division where the merchants were lower than the warriors (*Phaedrus*, 248*d*) who were not permitted property (*Republic* IV). Traditionally, the warrior class favors the son; the merchant class, the daughter. By slapping

---

10. On the slapping accident, see Brig. Gen. Brenton Wallace, *Patton and his Third Army* (Westport, Conn.: Greenwood, 1946), 207–9; Province, *The Unknown Patton*, 71–86, 91–92; Herbert Essame, *Patton: A Study in Command* (New York: Scribner's, 1974), 103–17.

his soldiers, Patton was treating them as sons; the civilian (i.e., merchant) reaction experiences them as mistreated daughters.

Although the office of President does combine civil and military, head-of-state and commander-in-chief, and though that office has been held by notable generals—Washington, Jackson, Grant, and Eisenhower—and men with military careers, it has been the habit in recent years for the presidency to founder upon this double role: I think of Truman and Korea, Kennedy and the Bay of Pigs, Johnson and Vietnam, Carter and Iran, Reagan and Central America. Unlike the Roman Republic where Jupiter and Mars could rule together, our republic pretends to have no God of War, not even a department of war. This repression rather than ritualization of Mars leaves us exposed to the return of the repressed, as rude, eruptive violence, as indulgent military expenditures, as rigid reaction formations disguised as peace negotiations, and as paranoid defenses against delusional enemies.

So far I have been stressing the distinction between the military and civil imaginations. I have considered each to be moved by its own arche-typal power, powers that do not easily accommodate in a secular, mono-theistic consciousness, because that consciousness identifies with a sin-gle point of view, forcing others into opponents. Oppositional thinking and true believing collaborate in narrowing consciousness.

Now, let me make a second distinction: between the military and nuclear imaginations. The martial is not necessarily nuclear nor is the nuclear necessarily martial. The civilian rejection of Mars, however, has so pushed the martial over into the nuclear that we can't think of war without thinking nuclear war. Mr. Reagan, in fact, called war "the unthinkable," a mystic's notion of a god beyond thought, beyond image. War is not unthinkable, and not to think it, not to imagine it, only favors the mystical appeal of apocalyptic nuclearism. Remember Hannah Arendt's call to thinking? Not to think, not to imagine is the behavior of Eichmann, said Arendt. So let us go on thinking all we can about Mars, now in distinction with the nuclear.

Mars in the Roman Republic, where he was most developed as a dis-tinct figure, was placed in a Champs de Mars, a field, a terrain. He was so earthbound that many scholars trace the origins of the Mars cult to agriculture. This helps my point: Mars did not belong to the city. Not until Julius Caesar and caesarism were troops allowed in the city.

The focus of martial activity has usually been less the conquest of cities than of terrain and the destruction of armies occupying terrain. Even the naval war in the Pacific (1941–45) followed this classical intention of gaining area.

The martial commander must sense the lay of the land. He is a geographer. The horse (an animal of Mars) was so essential for martial peoples because horses could realize the strategy of winning terrain. Martial strategy is archetypally geopolitical.

The nuclear imagination, in contrast, calculates in terms of cities, and its destructive fantasies necessarily include civilians. The city (and thus the civilization, whether taken out by ICBMs or kept as intact prizes by the neutron weapon) is the main focus of the nuclear imagination. The land between Kiev and Pittsburgh (hence Europe) is relatively irrelevant.

A second contrast between the martial and the nuclear: Mars moves in close, hand-to-hand, Mars *propior* and *propinquus.* Bellona is a fury, the blood-dimmed tide, the red fog of intense immediacy. No distance. Acquired skills become instantaneous as in the martial arts. The nuclear imagination, in contrast, invents at ever greater distance—intercontinental, the bottom of the sea, outer space. Because of the time delay caused by distance, the computer becomes the essential nuclear weapon. The computer is the only way to regain the instantaneity given archetypally with Mars. The computer controls nuclear weapons, is their governor. Whereas the martial is contained less by fail-safe devices and rational computation than by military ritual of disciplined hierarchy, practiced skill, repetition, code, and inspection. And by the concrete obstacles of geography: commissary trains, hedgerows, bad weather, *impedimenta.*

Our civilian republic has not become fully conscious of the distinction I am laboring. The civilian soldier rebels against military rituals as senseless. He does not grasp that they serve to contain the God of War and so must be obeyed—as Patton insisted—religiously, as if the military were a religious order.

So, too, our civilian republic is not enough aware of the distinction between military and nuclear, thereby entrusting the control of nuclear explosions to the military in the person of General Grove. Considering the volatile commixture of the God of War with the spiritual, apocalyptic appeal of nuclearism, it is miraculous that we have had only test blasts.

A further difference between martial and nuclear is in their visions of transcendence. They show two elemental imaginations of fire: war and the fire of earth; apocalypse and the fire of ether or air. And two different animals: the ram of territory and head-on collision; the eagle of piercing surprise and the uplifting rapture of nuclearism.

The nuclear imagination, further, is without ancestry. Nothing to look back on and draw upon. History provides no precedents. There is a broken connection, to use Lifton's phrase, between sudden, hideous, and collective extinction and deaths modeled by the ancestors. The martial imagination is steeped in memorials. Past battles and military biographies are the ongoing texts. We tramp the battlefields, ponder the cemeteries. There are Swiss depictions of battles, for instance, showing skeletons in the ranks: here are the ancestors fighting in our midst.

The rhetoric of Mars in war journals, poems, and recollections speaks of attachment to specific earthly places, comrades, things. The transcendent is in the concrete particular. Hemingway writes that, after World War I, "abstract words such as glory, honor, courage...were obscene beside the concrete names of villages, the numbers of roads, the names of rivers, the regiments and dates." How rare for anyone to know the date of Alamogordo (or even where it is), the date of Hiroshima, of the first hydrogen bomb explosion, or the names of people or places or units engaged. Gone in abstraction. Glenn Gray writes: "Any fighting unit must have a limited and specific objective. A physical goal—a piece of earth to defend, a machine gun nest to destroy, a strong point to annihilate—more likely evokes a sense of comradeship."[11]

Martial psychology turns events into images: physical, bounded, named. Hürtgenwald, Vimy Ridge, Iwo Jima. A beach, a bridge, a railroad crossing: battle places become iconic and sacred, physical images claiming the utmost human love, worth more than my life.

Quite different is the transcendent experience of the nuclear fireball. The emotion is stupefaction at destruction itself rather than a heightened regard for the destroyed. Nuclear devastation is not merely a deafening cannonade or fire-bombing carried to a further degree. It is different in kind; archetypally different. It evokes the apocalyptic transformation of

---

11. Gray, *The Warriors*, 42–43.

the world into fire, earth ascending in a pillar of cloud, an epiphanic fire revealing the inmost spirit of all things, as in the Buddha's fire sermon:

> All things, O priests, are on fire...the mind is on fire, ideas are on fire...mind consciousness is on fire.

Or like that passage from the *Bhagavad Gita,* which came to Oppenheimer when he saw the atomic blast:

> If the radiance of a thousand suns
> Were burst at once into the sky
> That would be like the splendor of the Mighty One.

The nuclear imagination leaves the human behind for the worst sin of all: fascination by the spirit. *Superbia.* The soul goes up in fire. If the epiphany in battle unveils love of this place and that man and values more than my life, yet bound with this world, and its life, the nuclear epiphany unveils the apocalyptic god, a god of extinction, the god-is-dead god, an epiphany of Nihilism.

Apocalypse is *not necessary to war.* Let me make this very clear: apocalypse is not part of the myths of Mars. Mars asks for battle, not wipeout, not even victory. (*Nike* belongs to Athene, not Ares.) Patton supposedly said: "I like making things happen. That's my share in Deity." Apocalypse is inherent, not in the Martial deity, but in the Christian deity. Fascination with a transcendent Christ may be more the threat to the Christian civilization than the War God himself. Are not civilizations saved by their gods also led to destruction by those same, their own, gods?

There is one more distinction, one that may be of the most therapeutic significance. If nuclearism produces "psychic numbing," stupefaction, stupidity, Mars works precisely to the contrary. He intensifies the senses and heightens fellow-feeling in action, that energized vivification the Romans called "Mars *Nerio*" and "Mars *Moles,*" molar, massive, making things happen. Mobilization. Mars gives answer to the hopelessness and drifting powerlessness we feel in the face of nuclear weapons by awakening fear, Phobos, his Greek companion or son, and rage, *ira,* wrath. Mars is the instigator, the primordial activist. To put the contrast in eschatological terms, Mars is the God of Beginnings, the sign of the Ram. March is his month, and April, Mars *Apertus,* opening, making things happen. Apocalypse may lift veils, but it closes down into the truly final solution, after which there is no reopening, no *recorso.* Broken the wheel.

I seem to have been making a case for the lesser of two evils, and to have so favored Mars that you may have heard me as a warmonger. But this would be to hear me only literally. Rather than warmonger, see me as ram-monger, Mars-lover. Take my talk as a devotional ritual of imagination to constellate his awakening power. In this way we may call him up and yet deliteralize him at the same time.

It was an ancient custom and is still a modern psychological technique to turn for aid to the very same principle that causes an affliction. The cure of the Mars we fear is the god himself. One must approximate his affects in order to differentiate them. The *Homeric Hymn* to Mars (Ares), in Charles Boer's translation, makes this clear:

> Hear me
> helper of mankind,
> beam down from up there
> your gentle light
> on our lives
> and your martial power
> so that I can shake off
> cruel cowardice
> from my head
> and diminish that deceptive rush
> of my spirit, and restrain
> that shrill voice in my heart
> that provokes me
> to enter the chilling din of battle.
> You, happy God
> give me courage
> to linger in the safe laws of peace
> and thus escape
> from battles with enemies
> and the fate of violent death. [12]

It seems that the more we can love Mars, as in this hymn, the more we can discriminate (to use its words): the deceptive rush of the spirit, the shrill voice that provokes into battle, and at the same time shakes off cruel cowardice from my head.

---

12. *The Homeric Hymns,* translated by Charles Boer (Dallas: Spring Publications, 1979), 60–61.

This imaginative devotion to Mars provides a mode of deliteralizing beyond interpretation of the meaning of the god, beyond a mental act of seeing-through. By deliteralizing I mean here: to be fundamentally penetrated by an archetypal power, to participate in its style of love so that its compulsion gives way to its imagination, its angelic, message-giving intelligence. Then the god is experienced in the event as its image, the event no longer requiring my psychologizing for the image to be revealed.

Just this is my aim now, right now as I am speaking: not to explore war or apocalypse in the service of prevention, but to experience war and apocalypse so that their imaginations become fully realized, real. We cannot prevent; only images can help us; only images provide *providentia*, protection, prevention. That has always been the function of images: the magic of sacred protection.

We do not know much nowadays about imagining divinities. We have lost the angelic imagination and its angelic protection. It has fallen from all curricula—theological, philosophical, aesthetic. That loss may be more of a danger than either war or apocalypse because that loss results in literalism, the cause of both. As Lifton says, "The task now is to imagine the real." However, like so much of our imagination of the archetypal themes in human nature, the wars we now imagine are severely limited by modern positivistic consciousness. We imagine wars utterly without soul or spirit or gods, just as we imagine biological and psychological life, social intercourse and politics, the organization of nature—all without soul, spirit or gods.

Wars show this decline of ritual and increase of positivism, beginning with Napoleon and the War Between the States (1861–65). The Great War of 1914–18 was stubborn, massive, unimaginative; the dark Satanic mill relocated in Flanders, sixty thousand British casualties in one single day on the Somme, and the same battle repeated and repeated like a positivist logical argument. The repetition of senselessness. Our wars become senseless when they have no myths. Guadalcanal, Anzio, My Lai: battles, casualties, graves (at best); statistics of firepower and body-count—but no myths. The reign of quantity, utterly literal.

Lacking a mythical perspective that pays homage to the god in war, we run the dangers of both war "breaking out" and "loving war too much"—and a third one: not being able to bring a war to a proper close. The Allies' demand for "unconditional surrender" only prolonged World War II, giving "justification" for the atomic bomb. Polybius and Talleyrand knew better: masters of war know how and where and when to ease out the god's fury. The very idea of an unconditional surrender evokes the blind rage of Mars *caecus, insanus,* the last-ditch suicidal effort. Surrender requires ritual, a *rite de sortie* that honors the god and allows his warriors to separate themselves from his dominion.

My thoughts have been intended to regain the mythical perspective. My thoughts have not been aimed at finding another literal answer to either war or nuclearism. We each know the literal answer: freeze, defuse, dismantle, disarm. Disarm the positivism but re-arm the god; return arms and their control to the mythical realities that are their ultimate governances. Above all: wake up. To wake up, we need Mars, the God of Awakenings. Allow him to instigate our consciousness so that we may "escape the fate of violent death" and live the martial peace of activism.

A Frenchwoman after World War II tells Glenn Gray: "Anything is better than to have nothing at all happen day after day. You know I do not love war or want it to return. But at least it made me feel alive, as I have not felt before or since."[13]

Imagine! Is she not saying that war results less from the presence of the god than from his absence? For we long for purposeful action, hand-to-hand engagements, life lived in terms of death, seriousness and lightheartedness together, a clearing. The Frenchwoman's "nothing at all...day after day" is the nihilism of the nuclear age. Nuclear doom occurs not only in the literal future out there when the bomb goes off. Doom is already there in our numbed skulls, day-after-day, nothing-at-all. Mars's *phobos,* fear, can awaken us out of this nihilism and its realization in an Apocalypse. Fear may be our most precious emotion. We have everything to fear, except fear itself.

I have tied our numbing with a blocked imagination and the blocked imagination with the repression of Mars and his kind of love. But fifty minutes, as we know from psychotherapy, isn't going to lift very much repression. I hope, however, that I have been able to evoke enough of Mars for you to feel him stir in your anger and your fear, and in the out-

13. Gray, *The Warriors,* xii.

ward extension of imagination that will probe such questions as: How can we lay out the proper field of action for Mars? In what ways can martial love of killing and dying and martial fellowship serve a civilian society? How can we break apart the fusion of the martial and the nuclear? What modes are there for moving the martial away from direct violence toward indirect ritual? Can we bring the questions themselves into the postmodern consciousness of imaginal psychology, deconstruction, and catastrophe theory? Can we deconstruct the positivism and literalism—epitomized by the ridiculous *counting* of warheads—that inform current policies before those policies literally and positively deconstruct our life, our history, and our world?

Let us invoke Mars. At least once before in our century he pointed the way. During the years he reigned—1914 to 1918—he destroyed the nineteenth-century mind and brought forth modern consciousness. Could a turn to him now do something similar?

Yet Mars wants more than reflection. The ram does not pull back to consider, and iron takes no polish in which it can see itself. Mars demands penetration toward essence, pushing forward ever further into the tangle of danger, and danger now lies in the unthought thicket of our numbed minds. Swords must be beaten into plowshares, hammered, twisted, wrought.

Strangely enough, I think this deconstruction is already going on, so banally that we miss it. Is the translation of war from physical battlefield to television screen and space fiction, this translation of literal war into media, mediated war, and the fantasy language of war games, staging areas, theaters of war and theater commanders, worst-case scenarios, rehearsals, and the Commander-in-Chief, an actor—is all this possibly pointing to a new mode of ritualizing war by imagining it?

If so, then the television war of Vietnam was not lost. The victims died not only for their cause (if there was one) or their country (if it cared). They were rather the sacrificial actors in a ritual that may deconstruct war wholly into an imaginal operation. Carl Sandburg's phrase, "Someday they'll give a war and no one will come," may have already begun. No one need come because the services for Mars are performed nightly at home on the tube. In a media society, will not capitalist war-profiteering shift its base from a military-industrial complex to a military-communications/information complex, the full symbolization of war?

If war could be contained in imagination, why not as well the nuclear bomb? A translation of the bomb into imagination keeps it safe from both military Martialism and civilian Christianism. The first would welcome it for an arm, the second for an Apocalypse. Imagination seems anyway to be the only safe place to keep the bomb: there is no literal positive place on earth where it can be held, as we cannot locate our MX missiles anywhere except as images on a drawing board or dump the wastes from manufacturing them anywhere safe.

However—to hold the bomb as image in the mind requires an extraordinary extension, and extraordinary daring, in our imagining powers, a revolution of imagination itself, enthroning it as the main, the greatest reality, because the bomb, which imagination shall contain, is the most powerful image of our age. Brighter than a thousand suns, it is our omnipotent god-term (as Wolfgang Giegerich has expounded), our mystery that requires constant imaginative propitiation. The translation of bomb into the imagination is a transubstantiation of god to *imago dei*, deliteralizing the ultimate god-term from positivism to negative theology, a god that is all images. And, no more than any other god-term can it be controlled by reason or taken fully literally without hideous consequences. The task of nuclear psychology is a ritual-like devotion to the bomb as image, never letting it slip from its pillar of cloud in the heaven of imagination to rain ruin on the cities of the plain.

The Damocles sword of nuclear catastrophe that hangs upon our minds is already producing utterly new patterns of thought about catastrophe itself, a new theology, a new science, a new psychology, not only burdening the mind with doom but forcing it into postmodern consciousness, displacing, deconstructing, and trashing every fixed surety. Trashing is the symptom, and it indicates a psychic necessity of this age. To trash the end of the century of its coagulated notions calls for the disciplined ruthlessness and courage of Mars. Deconstructing the blocked mind, opening the way in faith with our rage and fear, stimulating the anaesthetized senses: this is psychic activism of the most intense sort.

Then—rather than obliterate the future with a bomb, we would deconstruct our notion of future, take apart Western Futurism, that safe repository of our noble visions. Care, foresight, renewal, the Kingdom—these have been postponed forever into the future. Rather than blast the material earth with a bomb, we would deconstruct our entombment in materialism with its justification and salvation by economics. We would bomb the bottom line back to the stone age to find again values that are sensate and alive. Rather than bring time to a close with a bomb, we would deconstruct the positivistic imagination of time that has separated it from eternity.

In other words: explode the notions; let them go up in a spirited fire. Explode worldliness, not this world; explode final judgments; explode salvation and redemption and the comings and goings of Messiahs—is not the continual presence of here and now enough for you? Put hope back into the jar of evils and let go your addiction to hopeful fixes. Explode endings and fresh starts and the wish to be born again out of continuity. Release continuity from history: remember the animals and the archaic peoples who have continuity without history. (Must the animals and the archaic peoples go up in flames because of our sacred writ?) Then timelessness could go right on being revealed without Revelation, the veils of literalism pierced by intelligence, parting and falling to the mind that imagines and so welcomes the veiling. No sudden rendering, no apocalyptic ending; timelessness as the ongoing, the extraordinarily loving, lovable, and terrifying continuity of life.

6

... AND HUGE IS UGLY:
ZEUS AND THE TITANS

I

"**S**mall is Beautiful," as E. F. Schumacher wrote, but may I start off Big? I want to begin by recalling the enormities of events during the last half-century, the fifty years from the thirties through the eighties. So I am calling this Schumacher lecture, "...And Huge Is Ugly."

Let us recall: the Great Depressions and the vast displays of totalitarianism; World War II, its massive battles with thousands of tanks and hundreds of thousands of prisoners; the armadas and invasions. Hiroshima, Nagasaki, Bikini, brighter than a thousand suns. Religious wars in India and Palestine, roads packed with refugees, displaced persons. Superpowers, superhighways, supertankers, supermarkets, Super Bowls. Olympian spectaculars, the whole world watching TV at once. Urban conglomerations of twelve, fifteen, twenty million persons. Extermination of people in Biafra, Bangladesh, the Sudan, Ethiopia. Titan missiles, space shots, megatons of thrust. Defoliation, mile-long accelerators, high-energy physics, fission, fusion, and superconductivity. Corporate multi-nationals. Gigantism in agriculture, in commerce and trade, in architecture. Universities of 60,000 students. Trillion-dollar budgets and calculators that can bite off and chew these enormities. Mind-expanding drugs, cocaine highs, mushroom visions, and mushroom clouds. Decibels of rock. Annual broken records in pole vault and discus and 100 yard dash—higher, farther, faster. Population explosion. Suburbia sprawling, miles and miles of urban squalor, burning cities,

Presented as a 10th Annual E. F. Schumacher Memorial Lecture for the Schumacher Society, Bristol, England, November 1988. First published in *Resurgence* 123 (May/ June 1989).

burning forests, homelessness, and hunger. Gargantuan consumerism. Garbage barges, garbage dumps, dead fish, dead skies, and ageless species extinguished *en masse*.

These enormities have had a counterpart in the realm of ideas—vast eliminations in theology, in semantics, in cosmology. In theology, Harvey Cox's *Secular City* and John Robinson's *Honest to God* brought God into the humanistic, personal world, dethroning and emptying out the Lord of the universe, as Bultmann had demythologized god. And Thomas Altizer announced a post-holocaust theology: God is dead. This, feminism has further defined by putting the *coup de grace* to all patriarchies everywhere.

In semantics, we suffered a huge decomposition of meanings. Logical positivism and radical nominalism reduced statements about the world and life to language only and then cut off the signification of the language from significance beyond language, leading finally to deconstruction and postmodernism's little jokes on a pompous scale.

Cosmology has been fascinated with black holes, antimatter, catastrophe theory, Heidegger's dread, Levinas's absence, and Buddhism's profound insistence on the void.

I have not mentioned many other events that might give us cheer. These are easier for our minds to cling to and by means of them see into a New Age. I am staying with the enormities, not because I am an accountant of Saturnian doom; but rather because these same enormities have dwarfed our sensitivities to that condition which Robert J. Lifton calls "psychic numbing," a term which more fits our time and so replaces Auden's "age of anxiety."

"Verweile doch, du bist so schön," says Faust to the vision of his soul. "Stay a while, linger, you are so lovely, so beautiful," but we cannot perceive Gretchen or Helen, or the loveliness of the world, the beauty of which Schumacher urged us toward, if our senses are numbed by mind-blowing enormities.

Therefore, our task begins where we actually are right in the midst of the huge and the ugly and ourselves numb to it. For a rule of archetypal psychology is, "start right where you are." Don't escape by looking for origins or solutions. Just begin in the midst of the mess.

As a psychoanalyst my job is to lift repression from the psychic numbing that best describes our current malaise, the anesthesia of our current sensibility. I ask you to keep this idea of psychic numbing in mind for we shall return to it soon in full strength.

II

The emblem of this huge devastation or devastating hugeness suffered by our culture in the past fifty years is commonly called The Holocaust. Our collective mind ever and again returns to it as if fascinated by those horrifying images of Nazi concentration camps.

I used to analyze away this fascination. I used to think we were so numb that it took shocks of this worst sort to electrify our sensibility. I used to think that focus upon the Holocaust of the earlier part of the century was a displacement for the current holocausts actually going on in Salvador and Nicaragua, Cambodia and the Sudan, South Africa and the testing atolls of the Pacific, and in the breasts of those Christians who look to an explosive end of the world so they might be saved.

But now I think the Nazi extermination camps present the truest, ugliest image of the end of our epoch, end of our civilization from the Middle Ages forward, by authentically and accurately depicting that the God of our Western civilization is dead.

There is no recourse to the old religion: its myth is now an antique fable; its devotees, members of a quaint cult; its priests, like Druids of old. We cannot escape the truth that the camps and the killers as well as the trusting victims were members of the old faith, believers in the old gods, Jesus and Jahweh—all to no avail—except to reveal now to us what Jung saw in his *Answer to Job*: the present face of the old God is monstrous like Leviathan. Heraclitus calls this psychic reversal of virtue into vice, enantiodromia, the reversal into the opposite. The most vicious acts are committed by those most virtuously faithful.

The victims and the perpetrators were not only believers in the old faith. Their faith was Belief. They believed in Belief. "Credo" was their fundamental religious statement, their witness to the reality of their god. Their gods asked to be believed in and were sustained by the faithful. After the Holocaust these gods could not be believed in and so the gods died. More: Belief itself died, leaving open other modes of being with the gods, as we are daily with the world, as animals are with events. The world does not ask for belief. It asks for noticing, attention, appreciation, care.

Because of the end of the era of Judeo-Christian belief, it is quite reasonable to find many in our day welcoming an Apocalypse. Once belief itself collapses, the end of the previous world sustained by the old gods is already here. Only by an end of the world—as it is written in the Gospel of John and preordained by the myth of our Christian civilization—can the gods return, so say the true believers.

Let us be quite clear: our civilization has horrific huge monstrous destruction written into its Holy Book. There, in every hotel room, by every bedside, part of every confirmation, every marriage, funeral, and swearing into office is the Book to which the enormity of an Apocalypse provides its concluding chapter. *The Late Great Planet Earth*, which lays out in detail the historical enactment of the coming end of the world as announced by John in Revelations, was the bestselling book in English during the 1970s.

When we look at the fifty years through the lens of Divine Absence, absence of the divine, absence of the gods—that the old gods were not present at Treblinka and Maidenek, Dachau and Buchenwald, or at Hiroshima and Bikini—that the gods of our culture were themselves suffering from psychic numbing, utterly insensitive to the world, then we can draw at least one major conclusion: In the absence of the gods things swell to enormities.

A sign of the absence of the gods is hugeness, not merely the reign of quantity, but enormity as a quality, a horrendous or fascinating description, like Black Hole, Conglomerate, Megapolis, Trillions, Gigabytes, Star Wars. Whether presented in the images of multi-national corporations, polluted oceans, or vast climatic changes, hugeness is the signature of the absent god. Or, let us say that the divine attributes of Omnipotence, Omniscience, and Omnipresence alone remain. Without the benevolent governance of qualifying divinities, Omnipotence, Omniscience, and Omnipresence become gods. In other words, without the gods, the Titans return.

Are we re-enacting the beginnings of things as recounted by the *Theology* of Hesiod? The first great task of the gods was to defeat the Titans and to thrust them in Tartarus where they were to be kept away from the human earth forever. Zeus then married Metis (intelligence or measure); lay with Themis (who bore him Hours, Order, Justice, Peace, and the Fates); lay with Eurynome, through whom came the Graces; with Mnemosyne, mother of the Muses, and with Leto, mother of Apollo and Artemis. These archetypal principles and powers come into the world only when titanism is safely kept at bay. The cultured imagination and the imagination of civic order begins only when excess is encompassed.

Titans were imagined as Giants; in fact, the popular imagination, says Roscher,[1] never distinguished between Giants and Titans. The root of the word titan means: to stretch, to extend, to spread forth, and to strive or hasten. Hesiod's own etymology (*Theogony,* 209) of *titenes* is "to strain." This straining, striving effort suggests that the major contemporary complaint of stress is the feeling in the Promethean ego of its titanism. (Prometheus is perhaps the most well-known of the Titans, the figure whom Kerényi[2] has called "the archetype of human existence," thereby pointing to the titanic propensity in each of us.) Stress is a titanic symptom. It refers to the limits of the body and soul attempting to contain titanic limitlessness. A true relief of stress begins only when we can recognize its true background: our titanic propensity.

We may note a difference between titanism and hubris. Hubris is a human failure to remember the gods. When we forget or neglect the gods, we extend beyond the limits set by the gods on mortals, limits given mainly by Zeus through his union with Metis, Themis, and Mnemosyne.

Titanism, however, takes place at the level of the gods themselves. We are not Titans nor can we become titanic—only when the gods are absent can titanism return to the earth. Do you see why we must keep the gods alive and well? Small is beautiful requires a prior step: the return of the gods.

Besides Zeus, an especial enemy of the Titans was Dionysus, who was torn by them to bits. What does this say to our condition now? If Dionysus is "Lord of Souls" as he was called and *"Zoe,"* the vitality of life itself, the moist green force infusing all plants and animal nature with a savage and tender desire to live, then this urge can be rent to shreds, atomized let us say, by any procedure, any ambition, any universal law that goes beyond the bounds. Even the Promethean impulse to benefit mankind with high-minded actions can be destructive to the delicate

---

1. W.H. Roscher, *Ausführliches Lexikon der griechischen und römischen Mythologie* (Hildesheim: Olms, 1965), 5: 988.

2. Karl Kerényi, *Prometheus: Archetypal Image of Human Existence* (Princeton, N.J.: Princeton University Press, 1963).

strength of the soul whose Lord is Dionysus. Global solutions and thinking in universals is part of the enormity that I have calling titanic. Here we might recall Yeats's caution: "The mind that generalizes continually prevents itself from those experiences which would allow it to see and feel deeply."

The mind that toys with life also serves the Titans. Gizmos, gadgets, and games, distractions and entertainments, the huge profligacy of available trivialities waste the very stuff of life. When the Titans came to rip up little Dionysus they first distracted him with toys and while the child was looking into a mirror, he was dragged off and torn limb from limb (only to be rescued and reborn by Zeus).[3]

Why and how did Zeus become the first among his brothers and sisters? Why Zeus? And why Zeus for rescuing the world from the Titans? I think it is not his strength, his thunderbolts, his wily cleverness, nor his law and order, but rather his wide imagination. When we look at his dozen or more matings and his progeny—Apollo, Hermes, Dionysus, Hercules, Perseus, Artemis, Athene, and many others—he clearly could imagine these existential possibilities, these styles of consciousness. His range of fantasy was comprehensive, large, generous, and differentiated. He was indeed a sky god; he covered all with his breadth of imagining power, equal in articulated grandeur to titanic enormity. Titanic hugeness can be encompassed and contained only by an equally large capacity of inspired image-making.

Moreover, Zeus was born in daylight as they say, out in the open; his mother bore him on the wide earth. Zeusian consciousness is active; on the earth, there, in the open. He fathers activism, which tells us something about how to meet titanism. Not retreat, mediation, psychoanalysis, or hope in the Kingdom Come.

Despite evidence of flagrant titanism all around us, the Titans themselves are invisible, like the black night sky of Uranos, their terrible father, and hidden by their mother, Gaia, in her deepest womb. They are sometimes imagined as ghosts.[4] They work invisibly in darkness and

---

3. Walter Burkert, *Greek Religion,* translated by John Raffan (Cambridge, Mass.: Harvard University Press, 1985), 297.

4. Karl Kerényi, *Dionysis: Archetypal Image of Indestructible Life* (Princeton, N.J.: Princeton University Press, 1976), 243.

in the impulses and fantasies arising from the depths. Lopez-Pedraza[5] points out, referring to the mythologists Nilsson and Kerényi, that the Titans—because they are invisible or unimaged—therefore do not have limits. Without image they become pure expansion. Hence, their punishment requires severe limitations: the chains that bind Prometheus; incarceration in Tartarus.

Limitation in our society tends to mean repression. We imagine the defeat of excess by means of tougher laws, harder education, severer systems of management control. However, the cure of enormity through more discipline is but an allopathic measure, a cure through the opposite which often leads to a righteous puritanical totalitarianism. The correction of one titanism can easily convert into another sort, e.g., totalitarian moralism, unless we understand what Zeus is truly about: the ordering power of the differentiated imagination: polytheism.

III

I have not mentioned in my catalogue of twentieth-century horrors, Depth Psychology. Concurrent with the titanic enormities I have listed, is the rise, spread and penetration of depth psychology all over and throughout civilization—like kudzu vine, thriving as a parasite, clinging to the trunks of dying trees, falling temples, and crumbling institutional walls, depth psychology sends out more shoots and branches and strives towards every more light.

Depth psychology is everywhere. As the gods died, the Self emerged. Heinrich Zimmer, at the beginning of this period in the nineteen thirties said, "All the gods are within." So, depth psychology became the religion or theology and ritual of the inside—dream, vision, reveries, feelings, insight, personal remembrances of things past. We explored the within, but did we find the gods?

Like the retreats in the countryside to which Roman patricians fled during the decline and fall of that epoch and its dying gods, our educated and affluent class has gone into similar retreat, inside our private nature, inside the walls of our skins.

---

5. Rafael López-Pedraza, "Moon Madness—Titanic Love," in *Images of the Untouched*, edited by Joanne H. Stroud and Gail Thomas (Dallas: Spring Publications, 1982).

The justification for retreat from the disordered world has been given by ancient wisdom of shaman and rainmaker and oriental sage and Christian saint; put yourself in order and the world follows. Concentric circles—the smallest interior act in the mediating mind has ripples beyond itself. Eventually the wide world is affected—so runs the introverted (shall I say paranoid?) argument. Jungians have sometimes led the way away from the world soul into the private soul, quoting Jung[6] who said we are each makeweights in the scales of world history; on the individual the destiny of the world depends. I think this statement can be reversed and be equally true, especially true today: on the destiny of the world, the fate of the individual depends.

I now want to connect the titanic enormities of the last fifty years with the pervasive influence of depth psychology or psychoanalysis during the same period, and the emphasis of analysis upon self-development and individuality. There are several ways of making this connection. First, we may say they are merely unrelated concurrent occasions with no significant relation. Second, we may say they show a compensatory relation: the more horrific the vision of the world out there, the more beatific the vision of the interior castle. As impersonal enormities increase out there the more attention we devote to the minutiae of personal dreams, fantasies, feeling and relationships. Small is beautiful restricts its meaning to the private and personal.

Our everyday language gives evidence of this shrinking away from the world and into our private functions. The adjectives we use to describe events have become more and more self-centered. To the question, "how was the evening (or party, or lecture, or plane trip), we reply: "dreadful, exhausting, boring, fascinating, etc." We tell of ourselves, our feelings instead of describing the actual world, e.g., overcrowded, slow-to-get-going, full of strange people, noisy, etc.

There is a third way of connecting the enormities and depth psychology. This third way is by means of the when/then move, i.e., seeing both as part of one image and therefore necessary to and coterminous with each other. When the external world grows enormous, then we turn to the internal self; and also, when we turn to the internal self, then the external world grows enormous.

6. *CW* 10: 586–88.

This last co-relation we psychoanalysts have not been willing to explore: this possibility, this shocking possibility, the more I focus on the interior psyche, the more I may actually be contributing to the world as holocaust, to the Apocalypse, to the end of our civilization.

IV

I have long been critical of the disastrous self-centeredness of therapy. The fascination with self, however, cannot move until we recognize that the psyche, ever since Plato, has referred to an encompassing soul outside and beyond the borders of "me," beyond my intra- and interpersonal relationships, beyond even the world as my ecological environment or my projective field. As Jung said, the psyche is not in me; I am in the psyche.

This sense of the world as an animated being, as a living animal, is the first component of curing enormity. The animal sense engages the world as highly specific and particular. This William James called "each-ness," rather than wholeness and generalities. This beech tree, that hay field, that clump of wild flowers, this street corner, that smell, the taste of this water. The more animal our noses, the more the world presents itself to the senses as animal, and like tribal peoples, we take note of the specific values and powers of each event, each thing. Then, the Holy returns from Rudolf Otto's Wholly Other and theological vastness to this specific stone, medicine, frog or bird, pouch or pot.

The second component of the cure of enormity begins by trusting the heart's reactions of desire and anger, which the Scholastics and Church Fathers named *cupiditas* and *ira.* To these I would add fear, Phobos, the son of Mars/Ares, and also shame, the *aidos* of Artemis. These deep emotions of the bowels, liver, genitals, and heart, these responses of the animal blood keep us in tune, in touch with the world around—its beauty, its insult, its danger.

Analysis derogates these powerful bonds that keep us alive to the world and the world alive to us by calling them "affects" filled with "projections." Eastern wisdom teaches us to overcome them for they attach us to the wheel, to the illusions of existence. But these "divine influxes," as Blake called emotions, are not ours. Desire, rage, fear, and shame are echoes of the world's soul, presentations of qualities in the world informing our bodies and spirits how to be, what stance to take, what to have and what to hate, which way to turn.

When we hold a titanic view of emotions, we send them to Tartaros. Control. Repression. Curb your appetites; just say no; count to ten; stand tall; be not ashamed. Then, when the repressed returns as it must, it comes back as predicted with ruinous titanic power. Again, however, from a Zeusian perspective, desire, anger, fear, and shame open the soul out and toward the stimuli from the world under his sky.

Rage in particular is important here. Remember: Zeus and his brothers and sisters overcame the Titans and Giants in battle! Under the sign of Mars/Ares, the god of battle rage, intensity, fury. Emotions seek just what the word says: *ex-movere*, to move out, and rage is actually internalized or frustrated outrage. Outrage then becomes primary. When prevented from action, from moving out, it becomes *ira*, anger, rage. Let us recognize that outrage has a social intention. It leads us into the fray, into community engagement with our sisters and brothers. It notices moral insults and aesthetic injuries. It roars in protest. As Wallace Stevens said, "the lion roars at the enraging desert."[7]

Similarly, desire has been frustrated and psychologized into need, so that it too becomes internalized and we forget what D.H. Lawrence said: "desire is holy." Desire is holy because it is the emotional response to Venus's luring beauty in the world. The world is a great seducer. Whether to the scientist of nature or to the plain man on a ramble, the world draws us to it. And strongly! Else there would not have to be so many warnings against its Venusian lure, such as "the world, the flesh, and the devil." In the same way fear, the crucial emotion for survival, has been deprived by psychology of its objective correlative—the fearful giants out there—and become objectless, free-floating anxiety.

Anxiety, Need, Rage: these are substitutions on which psychology lives, having taken them into its province by internalizing fear, desire, and outrage. The return to the world, and the return to a world ensouled, requires the return of the primacy of these life-giving, life-protecting, and world-recognizing emotions. The psychological task is much like that which we have to perform on Newton's and Locke's

---

7. See my *The Thought of the Heart and the Soul of the World* (Putnam, Conn.: Spring Publications, 2004), 64–68, for an explication of the Stevens line.

qualities: returning color and taste and sound and texture to the things of the world, no longer pretending that these phenomena take place only in the subjective sensorium.

Of these four emotions, a word about shame. Until rather recently it too has been degraded to guilt, an emotion located in the ego or the super-ego; whereas, in fact, shame invades us, flushes through us, indeed a divine influx. Shame seems to be *the* emotion of ecology, as *aidos* is a characteristic word appropriate to Artemis, that lovely elusive lady of the woods, springs, hills, and clearings. A Navaho chant says:

> I am ashamed before earth
> I am ashamed before heavens
> I am ashamed before dawn;
> I am ashamed before evening twilight
> I am ashamed before blue sky;
> I am ashamed before darkness
> I am ashamed before sun
> Some of these things are always looking at me.
> I am never out of their sight. [8]

To litter the world with trash, to construct monstrous structures, to consume and waste as distraction from boredom is not merely illegal, immoral, or anti-social and unhealthy. It is shameful; offensive to the world itself, harmful to the soul.

V

The third component of the cure of the enormity—following upon the other two of locating soul in the world, and of freeing the animal blood's passions of desire, outrage, fear, shame—takes us directly to the founder of these lectures, Schumacher, and his aesthetic formulation: that word, "beautiful." Let us appreciate the courage shown by Schumacher in placing the word beautiful in the title of his book. Not small is efficient; not small is right, or good, or healthy, or natural, or redemptive: but small is *Beautiful*.

This shows courage, for to speak of the beautiful is to lift the major repression of the day. Not horror, not cruelty, not our personal lives and

8. Quoted in Patricia Berry, *Echo's Subtle Body* (Thompson, Conn.: Spring Publications, 2017 [1982]), 12–13 (trans. Washington Matthews [1894]).

their sexual vicissitudes, their family memories, their needs and greeds are repressed today. The last one hundred years of psychotherapeutic solitude has lifted the repression from the private shadows of our interior lives. We know every square inch of childhood, the molestations and abuses, the alcohol and beatings: we know all about gender differences, every nook and cranny of our *mauvais foi*, misery and narcissistic complaints. We even have explored our birth canal traumas and our previous lives long ago and far away from today's immediate mess. Today the Great Repressed, the taboo that never is mentioned in therapy or analytic theory, is beauty. The unconscious does not stay in the same place. What was unconscious is no longer unconscious. As psychoanalytic light proceeds through the forest, making clearings, new shadows spring up behind. The unconscious is always where we are not looking. Today we are unconscious of beauty. We are unaesthetic, anaesthetized, physically numbed.

Moreover, there is a huge and ugly, and evil, empire at work day and night to keep us this way. Manically charged, hyper-loud and strong TV; sensationalist media news; drink and sugar and coffee; developers, improvers and entertainers; the health industry building muscles not sensitivity; the medical industry as drug dispensers, sleeping pills, uppers, downers, lithium for children; and shopping, shopping, shopping. We are not even mummies or zombies in our psychic numbing, for we have not been to the Underworld, the land of the dead. We are simply in Plato's cave, drugged out of our gourds, shut down, numb.

Though the Titans may be invisible, an unimaged limitless greed locked inside human nature, titanism is all around. It strikes the ears, the membranes and eyeballs and fingers. Our senses touch and recoil. Repulsed by the huge and the ugly, we close off the world. We grab a bite on the run, drive thru our days. The common world is lost to sense, and too, the words of sense, the common descriptive language of adjectives and adverbs that give texture and shading. Instead, a titanism of acronyms and the justification for the ugly and the huge with abstract imageless reasons named economy, practicality, time-saving, comfort, accessibility, convenience, and national security. The cure? Not love; not relate, only relate; not arise from your chains—but "O Taste and See!" (Psalm 34). Let Zeus, born in the open, awake to all under the sky; ever-watchful, ever-noticing be exemplar for responding to all that the senses present with a richly elaborating imagination. Only well-shaped images fed by the senses can contain and differentiate our innate titanism.

In review, then, my three components of the cure for titanism interlock. Reawakening the sense of soul in the world goes hand in hand with an aesthetic response—the sense of beauty and ugliness—to each and everything, and this in turn requires trusting the emotions of desire, outrage, fear, and shame as the felt immediacy of the gods in our bodily lives, and their concern that this world, our planet, their neighbor, does not become the late great planet earth.

7

OEDIPUS REVISITED

Myth and Psychoanalysis

T o take up the theme of Oedipus is a heroic engagement. Can you imagine the weight that falls when opening yet again the pages of Sophocles's play, the play that Aristotle used for explaining the nature of tragedy, that Freud used for explaining the nature of the human soul, the volume that drowned with Shelley off Lerici, a tale of a hero told by Homer and Aeschylus and Euripides as well, and retold by Seneca, Hölderlin, Hofmannsthal, Voltaire, Gide—and add to that the shelves of scholarly apparatus, interpretations, commentaries, arguments; and then, to bring this inhumanly heroic theme in public ostentation to our annual *convivium* here—the heroism, or *chutzpah*, is beyond all decent proportion.

So it is necessary before we begin to acknowledge a god in today's work, Apollo, and his hero, Oedipus, so that they do not devastate us with surprise. We confess at the outset to the lure of the Apollonic hero so as not to fall prey to the myth itself, to its self-blinding propensity, its badgering persistence to discover and expose, its patricidal impulse to kill old kings, and to its incestuous inflation that could produce as progeny yet another incestuously psychoanalytic paper on the Oedipus complex. By this opening propitiation, I beg that the myth not be mine. May Apollo stay distant as is his nature, as well Oedipus and Laius, and even Teiresias, and the ancestors, Sophocles and Freud, too. Allow me to accord you reverence, yet kindly afford me safety from your sway while in your presence.

A Lecture first delivered at the Eranos Conference "Crossroads," August 1987, Ascona, Switzerland, and subsequently published in *Eranos Yearbook 56* (1987).

This gesture at the beginning is made in recognition of the power of myth. The *Wirksamkeit* of myth, its reality, resides precisely in its power to seize and influence our psychic life. The Greeks knew this so well, and so they had no depth psychology and psychopathology such as we have. They had myths. And we have no myths as such; instead depth psychology and psychopathology. Therefore, as I have repeatedly said, psychology shows myths in modern dress and myths show our depth psychology in ancient dress.

The first to recognize this truth which is foundational for modern depth psychology was Sigmund Freud. The first to recognize the implications of Sigmund Freud's recognition of the relation between myth and psyche, between antiquity and modern psychology, was C.G. Jung. Hear this passage, which I have abbreviated from the opening page of Jung's pathbreaking work, *Wandlungen und Symbole der Libido (Symbols of Transformation)*. Although published in 1912, Jung retained this opening passage intact in his 1952 revision of the book:

> Anyone who can read Freud's *Interpretation of Dreams*...[and] can let this extraordinary book work upon his imagination calmly and without prejudices, will not fail to be deeply impressed at that point where Freud reminds us that an individual conflict, which he calls the incest fantasy, lies at the root of that monumental drama of the ancient world, the Oedipus legend...We suddenly catch a glimpse of the simplicity and grandeur of the Oedipus tragedy, that perennial highlight of the Greek theatre. This broadening of our vision has about it something of a revelation...when we follow the paths traced out by Freud...then the gulf that separates our age from antiquity is bridged over, and we realize with astonishment that Oedipus is still alive for us...This truth opens the way to an understanding of the classical spirit such as has never existed before... By penetrating into the blocked subterranean passages of our own psyches we grasp the living meaning of classical civilization, and at the same time...gain an objective understanding of [our own] foundations. That at least is the hope we draw from the rediscovery of the immortality of the Oedipus problem.[1]

---

1. *CW* 5: 1–2.

Now hear Freud's words:

> Falling in love with one parent and hating the other forms part
> of the permanent stock of the psychic impulses...of early child-
> hood...Antiquity has furnished us with legendary matter which
> corroborates this belief, and the profound and universal validity
> of the old legends is explicable only by an equally universal valid-
> ity of the above mentioned hypothesis regarding the psychology
> of children. I am referring to the...*Oedipus Rex* of Sophocles.[2]

Freud recounts the plot, the *mythos*, briefly. Then he says:

> The action of the play consists simply in the disclosure, ap-
> proached step by step and artistically delayed (and comparable
> to the work of a psychoanalysis) that Oedipus himself is the mur-
> derer of Laius.[3]

This analogy between the poetic art and the artfulness of psychoanalysis
Freud states again:

> As the poet, by unraveling the past, brings the guilt of Oedipus
> to light, he forces us to become aware of our own inner selves.[4]

Then this:

> If *Oedipus Rex* moves a modern audience no less than it did the con-
> temporary Greeks, the only possible explanation is that...there
> must be a voice within us which is prepared to acknowledge the
> compelling power of fate in the *Oedipus*...His fate moves us only
> because it might have been our own, because the oracle laid upon
> us before our birth the very curse which rested upon him.[5]

These passages show that the particular myth uniting psychoanalysis
with Greek antiquity is the *Oedipus Tyrannus* of Sophocles. It is therefore inescapable—please note my language already takes on the Oedipal
vocabulary—if we would be faithful to the project of an archetypal revisioning of depth psychology, that this Oedipus be revisited.

By an "archetypal revisioning" I mean tracing the imaginal roots that
govern the ways psychology thinks and feels. I mean restoring behavior

---

2. Sigmund Freud, "The Interpretation of Dreams," in *The Basic Writings of Sigmund Freud*, translated by A.A. Brill (New York: Modern Library, 1938), 306–7.

3. Ibid., 307.

4. Ibid., 308.

5. Ibid.

to its fictions, an *epistrophé* of life's blind enactments and sufferings called abnormal psychology, an imagining of our field and its work in terms of *archai, daimones,* and gods. My project of imagining follows directly from Jung's most extraordinary and foundational statement, ontologically and methodologically foundational for whatever may justly be called "Jungian": "The psyche creates reality every day. The only expression I can use for this activity is *fantasy*... Fantasy, therefore, seems to me the clearest expression of the specific activity of the psyche."[6]

I follow Jung here most assiduously, believing that psychology is truly psychological only when it awakens to the fantasies objectified in its observations. Analysts in practice are obliged to notice the fantasies we have in reading our patients: so, depth psychology is obliged to notice its fantasies in reading its theories. A psychology that observes, reports, formulates, and explains the patient, or the psyche in large, remains like the patient who observes, reports, and explains—that is, projective or, let us say, blind, not seeing the very eye it is seeing with. Hence, we turn to the bedrock of fantasies, the myths, for how else can psychology as it is now conceived awaken to itself.

The project of course has a heroic cast; for how imagine projects except as heroic projections, redemptive, culturally liberating, yet always in service to the founding fathers by continuing their line. The project would lift or deepen human life from its horizontal wanderings and labyrinthine riddlings always to something more-than-human, at times animal, at times alchemical, at times cultural, at times mythical. It would restore to insight its origins in the epiphanic, even theophanic, moment, authenticating interpretation with the truth of beauty and the sudden joy of recognition, truth and beauty as one. Indeed, the thrust is heroic because it is so fiercely anti-humanistic, as if parented by a divinity and with a desire to return all things to that divinity; yet, just as equally heroic because the other parent is humanly mortal, naive, foolish, anchored in the ordinary world of community and *polis.*

So, we shall be continuing the line of Freud and Jung, drawing further parallels between myth and psychoanalysis. And we shall try to go beyond Freud's concentration on incest and parricide which narrowed his insight. Our first aim is to unearth other relevances for depth psychol-

---

6. CW 6: 78.

ogy in the Oedipus story for that is where the theater of Oedipus continues to be performed.

Family as Fate

Freud has been attacked for reducing the noble Greek notion of heroic
destiny to the banal intimacies of family. To Fliess, Freud wrote: "The
Greek myth seizes on a compulsion which everyone recognizes because
he has felt traces of it in himself. Every member of the audience was
once a budding Oedipus in phantasy."[7] Moreover, detractors say, Freud
got it completely wrong. He tells the tale so that the murder of the
father results from desire for the mother. Whereas in play and legend,
first came the murder and then the incest, and an incest without lust.
Freud emphasized the mother, providing the ground for his materialist
reductions. However, according to the legend, we fall into the arms of
the mother only after killing the father: the seduction of *mater* and mate-
rialisms of whatever sort are consequent to the murder of the unknown
father. When we kill the father we are Oedipal.

Who, what, where is this unknown father in actual psychology? I
have to assume that any contrary spirit that cannot be evaded may be
an unrecognized father. Do we not meet a "father" in those moments
of obstruction which narrow the path to single-mindedness, those
moments of resistance when we will not give way to what crosses us?
Jung once defined God with these words:

> To this day God is the name by which I designate all things which
> cross my wilful path violently and recklessly, all things which
> upset my subjective views, plans and intentions and change the
> course of my life for better or worse.[8]

By resisting the unknown that crosses "my subjective views, plans, and
intentions," I kill the father. I do not let myself be moved by the chance
spirit which blows for ill or good, or both. Resistance is indeed central
to analysis for it is essential to Oedipus's heroic style.

Yet, at the same time, this style accords a fathering power to the other,
unconsciously acknowledging that the other crossing my way has the

---

7. Sigmund Freud, *The Origins of Psychoanalysis: Letters to Wilhelm Fliess* (London:
Imago, 1954); letter dated 15 October 1897.

8. Cited from an interview with Jung, December 1961, as quoted in Edward F.
Edinger, *Ego and Archetype* (Harmondsworth: Penguin, 1973), 101.

fathering power to change my life. It is my King. The other's great "No" fathers me by standing in my way. *Eris, polemos,* strife, war, said Heraclitus, is the father of all things.

The critics also say, because of Freud, every family reduces to the single same account, a monomyth, and myth itself reduces to compulsions and repressions derived from family. The battles with cosmic fate then become the repression of desires. A human life is not called by fate but compelled by desire, say the critics. The tragic hero Oedipus becomes Little Hans with a phobia. And the Oedipus which is in us all becomes a five-year-old child, a little bud of lust and murder. And what a curse Freud put on family life. "I will never come near my parents," swears Oedipus (Grene, 1007)[9]—separation, suspicion, ignorance, abandonment, incest, infanticide, suicide, mutilation, and cursing into the next generation when old Oedipus at Colonus turns his wrathful back on his fighting sons.

Of course, Freud got it wrong—but I am not joining with his critics. Freud "got it wrong" because it is the genius of psychology to get it wrong, to disturb, pervert, dislocate, misread, so as to lift the repression of the usual sense. Psychoanalysis goes wrong in order to keep close to the wrongness in the case, whatever the case may be. Pathologizing is homeopathic: like cures like. There must be madness in the method if the method would reach the madness.

Besides, there are other ways of reading Freud. Yes, he did secularize fate into ordinary family emotion and cast his dark pathologized eye on family phenomena. Yet Freud ennobled family with a mythical dimen-

---

9. The Sophocles texts of *Oedipus Tyrannus* and *Oedipus at Colonus* referred to are those published in the Loeb Classical Library. Translations into English quoted are those of: Albert Cook, in *Greek Tragedy: An Anthology* (Dallas: Spring Publications, 1981); Francis Storr, *Oedipus the King, Oedipus at Colonus, Antigone* [1912], Loeb Classical Library, vol. 1 (Cambridge, Mass.: Harvard University Press, 1981); E. F. Watling, *Sophocles: The Theban Plays* (Harmondsworth: Penguin, 1950); Robert Fagles, *The Three Theban Plays: Antigone, Oedipus the King, Oedipus at Colonus* (Harmondsworth: Penguin, 1984); David Grene, *Sophocles I* (Chicago: The University of Chicago Press, 1991); Sir George Young, *The Dramas of Sophocles in English Verse* (London: J.M. Dent & Sons, 1906ff.); William Moebius (*Oedipus at Colonus*) in *Greek Tragedy*. Also consulted were A.C. Pearson, *Sophoclis Fabulae* (Oxford: Clarendon Press, 1923); my line enumerations attempt to follow those of Pearson and Storr.

sion, for his pathologized view was at the same time a mythologized view, confirming once more the root metaphor of depth psychology: mythology presents pathology; pathology, mythology. We require both to grasp either.

The infusion of Greek myth into the medical, academic, commercial, and often Jewish Vienna of the 1890s—Freud's world and the world of his clientele—brought to family a transparency beyond bourgeois materialism and its hysteria. While Oedipus collapses into Hans down the street, there glimmers through little Hans the radiance of Oedipus, Sophocles, Greece, and the gods. As Freud says: "Hans was really a little Oedipus who wanted to have his father 'out of the way.' to get rid of him, so that he might be alone with his handsome mother and sleep with her."[10] *Really,* that is Freud's word. What is *really* at work in the case is myth; what is really going on in family is myth: to feel myth in the daily world, just stay home with the family. Of course, it drives one crazy.

By returning family back to mythic figures, Freud performed an *epistrophé.* He reimagined our desires, our phobias, our childhoods. He relocated the human world in the mythical imagination. The World Parents of creation myths became the parental world: the parental world became our culture's creation myth, at once personal, secular, and historical. Parents gain supreme authority in the generation of the psychic cosmos. Whether actual, whether imagos, whether archetypal Mother and Father, parents become the great dominants. A father's terrifying authority arises—not because of introjected conventional religion which Freud abjured or because of patriarchal social norms—but because of myth: in the father is Laius and Apollo and the myth embroiling Laius, and in the mother is the Queen, the throne, the city.

Ever since, psychoanalysis performs this *epistrophé*—if we read it in this light. Ever since, psychoanalysts are the myth-preservers in our culture. They go on ritualizing the Oedipal tale, go on affirming the cosmic power of parents and childhood for discovering identity. By divinizing the parental world, each patient discovers a budding Oedipus in the soul. We believe we are what we are because of our childhoods in family, but this only because the actual family is "really" Oedipal—that is,

---

10. "Analysis of a Phobia in a Five-Year-Old Boy," *CP*3: 253: "Er ist wirklich ein kleiner Ödipus..."

mythical. Even as actual, sociological, statistical family life dissolves, psychoanalysis retains the myth. Early years and repressed memories are so fateful in our culture because psychoanalysis dominates our cult of souls and Oedipus is the dominant myth practiced in the cult. Depth psychology believes in myth, practices myth, teaches myth. That myth hides from recognition and lies disguised in literal and secular case histories is appropriate to the very myth they teach—the tale of Oedipus, its disguises and pursuit of self-recognition.

We must see this clearly, and here again I use Oedipal heroic language. The fact that literal family holds such sway in analytic considerations is because we are each "really Oedipus;" and this not because our psyches want our mothers but because we are, in soul, mythical beings. We emerge into life as creatures in a drama, scripted by the great storytellers of our culture. And, as budding Oedipus we immediately transpose the stock figures of Mom and Dad, or the absent Mom or Dad as is mainly the situation today, or aunt or stepfather or daycare lady—whoever plays their stand-ins—into Jocasta and Laius, ennobling desire, parents, memory, forgetting, foretelling, early family scenes, early abandonments, abuses, and mutilations, little boy and little girl wishes, and endowing these small, pre-initiatory events with salient inevitable determinacy.

But none of this is literal. We must see this clearly: none of it can be taken at only this one level of historical fact. Not what happened in childhood, not your recollections of lust and hatred, not even what is recalled or not recalled but buried, nor your parents as such. All these emotions and configurations are ways in which we are remythologized. And that is why these emotions and configurations carry such importance. They are doors to Sophocles and Sophocles himself a door. Their importance rises not from historical events but by mythical happenings that, as Sallustius said, never happened but always are, as fictions.

For the same reason Freud's basic theory still dominates—and will. It too is myth, wearing the costume appropriate to the *nigredo* rhetoric of science's materialism. What holds us to Freud, provoking countless retellings and commentaries such as this one now, is not the science in the theory but the myth in the science. Freud wrote to Einstein in 1932:

> All this may give you the impression that our theories amount
> to species of mythology and a gloomy one at that! But does not

every natural science lead ultimately to this—a sort of mythology? Is it otherwise today with your physical sciences?[11]

Individual patients struggling with self-knowledge are so convinced by the fictions of childhood because they are Oedipus, who finds who he is by finding out about his infancy, its wounds and abandonment. The entire massive apparatus of counselling, social work, developmental psychology—therapy in every form—continues rehearsing the myth, practising the play in its practices.

Sick City

Freud is little concerned with the relation between the tragedy of Oedipus and the tragedy of the city. For Sophocles, *polis* is central to the play. The play is filled with longing to find the father *and* to cure the city. The mystery of parricide and of the *polis* are inseparable. Only that resolution which cures the city can satisfy. For Oedipus—or any one of us—to find one's father and the truth of oneself is not enough, because there is a murder in the order of the world, and the world and the soul are inseparable. That is why the longing in the play is so intense: the world must be restored, not only its men and women. So the play is called *Oedipus Tyrannus*, Oedipus, ruler of the city, *rex*, king.

The play opens with the presenting complaints of a sick city. A priest of Zeus appeals to Oedipus:

> The city, as you see, wastes in blight,
> Blight on earth's fruitful blooms and grazing flocks,
> And on the barren birth pangs of the women.
> The fever god has fallen on the city,
> And drives it, a most hated pestilence...
> (Cook, 22–30)

Oedipus replies:

> I am not ignorant
> ...Well I know
> You are all sick, and in your sickness none
> There is among you as sick as I,
> For your pain comes to one man alone,

11. *Einstein on Peace,* edited by Otto Nathan and Heinz Norden (New York: Schocken Books, 1960), 186–203.

To him and to none other, but my soul [*psyché*]
Groans for the state, for myself, and for you...
...Know that already I have...
...sought, and found one remedy.

(Cook, 60–69)

The King has taken on the city and its people as himself. He calls them his children, *tekna*. He identifies his condition with theirs. He *is* the city and its people. We are dealing, however, with something beyond the symbolic significance of kingship, and rather with the interpenetration of sickness among the *polis*, its people, and the individual. All are sick together: individuals, community, and government. Private and public cannot be separated. The gods do not affect individuals and families alone, or only human beings: they affect the land, the crops and herds, the institutions of state. A city, too, can be pathologized by mythical factors—exactly what Jung said in "Wotan" in 1936. The gods live in the *polis*.[12]

Depth psychology has drawn conclusions from the play about the suffering of soul in the family. Depth psychology can draw further conclusions about the suffering of soul, psychopathology, in the city. How does a city act when it is sick? What moves do its rulers make? What notions of remedy arise from a sick city?

First, the sick city calls upon the leader to find remedy, equating King with City, Oedipus Tyrannus. The government is responsible. The people are children.

Second, the leader calls on Apollo to reveal the cause and the cure:

And this I did...
Creon, my brother-in-law, I sent away
Unto Apollo's Pythian halls to find
What I might do or say to save the state [*polis*].

(Cook, 70–73)

The government turns to Apollonic consciousness, Apollonic means of diagnosis and correction. And the government speaks in God's name:

God proclaimed him now to me...
...for me, for the God, and for this land of ours...

(Grene, 244–54)

---

12. "Wotan" was first published in the *Neue Schweizer Rundschau*; now in CW10: 371–99.

Third, the sick city summons the seer, shaman, or prophet for clearly seeing the nature of the ills. Oedipus sends for Teiresias, because

> ...what the Lord Teiresias sees,
> is most often what the Lord Apollo sees.
>
> (Grene, 285–87)

Fourth, the city purges. Oedipus says, "I will disperse this filth" (Cook, 138). Creon says:

> Lord Phoebus clearly bids us drive out,...
> A pollution we have nourished in our land.
>
> (Cook, 97–99)

Oedipus speaks of purification, expulsion, punishment; he curses those who would not obey him. As there is one remedy, the oracle of Apollo, so there is one villain, the scapegoat murderer. Creon, returning from the Pythian oracle, speaks of robbers in the plural (123), and Oedipus in the next speech contracts the plural to the singular. The indefinite plural "murderers" become the single scapegoat on whom all blame shall fall,

> I forbid that man, whoever he may be, my land,
> ...and I forbid any to welcome him
> or cry him greeting or make him a sharer
> in sacrifice or offering to the gods
> or give him water for his hands to wash
> I command all to drive him from their homes
> since he is our pollution.
>
> (Grene, 236–43)

Fifth, the sick city makes edicts. Oedipus says: I forbid, I command, I in-voke this curse. In these early passages of the play, he speaks as the voice of the city whereas Teiresias uses *ego* eight times in their exchange, referring to himself as a person.[13] Oedipus Tyrannus is the state, an utterly public figure: *l'état c'est moi.*

These five solutions—and let me repeat them *en bref:* a single answer to a complex problem, the appeal to Apollo, the reliance upon the prophetic seer, the language of pollution and expulsion, and apodeictic declarations in God's name—these supposed solutions are actually manifestations of the city's sickness. They are diagnostic signs. The solutions

---

13. Seth Benardete, "Sophocles' Oedipus Tyrannus," in *Sophocles,* edited by Thomas Woodard (Englewood Cliffs, N.J.: Prentice-Hall, 1966), 109.

imagined by a patient for his illness belong to the image of the illness. That is why therapists listen closely to what the patient wants at the beginning of therapy. How the patient imagines remedy and what measures he is already pursuing show how the patient is constellated by his condition. The *solutions* to the problem of Thebes present *the problem* of Thebes. The city suffers because of Oedipus, of course. Every playgoer knows that.

The city suffers more profoundly, however, from the Apollonic way in which it reflects on its suffering. Oedipus is the scapegoat because the city imagines itself in the manner of expelling evil. And it finds the scapegoat as prophesied because its consciousness fulfills its prophetic structure. "Phoebus who proposed the riddle, himself / Should give the answer—who the murderer was," says the Chorus (Storr, 279).

The Chorus, however, does not altogether follow the Apollonic mode; The Chorus extends the divine background. It mentions Zeus, Fates (*keres*), nymphs, Pegasus. It refers the pestilence to Ares (1911) and calls on Athene (158), Artemis (161), and Dionysus (212) for protection, even suggesting for Oedipus fathering gods other than Apollo: Pan, Hermes, Dionysus. So, the Chorus embraces a vision wider than an Apollonic notion of government and cures for its ills. The city is sick; "shipwreck" is the term, the marketplace in turmoil, the youth in the streets, the crops, the herds, the women barren, to all of which there is one appeal and one solution, according to the Oedipal and Apollonic mode: "Lay on the King."[14]

There could be other ways than the five measures we have just specified. If we listen to the Chorus, then we would look for the other remedies backed by other gods. When the institutions of the state are in shipwreck, then turn to the institutions themselves. If the crops, then why not a Demeterian remedy; if the women, then the protections of the marriage bed and childbirth. Concrete measures conceived in response to concrete cases. A differentiation of the single illness according to its multiple manifestations. This pragmatic non-heroic approach is much as in a modern city: the problems reside not just in City Hall or the White House. Kicking out the King will not change the school system or the excessive costs of highway repair. But: alter the architecture, the

---

14. William Shakespeare, *Henry V* (4.1.213–14).

water works, the market places, the child care, the traffic patterns—and the city itself changes. Healing takes place without a master plan or edicts from above but by honoring the varieties of gods in the specific concrete places of their presences.

Identity and Landscape

Oedipus is born in Thebes of his natural parents, Jocasta and Laius. He is raised in Corinth by his foster parents, Merope and Polybus. But his native land is neither, since he is expelled from the home of Thebes and leaves the home of Corinth. His landscape is in-between. The in-between place appears in the story as the crossroads that is neither Thebes nor Corinth and the in-between place appears also as the landscape of Mount Cithaeron. The Theban shepherd takes the infant Oedipus to this mountain where he is rescued by the Corinthian shepherd. The Chorus, addressing Cithaeron, calls Oedipus a "native of our Land" (Cook, 1093); Cithaeron is his "nurse and mother" (Cook, 1094). Teiresias predicts that this mothering mountain shall provide no harbor, offer no corner for his cries, when Oedipus is blind and in exile (421). Aeschylus says blind old Oedipus wandered the mountain. Natives there were said to show a spot that, following the text (1455), is his grave. Oedipus himself says, near the end of the play: "Cithaeron, why did you receive me?" (Grene, 1391), then turning to it finally: "Leave me live in the mountains where Cithaeron is, that's called *my* mountain…" (Grene, 1452–54).

What is Cithaeron? Why there his home, his infancy, his despair, his grave? What has that landscape to say about Oedipus, and what does "my" landscape say about any human nature?

There are many stories told of the mountain by mythographers from Pausanias through Kerényi—and it is appropriate to mention here again the extraordinary service Kerényi performed, collecting the tales and their depictions on vases and graves, and retelling the stories. Cithaeron is a wild place,[15] a killing field, rugged and rocky, though rich, moist,

---

15. Cf. Richmond Lattimore, "Sophocles: *Oedipus Tyrannus,*" in *Oedipus: Myth and Dramatic Form,* edited by James L. Sanderson and Everett Zimmerman (Boston: Houghton Mifflin, 1968), 295–97. The stories of Cithaeron are collected in W.H. Roscher, *Ausführliches Lexikon der griechischen und römischen Mythologie* (Hildesheim: Olms, 1965), II/1: 1208–9.

and grassy on its lower slopes. The lion that Hercules first killed and whose skin he wore may have come from here. Teiresias saw the coupling snakes on Cithaeron, killing one, and was cursed to lose his sight therefore. Another murderous snake story says the mountain is named for a youth who rejected the seductive appeal of the Fate, Tisiphone—a fate who instigates men to kill each other.[16] She killed him with one of her poisonous serpentine hairs. Babies were exposed on Cithaeron—for instance, Antiope's twin sons. Other brothers with brutal histories gave names to this pair of mountains, Cithaeron and Helikon. Cithaeron, envious and greedy of his father's domain, pushed his father off the mountain and then he, too, fell from the same cliff. Or, the brothers killed each other; and Helikon, the mild one, gave his name to the brother mountain inhabited by the Muses. Deep incestuous passions haunt this earth: Zeus and Hera there consummated that sacred, and incestuous, wedding. On this mountain Pentheus followed the troop of Dionysus and there, on Cithaeron, he was torn apart by the Maenads, among whom was his mother. Deep passions, killing fields, madness.

Concerning this madness: "On one peak of Cithaeron," says Plutarch (*Aristides* 11), "is the cave of the Sphragitidian nymphs...and many of the natives were possessed,...*nympholepti* (seized by the nymphs)." Frazer comments on the passage, saying that the nymphs were mischievous at noon, especially at summer noon. The places of great danger, of being seized by nymphs and so made mad, were wells, springs, rivers, shadow of trees, and "at cross roads for these places are [their] mid-day haunts...and a man who lingers there may be struck by a nymph, the consequences of which would be some mental or bodily ailment, generally the loss of reason..."[17] Frazer goes on, referring to another sanctuary of nymphs where "to cure such cases it is customary to prepare and place at a spot where three roads meet (*tristrata*)...some bread...honey, milk, and eggs to appease these nymphs."[18]

The plot thickens: like Sophocles's play, like Freudian analysis, we begin to detect a repressed or forgotten clue. Again the Oedipal imagination catches us in its atmosphere. Our very way of pursuing the topic seeks

---

16. Roscher, *Ausführliches Lexikon*, V: 207–10.

17. *Pausanias's Description of Greece*, translated with a commentary by J. G. Frazer, 6 vols. (London: Macmillan, 1898), 5: 20.

18. Ibid.

to bring to light the buried "real story." And the clues are so evident: for Laius's route lay hard by Mount Cithaeron: "a narrow crossroad between Kithairon and Potniai," says Kerényi.[19] Neither would give way; a violent fight; son kills father. The place is several times called a "triple way." As to the time of day the men met, the play does not say. But Phoebus Apollo, the bright solar god, is its tutelary spirit throughout; the entire drama is under the blaze of noon when nymphs are most dangerous.

No appeasing bread, honey, milk, or eggs, no soul food, at this crossroads. What sudden madness, what "loss of reason," overcame them? Was it nympholepsy? Did the nymph of the place seize the two men, so much alike as Jocasta says (743), the elder one, Laius, sterile, who had repeatedly been to the oracle to request a child, and then, siring one, orders him slain, and who has taken another man's son as his lover—of which we shall have more to say. And the other man, Oedipus, who had overcome the Sphinx with his "wit" as he says (397), solved the *ainigma* as a riddle, a problem—hey, no problem—not ever seeing, as Jung says,[20] that she herself was the problem, not ever seeing the monstrosity, having so very little wit that he hears no warnings, lives and breeds with his mother without ever seeing, without ever knowing.

Were they both, father and son, susceptible to nympholepsy, to noon's shadow, that high solar madness called *superbia,* a soullessness or absence of anima, psychologically inept? Like the play and like an analytical session we shall have to postpone the denouement of this anima question until the end of our analysis.

Beside this particular theme of the nymphs and the anima, there is a wider inference to draw. The nymph who strikes is the mood of a place, the face and form of a landscape. Gestalt psychology calls this embodiment of mood in a geography its "physiognomic character."[21] An actual

---

19. Karl Kerényi, *The Heroes of the Greeks* (London: Thames & Hudson, 1959), 92.

20. *CW* 5: 264: "Little did he know that the riddle of the Sphinx can never be solved merely by the wit of man"; 265: "The riddle of the Sphinx was *herself*—the terrible mother-imago, which Oedipus would not take as a warning." *CW* 10: 714: "Oedipus...fell victim to his tragic fate, because he thought he had answered the question. It was the Sphinx itself that he ought to have answered and not its facade."

21. Kurt Koffka, *Principles of Gestalt Psychology* (London: Routledge and Kegan Paul, 1936), 407; discussed in my *Emotion: A Comprehensive Phenomenology of Theories and their Meaning for Therapy* (London: Routledge and Kegan Paul, 1960), 139–41.

physical setting—well, spring, tree, crossroad—is animated; the airs, waters, places are ensouled. Our souls on earth receive the earth in our souls, an idea once expressed as the individuating effect of matter.[22] Oedipus of Thebes and Corinth and Colonus is also of, mainly of, Cithaeron. Do we not learn something more from Sophocles than Freud transmitted? Is there not a shaping of human natures, and thus our human destinies, by the shape of the nature in which we live? Geography, too, parents us. Freud[23] rewrote Napoleon so as to say "Anatomy is Destiny"; but Napoleon's original, "Geography is Destiny," is today more psychological. What we do for and with and to this nature, how we live our ecological life, affects the soul's animal, vegetative, and mineral substance. Ecological life is also psychological life. And if ecology is also psychology, then "Know Thyself" is not possible apart from knowing thy world.

Laius, Infantacide, and Literalism

Freud says, "The oracle laid upon us before our birth the very curse which rested upon him." The Oedipus complex pre-exists our birth. I suppose Freud to mean it is archetypal. In Oedipus's own case a curse was already on his father, Laius, that he would be killed by his son. The tragic career that leads Oedipus and Laius to the crossroads and the subsequent tragedies to all—Jocasta, their sons, Creon, Thebes—begin in the father's fear he will be killed by his son. So, Laius, to avoid the oracle, pinions the boy-child's feet, and he is exposed on Cithaeron (717). To save his own life, Laius orders his son's death. The plot begins in infanticide. Parricide is a consequent. In fact, Oedipus left Corinth so as not to kill his father.

But Laius wished to kill, tried to kill his son. Freud emphasizes parricide, both in regard to the Oedipal urge and to the primal horde, where sons kill the father. He says less about infanticide, about fathers killing sons. This desire in the father to kill the child we ignore to our peril, especially since psychoanalysis descends from fathers. If this myth is foundational to depth psychology, then infanticide is basic to our practice and our thought. Our practice and our thought recognize infanticide in the archetypal mother, its desire to smother, dissolve, mourn,

---

22. I refer here to the *materia signata* or *materia individualis* of Thomas Aquinas.
23. *SE* 19: 178.

bewitch, poison, and petrify. We are aware that inherent to mothering is "bad" mothering. Fathering, too, is impelled by its archetypal necessity to isolate, ignore, neglect, abandon, expose, disavow, devour, enslave, sell, maim, betray the son—motives we find in Biblical and Hellenic myths as well as folklore, fairy tales, and cultural history. The murderous father is essential to fathering, as Adolf Guggenbühl has written.[24] The cry to be fathered so common in psychological practice, as well as the resentment against the cruel or insufficient father so common in feminism—whether as cruel or insufficient ruler, teacher, analyst, institution, program, corporation, patriarchy, or god—idealize the archetype. The cry and the resentment fail to recognize that these shadow traits against which one so protests are precisely those that initiate fathering.

This because: first, they kill idealization. The destructive father destroys the idealized image of himself. He smashes the son's idolatry. Whenever, wherever we idealize the father, we remain in sonship, in the false security of a good ideal. A good model, whether kind analyst, wise guru, generous teacher, honest chief, hold these virtues of kindness, wisdom, generosity, and honesty fixed in another, projected outside. Then, instead of initiation, imitation.[25]

---

24. Adolf Guggenbühl-Craig, "Der nur gute Vater," *Gorgo: Zeitschrift für archetypische Psychologie und bildhaftes Denken* 12 (1987): 31–42.

25. Imitation (*mimesis*) may serve as a first entry into initiation, as an exercise in behaving in advance of oneself. One copies or identifies with an idealized model (*eikon*), devoutly hoping the image will carry one into a desired state of soul. The model remains effective as long as we attend it with observances (*devotio, dulia*). Imitation, therefore, keeps us ritually tied to an icon, in its cult and enhanced by its power. Initiation, however, begins in bewilderment and set-back, a darkness characterized by *loss of model* and loss of power. Naked, toothless, bleeding, in pain, alone, unequal to the task and in need of elders, feeling terrifyingly young—these are the initiatory experiences. They shatter the icons of remembrance, and devotions provide no protection. These experiences, ritualized in ceremonies, recounted in fairy tales, and lived in a psychoanalysis, are behaved in the crises brought especially by the underworld divinities, or the chthonic aspect of others, gods of love and combat, of risk and disease, of childbirth and marriage, and by the angels of the biblical Lord. One endures in the midst of an event in which is the god. The only model remaining is the event and its images that govern behavior in the event. One becomes who one is, finds one's name, by having nothing other than the being one is, a being who behaves images. In Gabriel Marcel's terms, we are moved from *having* to *being*, and in Jung's, "being in soul," *esse in anima*.

Then the son remains tied to the person of the idealized figure. Keats, whose father died when the boy was eight, said that he who would create— let us say "father"—must create or father himself. This seems to happen naturally, for the broken ideal does not simply disappear. It lives on like an aura, like an inspiration rising up from mourning the father's corpse. He is gone. He never really was; or, he was rotten. The *putrefactio* of the idealized image experienced as mourning the father begins early and continues long, because it is essential to the initiation of idealizing child into man of ideals. For the ideals return; released from imprisonment in idealizations of a father image, they settle into the work of life or the life of work. They begin to be realized in those fathering acts that Keats[26] called "soul-making," and the *opus* becomes father, teacher, master.

Second, the terrible traits in the father also initiate the son into the hard lines of his own shadow. The pain of his father's failings teaches him that failing belongs to fathering. The very failure fathers the son's failings. The son does not have to hide his share of darkness. He grows up under a broken roof which nonetheless shelters his own failings, inviting him, forcing him, to be dark himself in order to survive. The commonality—and commonness—of shared shadow can bond father and son in dark and silent empathy as deep as any idealized companionship.

Third, the terrible traits in the father provide a counter-education.[27] How better bring home a true appreciation of decency, loyalty, generosity, succor, and straightness of heart than by their absence or perversion? How more effectively awaken innate moral resolve than by provoking moral outrage at the father's bad example?

The prophecy before the birth of Oedipus states the result of Laius's attempt to avoid the prophecy. Taking action to avoid the prophecy fulfils the prophecy. Hence the feeling that oracles are inescapable, foredooming. But the doom is not in the prophecy; it is in the action taken when one hears the oracle literally. Laius hears literally and so literally tries to kill his son so that literally he is killed by his son. Laius is cursed not by the oracle but by the literalism of archetypal pronouncements—a

---

26. *The Letters of John Keats*, edited by H. Buxton Forman (London: Reeves & Turner, 1895), letter of April 1819 to his brother. I have expanded on "soul-making" in my *Re-Visioning Psychology* (New York: Harper & Row, 1975), 50–51, 110–11, *et passim*.

27. The idea of "counter-education" derives from Marsilio Ficino; cf. my *Re-Visioning Psychology*, 201, 133, 163.

topic we discussed here two years ago regarding paranoia. Prophecy is a "forthtelling" (to use David L. Miller's term), stating in dark speech what is archetypally present as a dark potential and which *may* become acted in the day-world in time. Only then does forthtelling become foretelling.

By this I am not saying what Laius should have done. We do not read a myth to correct it, to fault its figures. We read a myth to learn what it tells about psychic figuring, how the psyche configurates, figures out patterns of life. We read *Oedipus* to learn what it is to be a killer, not only of one's father but also, because of Laius, of one's son. We read *Oedipus* also to grasp something of the relation between what Sophocles calls a bad, ugly, or evil oracle—the literal understanding of an oracle—and the killing.

The myth is replete with oracles, even depends on oracles for its tragedy. First, the oracle to which Laius went several times so as to have a son, then the oracle to which Creon goes to find what is wrong with the city, then there is the Sphinx, and Teiresias. How do oracles fit into the tragedy? Why do oracles belong to the action of the *Oedipus*?

Therapists may listen to dreams as oracles and turn for insights to horoscopes, Tarot, and the *I-Ching*. They want to caution a patient (supplicant) from a course that they foresee will otherwise blindly lead to tragedy. This oracular way of hearing may indicate neither the therapist's shamanistic insight nor his practical perspicacity, nor even a Jungian belief in the unconscious. Rather, it may be showing the undying effect of Oedipus upon analysis. With Oedipus come the foreboding feelings of tragedy and the search in blindness, the blind search, for a way out. I will kill the father, so I'll get out of Corinth. The city is sick, so I'll drive out the culprit. In the heroic ear, the message is clear. Apollonic clarity. Apollonic oracles, Apollonic anxieties. The oracular approach would ward off with its literalism the tragedy that its literalism predicts. The oracular approach to the psyche defends against its measureless depths (Heraclitus) with literalist measures. Because the forebodings of incurable tragedy—suicide, homicide, psychosis, cancer, etc.—that arise during an analysis belong to its myth, these fantasies remain an inherent part of its feeling. They are themselves incurable because they reflect the tragedy in its depths. Both Freud and Jung remained true to this tragic sense. Neither attempted to cure analysis of its tragic component. They incorporated the feeling into their theory — theory as therapeutic because it embraces tragedy whether as shadow and evil (Jung), or as the foreordained and inescapable Oedipal complex itself (Freud).

Laius and Oedipus share more than Jocasta and the throne of Thebes. Father and son share a literalist psychology. (Jocasta says Oedipus
resembles his father [774].) This is why they must "oracularly" meet
at the crossroads and act the oracle literally. Both take oracles literally: the father abandons his son, the son flees from his assumed father
(Polybus). Both actions aimed not to fulfil the oracle, yet thereby they
rush headlong into fulfilling it. Neither reflects the darkness in divine
speech. They hear language in the same straight way. They are locked
in tragedy and act the darkness. It is as if both heroes were missing
anima, as if both were unaffected by psychology, by which I mean
Greek psychology in the tradition of Heraclitus who says how to read
and hear oracles.[28]

Oedipus had an early chance with the Sphinx to practice the psychological ear. He heard the Sphinx, however, as a riddle, setting him
a problem. He heard with a heroic ear. "I stopped her mouth" (Storr,
397). "I solved the riddle by my wit alone" (Grene, 398). In this passage,
he intensifies his heroic stance by speaking of himself—until then rarely
in the text—as *ego*.[29] Stopping the mouth of the Sphinx, another way of
stopping his own ears, is the signal deed for which the chorus praises
him in the last verses of the play: "...behold this Oedipus, Who solved
the famous riddle [*ainigma*], was your mightiest man" (Cook, 1525). For
the mightiest man, an enigma becomes a problem to be solved, van-
quished. Yet an *ainigma*, as Marie Delcourt notes, refers to "everything
that has a secondary sense or meaning: symbols, oracles,Pythagorean
counsels."[30] An enigma is like a mantra or a koan or a Heraclitean
gnomon to carry with one and learn from; sphinx as emblem on a
gemstone or mounted upon a pillar to be regarded, not shattered at the
bottom of a cliff.

Commentators often point out that Oedipus did not hear Jocasta,
Teiresias, or the herdsman, warning him to leave off his single-minded
pursuit. More important, Vernant says he did not hear, "the secret dis-

---

28. Heraclitus, fr. 93 (Diels-Kranz): "The lord whose oracle is that at Delphi neither speaks nor conceals, but indicates."

29. Cf. Benardete, "Sophocles' Oedipus Tyrannus."

30. Marie Delcourt, *Oedipus; or The Legend of a Conqueror,* translated by Malcolm
DeBevoise (East Lansing: Michigan State University Press, 2020), 276 n. 1.

course...at the heart of his own discourse."[31] *That* is his tragedy; not hearing the second sense: literalism. Perhaps literalism is at the heart of tragedy itself. "No literary genre in antiquity, in fact, uses so abundantly as tragedy expressions of double meaning, and *Oedipus Tyrannus* includes more than twice as many ambiguous forms as the other plays of Sophocles."[32] Ricœur says, "Sophocles' tragedy reveals,...in the work of art itself, the profound unity of disguise and disclosure."[33] The hero hears only half, intolerant of ambiguity. He takes disguise literally as concealment and so insists upon literal disclosure as revelation.

Oedipus did have a second ear, which opens after blinding at Colonus. But already in the *Tyrannus* he can hear otherwise. Right in the mathematical middle of the text, at its hinge, Oedipus tells that back in Corinth "a curious chance befell me...curious indeed...There was a dinner and at it a drunken man accused me in his drink of being a bastard...this thing rankled always" (Cook/Grene, 776–86). He had begun to hear of himself differently, and it goes on echoing. An ambiguous Dionysian element is at work unconsciously. Much as it was at his conception; for let us remember, Laius conceived Oedipus at night while drunk. There is another fathering spirit in Oedipus's nature like the

31. Jean-Pierre Vernant, "Ambiguity and Reversal: On the Enigmatic Structure of Oedipus Rex," *New Literary History* 9, no. 3 (Spring 1978): 477–78.

32. Vernant credits the idea to W. B. Stanford's study *Ambiguity in Greek Literature* (Oxford: Blackwell, 1939).

33. Paul Ricœur, *Freud and Philosophy* (New Haven: Yale University Press, 1970), 519. That ambiguity should be the hallmark of Greek tragedy, especially its heroic singlemindedness (e.g., Oedipus, Hippolytus, Ajax, Medea, Antigone, Pentheus), belongs appropriately to the god of theater, Dionysus. His epithets and images—the "womanly man," both little child and dark-bearded wild man, god of both black and white maenadism (Dodds), of comings and goings (Otto), and of borderline situations (Kerényi), who is both a phallic force yet never a hero—express the double-tongued ambiguity of life (*zoe*) where generation and decomposition are inseparable, and of theatre where every word is addressed both to the characters in the play and to the audience outside the play. Because this loosening of "unilaterial meaning" (Vernant, *op. cit.*) threatens rational mentality, Dionysus, God of Ambiguity, is called the "loosener," the "undivided," and mad, since he does not separate the "both" into an either/or. See further on Dionysian epithets and images in my *The Myth of Analysis: Three Essays in Archetypal Psychology* (Evanston, Ill.: Northwestern University Press, 1972), 258–85.

mothering Mount Cithaeron, a Dionysian place, too, which resonates within and undoes the relentless course of his heroism.

If we imagine a second sense in the oracle, then Laius might have heard: "watch your son deeply, study his heart, grasp his ways for he has the potential for your end. He is the one who can show how your life ends, the ends of your life." The son offers another way than the father's. The son is the ruling mind's potential for a second sense. He *is* the next generation, a generative understanding beyond the literalism of a king's kind of consciousness, which hardens into single meanings when the bounds of any kingdom are defined, uniting into one dominion—land, state, people, king: *tyrannus.* The tyranny of unity.

So Laius puts the son away, as Sophocles phrases it. Oedipus put the Sphinx away too, for that's what heroes do. They take action against the curses, monsters, evils that are necessary for their action. What's a hero without an evil empire to oppose? Curses, monsters, evils become "problems" that have no second sense. But there is no "away," no permanent place to put a psychic content, as Freud said. The repressed returns—in this case from that murderous *topos,* Cithaeron, the unconscious as a landscape of killing. Oedipus returns to kill the father who intended to kill him, even though Oedipus says (Grene, 1001), "I did not wish to kill my father." This Laius could not have said about his wish toward his son. In both cases, wishes and intentions are irrelevant. Tragedy comes from oracular literalism and the literal flight from it. Oracular literalism, heroic action, and tragedy twist into one knot.

The two ways—the father's and the son's—come together at the crossroads. The text uses the word "triple" for this place (716, 730, 800, 1399–1401). Three. Not opposite roads at cross purposes; triple, several paths, various senses of direction, as the French: *sens, sentier.* This crossroads, this metaphorical place could be the place of metaphor, generative of *various* senses of direction, ways to go, ways to be, a crossing into a symbolic, gnomic darkening of understanding, even a way below to Hecate's mystification.[34] But Laius and Oedipus, and the play, belong to

---

34. "It was good to invoke her in haunted places, because she could send up forms of terror or benign apparitions; it was important to have her image at the cross-ways, probably because they were considered likely places for ghosts." Lewis Richard Farnell, *The Cults of the Greek States,* 3 vols. (Oxford: Clarendon Press, 1896), 2: 515. Cf. Plato, *Laws* 873b: "Murderers are to be thrown down naked at specified crossroads outside the city."

heroic tragedy—particularly to Phoebus Apollo. Apollo as raven, wolf, and killer are not seen or heard in the sunlight of heroic action. The crossroads narrows into opposites and the literal darkness of blinding.

If Oedipus be our myth, analysts cannot be wary enough about reading dreams as foretellings and counseling actions from them. Just when we seem most on the track of clearing riddles we may be on the road of tragedy. The conversations in analysis are always more than secular. There is a further sense, once called anagogic, in every analytical utterance, because Freud brought in myth, and myth brings in gods. Each time we read literally in an oracular way, attempting to do Hermes's job of connecting worlds (and Hermes is not an oracular god)—whether we call these worlds life and dream, inner and outer, objective and subjective, psyche and reality—we follow Laius. We have lost the second sense in the literalism of the attempt. Hermes makes the connection; and hidden connections, as Heraclitus said, are the best. The clear unambiguous connection may kill the child, the next generation.

I am proposing that infanticide is a mythic manner of imagining literalism. I am elaborating further an equation (offered above in "Abandoning the Child"): archetypal child personifies imagination. If infanticide means killing the second sense, then infanticide is the mythical equivalent of literalism. This further implies that literalism, when it is the father's desire to kill the child, is the semantic equivalent of the father-son conflict. The father-son conflict, discovered in myths the world over and often presented as the key to *Oedipus Tyrannus* itself, is not its tragic *archē*. Rather, the father-son conflict will be seen as the root when we stay Oedipal in our imagination, assuming all things start in family. *Prior to that conflict is Oedipal discourse that does not hear into its own speech.* A literal discourse, a single meaningness would do away with the ambiguity that necessarily arises when sharing a kingdom with the next generation.

To go yet further: as I discussed regarding Hercules and the underworld,[35] literalism accompanies heroic action. Because the hero begins often an object of infanticide, as an abandoned, endangered infant, the repression of the second sense is how heroism begins. Therefore, our culture's current focus on abandoned, exposed children is but another part of our culture's heroism.

---

35. *The Dream and the Underworld* (New York: Harper & Row, 1979).

I am suggesting that heroism forms discourse itself, not merely with verbs of action or muscular prose, but as a literalistic opposing sense. The second sense, when abandoned by the first, is now single and itself becomes literal. The second sense then returns from repression as a literal opponent to the ruling meaning, rather than as the son renewing the realm with connotative extensions.

Myths take place in discourse. They are enacted in how we speak. Is that not what the very word *mythos* implies? Alchemy knew this. The motif of king-and-king's-son plays there such a part, for without the second sense alchemy itself would perish. None of alchemy has only one sense: it cannot be read literally. So the conjunction of Rex and Regina, the *opus major*, depends on the prior cohesion of king-and-king's-son.[36] We hear alchemy with the metaphorical ears of a bearded Rex who is also a beardless *filius philosophorum*. Otherwise alchemy literalizes into either primitive chemistry or spiritual magic.

The infanticide, the desire to kill the next generation, explains something of Laius's history previous to our text. Aeschylus named the first of his Oedipus tetralogy *Laius* (ca. 467 B.C.) and Euripides produced a *Laius* (ca. 411–409 B.C.). Neither is extant, though they are said to tell that Laius fell in love with the ravishing beauty of the son of King Pelops, the lad Chrysippos, and abducted him to be his lover. To Laius is attributed the first homosexual ravishment. He is called the inventor of pederasty[37] in the tradition of assigning the origin of a human trait, skill, or natural product to a god, a legendary figure, or community; that is, all things have an imaginal source in archetypal personifications. As punishment for this abduction, the oracle, or Pelops, cursed Laius to be killed by his own son.

Laius loved a boy and tried to kill his own boy. He could not generate, which was his reason for going to the oracle and for hearing it literally. His kingdom was barren already before Oedipus, before the Sphinx. Freud says boys want to be love objects of their fathers—a desire appearing in the clinical complaint and resentment we spoke of earlier:

---

36. The union of king-and-king's son—as, for instance, depicted in "The Book of Lambspring," in *The Hermetic Museum,* 2 vols. (London: Watkins, 1953 [1893]), 1: 296-305, shows the importance of the *senex-et-puer* motif in alchemy. Cf. *UE* 3: *Senex & Puer.*

37. On Laius and the invention of pederasty, see K. J. Dover, *Greek Homosexuality* (New York: Vintage Books, 1980), 198–200.

"my father didn't love me." Plato's dialogue, *Laches,* a "dialogue in which fathers consult Socrates about the education of their sons," reports (180*b*) that "everyone who is occupied with public affairs...[is] apt to be negligent and careless of [his] own children."[38]

Fathers neglect their sons, do not fulfil the erotic bond, because of the incest taboo.[39] Fathers like Laius hear the taboo only literally and so may love only other men's sons. Greek education, notoriously so tied with Greek love, portrays fathers loving other men's sons. As Eva Keuls writes: "The archetypal homosexual relationship was that between a childlike...boy and a mature man. The contact had strong paternal overtones."[40] If Laius is cursed for pederasty, his abducting Chrysippos from Pelops, this pederasty results from his literalism. *He hears the prohibition against incest as a prohibition against eros.*[41] The repressed returns as homoeros.

The father may not, dare not, cannot love his own son as his son would ideally be loved, not only because of the incest taboo, not only because of the public preoccupation of fathers as the *Laches* says, not only because the second sense is death to the tyrannic king. There is yet another reason shown by Laius. In fathering lurks infanticide. The father avoids or neglects his son because of the archetypal urge to kill him. If Oedipus be our myth, then Laius plays a part in it: to come close in love between fathers and sons also brings murder near. That cry for father, for a first principle, a creation myth, a roof that guarantees, an altar with sustaining presence, a base, a rock, pillar, platform, sheltering portal, a bright good sky, land of one's fathers, patrimony, inheritance, endowment, that cry for substance and structure to found one's spirit and protect one's life, that cry for a fathering god, can never be fully satisfied because father brings murder near. "Eloi, eloi lema sabachthani" (Mark 15: 134) is indeed the archetypal cry of sonship witnessing the truth of the murderous father.

---

38. Paul Friedländer, *Plato,* 3 vols. (New York: Pantheon, 1964), 2: 38.

39. Robert Stein, *Incest and Human Love* (Dallas: Spring Publications, 1984), chap. 7 on Oedipus.

40. Eva C. Keuls, *The Reign of the Phallus: Sexual Politics in Ancient Athens* (Berkeley, Los Angeles, and London: University of California Press, 1993 [1985]), 299.

41. Stein, *Incest and Human Love,* chap. 4: "The Incest Wound."

The killing father, whether repressed, enacted, or sublimated, permeates the psychoanalytic movement, obsessing Freud, too, in regard to his pupils and to the second sense, the next generation, brought by the sons to analytic theories. The murderous aspect continues on in each analysis, even if euphemistically named negative transference and counter-transference, or resistance, aggression, hostility, or rage. And, it appears among the schools of analysis as violent revisionism and bitter orthodoxy. Scapegoats, expulsions, pinioned feet, sterility, narrowness at intersections, and oracular readings which curse the other by discovering what is truly wrong with the other: all this keeps the configuration of Laius very present in our field. Psychoanalysis walks in its own shadow and perpetuates the shadow of its tragic myth.

Myth and Method

Our route has passed dangerously close to the Sphinx. Was Freud wrong about Oedipus or right—as if like a hero we had to choose. We are still in Sphinxian territory, though I think we now can see why the riddle appears. We have been misled by the intentional fallacy, misled into reading Freud according to his intentions. That is, Freud intended to establish that the core complex of every analytic drama is Oedipal. The basic content of the conflicted soul lies in childhood and its passions in regard to parents. Self-knowledge consists in uncovering this truth.

We have been misled in following Freud's belief that the *contents* of the myth are the essentials of analysis. We have been driven either to accept that we, like Little Hans, are really Oedipus, and then prove that this Oedipal core is universal; or we reject this core content, thereby seeming to be free of Freud and Freudianism.

It is not, however, the contents of the myth that keep analysis Freudian. It is the method. Analysis is Oedipal in *method*: inquiry as interrogation, consciousness as seeing, dialogue to find out, self-discovery by recall of early life, oracular reading of dreams. The methods of an analysis are the *methods* of this myth. Here we connect again with the theme: Crossroads.

The Greek word for road is *hodos*, from which our "method," *meta-hodos*, is derived. Can we imagine a way beyond the narrow and killing road by Cithaeron, a way that would leave behind the dilemmas of this drama not only in content but in procedure, a way of analysis that remains a therapy, but not Oedipal, not Apollonic?

Some years ago I tried to find another road. I turned to Dionysus, and to Hades, suggesting a post-Apollonic consciousness.[42] I had earlier also suggested Psyche and Eros as the myth of analysis.[43] But to my ignorance, I remained Oedipal. I was still blind to the overriding importance of method, that the deepest myth of any analysis lies in its method.

And so Jung, too, does not offer a way out. The 1912 passage, which opens *Wandlungen und Symbole* (and which I quoted earlier), pays tribute to Freud and Oedipus in order to leave Freud and Oedipus. Jung introduced many new methods: amplification rather than association, synthetic and prospective understanding, typological relativity, the chair rather than the couch, one or two hours rather than five, participation of the analyst rather than an impartial screen. Nevertheless, the myth of Oedipus remains in the *meta-hodos* of Jungian analysis: becoming conscious through insight, a journey to self-knowledge, a dialogue with wiser Teiresian figures, consciousness as self-awareness, dream as oracle.

Maybe I need to demonstrate more fully what I mean by the myth in the method, and why analysis in actual practice remains Oedipal because of its methods. To do this, let us turn once more to Freud as practising analyst talking with a patient. The patient is again Little Hans. One of Freud's pupils then was the father of the boy. (The mother, too, had been analyzed by Freud.) The father recorded the little boy's fantasies, anxieties, behaviors, and remarks, and also what he, the father, also the mother, replied. A long diary, verbatim, over many months. Freud consulted regularly with the father, seeing the actual boy only once. Freud analyzed this case, foundational for the field of child analysis, at one remove. His clarity about the child psyche comes from an Apollonic distance.

We now listen in on Freud's record of that one conversation when Freud saw and spoke with the boy. Father and Hans together come to the Doctor. (I shall abbreviate here and there.)

> That afternoon the father and son visited me...The consultation
> was a short one. His father opened it by remarking that in spite
> of all the pieces of enlightenment we had given Hans, his fear

---

42. "First Adam, then Eve: Fantasies of Female Inferiority in Changing Consciousness," *Eranos Yearbook* 38 (1969): 349–412; and *The Dream and the Underworld*.

43. "On Psychological Creativity," *Eranos Yearbook* 35 (1966): 349–409, which became Part 1 of *The Myth of Analysis*.

of horses had not yet diminished...As I saw the two of them sitting in front of me and at the same time heard Hans's description of his anxiety-horses, a further piece of the solution shot through my mind...I asked Hans jokingly whether his horses wore eyeglasses [Freud refers to the blinders of which Hans was particularly afraid] to which he [Hans] replied that they did not. I then asked him whether his father wore eyeglasses, to which, against all the evidence, he...said no...I then disclosed to him that he was afraid of his father, precisely because he was so fond of his mother... Long before he was in the world, I went on, I had known that a little Hans would come who would be so fond of his mother that he would be bound to feel afraid of his father.

Freud concludes the paragraph by recounting a little scene between father and son prior to their consultation with him; the next paragraph opens with this amazing sentence:

"Does the Professor talk to God," Hans asked his father on the way home, "as he can tell all beforehand?" I should be extraordinarily proud of this recognition out of the mouth of a child, if I had not myself provoked it by my joking boastfulness. From the date of this consultation I received almost daily reports of the alterations in the little patient's condition. It was not to be expected that he should be freed from his anxiety at a single blow by the information I gave him; but...from that time forward he carried out a programme which I was able to announce to his father in advance.[44]

"Does the Professor talk to God, as he can tell all beforehand [*Spricht denn der Professor mit dem lieben Gott, daß er das alles vorher wissen kann*]?" The case of Little Hans is not only the first analysis *of* a child; it is the first analysis *by* a child, for Hans sees through the Professor's clothes, laying Freud's case bare. Freud believes he sees into Hans, past and future: before Hans was born he loved his mother. And soon after the "information I gave him," Hans could carry out "a programme which I was able to announce to his father in advance." But Hans sees through to Freud's essential nature, Freud's Moses beneath the beard.

Where Freud sees Hans's blindness—that his father quite evidently does wear glasses so that fear of the horse with blinders reduces to fear of the Father; Hans reads Freud's inability to see that he stands in the

44. *CP* 3: 184–85.

middle of myth, unseeing. Even the phrase, "a further piece of the solution shot through my mind [*schoss mir ein weiteres Stück der Auflösung durch
den Sinn*]," comes suddenly during the exchange about eyesight and
blinders. Was what shot through his mind an Apollonic arrow? Is this
how Apollo affects analysis: sudden insights, resolving clarities, blinding
revelations? Where Freud sees the Oedipal contents in Hans, Hans sees
the Oedipal method in Freud. Freud the oracle: the Professor talks with
God and knows "beforehand," like Teiresias, like the oracles to which
Oedipus, Laius, and Creon turn in order "to carry out a programme."

In the very moment of insight into Hans Freud is blind to the process
of insight itself because he is seized by the content of it. This is precisely
how insight blinds. We are so fascinated by what we see, we do not see
our seeing: the objective content of the insight stands forth and we lose
the subjective factor that makes this content visible in the first place.
This is the Oedipal moment in the analytical method—when surety
seizes, epiphanic, following upon a long coil of unravelling and piecing
together. Freud sees Oedipus in Hans because Freud's method is Oedipal. As he said: "The action of the play consists simply in the disclosure,
approached step by step and artistically delayed (and comparable to the
work of a psychoanalysis)."[45] What Freud sees is the objectification of
the myth he has imported into analysis by means of his method, that
art of detection towards clarified solutions. Freud is Oedipal, our field
of psychology is Oedipal, because, according to Teiresias, the dominant
characteristic of this blind man, Oedipus, lies in how his mind works,
his superior *heuriskein* (440): discovering, finding, or figuring out. Precisely this analytic method of figuring out keeps us Oedipal. We must
pursue further this theme of psycho-analytic blinding.

Psychoanalytic Blindness

Blindness is the prerequisite of the Oedipal method in depth psychology
for it initiates self-searching. We start in the dark, unable to see what
to do, which way to go, as if at a crossroads. We ask for light on the
problems and insight into our natures. We want to see clearly what is
wrong and rid our states of soul of their barrenness and blight, and thus
find truly what we are. We turn to dreams as gnomic guides and piece

---

45. Cf. note 3 above.

out the puzzle step by step. Yes, to be in analysis we must be blind. That blindness is today called unconscious.

There are ways of being blind: as Oedipus whose eyes are open and cannot see, as Teiresias whose eyes are closed and is a seer. Still, both are blind. The language of light and sight and eyes permeates the play. Oedipus's self-blinding at the end of the *Tyrannus* is commonly understood as the revelation of his true character. He is concretely blind at the end because he is psychically blind at the beginning. Oedipus's blinding at the end, however, is the outcome of his method of proceeding—pursuit, questioning, getting to the truth of himself, self-discovery. Know Thyself, here, equals blindness: when, by pursuing the Oedipal method, finally I know who I am, the result is blinding, and blindness.

What Teiresias calls the "double-striking curse from father and mother both, shall drive you forth...with darkness in your eyes" (Grene, 416– 17) results from the Oedipal attempt to see by interrogation and interpretation. Content results from method. The "what" that is discovered is utterly tied to the "way" it is discovered. The parental curses unfolded in an analysis follow from the tale into which we are enfolded by entering the original blindness that is the analytical premise: its fantasy of a journey, a *hodos,* from unconsciousness toward self-discovery via enlightenment.

For there to be an analysis at all, we must find ourselves tied to the parental world as unconsciousness, incestuously (Freud), uborically (Jung), desiring heroically to free ourselves through insight. "I will hear nothing but of finding out the whole thing clearly" (Grene/Cook, 1065), declares Oedipus, while Jocasta's final response pleads for unconsciousness: "O Oedipus, God help you! May you never know who you are!" (Grene/Cook, 1068). Finding out who you are overcomes incestuous unconsciousness, and the analyst guides by having wider, deep-set eyes—Teiresian eyes. Analysis aims to open those of the patient by placing concrete life in the vessel (*temenos,* process, transference, etc.), putting out the eyes of the physical view so as to see life more clearly as a field of ignorant projections, as shadows on the wall of the cave.

The outcome is tragedy, since the I's heroic effort to see is the symptom itself trying to see, and a symptom cannot see itself. That is why it is a symptom. The tragedy of Greece becomes the tragedy of psychoanalysis. As Freud said: "Every member of the audience was once a budding

Oedipus in phantasy and this...causes everyone to recoil in horror."[46] The tragic realization that the very instrument I call my consciousness, and which I am using right now to analyze the tragedy of Oedipus, is itself Oedipal makes me recoil, not because of my fantasies, but because the horror is my own consciousness.

So analysis cannot help but confirm with case after case as empirical evidence the terrible impact of the desires, fears, hatreds, and abuses of childhood. And analysis cannot help but propound every few years new theories regarding the cursing causality of the parental imagos and the formative dynamics of early childhood. Every new theory from Freud's immediate disciples, through Klein, Kohut, and Lacan, including modern Jungianism's fascination with developmental psychology, the mother and father archetypes, sand play and child analysis, turns to the same Oedipal ground. The empirical findings and the revelatory theories confirm the myth on which analysis, as Freud said, bases itself. Because we proceed like Oedipus, we think like Oedipus, and we find what he found.[47]

---

46. Freud, *Origins of Psychoanalysis.*

47. The core of blindness is belief. Seeing is believing. What we clearly see convinces us that we see clearly. The core belief of analysis states that personal disorder develops within family. The myth of family fuses with the method of analysis as the reconstruction of personal development. When "I summon up remembrance of things past" (Shakespeare, *Sonnet* 30), my analysis is secular and bourgeois, because those things, that past, are bound in the myth of family and of a particularly European variety. That family may exist still in white middle-class districts that provide the population for the Oedipal cult of therapy, but that family is hardly present in the city at large. That city of black, brown, beige, olive, yellow—and tinged all through its soul with blues—seeks its cure less in self-searching sessions of sweet silent thought than in the streets.

"Secular" and "bourgeois" are other words for the fallen soul exiled in facticity. As long as the soul is in exile, as Henry Corbin has said so often and so fervently, we see things only with the eyes of the exiled, remember the past only in its facticity, and imagine the way out only as progressive development. (Cf. Corbin's *"L'Imago Templi* face aux normes profanes," *Eranos Yearbook* 43 [1974]: 183–254, translated as "The *Imago Templi* in Confrontation with Secular Norms" by Philip Sherrard in *Temple and Contemplation* [London, Boston and Henley: KPI, 1986].) But there is no development out of exile, since exile does not progress and the notion of development itself is the secular expression for the hope to return, for restoration. So, the therapeutic task is not reconstruction of the past and the family, but reconstruction of "the Temple,"

Were we to imagine therapy differently—say, as a work in love with the mythologem of Eros and Psyche paramount; or as a work in generativity and marriage with the myths of Zeus and Hera and their struggles and their progeny; or as a work in imaginative flying and crafting with Icarus and Daedalus; or of Ares and the world of combat, anger, and destruction; or as a world of mimesis where art becomes life through desire with Pygmalion; or a work in which Hermes or Aphrodite or Persephone or Dionysus plays the principal—therapy's methods would display an altogether different nature. Would we still be assessing a human soul in terms of its origins, and would origins be equivalent to parents and childhood? Would we still be trying to 'find ourselves; our true story, our identity? Would we still be solving riddles, reading predictions out of our dreams, treating our fantasies as oracles to tell us who we really are? Were the methods derived from other myths, analysts would less be fathers and mothers, seers and prophets. Incest and child abuse would not be prime theoretical concepts and experiential anchors. And blindness would be relocated from the definition of unconsciousness to the very act of analyzing that unconsciousness. Like Oedipus, our blindness appears in the methods we employ to see.

While Oedipus is wholly engaged in the pursuit of himself, different methods would free us from similar subjectivism. Our sufferings and pathologies would be less about ourselves. Instead, they might refer to the inherent difficulties of flying and crafting, say; to the art of skillful loving; to the heart-work of marriage; to the isolation of research; the pain of fighting; or to living right with Gaia's earth. The weariness, the fever, and the fret that harassed the task of writing this paper would be attributed to the paper—the *daimones* of writing, of public speaking, of Eranos, of Oedipus—not to the "me" and "my problem." Unless we let go of subjectivism, how will the soul ever return to the world, to things as they are, so that they receive the attention they need from us? There are other pursuits, other urgencies than those of Self. What is it to make beauty? To serve my city? Be a friend, die with dignity, love the world, remember the gods?

which restores the city to remembrance of its soul. Consequently, the urge to go into therapy in order to get out of family presents the soul's desire to return from facticity in which it feels daily exile.

I named a few themes and a few mythical personages at random. Countless tales move through the forest. The soul's meadows are carpeted with interlacing fictions. Sophocles himself, says E.R. Dodds, "held various priesthoods."[48] And the Chorus in Oedipus invokes many other gods in contrast to the monomythic hero who maintains a self-righteous devotion to one god only. The Chorus asks: "O doer of dread deeds... What daimon drove you on?" Oedipus replies: "Apollo it was, Apollo, friends,/Who brought these ills" (Cook/Storr, 1318–21).

The play itself adumbrates another way of coming to the truth of one's nature. The origin of Oedipus is told by a drunk in a tavern, making superfluous the entire procedure of oracles, prophets, oaths, and inquisitions. Gossip, drunkenness, and the ordinary fellowship of demos reveal character and fate without the Oedipal method of self-searching inquiry. Others tell you who you are. The play follows this Dionysian track, for it stages in public for all to see the agonizing intimacies of soul.

The constraints of our Oedipal fiction, nevertheless, prevent me from exploring these possibilities. As long as I am doing a psychoanalysis of psychoanalysis, my thought is limited by the Oedipal method: insight, clarification, discovery of what is wrong, tracing back to parents and childhood—Apollo, Sophocles, early Freud, Little Hans. I cannot chart the routes for other therapies—of craft and skill, of service, of expression, of camaraderie, of worship, of the discipline of beauty, whatever—because the Oedipal method has defined even the meta-hodos: becoming conscious as finding self. Whatever myths may operate in the psyche, whatever contents we might disclose, as long as our method remains search for self, these other tales will yield only Oedipal results because we turn to them with the same old intention. We are still seeking a subjective identity by understanding ourselves, locating this understanding and this identity in a narrative of personal development. We can't get out of this play, this tragedy.

Pop-polytheisms and astro-mytho-typologies delude us by offering fresh new contents for identifying ourselves. The new contents are nonetheless constrained by the old method of self-discovery. We turn to a goddess not for her sake, her therapeia, but for our self-realization. The

---

48. E.R. Dodds, "On Misunderstanding the Oedipus Rex," Greece & Rome 13, no. 1 (April 1966): 37–49.

transpersonal ideals of new-age psychologies defend against Apollonic anxieties with Apollonic idealizations. These serve as counterphobic denials of the tragedy inherent in their search for self. Hence, the desperate desire to leave the Greek world altogether for Native American healing rites, Eskimo shamanism, Balinese movement, Zendo sitting, African drumming, Hindu breathing, Tantric sex. Therapy wants to leave Greece to escape Oedipus.

How much this myth is ours, how thoroughly it characterizes our psychological age, shows in the accounts we give of our miseries. What other culture—Egyptian, Hindu, Roman, tribal, traditionally Catholic, let alone that of Greece—would attribute to actual parents and actual childhoods the reason that one goes insane, is depressed, falls ill with psychic complaints, or falls out of society? And what other culture would seek the cure to those ills—not in gods, ancestors, or cosmic forces, not in rituals, curses, demons, names, places, foods, airs, waters, that is, actual things visible and invisible—but in calling up your personal childhood and parentage from long ago and far away. What an irony that the psychology of our culture is fixated in the idea of development, thereby preventing psychology, and our culture, from the very development espoused by its idea.

Psychoanalysis offers consciousness. (I use "psychoanalysis" for the entire psychotherapeutic movement regardless of school.) Consciousness is the salvational term. Consciousness may protect, or at least give *providentia,* in regard to disaster, disease, destiny—especially the destiny of Oedipus. If we have psychological consciousness, we will not be blind. That is the assumption. The practitioners of the cult of consciousness perform its rituals at appointed hours, appointed places. In this practice, the Oedipal contents of history as determinants of fate are attested, witnessed, and confirmed by priest and penitent in emotionally gripping communion. Claiming that the practice of the cult may open the eyes through its method of subjective examination, psychoanalysis maintains a blinding to its myth that requires blindness as its premise, even defining its own blinding as insight. Furthermore, by exclusively defining consciousness as the product of its method, psychoanalysis preempts the method of becoming conscious. Its hubris is Oedipal: self-awareness is the only definition of consciousness. There is only one way: the method of subjective investigation. Outside the church, no salvation. (*Extra ecclesiam, nulla salus est!*)

Yet analysis itself is only one way, a way that offers a disciplined contribution to the skills of psychological reflection, imagination, and conversation. No small skills these, but they hardly encompass consciousness. The fisherman with his net, the soul singer's voice with the blues,
the attorney's awareness in argument, the kindergarten teacher and the
nurse moving among their charges, the gardener's sense of sun, shade,
soil, and moisture—these exquisitely attentive consciousnesses require
no examination of subjective history. Analysis would say for them to be
conscious they must enter the church, go into therapy. I would rather
say *the unexamined life* is indeed worth living. More: life is not a riddle; how
monstrous to consider it so! "O taste and see!"[49]

Analysis at Colonus

I seem to have doomed psychoanalysis by maintaining its tie to Oedipus
from whose tragedy, according to the tragedy, there is no escape. We
have learned that substituting another myth or any number of myths
will only lead back to Oedipus because of the analytical method. Fortunately, this very same myth offers a way forward. Freud stops in Thebes,
with the *Tyrannus.* Sophocles dreams the myth along, as Jung advised us
all to do. Let us move then from Freud to Jung by going with Oedipus to
Colonus, that second *Oedipus,* written by Sophocles in his nineties, soon
before his death in this same city, Colonus.

There can be, however, no way forward until psychoanalysis takes
into itself, as thoroughly and completely as does. Oedipus, the reality
of its own blind inflation: that inflated insistence that it is the doctor of
the sick city, of the barrenness and blight lying all around its carefully
framed consulting rooms. Our location of psyche in psychology and
thus our imprisoning control of it, our self-centered view of consciousness depriving the world of its mind, our reduction of the unfathomable *hodos* of the soul to the little tracks of childhood, hearing the gods
only in oracles, and that presumption that were we to set an individual
consciousness straight then the city will be well again—this is delusion
and this is hubris. Like Oedipus, we move to Colonus only when we
recognize the blinding eye-opening truth that we are the culpable and
not the cure.

---

49. Psalm 34:8.

The first description of Colonus comes from Antigone:

> As for this place, it is clearly a holy one,
> Shady with vines and olive trees and laurel;—
> A covert for the songs and hush of nightingales
> In their snug wings.
>
> (Fitzgerald, 16–19)

The Chorus says further of the holy place:

> In the glade where the grass is still,
> Where the honeyed libations drip
> In the rill from the brimming spring.
>
> (Ibid., 157–59)

And in the famous choral poem describing Colonus, the nature of Cithaeron is utterly transformed:

> ...leaves and berries throng,
> And wine-dark ivy climbs the bough,
> The sweet, sojourning nightingale
> Murmurs all day long.
>
> ...ever through the shadow goes
> Dionysus reveler,
> Immortal maenads in his train.
>
> (Ibid., 672–80)

The verses go on telling of clusters of narcissus, crocus, olive trees and gray-eyed Athene, of the Muses and Aphrodite. There is much about taming horses. Bird song, the sound of waters, the limpid poems themselves show a shift from seeing to hearing. The opening line of the play is a question, the key question to resolving the Oedipal complex. Oedipus asks Antigone: "My daughter...where have we come to now?" In the next eighty-one lines of the play, Oedipus asks nineteen questions. These differ from the questions he asked in Thebes or were asked him by the Sphinx or asked of the oracle. He is no longer the furious inquisitor, twisting the shepherd's arm to get the full story (*Oedipus Tyrannus* 1152).

He asks about the place, the nature and behavior of where he is now and how to adapt to it. "Hide me in the wood, so I may hear / What they are saying" (Fitzgerald, 114), he says to Antigone. The Chorus says to him in the first speech, "Wanderer can you hear?" Antigone advises him: "We should give in now, and listen to them" (Fitzgerald, 171). "Sounds are the things I see" (Fitzgerald, 139). To be alive is to hear: the Chorus describes death as "no music and no dance" (Fitzgerald, 1222). He learns the prayer from the Chorus by listening (*akousai*) (486). Where he could not see through in the *Tyrannus*, in the *Colonus* he can hear (*akoueté*) through Creon's deception (881). At the close, before he walks away to die, he hears his daughters wailing, hears the signal thunder and the call from the other world: "Oedipus! Oedipus! Why are we waiting? You delay too long...(Fitzgerald, 1627–28).

The reliance on oracles fades. He even refers to Apollo's oracle as ugly (*kaka*, 87). In anima country, the spiritual mode is passing. When one is in touch, who needs farsighted wisdoms? "There is no felicity in speaking/Of hidden things," says old Oedipus (Fitzgerald, 624–25). Fewer signs, seers, and prophecies: more listening close at hand. "Touch me," he says to Ismene (327), and to Antigone, "...let me touch you/Whom I had thought never to touch again!" (Fitzgerald, 1104).

Oedipus at Colonus suffers physically as did his people in Thebes. He has fallen out of his wits into the world of touch by striking out his eyes with Jocasta's pin. This opens his eyes by shutting them from light, from seeing clearly, and from knowing as seeing. Now he knows differently. He has descended[50] from the spiritual blinding of his hubris as savior, through the psychological blinding of obsession with family, into the underside of his god, blood-crime, and catharsis: Phoebus Apollo, now wolf and raven.[51] Only in this final fall is Oedipus revisioned by revisioning himself.

Aristotle, in the *Poetics* (XIV) when speaking of fear and pity and the *Oedipus*, says that "the mythos ought to be constructed that, even without the eye, he who hears the tale told will thrill with horror and melt to pity." Not the eye but the ear: *katharsis* depends not on what we see, but how we hear. Aristotle in this passage—despite the basically Apollonic meaning of *katharsis* as rational clarification[52]—has placed himself within the cathartic shift from *Tyrannus* to *Colonus*.

---

50. Cf. James Schroeter, "The Four Fathers: Symbolism in *Oedipus Rex*," in *Oedipus Rex: A Mirror for Greek Drama*, edited by Albert Cook (Prospect Heights, Ill.: Waveland Press 1982 [1963]), 131–33.

51. Cf. Karl Kerényi, *Apollo* (Dallas: Spring Publications, 1983), 56.

52. Cf. Martha C. Nussbaum, *The Fragility of Goodness: Luck and Ethics in Greek Tragedy and Philosophy* (Cambridge: Cambridge University Press, 1986), where she claims that the history of the term *katharsis* shows its "primary, ongoing, central meaning is roughly one of 'clearing up' or 'clarification'" (389).

The move from Thebes to Colonus moves the mind from seeing to hearing, moves questioning from what happened to *where are we now*, moves family from parents to children and moves children (*tekna* as he called the Thebans and now calls his daughters) from duty to love, moves the revelation of character from inquiry into origins to preparation for ends, moves saving the city by action to blessing the city by death, and moves piety from oracles to libations. These moves have brought Oedipus into anima country; Colonus is described as *argeta*: silvery, radiant, white (670).[53] This is the new land, a foreign land for a hero.

So these moves suggest another one: from Freud to Jung, a move within the myth of analysis which is our overt reason for revisiting Oedipus. In the *Colonus*, anima and images are more the method—the hollow pear tree where Oedipus sits down and undoes his filthy garments (1595–96). Antigone in the wild forest, without shoes, beaten by the rains (350); Ismene smiling, wearing a wide sun hat as she returns on a Sicilian pony (313–19); the simile for Oedipus's suffering like a wild wintery wrack of waves breaking over him, coming on forever (1242–44). Anima takes the lead in the person of Antigone who provides the *hodos* (113). He calls Ismene and Antigone "my children...and sisters" (329). Incest shifts from literalism and taboo to sister-daughter, an accompanying double sense that guides his way. Gods are invoked of whom we heard little before—Hermes, Persephone, green Demeter. Ares who brought anger on Oedipus and fiery plague on Thebes, and bright-burning Phoebus, too, fade their force. The blindness of Oedipus and of Teiresias are supplemented by the blindness of the unquiet soul. "My eyes are blind with tears / From weeping for you, father," says Antigone (Fitzgerald, 1709). "To wipe them clear of sadness is impossible" (Moebius, 1711). This land flows with waters. It belongs to Poseidon. Rather than detection of wrong and correction of it, submission—to his terrible life, to death, the gods, and to Theseus, the younger king.

The bond between Theseus and Oedipus repeats, and redeems, the homoerotic love so disastrous for Laius. Although the ancestral ("before

---

53. Cf. my "Silver and the White Earth," *Spring: An Annual of Archetypal Psychology and Jungian Thought* (1980): 21–48 and (1981): 21–66 on the alchemical and psychological significance of silver as color of anima.

his birth") curse of Thebes continues in Oedipus's cursing of his own sons who have driven him out, he gives his blessing to another man's son, Theseus. The feeling between them is conferred not by forceful passion in the style of Laius, but by submission. Oedipus transmits the power of blessing by surrender to his weakness. He says to Theseus, "I come to give you something, and the gift / Is my own beaten self [athlion demas]" (Fitzgerald, 576). Does this indicate how the old fathering analyst advances the homoerotic transference between junior and senior men? The relationship advances to a blessing, not because the elder confers status, wisdom, or protection, but by his beseeching refuge for his beaten self in the younger's territory. He says, "For Oedipus is not the strength he was" (110). Yet he says, "When I am nothing, my worth begins" (393).[54] Surrender as blessing.

Freud, too, says this is the way of passing the Oedipal complex: submission to the other without fear of castration. (Though the man to whom one submits, Sophocles might add, must be of virtue; for Oedipus submits neither to Creon nor Polyneices.) That passing, that dissolution, of the Oedipus complex—Freud's term is *Untergang*—occurs graphically in the *Colonus*. Oedipus leaves by way of a steep downward path (*katarrakten hodon*). Whether as submission, or as a second undersense (*byponoia*), or as underworld, the way down of Oedipus is the way up of the psyche. The messenger describes his going:

> Some gentle, painless cleaving of earth's base;
> For without wailing or disease or pain
> He passed away—an end most marvelous.
>
> (Storr, 1660–63)

In this play, analysis itself seems surpassed, for contentment yields understanding, rather than understanding, contentment. Finding out is not the way, does not yield meaning, nor does it save from tragedy. For as Oedipus says and as Freud repeats, the tragedy was all known long ago, before birth (970). The focus is no longer "remember what happened." Instead, Oedipus says in his final line, "remember me" (1553),

---

54. Some translations of line 393 are: "Am I made man in the hour when I cease to be?" (Watling); "When I am finished, I suppose I am strong!" (Grene); "So, when I cease to be, my worth begins" (Storr); "When I am nothing, then am I a man?" (Whitman). Refer to note 6 above for complete references.

himself passing away into *memoria,* into the marvelous, conscious of becoming myth. Neither knowing, nor truth, nor meaning matters so much in anima country. Instead, hearing, beauty, nature, blessing, loyalty, service, dying, and love. He says to Antigone:

> Press close to me, child,
> Be rooted in your father's arms; rest now
> From the cruel separation, the going and coming.
>
> (Fitzgerald, 1112–14)

And at the close to his daughters:

> Children,
> today your father is not with you anymore.
> Everything about him dies; this rigorous attention
> to his needs may now be dropped. Children, I know how
> it leaves you numb. But one thing can be said
> to alleviate all the soreness: love [*philein*]
> I felt for you
>
> (Moebius, 1611–17)

The Changeless and the Changing Ethos and Daimon

Many changes between *Tyrannus* and *Colonus,* but not the character of the main character.[55] Oedipus is still a savior-hero, before of Thebes, now of Colonus by protecting it with his tomb. He still asks questions, wants to know; still relies on wits, in dealing with Creon and Polyneices; still sent by Apollo (665), declaring himself a sober, wineless man (*nephon aoinos*) (100) who expects Apollo's word to be fulfilled (102). He still fights, heroically grappling Creon. The family pull remains; Creon and Polyneices remind him of mother and father, murder and Thebes. They want his daughters and his death to be located in the old place. He is still concerned with *polis,* saying to Theseus in a last blessing: "I pray that you and this your land and all / Your people may be blessed…" (Fitzgerald, 1553), still uniting king, land, and people in one. The trait of secrecy in his

---

55. "It has long since been recognized that Oedipus, in fundamental character, is still the same as ever…Not only his character but his external fate remains unchanged." "Apocalypse: *Oedipus at Colonus,*" in Cedric H. Whitman, *Sophocles: A Study in Heroic Humanism* (Cambridge, Mass.: Harvard University Press, 1951), 199.

character, from his origins in hiddenness and as paranoid counterpart to his public identity, also persists. For he commands Theseus in that same speech to come to the grave "Alone. Alone because I cannot disclose it/To any of your men or to my children/Much as I love...them/Keep it secret always,..." (Fitzgerald, 1528–30). A consistency of *ethos* or character remains (*Poetics* XV).

The distinction between what changes and what does not change is crucial to psychotherapy. To work on the changeless as if it could be changed or to miss the changes by fixing upon intractable complexes: these are indeed unhappy therapeutic errors. The *ergon* of analysis changes us and does not change us. The same and the different are indeed basic categories. They are not merely perspectives, as if with one eye we can see all the differences a psychoanalysis makes, while with the other eye everything seems to have stayed the same. Oedipus provides a background for this crucial distinction between what does and what does not change. The tenor, the landscape, the images, the method all change. Preparing for death, he has been moved into anima country. The sister-daughter "who served my naked eyepits as their eyes" (Fitzgerald, 867) has given him a different vision.

Analysis can learn from this that its work is less to change character than to release soul from the tyranny of character, to distinguish between *ethos* and *daimon*, and so to serve *daimon*, a *therapeia* of *daimon*. As Henry Corbin said: not your individuation is the aim of the work but the individuation of the angel. Hence, at the end, Oedipus vanishes and the daughters remain visible—Jung's *esse in anima*, being in soul (*CW* 6: 77), displayed as dramatic reality.

The process of analytical work is artistically delayed, as Freud said, though not, as he said, to unravel and disclose. Step by step, the vision of the *daimon* leads the blindness of character, as Antigone leads Oedipus, into a foreign land, the white city, *la terre pure*. "He died as he had wished, in a foreign land," says Antigone (1708). Of course, his questions are all about this foreign land rather than about himself, for the habitual ethos of self-study, the psychodynamics of Oedipus, offers nothing about where he is now. The land has changed because the anima *daimon* has changed from killing mother mountain to benign grove of goddesses, from Furies to Eumenides, from suicidal queen mother-wife and suicidal Sphinx, and possible nympholepsy, to loving sister-daughters. With the death of Oedipus at Colonus, psychoanalysis based in this myth passes from *ethos* to *daimon,* from psychodynamics to psychodaimonics. Character and soul go their separate ways. Apollonic kingship and its blindness, family history cursed with literalism and prophecy, the method of inquiry for problem solving—all leave this earthly scene. The daughter-sister and the city go on.

If the eternality of Oedipus as a hero, as a drama, and as a timeless myth of the psyche is assured at the close of the *Colonus* by traditional signs of immortality—lightning, vanishing, opening to the other world[56]—the *actual immortality is presented as continuity,* as attachment to the *agon* of life. Antigone goes back to Thebes. That's what actually goes on: the soul and the city. In her last speech, at the very end of the *Colonus,* she says: "Return us to the other world of Thebes," which she calls *Ogygious* (1770),[57] locating the mythical, primal, imaginal place in the actual city of Thebes, that cursed pathologized place. *For the soul, the other world is in this world, visible, continuing, and here.*

Postscript

I ask to conclude with a postscript about the act of speaking, to give an account of my reasoning in accepting to speak of psychoanalysis at Eranos yet again. How much does one have to say, after all? Do we not revolve around the same themes, strike the same chords, even if in different keys and rhythms? But I did not come here for the reason of newness, because of something new to say. This theme of Apollonic blindness was addressed often in earlier papers. Moreover, Freud and Jung have been the pivotal figures for my twistings and turnings year after

---

56. See Gregory Nagy, *The Best of the Achaeans: Concepts of the Hero in Archaic Greek Poetry* (Baltimore and London: The Johns Hopkins University Press, 1979), 190–95 on thunderbolts and gusts of wind, both of which are mentioned by denial in *Colonus* (1558–59), and thunderbolts directly in 1515.

57. "Ogygos," in Roscher, *Ausführliches Lexikon,* III/1: 683–94. Besides being a name of the first king of Thebes, a general epithet for its founding patron (or pattern), for the city of Thebes itself, and one of its seven gates, Ogygos is a name of Dionysus, Poseidon, Okeanos, and of a Titan (689), as well as of the tempting waterworld of Kalypso's isle. The word suggests the hidden deeps of the oceanic imagination, the titanic aspect of the primordial *Urwelt,* or the Imaginal as "das Unermessliche und Ungeheure" (693).

year. And certainly I do not join with you to help maintain a tradition, that is, for reasons of oldness. A tradition lives in the silent devotion of attendance: it does not require speaking. Time, neither as newness nor oldness, provides justification.

At first I accepted out of loyalty and affection and a need for the nourishment given by this picnic, this *eranos*. I have since recognized that the presentation of this paper is a presentation of self, of Oedipal self, of a blind man in a sick city, struggling with the Apollonic curse of his world, psychoanalysis. The play brought words of self-revelation; I did not realize at first that I was in the play, that the drama was so powerful, Freud so keen-scented, and that this play plays through the inquiring mind and heuristic method of our culture from which I have not escaped. I did not recognize that it was I who could not hear to the heart of my own discourse. Even my asking and answering, "Why did I come, why do I speak?" is Oedipal.

Only when Oedipus goes under the hill, only as he walks away from us, might the nightingales, the freshening waters of Poseidon, and the greening of Demeter touch our field, a psychology of anima released from the tyranny of Oedipus. "Oedipus! Oedipus! Why are we waiting?...You delay too long to go!" (Fitzgerald, 1627–28).

8

PINK MADNESS, OR
WHY DOES APHRODITE DRIVE MEN CRAZY
WITH PORNOGRAPHY?

> Now, you will agree that to prefer the soft to what is
> hard is proof enough of... Eros."
> —Plato, Symposium, 195*d*

Aphrodite's Complaint

I f you had been put in a closet for hundreds of years by priests, philosophers, and prudish women who loved their religions more than
their bodies, what would you do to let mortals know that you are
still vibrantly alive and well? And if you were banned from actual life,
except for occasional opportunities in certain circles dedicated to you
or at specified times or occupations, finding no societal frame in which
to fit into the literal realities of medieval piety, reformational capitalism,
iron-age industrialism, ceremonial colonialism, scientific progressivism
(as it transformed into therapeutic salvationalism)—if there simply was
no dignified place for you in the big literal world, what avenue would be
left except fantasy?

Remember, this lady's terrain is the evocation of desire, the provoca-
tion of attraction, the invocation to pleasure. But long hair is not allowed
on the production line. Gets caught in the cogs. Botticelli's lovely lady
would have to wear a white hygienic cap. Managerial women cover the

Parts of this essay were delivered as the Opening of the Festival of Archetypal Psychology, Notre Dame, Indiana, 1992; at the Myth and Theatre Festival in Ville-
neuve lez Avignon, France, 1993; and on occasions in Berkeley, California; Omaha,
Nebraska; and New York City, 1994. It was first published in *Spring: A Journal of
Archetype and Culture* 57 (1995).

pulses of throat with high collars, like clergy. Skin shall be clothed to protect from cancer. Toes shod; nails clipped. Musty odors of the warm-bathed flesh astringently banned with deodorants that last all day into the sweet hours, *cinq a sept.*

To raft the wild waters with Artemis is OK; to bring a present home for Hera is OK; to plan strategy against competitors with Athene is OK; so, too, to jog with Hercules for muscle tone and circulation to defeat Geras, old age. OK. Remember social Darwinism says survival of the *fit-test*, not of the loveliest. So, I, ruler of beauty and desire, how do I bring my cosmos into the actual world where the gestures I provoke are called sexual harassment, the lust I instigate called date rape, the body I make concupiscible called a mere sex-object, and the images that pullulate from my teeming greenhouse of erotic imagination called pornography? What shall I do? Well, she said, I have my method: I shall make men crazy; I shall afflict them with pink madness.

By crazy I do not mean insane, violent, deluded, paranoid. I mean crazy as cracked: crack the veneer, crack containment in correct frameworks. Breakdown as breakthrough. And by *pink* madness I mean putting on rose-tinted glasses to see allure in the flesh, aurora in the vulva, *hortus inclusus, rosa vulva, fons et origo, cunnus mystica, fons et puteus, rosa mystica.* Porno-graphy shall be my path—the path of libidinal forbidden fantasy.

I shall invade every nook of the contemporary world that has so refused me for so long with a pink madness. I shall pornographize your cars and food, your ads and vacations, your books and films, your schools and your families. I shall be unstoppable. I'll get into your T-shirts and underwear, even into your diapers, into teenie boppers, their slogans and songs, and into the old ladies and gents in retirement colonies, on walkers in San Diego and Miami Beach. I'll show you—by *showing,* until your minds are fuzzed pink with romantic desires, with longings to get away—trysts, nests, sweets. That is, the civilization will be crazed to get into my preserve, my secret garden. I will excite your entire culture so that even those attempting to cure their neuroses, as well as their sober psychoanalysts, will have nothing better to talk about than desire, *jouissance,* seductions, incest, molestations and the gaze into the mirror. Remember: what you call advertising, I call fantasy.

Oh, it wasn't always this way. I wasn't always excluded. Rome was my city, founded by my son, Aeneas; and Paris has a name like that of that wise boy who saw my beauty. Troy, too, was my city. New Orleans, Kyoto, Shiraz, Venice. No, it wasn't always as it is today. I once had plenty of room in the daily world until those fanatic martyrs took over with their nails and thorns and burlap suits, and those rabbis with their wondrous words and woolly hats. But now that I am driven from the public realm, I shall rule what has been left to me, the private, the privy secrets, the privates.

So let's start talking of the privates, and I shall let the lead go to one of my sons, not Aeneas, the hero; not Hermaphrodite, whom I conceived with Hermes; and not Eros, but another son, disfavored and disproportioned, Priapos.[1] I ask him to take the lead now, since the incantation of him, celebration of him, attempt to erect him from neglect is a principal aim of pornography. It is the figure of Priapos that makes pornography and the contention about it so fascinating. (Fascination is the right word, since *fascinum* was a standard Roman term for the male member, as amulet, gesture, graffito, or trinket, to ward off evil and bring good luck.)

First, more about our leader, my son Priapos. Several facts—the kinds scholars use to suppress me by their scholarly distancing. Priapos was, they like to say, a god of fertility. He played a "role in nearly all mysteries," says that conservative and distinguished classical scholar, Walter Burkert.[2] Processions with huge *phalloi* were the most public form of Dionysian worship. The priapic was a way to honor Dionysus and even to represent him. Since (as Heraclitus says) Dionysus and Hades are the same, the *phallos* triumphant belongs as well to Hades, and therefore has a subtext, an intention below what is blatantly exhibited.

Something mysterious goes on during arousal. Since pornography aims at arousal, it must also have an underworld meaning of mystery and not merely an underworld meaning of criminality. Or, perhaps we must accept that both underworlds go together—the mysterious and the criminal. The very subject, pornography, let alone its images, disturbs our conventional reason because pornography invites both Dionysian ecstatic vitality and Hades's rape and death. The erected *phallos* acts as a fascinating emblem of both desire and terror.

---

1. For a superb chapter on Priapos, see Rafael López-Pedraza, *Hermes and his Children* (Zurich: Spring Publications, 1977).

2. Walter Burkert, *Ancient Mystery Cults* (Cambridge, Mass.: Harvard University Press, 1989), 105.

Of course, humans are never able to state just what is pornography. Even the august United States Supreme Court cannot speak of it clearly. As Heraclitus also said, omens and oracular mysteries do not speak clearly; they give only signs because "nature loves to hide." Even if arousal and erection speak loud and clear, the epiphanic nature of the arousal remains mysterious, rising as it does from a bed of images. That's why sexual imagery plays such a vivid role in mystery cults and why sexual imagery fertilizes creativity (by which I mean any originating impulse). Arousal is at the origin of life and like all origins is fundamentally concealed from the clarity of understanding. We can never know how anything started. All beginnings are fantasies...maybe, even, sexual fantasies. Am I saying that the world begins in pornography?[3]

So there is a mystery to this day: about the *phallos* in the basket and the rape of Persephone. These sexual and violating images were central to the Eleusinian cult that lasted as the major religious devotion of the Mediterranean for at least a thousand years. So, too, the sadistic eroticism of the Villa dei Misteri in Pompeii.[4] Not a virgin birth and an immaculate conception—a *phallos* in a basket! Why the porn imagery, the rape, the *phallos* at the heart of these cults, which were mainly mysteries for women? What was going on?

Perhaps the mysterious moral was Aphroditic. Maybe these cults were saying, especially to women so easily captured by Hera and Hestia, by Artemis, Athene, and Demeter: Women keep sexual fantasy alive! Imagine! Imagine! Imagine! At the heart core is a hard-core porn image— a *membrum virile.* Keep lust awake in your mind—or as in India, deck the parts with boughs of flowers, bring them oils, tribute, tapers, coins. Don't lose your sexual erotic imagination. That's what "fertility" as the scholars call it really means. Keep your fantasy fertile. Don't cave in to sexual shames and secular fears about disease, abortion, and menopause.

All that I am revealing to you comes from her, what she told me, much as the voice of a lady philosopher consoled Boethius in his prison cell

---

3. The Gnostic Justin of Monoimos considered Priapos and God the Father to have been one and the same. Cf. Geoffrey Grigson, *The Goddess of Love: The Birth, Triumph, Death and Return of Aphrodite* (London: Constable, 1976), 81.

4. Linda Fierz-David and Nor Hall, *Dreaming in Red: The Women's Dionysian Initiation Chamber in Pompeii* (Putnam, Conn.: Spring Publications, 2005).

and as Diotima spoke with Socrates about the nature of Eros. So, I am recounting what she—I hope it was she, Aphrodite[5]—indicated to me, a retired psychoanalytic man who saw hundreds and hundreds of dreams and fantasies and obsessional thoughts that we call pornographic in the psyches of what are called "patients," i.e., those humans so often suffering from the absence of Aphrodite in their actual lives and therefore victims to her incursions and her revenges.

To go on with her appeal. I am not happy, she said, and it is my nature to be happy. No, I am not happy allowed only this one access of fantasy, so I am a bit spiteful, revengeful. After all, my sister, or half-sister, was named Nemesis, and Nemesis or Retribution and I are linked closely; where I come into a human's fate Nemesis usually comes, bringing some sort of retributive justice. For instance, Paris preferred me to Athene and Hera—and out of that came terrible marvelous retribution: the Trojan War and Homer. So, pink madness is my retribution. My avenue of return.

I do want to tell you more about my extraordinary boy, Priapos, or my boy with the extraordinary equipment; actually not a boy now, but a rather heavy-set, balding, ruddy, bearded, full-grown man—though for me he will always be my boy.

According to some tales, Priapos was a "brother" of Hermaphroditos. Both were said to be offspring of Hermes and Aphrodite. But others say Priapos was sired by Dionysus; some tales say even by Zeus, directly. Finding the Father is never easy—even among the gods. And whom am I to tell, even if I knew! Whoever the lucky father was who had the pleasure of Aphrodite's bed and body, Priapos is definitely *her* son.

Aphrodite is always there, as a mother is always there in her son. Whenever, wherever Priapos raises his balding head, Aphrodite is also there. This suggests, vulgar as it may seem to those who cling to prissy pretty sex, every hard-on is mothered by Aphrodite and is somehow carrying out her intentions, her fantasies, as the mother instigates and inspires the activities of her sons.

Of course, as the stories go, Aphrodite was horrified by her well-hung baby boy. So hung up was she on her notions of beauty, that she saw his

---

5. The best contemporary guide to discovering Aphrodite's effects in human life is Ginette Paris, *Pagan Meditations: The Worlds of Aphrodite, Artemis, and Hestia* (Putnam, Conn.: Spring Publications, 2005).

body as deformity. She could not bear the sight of him. Isn't this interesting, the intolerance of excess by Aphroditic criteria of beauty. There is a lesson here for all you worshipers of the shapely, perfect, lovely, smooth, and pleasing ideas of beauty. But to go on: she bore him, but could not bear him, and so she exposed him on a mountainside. A shepherd found him. A marvelous figure, the shepherd, always finding foundlings: like Oedipus, and the one in Shakespeare's *Winter's Tale* who found Perdita. Christ, too, was a shepherd who saved abandoned ones, the lost lamb-skins, and we all go on with this mytheme.[6] Today, the good shepherd is the analyst-therapist caring for our abandoned inner child. And how betrayed and enraged and vindictive is that inner child when it discovers the archetypal link of shepherd to Pan and Priapos.

Now, this shepherd is able to save Priapos, not because he is a com-passionate redeemer, but because the shepherd is himself perverse, as crooked as his crook. The shepherd's god is Pan, the goat-god, who, among other things invented masturbation—panic also. A freakish fig-ure, like Priapos, Pan lives his life at the edge of civilization, in the pagan zone, and like Priapos provides a main stream of our humor. For instance: what is virgin wool? It comes from sheep who run faster than the shepherd.

But back to Priapos exposed. Exposure. His whole life condenses into that acorn of exposure. For, ever after, he who was exposed on the mountainside, is the exposing one, the one who exposes his signifi-cant member in statuettes, cult objects, souvenirs, charms, murals. He exposes himself and yet is always undercover, under a cloak, a kind of shirt, leaves and foliage, a toga half-raised, exhibiting his erection.

As for that garden where Priapos is to be found (he is the god of gardeners[7]) come on, don't be conned or cozened. The garden is one of the oldest euphemisms for the genital region of women (*pudenda muliebra*),

---

6. Cf. David L. Miller, "'Christ, The Good Shepherd," in his *Christs: Meditations on Archetypal Images in Christian Theology* (New York: Seabury Press, 1981), 3–52, for a superb analysis of the shepherd figure.

7. One of the great gardeners of all time was Thomas Knight, younger brother of Richard Payne Knight, nicknamed "Priapus Knight" (1750–1824), who honored this god with the first modern treatise, *A Discourse on the Worship of Priapos* (1786). The money earned by Richard supported Thomas's endeavors—a gift of Priapos's fertil-ity? Cf. Grigson, *The Goddess of Love*, 80.

kepos in Greek, as we use the word "bush," and images of fruits and flow-ers, such as fig, melon, apricot, peach, cherry, plum, and of course, rose. So, of course, Priapos is the gardener who cares for the "garden"—a task which keeps him happily occupied. Scholarship has had to cover all this up with "fertility" because Priapos is himself covered in order to be dis-played; as I am doing here—and López-Pedraza did years ago in writing on Priapos.

With this we come to what's clinically called exhibitionism. Could it be Priapos who is displaying himself in this urge? Is this urge saying, "Look at my parts that Aphrodite rejected. I need to be seen, appreciated, taken in from abandonment, saved from this cursed orphaned condition. I am Aphrodite's son who was exposed by her and so I must return by the same route: exposure of the very part that caused my exposure." Is this what exhibitionists try to say to everyone they can show their genitals to? "Look at me. I mean you no harm. (Clinically, exhibitionists are not violent, not rapists, but usually mild and timorous men.) Receive me. See, I am proud and wonderful, despite what my Mother says."

About that curse at birth, there is more to say. About the gross genita-lia, porno grossness, excess, exaggeration that so horrified Aphrodite's sensitive good taste, that penis that surpassed the standard benchmarks for the standing male member—do you know the full story of how it happened?

Aphrodite, about to give birth, retired to Lampsakos, a town on the Hellespont, a place that later considered Priapos its founding Hero-God, for there he was born and there, later, his cult was celebrated, coins bearing his image cast and Priapean rituals enacted. Heroic Alexander wanted to destroy the town for its pornographic excesses. Heroes seem to be sexually shy: Hercules remaining on the Argonaut rather than dally with women; Bellerophon retreating from women who raised their skirts. Even the marbles (statues) carved to represent heroic figures and heroic gods like Apollo show modest appendages compared with the sizable grotesqueries of satyrs, Pan, and Priapos.

Now Hera was enraged at the trifling of Zeus, or of Dionysus, Zeus's son by Hera's rival, Semele. In Hera's mind this child to be born from Aphrodite was an insult in its very conception because it was directly or indirectly from Zeus. The child would be living testimony to her hus-band's philandering, the very progeny of the very behavior she, Hera,

Queen of Heaven, was ordained to oppose. Well, she, Hera, cheated and deceived in her own style by proffering aide to Aphrodite during her lying-in and delivery. She touched Aphrodite's belly with her finger, causing the child's unshapeliness. We must recognize the long finger of Hera in the gross genitalia of Priapos. Hera's normal straight measurement creates Priapic enormity.

Priapean enormity has many gods in it—lots of gods. It can't be read simply—as López-Pedraza says. Each Priapean excitation has in it the powers of Aphrodite, Dionysus, Hades, Zeus, maybe Hermes, and so on. But in all this let us never forget the finger of Hera. This is what a polytheistic psychology teaches about any event. There is a complex imagination released rather than a simple explanation that identifies and closes the question. We get a story rather than a reduction or a moralism, and each mythical story involves another. As the German Romantics said, "Never, never does one god appear alone."

I lay emphasis upon Hera because the other sons of Aphrodite as well as her favorites—Aeneas, Paris, Anchises, Eros, Ares, Adonis, Hermes, Dionysus—were certainly not misshapen. (Hermaphroditos was indeed peculiar, because of his doubled attractiveness; and although Aphrodite's husband, Hephaestus, was lame, this was a deformity intimately associated, again, with Hera.) Of all the beautiful goddess's sons and lovers, only Priapos was misshapen, only this one touched by Hera.

One touch of Hera and the priapic becomes "deformed," vulgar, gross. We turn from it, repulsed; we abandon it on the mountainside and call it uncivilized, pagan. ("Pagan" literally means "of the rocky hillside.") Hera would approve of only one kind of erection, that which serves the mating game, the coupling, husbandly kind. Here, then, is the authoress of the bans against hard-core porn that grossly shows erections and invites priapic erections in return. I suspect most of the goddesses are anti-porn: Athene took sides against the more potent forces of Poseidon and Dionysus, and she didn't like horny goats; Hestia refused Priapos when he came after her; and Artemis surely doesn't chase and hunt in gardens.

Hera would exclude the excessive sexual imagination so as to keep lust within conjugal bonds. It is she who makes it ugly, not that the genitals are themselves ugly. As Georges Bataille noted, and the French do note such things, the actual genitals are the most desirable and the most repulsive at the same moment. She causes the priapic to be placed outside the limits, marginalized to the red-light district, the porn shop, away from decent people with family values. It is Hera who has turned pornography into obscenity.

Now I am not here to blame Hera or to invite her enmity; I have enough troubles in her domain. In fact, dear lady, I regard myself as one of your devotees, having done obeisance at your sacred places in Sicily and Paestum and made notes for a short book favoring your virtues and their importance for our contemporary culture. Nonetheless, Hera, allow me this analytical moment of penetration into your preserve.

The localization of priapean sexuality in a red-light district is the literalization of a mythical domain. Priapos's garden remains outside the house, even if relocated in an urban porn shop. The perverse imagination—and you may recall that one of the marks of the priapic is the penis twisted to the rear, a metaphor, of course, and not simply a physical curiosity—does not belong at home where the twists of the imagination are to be laid straight. Hera's realm is where fires are cooled, following St. Paul's dictum that it is better to marry than to burn. Pornography can ignite the dormant images in the chill of domestic tranquility. When pornography enters the home, it appears asinine, again in accord with myth. For one tale says that when Priapos invades the house, attempting to take Hestia who is nodding by the hearth, an ass brays, waking her so she can fend him off. Priapos is not for domestication. Pornography cannot be safe and sane; it cannot abide by family values. Yet that same ass, given its due, is also central to the Isis mysteries of the psyche as told by Apuleius in *The Golden Ass.*

So when Sallie Tisdale[8] writes about her desire, a woman's desire, to visit porn shops, buy porn videos, and watch them, and then writes of the shame she overcomes to free her curiosity, it's not a shame brought on because porn-viewing is a male activity exclusively. Rather, her shame reflects the mythical fact that porn does not belong inside the consciousness of the normal community, its domesticity and conventions as defined by Hestia and Hera. The resistance Tisdale overcomes is not patriarchal conditioning (women keep out); it is the archetypal resistance of these goddesses to Priapos and Aphrodite. Is this why usual wives don't want to watch porn at home with their usual husbands: the sex of two couch potatoes in front of their screen. When Tisdale visits

---

8. Sallie Tisdale, *Talk Dirty To Me* (New York: Doubleday, 1994).

the shop, she is like one of the women who leaves the house for the mountainsides of Dionysian mysteries, women's mysteries, those exclusive women's festivals of which Kerényi writes: "At exclusive women's festivals, to which men are not admitted, the participants said the most shocking things to one another. At the feast of the *Haloa* there were not only obscene mockeries but some very indecent behavior. The married women were led on by means of ritual play to things forbidden in marriage."[9]

I have told the tale of Priapos, of Hera's finger on Aphrodite's belly, of his exposure and marginalization in order to show the archetypal curse on the priapic, and consequently on all vigorously erected image consciousness, that arousal of imagination pornography seeks to achieve. It is blamed for male violence, the beating of wives, sexual excesses and unnatural distortions, degradation of women, molestation of children, rapes...all this argumentation is part of the curse put on the priapic by Hera and by her minions in the domain of the domestic, the communal, the societal.

By the way, a recent intrusion of this mythic constellation in public life occurred at the exposure of Clarence Thomas (stocky, middle-aged, balding, swarthy if not ruddy) before the United States Senate Judiciary Committee. There he was, uncovered on TV, a kind of indecent exposure when he was accused of talking about the size of the penis of the porn actor "Long Dong Silver" with his female aid, Anita Hill, and there was mention of a seductive pubic hair on a Coke can. Of the many plants used in antiquity to honor Priapos with garlands was the *adiantum*, in Roman times known as the *capillus veneris* or maiden hair or our lady's hair, and "the hair implied in these names was that of the pubes."[10]

Images are Instincts

Sex education, sex talk shows, sex help books, sex therapy, sex workshops—Aphrodite's pink ribbons wrap our culture round. The billion-dollar porn industry is minor league compared with the haunting sexual

---

9. Karl Kerényi, *Zeus and Hera* (Princeton, N.J.: Princeton University Press, 1975), 99.

10. Thomas Wright, "The Worship of the Generative Powers" [1866], in Richard Payne Wright and Thomas Wright, *Sexual Symbolism: A History of Phallic Worship* (New York: Julian, 1957), 100.

obsessions endemic in the culture at large. But for a moment I want to move away from both politics and morality and into psychology—the psychology of the image.

First, to Jung's psychology of the fantasy image, which, after all, is precisely what porn is: lustful fantasy images. Jung places images and instinct on a psychological continuum, like a spectrum (CW8: 397–420). This spectrum, or color band, ranges from an infrared end, the bodily action of instinctual desire, to the ultraviolet blue end of fantasy images. These fantasy images, according to Jung's model, are the pattern and form of desire. Desire isn't just a blind urge; it is formed by a pattern of behavior, a gesture, a writhing, a dancing, a poetics, a coming-on of style, and these patterns are also fantasies that present images as instinctual behaviors.

Jung does something different from Freud. Freud regards the blue or mental end to be the sublimation of the red desirous instinct. The red transforms, civilizes, sublimates into the blue for Freud. Jung, however, regards the images to be the instincts themselves. Image and instinct are naturally inseparable. You always are in a fantasy when performing an instinct, and you are always instinctually grasped when imagining a fantasy. Since images and instincts are two faces of the one thing, Jung's model implies that any change in one is a change in the other. If you mess up your instinctual life, your imagination is also messed up; if you repress your fantasy images, your instinctual life is also repressed. This is important, very important. Instinct and image *are* each other. Your images are instincts in fantasy form; your instincts are the patterned behavior of imaginings.

If we split the red end from the blue, we get a blue imagination without vitality: Hallmark clichés as emotions, New Age spiritualized imagination without the coarse, the strong, and the lurid. And we also get the coarse, the strong and the lurid as violence; a red-end instinct deprived of formal containment and imaginative variety.

Example: Some years ago at the Kinsey archive in Bloomington, Indiana, I saw volumes of prison erotics on deposit—love letters, drawings, notebooks, artifacts, crayon sketches—the pornography made by inmates and confiscated by the guards. The blue end of the spectrum was forcibly repressed; imagination under lock and key. What then happens to the red end? Prison rape, buggery, and prostitution.

When the fireman in the Los Angeles fire station fought a legal battle against feminist firefighters to retain his right to look at porn magazines while on call in the firehouse, he was firing up his fantasy, keeping it lively, so that the instinct necessary for his job is also alive. (He won the case, by the way.)

There is a lesson here. The confiscation of the writings and drawings in the Indiana prisons indicates a great fear, the fear of imagination itself, the fear of the uncontrollable effusion of fantasy life that cannot be held within bars and walls. I need to explain this further. For this explanation, I turn to a book by a Columbia University Professor of Art David Freedberg, a mammoth masterly work: *The Power of Images.*[11]

Freedberg says, "images do work in such a way as to incite desire," and since, he says, "the eyes are the channel to the other senses," all pictures make us look. They seduce us into looking. The gaze stimulates the other senses and arouses. Arousal fetishizes the object. We are fixed by it, to it. What holds the gaze is this demonic power in the image, its superhuman or divine force. Images, not only sexually explicit images, make eros visible and are demonic, and so for centuries artworks have been said to lead to vice, their beauty corrupting.

Plato insisted in the *Republic* (3:401b) that the images of the arts must be controlled. This Aristotle restated in his *Politics* (7.17 [1336b]): "It should therefore be the duty of government to prohibit all statuary and painting which portrays any sort of indecent action."

Because images draw us into participation with them, that part of human nature for which Plato and Aristotle here speak—the Apollonic, logical, mathematical, idealized—is brought down by images and sullied by the emotions they arouse. The body is enlivened by images, by graphic images especially, and the fear of that enlivened imagination, falling to the image (Pygmalion), idol-worship, addiction, forces the higher mind to consider censorship, such as Plato and Aristotle mention.

Censorship is an inherent response to the libidinal potency of the image, and not to any particular content. As Freedberg says, "[The] potential for arousal immediately and irresistibly accrues from the interaction between images and people." Hence, all images are threatening because the potential for arousal is ever present.

---

11. David Freedberg, *The Power of Images: Studies in the History and Theory of Response* (Chicago: The University of Chicago Press, 1989).

Pornographic images present only one case of wider libidinal arousal. Holy images, too, have been savaged as, for instance, Michelangelo's *Pietà,* and bourgeois images, for example, Rembrandt's *Night Watch.* Defacing, stabbing, acid attacks on paintings by Poussin, Dürer, Mantegna, Rubens, Correggio belong to the history of art; so do also the thousands and thousands of images smashed and ripped by governmental edicts from ancient Egypt, Persia, the Greek Islands, and the Americas to small churches in rural England. The history of iconoclasm, of fear of the image and attempts to control it, says clearly that *all images are pornographic in their arousal capacity,* an arousal which recognizes the libidinal animation, the daimonic power, the active soul in the image.

When I say all images are pornographic, please let's recall that the definition of pornography depends not on what is depicted, but on its effect, the instinct in the image. As Webster says: Porn is material depicting erotic behavior that is *intended to cause sexual excitement.* Content is contingent upon effect: arousal. That's why the content has to be circumspectly, even privatively, defined, e.g., *without* scientific, aesthetic, etc., value. Content is insufficient for definition, because as the Supreme Court declared (Cohen vs. California, 1971), "one man's vulgarity is another man's lyric." We do not know pornography by what it is, but by what it *does.* That's why Justice Potter Stewart could say, "I know it when I see it." He knows what's porn because of what the images do to his instincts, his emotions; arousal. The question of definition becomes simply: does the image produce a *frisson;* does it stimulate instinctual reverberation. Again, the definition of porn given in Fowler's *Dictionary of Modern Critical Terms* is that which "depraves or corrupts," i.e., what it *does.*[12]

For orthodox monotheists who follow a pure and abstract spirit, any image depraves and corrupts, even a dream, and ought to be eradicated at its source in the mind. The history of iconoclasm is long and bloody (and I have already reviewed it in my *Healing Fiction*[13] in regard to Jung's courageous insistence upon images as the basic stuff of the psyche and therefore of its therapy). The history of iconoclasm continues in subtle

---

12. Cf. James Joyce, *A Portrait of the Artist as a Young Man* [1916] (Harmondsworth: Penguin, 1976), 205: "The feelings excited by improper art are kinetic, desire or loathing...The arts which excite them, pornographic or didactic, are therefore improper art."

13. *Healing Fiction* (Putnam, Conn.: Spring Publications, 2005).

forms by reducing images to allegories, interpreting them into concepts and by meditative techniques that seek to empty the mind for the sake of an imageless state.

Censorship

Since images are instincts, censoring images represses instincts. What then happens to the vitality of the citizen? Here, the issue of censorship shifts from one of personal expression and belief (freedom under the U.S. Constitution's First Amendment) to one of national vitality, even national security. It becomes an issue of the Constitution itself whose preamble states that our government aims to "insure domestic tranquility" and "promote the general welfare."

If tranquility of the general populace means tranquilized, then government censorship might be defensible. For, yes, pornography arouses. I submit that this potential for igniting an insurrection of the repressed instinctual imagination and for fomenting curiosity to pry into what is concealed may be the motives underlying the anxious scrutiny of pornography in our times by all three branches of government: Supreme Court, Congressional Committee, and Justice Department.

Notice, please, that we are now moving from myth to law in accord with an archetypal pattern of the human mind. As we move, deliberation begins to replace delight. Aphrodite dethroned; *nomos* and *themis* to the fore.

Right away, a definition of pornography: the stimulation of lust through imaging and the stimulation of imaging through lust. We may tighten this definition by omitting "stimulation" since arousal is always contextual, depending on variables such as time, place, mood, and taste. Many lustful images leave one limp and stupefied; some imagined lust provokes only revulsion. Thus, in sum, *pornography is lustful images and imagistic lust.*

I offer this definition to replace those of the dictionaries which link "pornographic" with "obscene"—meaning dirty, filthy, offensive to decency and modesty. Although the Greeks used the word *porne* for prostitute, in English "pornography" enters the Oxford English dictionary only in mid-Victorian times when it received its obscene qualification.

Can we clean up this mess that muddles obscenity with pornography? Let us try to keep in mind what Murray Davis says in his lovely book,

SMUT, "that no sexual activity is obscene in itself, but only in relation to a particular ideology. Therefore, the central question...should be shifted from 'What sexual activities are obscene?' to 'Relative to what [ideology] are some sexual activities obscene?'"[14]

Although the Justice Department has a National Obscenity Unit, precisely what obscenity is remains unclarified. Mainly, it is defined as *a)* depictions or descriptions of sexual activities or organs, *b)* appeal primarily to prurient interests offensive to local community standards, and *c)* without redeeming scientific, aesthetic, or social merit. The obscene is wholly sexualized. Nuclear dumps, leaching poisons, clear-cut forest lands, strangulated seals, disfigured toy monsters, TV tortures, platters of food dumped in restaurant garbage, bombing children in Iraq, George Bush walking through South Central LA, Richard Serra's rusty girders plunked down in public squares, McDonald's arches spanning the globe and the smell of fried grease—none of this is legally obscene, yet what of this has scientific, aesthetic, or social merit? Obscenity, dislocated from its actual daily occasions, has been displaced onto sexual acts and organs. But I have seen buildings more obscene than Marilyn Chambers and Traci Lords—and buildings can't be turned off; you are forced to enter them. Clearly our culture is more afraid of looking at Robert Mapplethorpe's photos of a penis than of Rambo's automatic rifle. We are more afraid of viewing an ordinary human anus than the assholes we watch nightly on TV.

The struggle with pornography in America is not about obscenity. It is about ideology; and, according to Leonore Tiefer, President of the International Academy of Sex Research, particularly the ideology condemning masturbation.[15] Anathema! And why? Since statistics say almost everybody masturbates, probably more citizens than brush their teeth, and certainly more than vote. Why so ideologically condemned? Partly because masturbation offers pleasure without dependence; it may even prevent shopping. Archetypally, masturbation invokes Pan, and we witness his panic when the President, employing the powers vested in him to defend the Constitution, summarily fires the Surgeon General

14. Murray S. Davis, *SMUT: Erotic Reality/Obscene Ideology* (Chicago and London: The University of Chicago Press, 1983), 238.

15. Cf. *The Sex Panic: Women, Censorship and "Pornography"* (New York: National Coalition Against Censorship, May 1993), 12.

(whom he had appointed) for stating that the youth of this nation (under God) should learn about masturbation at a time in this nation's history when HIV, gonorrhea, unwanted pregnancy, and date rape plague that same youth.

In the United States, about 2000 rapes occurred today and will occur tomorrow. One out of eight adult American women will be the object of a rape—the definition of which I shall leave aside. Child molestation, child prostitution, satanic sexual cults, venereal diseases—why enumerate? All too well known to you. Violent and pathological sexual fantasies have colonized our minds. We are a nation of lustful images, a pornographic nation. This is a hard-core fact. But our pornographic nation has yet to disentangle its violence and its obscenity from pornography. For violence is the enemy, not the sexuality that may occasionally accompany it. And obscenity of the nation's taste, values, language, and sensibility is only minimally and contingently represented by porn. The "problem" of what to do about porn begins first with the nation's hardcore devotion to violence and obscenity.

The way America deals with its hard facts is to make a law. As one commentator on America has said, *law is the myth of America.* Lawyers are our priests, our interpreters of the dominant myth that steers the civilization, codifies its practices and provides its rituals. Of course, lawyers must receive high tribute. So, to deal with pornography we outlaw it, and thereby blame it for inciting criminal behavior. Let us remember, however, that a definitive causal link between pornography and criminal sexual behavior has never been established. President Johnson's commission report published in 1970, and the Meese report (1986) and the Surgeon General's report all failed to find reliable evidence that significantly connects pornography with criminal sexual behavior.[16]

Despite these repeated inconclusive findings, the Senate Judiciary Committee deliberated many months over the Pornography Victims

---

16. The legal issues and their history are thoughtfully discussed and thoroughly documented in Edward de Grazia, *Girls Lean Back Everywhere: The Law of Obscenity and the Assault on Genius* (New York: Random House, 1992); Donald Alexander Downs, *The New Politics of Pornography* (Chicago and London: The University of Chicago Press, 1989).

Compensation Act. This bill, in its own perversely twisted way, gives backhand recognition to the power in the image to incite desire. For the Bill, as originally proposed, would have held producers and distributors of pornography legally responsible for illegal actions committed by the consumer of porn. Victims of sex crimes could file civil suits to recover damages from producers, distributors, maybe even actors, of "obscene" materials, if the victims could show that the materials caused (incited, sparked, initiated) the crimes. You would no longer be a citizen responsible for your behavior—you are rather a victim of *Penthouse* and *Screw*.

Just here we see the effects of Hera on our legal thinking. (Does Aphrodite write laws? What kind would they be? Does she engage lawyers, or has she other means of getting her own?) When the "nine old men" as Roosevelt called the Justices (and I include O'Connor and Ginzberg in that number) consider the cases of pornography brought to the bench, they retreat to an imaginative figure called "the average person" (sometimes called "reasonable person") who "applying contemporary community standards would find the work to be patently offensive."

Who is this fictional "person?" The statistically average person in the United States would be one of Hera's marrieds (or has been married), whose repressions would reflect the peer group, i.e., standard *petit bourgeois* standards. For this "person" the images of porn—as the law states —can appeal only to "prurient interests." Once the door to porn has been closed by local community opinion, the only opening is through the keyhole. The only access for a puritan is prurience. Then who buys porn? Where's the money coming from?

"Not me," says the average reasonable standard community person. It must come then from the non-reasonable (irrational, demented?), not average (fringe?), not following community standards (asocial?) persons. There must be an awful lot of them with fat wallets to maintain the ever-expanding multi-billion dollar industry.

Porn and prurience seem inseparable because when lustful images are uplifted into archives for the study of sexuality or collected as erotic art, no one seems to go. According to a recent report the Kinsey archives are "falling apart," the Museum of Erotic Art in San Francisco is "defunct," and access to the patchy assembly of material in other collections like that of the New York Public Library is desultory and complicated. Moreover, "serious" interest by the reasonable person also flags. The President of the

Institute for the Advanced Study of Sexuality complains: "It's difficult to get enough trained people to look at all the material we get in."[17]

That these images aimed solely to arouse must have other serious ends also takes us back to Hera (or the Roman Catholic Church) who insists all human sexuality must serve a high purpose. Do notice that pleasure, enjoyment, surprise, shock, curiosity, initiation—or just watching —are not serious enough. Priapean and Aphroditic values are judged by other values assumed to be superior. Hera raged at Zeus for not keeping within the service of marriage his philandering fantasies which generated so many extraordinary forms of existence, his progeny. And the Church has ruled for centuries that sexuality must serve procreation or marriage or God. Otherwise dalliance and the furor of the flesh belong to the Devil. The Supreme Court makes all this very literal, branding a red-letter warning into the lustful imaginings of every citizen: if you get into porn, it must only be for '"serious scientific, aesthetic, or political value."

Political? Isn't porn itself political? From the reactions of Jesse Helms and the storms unleashed whenever Aphrodite overtly invades the body politic via arts funding, museum exhibitions, or the bodies of politicians, she melts the borders between politics and pornography. Pornographic materials are *ipso facto* political in that they intend to arouse the suppressed body of the citizen in which is also the body politic.

The overlooked virtue of Andrea Dworkin's and Catherine Mac-Kinnon's lethal assault on pornography is their coupling of porn and politics. Their move is similar to mine; the consequences of the move, however, are completely different. The argument that they have succeeded in establishing into law in Canada and partly in Minneapolis and Indianapolis runs like this: Because pornography is sexual subordination of persons, the politics of porn moves from the rights of personal expression and belief (First Amendment) to the civil rights established by the Thirteenth and Fourteenth Amendments prohibiting involuntary servitude and deprivation of liberty. They further argue that as a demonstration of the subordination of women to men, pornography discriminates against all women. It is to be banned, not because it incites violence but because it is violating. Confining it to a red-light district not only condones this involuntary servitude, but legalizes a ghetto, a slave quarter.

---

17. Stacey D'Erasmos, "Pornography Archives," *Lingua Franca* (June/July 1992): 51–52.

So they say, abolish all porn because the First Amendment does not take precedent over the Thirteenth, the abolition of involuntary servitude, or the Fourteenth, which guarantees civil rights, or the Eighth, which forbids cruel and unusual punishment.

To advocate pornography is not to ignore the crudities and cruelties of some porn against some women. But it is to ignore some crude thinking about gender. Each time we use the word "women" in this context we need to realize that it subsumes within it billions of particular female persons, each with thousands of particular traits, likes, and dislikes that differ according to time and place, mood and taste.

The very question: "Is pornography harmful to women?" is harmful to women. The question ignores these individual differences. The question reduces all women to a class concept, and while elevating that class to "equality" actually oppresses individual women by the logic that forces them to be included *nolens volens* in that class.

Therefore, many feminists refuse to follow Dworkin and MacKinnon, finding them more oppressive than the porn they would ban. First, because sexual relations are relations and not *eo ipso* violations, force being only one form of that relation, not sex itself. Second, they psychopathologize all sex: whereas bondage, fisting, or fellatio may be for some at times not a deprivation of liberty but a practice of joy. Third, banning porn closes an industry and forecloses a person's pursuit of happiness to follow a vocation as a professionally trained actress, strip artist, writer, photographer, or prostitute. We did not close down the garment industry because of immigrant seamstresses in sweatshops or the dark satanic mills of Dickensian England because of laboring children. Protections were enacted, injustices corrected, conditions upgraded. And the industries themselves improved.

Fourth, Dworkin/MacKinnon have fundamentally distorted the male/female relation in porn. Men ogle and leer and spend not mainly because of patriarchal depravity and abusive power so rampant in the society. No, it is because men are entranced by the mystery revealed in porn, the naked Other revealed. They are, as Camille Paglia[18] says, in awe and under dominion of the feminine goddess. Porn reveals Her

---

18. Melanie Wells, "Woman as Goddess: Camille Paglia Tours Strip Clubs," *Penthouse* (October 1994): 58ff.

power. The abolition of porn would suppress the goddess and so, I conclude, against Dworkin/MacKinnon, that its prohibition is not in Her name. Indeed, Susan Griffin,[19] "the pornographic mind is the mind of our culture"—though not as you argue because of men's inflammations but because of Her infiltration.

Arguments back and forth—censor everything! censor nothing?—omit the principle I have been elaborating through these pages. Whatever the violence, whatever the cruel bondage or degradation that is displayed by porn, these images of exploitation are all images. Pornography, as the suffix *graph* explicitly states, belongs to an imaginal reality—theater and show, inked lines on a paper, paint on canvas, reels of micro-thin film. All are such stuff as dreams are made on, phenomena of lustful imaginings. Their reality is beyond the law. The actual literal humans who portray these imaginal scenes have recourse to the same measures that protect the citizen against injustice in any occupation or situation. Equal rights under the law for all, regardless of profession. But the imaginings themselves are unavailable to censorship, unreeling their shows in the dream and in the mind, day and night, as archetypal functions of the natural psyche.

So if we accept Susan Griffin's dictum, "woman who *is* nature," then the unceasing generation of pornographic images cannot be a male province or even a male perversion. As natural, they must be the gift of the woman who is nature, the gift of the goddess whom Griffin herself acclaims, in the shape of Aphrodite *porneia.*

Priapos and Jesus, Pothos and Shopping

We have attended so carefully to Priapos in this essay because he is instrumental in most hard-core porn, either as what is depicted or what aimed at. If there is a god in the disease, as Jung says, the god is Priapos. Is it not wiser to pay obeisance to the god than be obsessed by the disease? Porn aims to resurrect his erection. For the idea of divine resurrection needs to be recaptured from Christian usurpation and placed where today it actually occurs, the insurrection of the flesh, as St. Augustine called his libidinal desires, the resurrection of the pagan pow-

---

19. Susan Griffin, *Pornography and Silence: Culture's Revenge Against Nature* (New York: Harper & Row, 1981), 3.

ers who have been pressed into the flesh. The first sign of their unease is pink madness.

Three reasons why the gods return first via pink madness, all noted by Freud: a) the sexual libido is at the top of the pile of twothousand years of repressed contents; b) it is a most forcefully urgent instinct; c) and yet an instinct easily metamorphosed into devious vicissitudes. Pink madness invades especially the commercial world, pornographying shampoo, Hawaiian islands, coffee beans, and Velveeta cheese. Pink madness sells the skin of automobiles and the smooth hairless bodies attached to Nordic-trak machines. All these images we watch daily are varieties of soft-core porn. Romantically tinted, fuzzily sensuous, languidly arousing. However, the god or daimon here is less Hermaphroditos the freak or Priapos the prick than their lovely brother, Eros. His is the inflammatory appeal, the otherworldly seduction, the constant courting of the soul, tempting psyche to swoon with desire—follow me, come fly with me, I will give you voluptuousness. You recall Eros and Psyche had a child (Aphrodite was her Granny) called *Voluptas,* voluptuousness, defined by the *Oxford English Dictionary* as "of, pertaining to, derived from, resting in or characterized by gratification of the senses, especially, in a refined or luxurious manner; marked by indulgence in sensuous pleasures." Precisely that is what the aura of consumerism offers: indulgence in sensuous pleasures.

Consumerism of course appeals to the psyche, because Psyche is always entranced by Eros. She can't help but shop, if the mall and the catalogue are where Aphrodite works her seductions and where the tale of Eros and Psyche plays itself out in our time. Wherever we are lured, the psyche is caught in that myth. And I want to defend this soft sex selling against the proponents of hard-core. They want crotch shots and organ grinding. No wrappings and trappings, no romance, no chiaroscuro, no fuzzy fade-outs.

The crucial criterion of hard-core content is direct concrete presence; nothing hidden, nothing absent. The reverse of this utter one-sided sexual literalism are the prudish censoring cover-ups, i.e., utter one-sided moral literalism.

This war between the two aspects of Priapos continues through the centuries, because there is always the fear that the demon may jump from the image, off the page, dancing right into your lap, like that spark

Malraux says which leaps from one person to another via an art object. The spark of arousal lurks; your erotic imagination could be stirred. Hence censorship: notorious are those by the Church of Michelangelo's *Last Judgment* in the Sistine Chapel. Even the Bible has been found pornographic, censored, and parts banned.

Flaubert wrote of these fig leaves and veils so acidly that I cannot resist an excerpt. Flaubert says he would have

> given a fortune to know the name, age, address, profession, and face of the gentleman who invented for the statues of the museum of Nantes those fig leaves made of tin that look like devices designed to discourage onanism. Casts of the *Apollo Belvedere*, the *Discus Thrower*, and a flute player have been outfitted with these shameful metal drawers...affixed with screws to the members of these poor plaster figures now flaking away with pain...Amid the common stupidity which surrounds us, what a joy it is to find...at least one truly outstanding idiocy, one gigantic stupidity. [20]

My point is that the covering *verifies* the priapic, transforms the athletic discus thrower, for instance, into a pornographic figure. Asinine stupidity (the object of Flaubert's scorn) belongs with Priapos. The statues move from nude art to naked pornography by virtue of the "shameful metal drawers." The importance of covering for the lustful imagination of uncovering suggests that Mapplethorpe's nude images are less pornographic than the Apollo Belvedere who invites prurient peeking. Even Aphrodite stands at her bath partly turned away, partly covered, yet nude and bare. Presence and absence both, for absence makes the heart grow fonder.

Nonetheless, as I said, advocates of hard-core want full exposure. For instance, Pietro Aretino, Renaissance journalist and hip porn purveyor, writes:

> What harm is there in seeing a man mounting a woman? Should beasts, then, be freeer than we are? We should wear that thing nature gave us for the preservation of the species on a chain around our necks or as a medal on our hats; for that is the fountain rivers of human beings come forth from...That thing made you...it created me, and I am better than bread. It produced

---

20. Gustave Flaubert, *Voyages* (Paris: Les Belles Lettres, 1948), 1: 203 [my translation].

the Bembos, the Molzas, the Varchis, the Ugolin Martellis...the Titians, and the Michelangelos, and after them the Popes, emperors, and kings. It generated handsome boys and beautiful women with their "holy of holies." We should celebrate all this by establishing special holy days and festivities in its honor rather than confining it in a small piece of cloth or silk. Men's hands might be well hidden since they gamble money, swear oaths, practice usury, make obscene gestures, tear, punch, wound and kill.[21]

Aretino today would be among those who argue for more genitals on TV and fewer handguns.

I fear that neither Flaubert nor Aretino grasp that the tin fig leaf or small piece of cloth belong essentially with the priapic. Cover-up is essential to priapic arousal. Soft core, because it invites fantasy beyond what is presented, fetishizes even more strongly an arousing image.

This argument obliges us to re-read the most important of all coverings in our culture, the naked Jesus of the Crucifixion. Those veils, bits of fabric, and artfully placed screen figures between us, the viewers, and his genitals are not simply to be read as literal censorship of his literal sexuality, to ban sex from the mind of his devotees.[22] These guises that hide and yet indicate serve as a soft-core gesture on the part of a very sophisticated church (whose rules consciously controlled for centuries the image-making of religious objects). Suggestive, discreetly placed cover-ups fascinate the worshipers of this most holy icon of an all-but-naked god, binding us to the image erotically, passionately, arousedly, just by the very fold of cloth, the branch, or limb, or leaf, or cupped hand, closing off the literal and opening into the imaginable, the implied, sparking the fervor of fantasy. The determining icon of our culture's religious consciousness, because it is priapic in its genital presence and absence together, is a soft-core emblem par excellence. And I say this not as an insult.

For the soft brings in Eros, as Plato says. So I, Aphrodite, favor soft core. But do humans ever fully get the nature of Eros? Do they realize

---

21. Quoted from Pietro Aretino, "Lettere il primo e il secondo," in *I Modi. The Sixteen Pleasures: An Erotic Album of the Italian Renaissance*, edited by Lynne Lawner (Evanston, Ill.: Northwestern University Press, 1988), 9.

22. See the convincingly argued and carefully documented, sensational monograph by Leo Steinberg, "The Sexuality of Christ in Renaissance Art and in Modern Oblivion," *October* 25 (1983).

that part of its nature descends from that parent, Penia (need) who always wants, as told in the *Symposium* tale by Socrates (one of my all time lovers). This congenital unfulfillment reappears as an inner figure within Eros called *pothos*[23] or yearning, a longing for what is not here, hard, now, sure, known and red, but away, diffuse, rosy. Soft porn yearns toward the unattainable, suffusing commercial banalities with the promise of lascivious sweetness, like the girl on TV sucking her forbidden Frusen Gladje.

The dominant theme in all soft porn is the transgressive temptation, beyond the limits of the actual and the usual, like the romance pulp fiction on a drugstore shelf. Soft porn offers sex transfigured to mystery, the sacralization of sex redeemed from secular conformity by Aphrodite *charis,* the grace and charm of the unknown as the new. It frees the heart's yearning for a "first time" *in illo tempore,* a mythical time untouched by earthly burdens, a new person in a new way in a new place, clasped breathless bodies in sacred space, all absences now present in a bleak room off a roaring highway.

So, I, Aphrodite, and my boys, banned from secular civilization, return into its heart core through the allure of consumerism that makes us want, desire, reach out (*orexis,* the Greek word for appetite, coming originally from stretching out, as of the fingers). And appetite has in it *petere,* to seek, to go for it, (petition as seeking, begging) and petulance, that feeling when you don't get what you beg for. Inside the shopping appetite and reaching fingers of consumerism is *ptero,* the wing of a bird; our stretching hand, a bird's wing. The human hand is phylogenetically homologous with the structure of a wing, so that the reach of desire is the wing of a bird. As archaic as the pterodactyl are the flying fingers of the yearning spirit ransacking the discount tables in your local mall.

Quite simply: Aphrodite's pink madness runs the world *sub rosa* in the guise of the consumerist economy. Of course shopping and television viewing are the first and second leisure activities of the American people. By means of her seductions, she keeps the world running, out there shopping. Government enacts laws against drink, against smoking

---

23. I have discussed pothos at some length in *UE*3: *Senex & Puer.* On the relation between pothos and perversion, see Al Lingus, "Lust," *Spring: A Journal of Archetype and Culture* 51 (1991) and Davis, *SMUT,* 238, who writes, "Sex, in short, is not so much a worldly as an other-worldly desire..."

and promulgates a "no" against drugs. But who and how prohibit shopping? What—no more catalogues?

If truth be told, I, Aphrodite, *invented* soft core. It is how I catch a culture with a pink hope, a desire for wings. And it is far more effective than hard core because it has the power of a symptom: it both denies and offers what the psyche wants. Soft porn is a compromise, as Freud (another of my sons?) said of all symptoms. It invites the soul's yearning for the beauty and magic of Eros, but only tantalizes with fantasies of a ghostly lover unknown, unseen, like my boy Amor in Psyche's night, present and absent both.

Remember: beyond the cooled habits of lust in marriage, *performed* lust[24] has but two choices, the neurotic or the psychopathic. Either the sentimental idealizations of a screen romance or the zipless fuck of strangers without past or future. Freud himself said that the actual does not satisfy the sexual libido and Reich gave his life trying to get it "right" by literalizing cosmic *pothos* into orgone energy. Only *pothos* fulfills the soul's invisible complexities because *pothos* cannot happen. Like the alchemical conjunction, it is a dream, a miracle in the glass vessel of imaginal reality.

As I see things, soft porn is not an idealization of sex, as the Freudian greybeards (Anna, too) might say, and therefore a defense against hard reality. Rather it is the heavenly aspect given by me, this goddess, directly or via one of my sons, reminding the soul that it must always serve in my temple, where it will always be susceptible to a wondrous lifting up from this world and reminiscent of another, platonic, romantic, and rosy-fingered, filling this consumer world with the golden glow of Aphrodite Urania, that otherworldly radiance which was always the main purpose of my being and the main significance of my smile.

And so consumerism is far more effective and more pleasing than censorship, because it diverts rather than castrates desire. Do not the moralistic attacks on the hard-core porn industry serve, in fact, the retail trade? Business seems to recognize that were hard core more prevalent, frankly lustful images could drive pink madness from the market. Then shoppers might escape the trap of the consumer conundrum as phrased by Eric Hoffer: "You never get enough of what you don't really want."

---

24. See Lingus, "Lust," and his subsequent book, *Abuses* (Berkeley: University of California Press, 1994).

Curiosity as Courage

I would like to place what I am writing here within the field of psychological heroics as practiced by the founders of therapy—the psychoanalysts of Vienna and Zurich, the clinicians of Paris and Nancy, the
asylum psychiatrists of Germany and England, those pioneers who were
courageously curious about the vagaries of the human imagination and
whose province was the unacceptable and unrelenting moods, lusts, and
obsessions that feed the roots of imagination in each citizen, incarcer-
ated or in the streets.

Our work has always been in defense of the oppressed rather than
adjustment to the oppressor. Therapy takes the side of the victim. But
today it is hard to distinguish who is the victim and who is the oppressor.
Are we victims of pornography or is pornography the victim? The lustful imagination is persecuted by puritanical Victorianism whose roots
go deep into the fundaments of religious orthodoxy that does not allow
the mind its nature and the dream its sexual pleasure, condemning the
freakish and twisted to the public stocks of political correctness. This
persecution so splits lust from images and images from lust that images
lose their instinctual vitality and, worse, lust loses its imagination, finding substitute satisfaction in brute literal enactments. A vicious circle
of literalism creates what it seeks to prevent, so that the censor may be
more an underlying cause of sexual violence than that which is censored.

The seeds of this literalism were handed directly to Moses (Exodus 20)
in a commandment against graven images. The Almighty warned Moses
that any graven image—even of birds and fish—infringes His omnipotence and must therefore be more abominable in a cosmic sense than
such ordinary no-no's as lying, larceny, adultery, and murder. Clearly
any image at all is a grave threat to the monotheistic mind. Let us nevertheless remember that the edict says you must not fix in stone (graven
means chiseled) any fantasy whatsoever, including, then, the fantasy
prohibiting a graven image. This has always been recognized somehow
by Jewish observers who regularly present the Commandments iconically and ironically as two engraved stone tablets. So, to take the commandment against idolatry on the mono-level of a prohibition only is
itself a literalization of the very instruction not to literalize, therewith
setting the commandment itself in stone, turning it into an immovable
idol, perduring to this day in the stoneheads of fundamentalism.

But that's only half. The other half occurs in Matthew 5:28 where we are urged not to make any distinction between a lustful image in the mind and actual adultery in behavior. This was the passage that got Jimmy Carter in trouble. In a *Playboy* interview he admitted looking with desire. He courageously admitted to lustful images. For literalist readers of Matthew, Carter committed adultery for there is no fundamental difference for the orthodox between what one imagines and what one does.

May we not by now conclude that the basic issue of pornography becomes neither obscenity nor sexuality. It is literalism, the single-mindedness which reads images unimaginatively and is thereby threatened by them, and so is driven to control all images, especially those that are overtly vital, i.e., endowed with sexual potency.

By referring to Matthew and orthodoxy, I am reminding us of Christianity's investment in the control of lustful images, a never-ceasing concern that did not begin with the present Pope's dogmatic obsessions. It begins centuries ago when Christianity itself took shape vis-à-vis Paganism, as Christians called the contemporary religions by which they were surrounded. The struggle over pornography is the struggle with Paganism. And the pagan gods and goddesses return, as the repressed always return, said Freud, through the most vulnerable place in Christian doctrine: its *lacunae* in regard to pleasure, the body, and the mythic imagination. Aphrodite, Priapos, Persephone, Pan, Eros, Dionysus, Zeus—especially these are the gods returning. Pornography is where the pagan gods have fallen and how they force themselves back into our minds.

Owing to their presence I cannot support any censorship at all. I am obliged to validate all porn on the basis of its importance for resurrecting the archetypal imagination. I want to encourage curiosity in it, or what is now condemned as "prurient interest." (I stand against the Christian writers, such as François Fenelon [1651–1715], who elevated curiosity to the first of sins, above even pride.) Before we choose among the parts, let us first accept the whole, otherwise differentiation becomes one more insidious suppression. As Thomas Jefferson said, "Whose foot is to be the measure to which ours are all to be cut or stretched?" The statutes against assault and involuntary servitude and which protect minors and those in dependent positions sufficiently deal with the injustices wherever they occur in society, including the pornography industry. Pornography is not a worse case of the exploitation and abuse of children, of bodies, of women or of physical cruelties.

The war against pornography is only obliquely motivated by the pious defense of hapless children, the protection of exploited women, and the safeguarding of decent family values. The war is that ancient one of iconoclasm against images, of the spirit's high-mindedness against the soul's natural proclivities, of purity against pleasure, of sentimentalism against Saturn, of the rule of ideals against the facts of life, or in short, the high-minded Olympian gods against the powers of the field, the soil and the Underworld. Aphrodite combined both: *pornē* and *urania;* as Priapos was a protector against bad luck and a fertile gardener as well as a frighteningly phallic grotesque.

The suppression of pornography begins with confusing the sexually graphic with the obscene, thereby lowering our private bellies into privy filth. This is the main mode of iconoclasm in our time and, by the psychological law of *pars pro toto* (a part represents the whole), it pornographizes our nude bodies and degrades sexuality of any sort. This first obscene madness necessitates the secondary pink madness of consumerism. Also, this obscene madness creates the convention of shame, that interiorized censorship which inhibits serious rational community folk, like you and me, from talking about porn. It only can mean talking dirty.

Well, I want to talk dirty—to you—dirty politics. The political fight is about control of the responses of a human's body, or as Thomas Szasz says, control of the citizen's body by the state, otherwise known as slavery. Perhaps pornography needs a lobby comparable with the National Rifle Association. For the constitutional right to bear arms that so exercises citizens today depends first on an enlivened and personally owned body reclaimed from state control, so that the citizen can bear those arms with civic responsibility rather than random, resentful rage.

Pornography thus becomes as vital to our political present and future as other areas of bodily liberty; the rights of assembly and speech; to go unhampered to the polls; the abolition of bondage; abortion rights; the right to end one's bodily life; to ingest substances of one's own choosing; to be protected by law against physical assault, discrimination, exploitation, and unjust punishment.

To these fundamental liberties I am adding the right to fantasize. Fantasy is innate to human beings, as irrepressible as our other instincts.

As such, it is more than a private luxury, more than a basic necessity. Fantasy is as well a collectively human responsibility, calling for the conscientious, courageous, and joyful participation by the citizen in lustful imaginings. Pornographic fantasies require their place in the body politic as part of its instinctual vitality, else the psyche's life and the society's welfare is thwarted. If pornography, as we have defined it, finds no societal support and instead societal suppression, then the citizen and the nation decline into shamed, passive-aggressive victimization, tied by soft pink ribbons and whipped by the frenzies of consumerism.

Postscript (2007)

In the fifteen years since this essay first found form, Priapos has come on stage by means of popular advertisements for cure of Erectile Dysfunction (ED). But the god of erections does not appear full front and center. In keeping with postmodern notions, he is present in his absence. TV ads for pharmaceutical cures in fact explicitly warn against him, referring to "priapism" as an erection lasting four hours or more. Should that happen, call your doctor—or 911.

The actors shown on TV supposedly stand in for men with ED. But is it the men or the imagined situations where ads place them, which might be grounds of dysfunction. In a lovely natural setting, on a cruise ship, at a lakeside retreat, quietly dancing, cozying up with a middle-aged woman; discreet, sensitive surroundings, groomed, neatly appointed; domesticated pairs, friendly, understanding. Married. Coupled; but not coupling. No tawdry truck stop; no roadhouse with porn films running 24/7; no high-class call-girl club or lap dancer, gay bath house, spring-break beach scene, or communal military shower—places where Priapos is likely to pop up uninvited.

The subdued milieus of the ads are hardly hard-on country. More likely they bespeak the world of Hera who cursed Priapos *ab utero*; or the intimate interior domesticity of Hestia who rebuffed Priapos coming on to her; or the pristine woodlands of Artemis who let no eager pursuer get close; or, at best, the soft lovey-dovey world of Aphrodite-Venus, his mother, whose taste was so offended by his gross engorgement that right at birth she recoiled and rejected her son. Maybe ED is better conceived to be a dysfunction of the archetypal imagination than a defective pumping system.

Already Aristotle, Galen, and the physiology of the Stoics knew that erection depends on *"imaginatio,"* the airy element as a movement of the "animal spirits" (as the vital soul was earlier called). Galen said there was air in the *corpus cavernosa* of the penis, and Leonardo da Vinci shows in his anatomical notebooks sectional drawings of two urethral passages: one for fluids, the other for the pneuma.[25] Erection begins in fantasy. That's why the small-print information packaged with ED drugs says their product comes into play only after arousal and does not cause it. Sex starts in the mind, and the mind starts in *poiesis,* the fantasies in which the gods make their moves and play their games.

9

IN:
HESTIA'S PREPOSITION

I

One sure thing we have all learned doing analysis and that is the importance of the small and detailed. I began my Jungian journey—and I use the "J-word" accurately, for it was a geographical trip from Himalayan India, through Israel and Sweden eventually to Zurich—with giant steps. India, Typologies, Individuation, Big Dreams, Universal Symbols (I wanted to do my first thesis on the idea of Spirit, and a second one on Time), I mean BIG! But now I seem to be taking ant steps, teeny-tiny attention to the smallest things.

That's why the minute title, "In"—however, I don't know yet whether it will turn out smaller or bigger than big. That's already a dimension of the question: has "in" dimensions, size, shape, place?

Before we get to that: a reminder of what we all already know. "In" is no doubt *the* soul word. "In" is definitely "in" in depth psychology: *in* analysis, *in* therapy, *in* the transference, *in* love, *in* a relationship, *in* mourning, *in* your head and not *in* your body, and once upon a time "in a family way"—now "in" has got deeper, gone further, becoming "into," the key term for being thoroughly absorbed: into bird watching, into rap, into Mexican cooking.

The history of our field confirms these ordinary uses of "in" and "into." The locus of psychoanalytic preoccupations from its beginnings was with an interior topography and dynamics of regions, figures and forces, memories and feelings, flows and complexes, all of which are imagined to be internal.

Earlier versions of this paper were given at the national meetings of Jungian analysts in Boston and at the Pacifica Graduate Institute in Carpinteria, California. First published in *Spring: A Journal of Archetype and Culture* 63 (1998).

Especially feelings; they are kept in and let out. They are deep down inside, and they go on continually as the interior reflective coloring and rhythm to outer behavior. A major objection to behaviorism and behavior therapy on the part of depth analysts has been that behaviorism has no "inside." There's no "in" there.

In short, the main activity of analysis takes place inside. That's where the true person hides, the inner me. Sorting out this inner world—what did happen *in* the past and might happen *in* the future, means working through parental interjects, the complaining remnants of the inner child, going with the withdrawing introversion of the libido, and reductive investigations of the shadow—that "agenbite of inwit," as Joyce called remorseful self-examination. "In" is the key preposition in analysis, more important I believe than "with." "In" is the key direction of psychological movement, the key location of psychodynamics, and the privileged position of soul values.

Characteristic especially of Jungian analysis are such "in" words as *temenos,* container, *vas hermeticum,* sacred space, as well as the cautions derived from allegorical stories and myths about opening the bottle lest the spirit escape, opening the box rescued from the underworld, or opening the jar of evils.

"In" is a habit of mind we each share unavoidably. The way we conceive "in" partly results from institutionalization. I mean the hardening of originating ideas into paradigms by which we conceive experience. We analysts, despite our enhanced capacity to reflect and analyze, are not immune to the institutionalized mind. In fact we are more unfortunate than most other professionals precisely in regard to the collectivity of our reflections, since the tools of analysis and reflection we use to reflect on our profession are the very concepts furnished by the institution. We bear witness daily to the great impasse Jung often wrote about: the psyche's difficulty, if not impossibility, of becoming conscious of itself by means of psychology. How does the knower know itself?

Whether we condemn our institutionalism as dogmatic adherence or persona adaptation to our school and its training, or to the comfortable conservatism of the feeling function and its troubles with thinking, or whether we employ Václav Havel's definition of stupidity as the transmission of received ideas without thinking them, just passing them on—all these sins of the institutionalized mind, which we witness in government, academe, journalism, religion, or in our field, and which we so abhor, may well result from a prior, even primordial, sin, literalism. By literalism I mean the "natural and customary" meaning of something, just as it presents itself, without under-sense or second level, as the dictionary says, "without metaphor, exaggeration, or inaccuracy," or suggestion. Taking words in their primary sense.

Primary, however, implies secondary, otherwise why use the term primary? Primary implies a plural possibility, another further sense. "Literal" mythically means without Hermes/Mercurius, without the goddess Peitho who comes sometimes as Athene, sometimes as Aphrodite—the persuasive one. Literal means nothing tricky or subtle, nothing charming.

In regard to our specific topic, "in," we find "in" literalized as a defined place into which we go—the unconscious, the body; or to a definite time in the past. This literalization makes us forget what the master said: not the psyche is in me, but I am in the psyche. We forget and literalize the soul inside the skin, the mind inside the skull, the dream, the emotion, the memory inside the "me" to the neglect of the collective psyche, the *anima mundi* in which we live our lives all day long.

Let me here differentiate several main linguistic uses of "in." I do this partly that we become more conscious of the predicament "in" puts us in. And, as Jung said, becoming conscious requires differentiation. So, let's just run through these uses. You can find them in your dictionary or grammar book where I found them.

The preposition "in" means *within the limits of* space, time, condition, situation, circumstance. "In" as limited, bordered, defined. As I already said: in analysis, in love, in the soup, in court, in jeopardy, in a hurry, just in time. "In" as a state of limited being—whether in a garden, in a mess, or in analysis. Confinement. Shall we say "framed?" So, when we say the soul is in the body, we don't only narrowly mean "in" as literally inside the place of the body. We also mean more broadly limited by, confined to the circumstances of the body.

"In" is also a prefix bearing several meanings:

1) A negative, privative prefix: indecision, inarticulate, inadmissible, injustice, insane, incest (as unchaste), incapable. This negative or privative "in" substitutes for "un" as unconscious. (There was a nineteenth-century usage of "inconscious.")

2) The prefix "in" also means continuing a motion onward. Going in, into, getting into something, and then being within it or inside it. There was once a verb "to in," as "to in the harvest."

3) This continuing inward meaning blends with a third meaning of the prefix that coalesces Teutonic and Latinate meanings in words (via French) with such prefixes as enclosed, encompassed, embraced, enveloped, ensnared, enchanted; ingrained, ingested, innate, initiate—where we are both situated "in" and continuing the motion more and more inward into the state of being described.

In a nutshell: "In" is a trapping word.

It would seem the word "in" acts as an archetypal force—going *into* the unconscious gets you really and indeed deeper *into* your situation, your feelings, your memories, and encompassed by the transference.

From the preposition and the prefix it is but a little step to the noun, "in." Those who are "in;" the ins as insiders. An "in" person is privy to what goes on inside the privileged preserve within the borders of a particular state or condition, time or place. To be "in" is to hold a prime or "pre"-position.

Inclusion, the subject of our meetings, with all its vices and dangers, follows quite rationally from our professional service to "in." As the dominant of our profession, "in" prepositions us so that we seem driven to be worried about borders and frames, perhaps more than any other profession. "In" would seem to act as a semantic force pulling us continually further into inner work with consequences that are cultish, exclusive, and isolate, despite all efforts at community, social consciousness and emphasis on relationships.

The semantic, grammatical differentiation that I just put you through aims beyond prefix and preposition analysis. It aims at analysis itself, our work, Jungian work, and also the field populated by millions of sincere devotees engaged in the inner work of self-study and self-help therapy, and the concepts and attitudes that are at work in this work.

I am aiming also toward something beyond the deconstructive critiques, that abuse of analysis in which I have indulged these last years. *Deliteralizing* is necessary; seeing through is a fundamental psychological move. To keep psychotherapy therapeutic it needs constantly to deliteralize its support system—its concepts and attitudes. *Displacing* is also necessary. It keeps us at the edge of our chairs, forcing freshness from us.

Deconstruction is necessary because it can keep us from fundamentalism, from our being, but reissues in American editions of the standard works produced in Zurich fifty years ago. Maybe I am too personal here, for I began my training there in 1953, more than forty years ago, and my mind still prints out texts copied from the old Zurich hard-disk matrix. I am always resisting the fear of that influence.

I am pushing toward discovering not only what's *wrong*—a martial method that only entrenches you more rigidly in your defenses of analysis—I am pushing now to find the roots of what's *right* about analysis, and by means of different myths from those I searched in the past. All along I have been trying to get at the myths of analysis. What goes on has such power, a fascination that cannot be accounted for by secular, social, and reductive accounts. Analysis remains a mystery, and mysteries are best accounted for by myths.

Our search takes a further step and a smaller one—less erotic, less Dionysian, and also less Saturnian—into the myth of the "in." Once we have deliteralized the "in," we can recognize that it is more a confining concept than one of actual location here or there. Once we have liberated "in" from the Cartesian conundrums that catch it up in personal subjectivity versus the objective world, or mind versus matter, we can at last realize that anything anywhere offers its interiority and can deepen inward continually. Even when we recognize that depth psychological analysis is not the only depository of "in," we are left, willy-nilly, with the addictive attraction of analysis as the privileged office of interiority. As well, we are left with the classically observed procedures of analysis—the closed chamber, the calm distance and warm empathy, the appointed hour, the limited time, the ethical codes, the inquiry into family, the concentrated focus, the secrecy and anonymity—procedures that maintain the literalization of the "in" in the language spoken, the private practice, the professional codes, all of which combine to make the work ritual enactment.

II

W hat then is the power, who the god or goddess that draws us in, keeps us in? What is this archetypal insistence upon interiorizing and upon preserving the sanctity of the "in?" I believe the answer to "who?" is Hestia.

So now I am going to quote passages from material gathered mainly via five writers on Hestia who have already culled the classical sources and steeped themselves in her material. I shall be quoting from L.R. Farnell's *Cults of the Greek States*[1] (LRF), Ginette Paris's chapter on Hestia in her *Pagan Meditations*[2] (GP), Barbara Kirksey's piece on Hestia in *Facing the Gods*[3] (BK), and two essays from *Spring*: by Stephanie Demetrakopoulos[4] (SD) and by Paola Coppola Pignatelli[5] (PP). I will quote phrases from these authors, asking you to look at the excerpts in terms of analytical work.

But first a general word on Hestia. She was the first of all immortals to be honored in libations and processions—before Zeus, before Hera, before Demeter and Gaia. As we say, "Cheers, Prost, Santé, Salud, Kampei, L'chaim," Romans said, "Vesta!" She was the glowing, warmth-emitting hearth. That is her image, her locus, her embodiment. Hearth in Latin is *focus*, which can be translated into psychological language as the centering attention that warms to life all that comes within its radius. This is Hestia. Ovid speaks of Hestia as "nothing but a living flame." Her name probably derives from the Indo-European *vas*, inhabit. Another derivation is from the root of essence. In short, she is only "in," and like consciousness itself, not an object seen but an enlivening, enlightening focus, the soul essence that inhabits anything.

---

1. Lewis Richard Farnell, *The Cults of the Greek States*, 5 vols. (Oxford: Clarendon Press, 1896).

2. Ginette Paris, *Pagan Meditations: The Worlds of Aphrodite, Artemis, and Hestia*, translated by Gwendolyn Moore (Thompson, Conn.: Spring Publications, 2022 [1986]).

3. Barbara Kirksey, "Hestia: A Background of Psychological Focusing," in *Facing the Gods*, edited by James Hillman (Thompson, Conn.: Spring Publications, 2022 [1988]).

4. Stephanie A. Demetrakopoulos, "Hestia, Goddess of the Hearth," *Spring: An Annual of Archetypal Psychology and Jungian Thought* (1979): 55–75.

5. Paola Coppola Pignatelli, "The Dialectics of Urban Architecture: Hestia and Hermes," in *Spring: An Annual of Archetypal Psychology and Jungian Thought* (1985): 42–49.

Now the passages: Concerning the note-taking, diary keeping, journal entries, dream recordings that are the stuff of inner work—Plato's *Laws* says:

> ...judges of a criminal who sinned against the gods, parents, or state write down at the end of each day all things germane to the case and leave the scrolls on Hestia's altar. (IX, 856a)

Analysis as sustenance, as nourishment, as feeding the soul, as unconditional support, as positive mother: "On April 15 in Rome pregnant cows were sacrificed to Vesta to ensure plentiful supply of milk" (SD 67). Vesta also cared for supplies of the salt and the sacred flour (*mola*).

Analysis: one day at a time, one session at a time. Keeping it fresh:

> The [Roman] vestals were not allowed to keep water on the premises and were required to carry each day only what they needed in a strange vessel made especially for this purpose. The vessel had such a narrow base that it could not stand up [storage was not possible; old water not usable; the narrowness of the base = the strict discipline of the vessel] and [this vessel] was called a *futile*. (SD 65)

When does analysis as service to the "in" come to an end? Freud's "Analysis Terminable or Interminable [*Unendlich*]":

> Eternal was Vesta's most common adjective/attribute. (SD 72)

On couples therapy and conflict resolution. Analysis as refuge, as a safe place:

> Disputes were settled at Hestia's altar. (SD 63)

> The hearth was also a place of making peace and granting mercy. (SD 62)

> She takes no part in wars, grievances, or affairs between gods and mortals. (BK 105)

> Hestia is able to guard images. (BK 106)

The next group of passages attests to the impersonality of the work and its numinosity, the transference rather than the human relationship. Again, what follows are direct quotations from one or another of the five authors mentioned.

> A central aspect of Hestia consciousness in a proclivity for anonymity. (SD 60)

> When men swore by Hestia, they swore by the holy hearth, not necessarily by any personality. (LRF 361-62)

Least anthropomorphic of Hellenic divinities. (LRF 345)

A potent presence, not a personal individual. (LRF 364)

A numina rather than a divinity. (LRF 362)

On the privacy and safety of the analytical *temenos*:

The phrase, he is sacrificing to Hestia—became a proverb for a secret business. (LRF 357)

Sacred asylum where one could take refuge. (GP 168)

Sacrificial offering to Hestia is never a violent, blood-shedding one. (PP 44)

On the absence of personal intervention, i.e., Freud's idea that analysis proceeds by "abstention":

There were almost no stories about her. (BK 103)

She indicates no movement. (GP 167)

On the nature of analytical progress and the descriptions of the Self:

She is always seated on circular elements, just as the places where she is worshipped are circular. (PP 46)

On the primacy of the family in the analysis of the individual:

Specially connected with the life and law of the family and the clan. (LRF 355)

Only actual service performed in her honor...appears to have been a family meal. (LRF 356)

Without her humans would have no feasts. (*Homeric Hymn* to Hestia)

She presides over the famous progress from "raw to cooked," transforming nature into food. (PP 43)

We need to distinguish here different implications of family household. "Hestia" indicates neither the literal family household in the Hera sense, nor the family as childbirthing and childcaring, nor even a house as a building. Rather, Hestia more duly governs the inner psychic structure, which is sometimes today formulated as family system and family values which the Romans called the *gens*, that invisible spirit that reigns as a cloud, a mantle, an invisible net, the shared communal soul of a household present especially at a communal meal, the primary civilizing act. Again, a distinction: not the growing of food, nor the cultivation of taste (Demeter and Aphrodite), but the ritual of eating food together.

Eating out on the run, snacking, breakfast in the car alone on the way to work, these habits may do more to violate Hestia and invite harm to the hearth of soul than all other proposed causes of family dysfunction such as absent fathers, TV violence, drugs, child abuse, etc. The shared meal, let's remember, is central to Greek, Italian, Jewish, Middle-Eastern, Oriental, African-American, and Midwestern farm life so that eating together, and its neglect, may deserve more analytical attention than "sleeping together," if analysts wish to serve Hestia with their focus.

Back to the quotations:

> She does not leave her place; we must go to her. (GP 167)

> In Plato's *Phaedrus* (247a), when the eleven gods travel to Olympus, Hestia alone abides at home. (SD 61)

> To her is attributed the invention of domestic architecture. (GP 169)

> Her image is architectural. (BK 104)

> Her image and her place are identical. (BK 104)

From these passages I draw the conclusion that analysis as a Hestian ritual of the inner must take place in a closed situation. Only there can there be focus. The analyst doesn't make outside appointments, doesn't make house calls, because the ritual is one of place. From its beginnings on Bergstrasse and Seestrasse, analytical consciousness "takes place" in a sacred space giving focus to psychic contents. The architecture must make focus possible.

The inner reveals itself within walls and can be extracted from its misplacement in my past history, my personal life, and the literalism of my relationships. Getting to and entering the therapist's place and departing from it reverberate with the tensions of the ritual of going in and coming out of the Hestian confines.

Architecturally Hestia was paired with Hermes (PP *passim* & GP 169–70). He of the outside, she of the inside. As we move ever more into a Hermes hypertrophy—cyberspace, CD-ROMs, cellular phones, satellite, 300 cable channels, call-waiting, virtual realities—I can be connected everywhere "outside" and will require ever more desperately the centering circular force of Hestia to keep from evaporating into space. In this age of excessive Hermes, classical Jungian inward analysis as a ritual observation of Hestia may be more necessary than ever before.

On the specifically sexual wrongdoings in therapy:

> [Hestia] is immune to Aphrodite's power and…to Eros's arrows. (BK 104)

> Sexuality must be hidden from Hestia…her wish never to marry. (SD 56)

You are familiar with the story of Hestia nodding by the hearth when Priapos crosses the threshold into her domain to assault her, but she is awakened by the warning bray of an ass and wards him off. The fire of Priapos does not belong in the glow of the hearth. Direct rampant sexuality lacks interiority. This bugaboo that has erupted into analysis from its very first case with Josef Breuer, and the ethical purism with which it is resisted, belongs to the myth and ritual of Hestia. In Rome, for example, the vestal attendants in her cult were virgins. If any were sullied in any way, whether by seductive walking, longish hair, immodest dress, or even too flighty an attitude, they could be, and were, buried alive in a chamber in the earth, sealed off, and "deleted" (that's the word in the text), as our profession deletes the name from the list of analysts, excommunicates them from our society. Our quiet conformism enacts the rituals of an ancient cult, thereby affirming ourselves in that cult. Our sexual purity in regard to analysis is more than moral American puritan correctness; it is required by the goddess of the "inner."

A last set of passages may come as a surprise, because of our severely Manichaean ontology that so radically divides "in" from "out." Hestia, we might suppose, belongs wholly to the within, even if she is described as impersonal, unimaged, unemotional, and unerotic. These passages say something surprisingly different.

> With Hestia, we are in the collective domain. It is Artemis, not Hestia, who preoccupies herself with solitude. (GP 170)

> Her vantage ground in the Greek polis was the Prytaneion, the common city-hall. (LRF 347)

> …sacred fire…on the hearth of the city-hall; it may have been regarded as the soul and hence the luck of the state. (LRF 353–54) Hestia…is likewise the center of the *oikos,* which does mean residence and abode, but at the same time also means settlement on urban territory and agglomeration. Hestia is represented as sitting on the *omphalos* or navel of the city… (PP 44)

As domestic life belongs to the city, so public life belongs in the private sphere. Since Hestia who is first and center in all cases, city hall and household do not divide. Both call upon the same focus which recollects the governance of impersonal powers over private and public matters alike. To remember these powers our society is obliged to go into analysis to get focused again on the inward flame, but the way out of analysis would also be given by Hestia, that is, by tending that flame in city hall in the rituals of democracy.

III

In conclusion, I would like now to make clearer from this jumble of notes, half thoughts, and quotations just what I have been trying to demonstrate.

First, I wanted to establish the preeminence of the preposition and prefix "in" as a dominant of our analytical ontology. And so I took you through a review of the semantics of "in."

Then, I wanted to demonstrate the approach of an archetypal psychology, to enlist its method in saving the phenomenon, the phenomena in this case being the strong feelings and important values that remain attached to the word "in" even after we applied intellectually deconstructive acid. Even after deliteralizing "in" and recognizing that it is not literally anywhere—the appeal of interior, inmost, inward, introvert, within, would not go away.

I then justified this attachment to "in" as archetypally valid, that is, our love of the inwardness of analysis comes not just from the historical habit of locating soul inside the skin or from the excess of subjectivism and personalism that we have cultivated in our Christian-converted culture since Augustine and Descartes and most "pc" (psychologically correct) thinkers since, including Freud and even Jung. Instead, I claimed that the deep importance is given by Hestia, and that analysis, besides being an enactment in many cases of myths of Eros and Psyche, of Demeter and Persephone, of Hades, of Hermes, of Hercules, and especially of Oedipus in its self-destructive "figuring-outs," analysis is a ritual of Hestia, that attentive focus called "consciousness," and therefore analysis places its practitioners at her hearth.

For me, this uncovering of Hestia among the shards of my deconstructed analytical temple was an immensely helpful revelation, because she does not know the distinctions between public and private, between inner and outer in the sense of psychological insight and political activity, between self and community. In service of Hestia one could hardly be more secret and silent or more communal and societal. The discovery of Hestia among my ruins means also for analysts that if Hestia is she who makes our work sacred, then what a patient does, and what we do, in the city hall to keep its coals glowing is as much part of soul-making as any dream, any memory, any emotion, or any insight.

10

HERA, GODDESS OF MARRIAGE

Marriage involves two worlds—a world of huge ideals and a world of very mundane practicalities. These two sides of marriage symbolically bring together heaven and earth, the old imagery of sky god and earth goddess, or *vice versa*, so that we each suffer the pulls of that pair: "How do you bring together the ideals and the garbage, the wedding dress and the car repairs?" The "marriage problem" is stated in the archetypal image of the two worlds to begin with: not necessarily as gender difference but as directional pulls, one high and vertical and the other low and horizontal. No matter how mundane a marriage may be, anchored in the ordinary daily world, idealization is there all the time, not simply the wedding dress, but all the fantasies of how it could be, should be, desires to be. The home together in a house of your own, the idealized partner, the idealized couple—"aren't they a lovely couple?"—sex at home, double income (which even the government favors), and the feeling between wife and husband as brother and sister.

The other side of the ideals are the practicalities. How does a marriage exist in actuality? It is a convention of society, yes, but it is also a societal convenience. One person watches over the kids and the bags while the other goes off to the toilet in the airport or the mall; one of them holds the trash sack open so the other can put in the garbage. One drives the car while the other looks for the road signs. These are actualities of marriage that go with the wedding dress, the bridal showers, the ideal husband and perfect wife. How hold these parts together? What is the yoke?

A transcription made from a recording of a public lecture, Santa Barbara, California, February 1996. (Earlier versions were presented in Omaha, Nebraska, October 1994, and Berkeley, California, June 1994.)

When the local paper interviewed the people in my little town of Putnam in Connecticut, asking people in their sixties, seventies, and eighties what was best about marriage, the answer was the coupling. Sharing life, being together, coupling.

These two parts were known in alchemy as the fixed and the volatile. One of the early alchemical dictionaries says there is no term more frequent in use among the "philosophers" (those would be alchemists) than the word "marriage." Sun and moon, mother and son, bride and bridegroom, brother and sister, all these alchemical expressions have references exclusively to the joining of the fixed and the volatile. You can decide which one of you is the fixed and which one of you is the volatile or how roles change back and forth. So marriage becomes archetypal, beyond just you and me and our personal lives; and our "marriage problem," a place of enormous unhappiness. Fifty percent of our marriages go into divorce. In Michigan, they're going to start new laws to prevent this from happening so easily. In America, when there's something we don't like we deal with it by making a new law, and some Europeans say that the myth of America is law. Instead of having myths that sustain the culture, we make new laws, and so we need many lawyers because they're the priests of the system. To slow down divorce we write a new law.

The difficulty is that you go into marriage with the expectations both of the practical and the ideal. Then each partner wants to change the other one to fulfill the expectations, and the language becomes, "I can't" or "I won't," a battling between the "I can't change" and "I won't change." Either stuck depression or active warfare goes on all the time. The reality is never equal to the fantasy that one brings into the marriage. There's an excess of fantasy. We imagine this good marriage that includes everything—all the gods—communication, partnerships, support, fertility, friendship, sexual ecstasy, infatuation, creative imagination, loyalty, a place for madness, perversion, rage, everything shall be allowed. Marriage shall hold it all.

The largeness of the marriage fantasy comes partly from Hera because she was the great goddess, a queen who embraced a great deal, including her husband, Zeus, who embraced even more. Our American marriages should be fantastic and announced in *The New York Times*. The earlier marriages—Victorian marriages—certainly did not embrace that much. Mr. and Mrs. still called each other Mr. and Mrs. years after. They never showed themselves naked, did not use first names, had long silences in their relationship and kept apart great parts of themselves, their fantasies, their dreams; marriage provided a container for the quiet desperation of interior life. A man was a husband (as the word itself says), a good provider, who kept matters husbanded, under control; and the woman was a housewife (that is, she took care of the house).

Hera offers the desire to be married: this mad "wanting to be coupled" that comes over us at an early age, that carries a huge amount of archetypal meaning as if it were salvation. This is not the same as finding a "significant other," the right person, and so on. Rather, this driven necessity, the urge to mate, is not merely genetic, sexual; it is ontological; to be mated, to be coupled. Wanting a husband, wanting a wife—and the other side is a terrible fear. The fear of being coupled, the fear of being mated, which is the fear of the goddess. It comes up in a film, *Four Weddings and a Funeral*, where the main figure is afraid all the way along of marriage at the same time longing for it. These are two sides of Hera—the longing for coupling and the fear of it.

Another way she appears in the psyche of marriage is as a cow. She was worshipped as a cow, the nourishing, stable, receptive sense that once one's married, one has a cow. Hera's cow says there will be stability, there will be nourishment, there will be regularity, there will be calmness, there will be order, there will be a stable smell. She (cow-Hera) was called "cow-eyed."

The cow is also property, so a third aspect of Hera in marriage is property: dowry, prenuptial agreements, and so on. The laws of property; the tremendous value that we place on property in our American society. In the beginning in the United States you could vote only if you had property. We live in a Hera world in the sense of the importance of private property—you can kill to keep intruders off your private property. Property is already present in the trousseau, in the gifts that are given at the wedding, in the bridal shower, in the accumulation of property that begins with the engagement and the divisions of property (*your* checkbook and credit card, and *mine*). Remember Ulysses: the heroes of the Greeks were supposed to bring home trophies from their adventures to adorn the house; bring home evidence of victory, emblems, property. And heroes were "the glory of Hera," which is what the word Hercules (Herakles) means.

Hera's element was the element of air, and air has to do with atmosphere. Every marriage and every moment of the day has its own atmosphere, and when one of the partners comes home in the evening he or she feels right away the atmosphere in the house, and if you're not sensitive to the atmosphere in the home, you are inviting discord. There is a kind of quality, of mood, that is the atmosphere—not good to be breezy if a storm is brewing. It goes with running the household, it goes with the moods, the low and high pressures, the weight that hovers over the rooms, and it emanates neither from man nor woman but from the home itself. You can see it in some of Thurber's old cartoons about coming home where the house is like some giant beast or some tremendous encompassing octopus, a mood that overwhelms the movement from the street into the house.

One more of these vital factors that Hera governs is jealousy. Hera was noted in story after story for being a terribly jealous wife. Anything that threatens the couple makes Hera seize up. There are different kinds of jealousy—sexual jealousy, narcissistic jealousy about not getting the right attention, and there's a jealousy that has to do with threatening the couple and that's where Hera shows herself. A husband can be jealous of his wife's job, her friends; she can be jealous of his mother, his relation with their daughter, his work and travel—all can threaten the couple. It's not all sexual.

Here is a little poem by Robert Creeley. It's very subtle because it shows the movement from idealizations to deep coupling:

A Marriage

The first retainer
he gave to her
was a golden
wedding ring.
The second—late at night
he woke up,
leaned over on an elbow,
and kissed her.
The third and the last—
he died with
and gave up loving
and lived with her.

Creeley is saying there is something beyond the fantasies of loving. Simply living unto death would be the ultimate marriage, the deep aspect of coupling.

The idealizations in our culture are extremely difficult. We expect them to be fulfilled. I knew a man who was from the Sudan. One day he picked up the *London Times* and found out he had been married. He didn't know her yet, but he had been married to her. Another man I knew in India had tremendous ideals about marriage. He was a young man and he had romantic, beautiful images in his mind. He went through the entire ceremony and his bride was veiled. When the wedding ceremony was over and she was unveiled, she had had small pox and her entire face was scared with marks. For him the idealization of his image of marriage, of the bride and so on, was over at the moment of the wedding itself.

People go into marriages with different fantasies. One is that it's a sacrament that invites old age and invites death even in the words of the ceremony. Till death us do part. And marriage includes sickness and poverty—the worst. The sacrament contains the shadows of life. Another view, that Adolf Guggenbühl, in his book *Marriage Is Dead—Long Live Marriage!*, lays out very well, holds that it's a vocation, and only some people can do it. Marriage is a calling and not everybody is called to marriage. He claims it is a way of individuation for some people and not for all. So we ought not lay on people that they must be married all in the same way; some people have other sorts of callings. If Elizabeth Taylor marries eight times, it's clear that wasn't her calling. She's a serial marriager; she has another calling. It's not that she failed at marriage; it's that she has some other things to devote herself to.

Another view which I already mentioned is that marriage is a symbolic representation of heaven and earth, on the one hand, practical and, on the other hand, ideal. Hence divorce, from this view, is a radical cosmological horror; it splits heaven and earth. It's an archetypal violent rupture. A rending of the cosmos.

Then a fourth view, which will be amplified as we go further: marriage belongs to the state; it belongs to society, to the community. Zeus and Hera are social stability; they are the state in a way, so we can be married by a Justice of the Peace at City Hall, because marriage is also secular. We recognize that by having both church weddings and legal weddings. Our tax code, our inheritance laws acknowledge that a fundamental structure of the organization of society is marriage. Therefore some can claim it has nothing in particular to do with the persons who are engaged; it hasn't anything to do with God; it hasn't anything to do with symbolic representations. It is a fundamental structure of society belonging to the *polis* or the city or the community.

I said that Hera is the figure who wants us to be coupled, who urges coupling on us. And her coupling is with her brother, Zeus, so it's a very intense coupling, it's endogamous; it's as if her mate is within her own interior. Those feelings you have that your husband is your best friend. Your husband is as close as a brother or that sense that your partner is a sister. That kind of relationship of inner intimacy and familiarity is recognition of that Zeus-Hera feeling.

When Hera is uncoupled troubles break out. I can read you (from the *Homeric Hymn* to the Pythian Apollo) a little example of archetypal troubles. Hera had given birth to the monster Typhaon once when she was mad after Zeus himself was giving birth to glorious Athene in his head (he went off and gave birth to Athene out of the top of his head), and the lady Hera got angry then. To her, he was separating out from the marriage. Un-coupling. And the lady Hera got angry then and said this to the gods who were assembled. "Listen to me all you gods and goddesses how Zeus who gathers the clouds has begun to dishonor me after he has made me his dearly beloved wife. Without me he has given birth to bright-eyed Athene who stands out from all the blessed gods. But my own boy, Hephaestus, the one I myself gave birth to, was weak among all the gods and his foot was shriveled and it was a disgrace to me, a shame to me in heaven, so I took him in my hands and threw him out and he fell into the deep sea."

She's tough, Hera! Let's not forget that. When her mate did something on his own, she did something on her own. This goes on in our society today—"All right, you're going out to do this, I'm going out to do that." We each have our own necessary drives, we each have to take care of our own *daimon*. So Hera's made a lame son and she throws her son out. She's complaining that what came out of her was lame, whereas what came out of Zeus was bright-eyed Athene! "Well you crafty devil," she says, "What do you plan to do now? How did you dare give birth alone to bright-eyed Athene? Wouldn't I have given birth for you? At least

I was called your wife among the gods who live in this big heaven. Watch out now that I don't plan some trouble for you later on." Get that... Watch out that I don't plan some trouble for you later on.

"She said all this and went away from the gods. Her heart very angry. The lady Hera with her cow eyes prayed and struck the ground with the flat of her hand and said, 'Listen to me now. All of you. And give me a child separate from Zeus and yet one who isn't any weaker than him in strength. In fact, make him stronger than Zeus.'" "She cried this out and beat the ground with her thick hand and then Earth who brings us life was moved. When she saw it, she was very happy and she expected fulfillment. From that point on, for a full year she didn't go once to the bed of wise Zeus, she didn't even sit in her elaborate chair as she used to do giving him good advice." [That's another part of what Hera does.] "No! She stayed in her temples the lady Hera with her cow-eyes...and when the months and days were finished and the seasons came and went for the turning year, she bore something that didn't resemble the gods, or humans at all: she bore the dreaded, the cruel Typhaon, a sorrow for mankind. Immediately the lady Hera with her cow-eyes received it... and used it to do plenty of terrible things."

The three creatures that she brought forth on her own in the state of un-coupledness were Hephaestus, the smith, whose leg was twisted and on backwards; Ares, Mars, the god of fury, battle rage; and this monster, Typhaon. Clearly when Hera is un-coupled all hell breaks loose. And that is the fear of Hera. That fear runs through marriage about breaking the marriage. Let's say men pick up the fear (we joke about men being henpecked, and so on), saying they're afraid of their wives. They're not afraid of their wives, they're afraid of the Hera element. If you break, in some way or another, this marriage situation, all hell will break loose. What happens when the un-coupling happens? Out of the goddess of marriage itself comes this violence; the Mars, Hephaestus, and this monster, Typhaon.

There's another subtle important aspect in the myths of Hera: she has three phases or three faces. Hera the young, virgin, bride who is called Hebe. Hebe didn't make it into our culture except pathologized as "hebephrenia." That diagnosis no longer means much in the DSM, merely a disordered subform of schizophrenia. Earlier, hebephrenia referred to a juvenile dementia, usually "found" in a young girl who was silly, laughing a lot, light-headed. The mythical figure, Hebe, was the young form of Hera, and the word also means *pubes* in ancient Greek: hence a form of schizophrenia with early, adolescent onset. In many stories Hebe is the bride of Hercules, that is, the Hebe aspect of Hera marries Hera's hero who even contains her name in his. The Hebe-Hercules couple goes on still when the light-headed cheerleader dates the football star.

The next layer of Hera, the second face or phase, is the matron, the powerful woman who rules in society, the married woman. There was a time in our society when unmarried women, divorced women, widowed women couldn't quite join society. The matrons who were coupled didn't want any threat to the coupling. This is the powerful Hera who continues in our notion of the married matron. The third face of Hera was called Chera; she is the left one, the one who is not necessarily old yet she belongs to Hera as the aspect who is either deserted or left alone or is simply left. In Paestum the three phases were represented in topology; three levels of temples from hillside down to seashore.

If you consider these phases as a progressive narration then a woman starts girlish and happy, and then becomes a powerhouse in society, and then her husband runs off and she is left: that cheapens the story. The implication is rather that where Hera is, there is always the giddy young girl, a happy innocent, and there is always the mature woman, and the one who is left alone. There is always a loneliness, there's always a left part. If one lives that as a literal fear then one is living a marriage in which one is always afraid of being left and always having to suppress youthful silliness, the young Hebe. Whereas all three are faces of the goddess.

Now let's be clear, the archetype of the wife is not necessarily a woman—we're in an archetypal psychology and not a gender psychology or a moralistic psychology. Of course, it's very difficult to talk without using everyday language. But the archetype of wife can possess anyone. I mean there are many husbands who are more wives than they are husbands—in their demands, and in their fears, and in their sense of marriage. Besides, gay pairs offer varieties of couplings. The heavenly urge to marry occurs in men as well. I had a man working with me years ago who had already been married twice. He was in his late thirties. He had begun with a new woman whom he wanted to marry, but it wasn't so much *her* as it was getting married. When he walked down the streets, he looked in all the shop windows at dishes, pots, and household goods, and that was his favorite part of window shopping. He went to furniture, went to curtains, he was absolutely obsessed with the housekeeping world of marriage. He wanted to be married. It isn't just women who can be possessed by the coupling, mating, establishing domestic life.

The problem that marriage sets up of course is this coupling, uncoupling—as soon as someone is coupled they want to be un-coupled and soon as they're un-coupled they want to be coupled again—back and forth, back and forth. It is an essential part of marriage because one part of Hera is un-coupled. Part of the time there is a fury when the marriage is broken, but another part of her is archetypally left and is always alone.

It is all there at once. At the moment of marriage, the widow is also there and the divorcee is also there. That psychological fact is not recognized because we put all of our lives into a process of time, so we're afraid of the way it is going to come out at the end. Rather, Hera tells us that the "end" is there on the day of the wedding. A piece of you is left out, archetypally divorced, abandoned.

What Hera cannot stand is a token husband. This doesn't mean that she wants children with her husband, in fact Hera is not called "mother" and has no mother part to her mythology. She is not one of the mothers. Athene was called *mater.* So, mother has a whole other meaning than wife. Hera is insistent upon the *gamos,* the marriage, the union with the husband, the pair, the coupling. So, she doesn't want a token husband because that frustrates the deepest meaning of the union, making her furious and enraged with Zeus, because he is so cavalier about the union at times. She doesn't want an official husband, she wants a mate.

This fact that this old one, or the left one, is there at the beginning shows even in a very young couple when the man turns to his fiancée or his bride or his young wife, who may be only nineteen years old, for perceptions, for insights, for advice—he's asking for and sensing that third person of Hera in his young wife. She may only be nineteen but she's not only Hebe; she's also the matron and she's also the left one. It's already there in her judgment, in her hesitations, or decisiveness, in her perceptions, in the talk they have in bed—which used to be called a "curtain lecture." In Holland and England it was a "curtain lecture" because they drew the curtains around the bed and that's where the wife could really tell the husband what was going on because he didn't know what the hell was going on.

It's interesting to see this development from Hebe to the full matron, and how clever Hebe is under the girlishness. If you saw the movie "The Age of Innocence," Winona Ryder plays this young Hebe girl and she has to deal with her husband who is attracted to Michelle Pfeiffer, a woman with a past, who comes from Paris, who wears strange clothes, who's exotic, romantic, who has Persephonic qualities, who has Aphroditic qualities, and who had made a bad marriage. What deep interesting stuff was in her compared to little Winona Ryder! The movie shows how Winona Ryder maintains her Hera coupling power by becoming pregnant. There can be no divorce, no separation. She has outwitted Michelle Pfeiffer and become a very strong woman at the end of the movie. She's able to hold him within the social setup, and that is the crucial aspect of Hera which we have to come to next.

There is loyalty to society and the function of upholding society and being able to manipulate the social to work within the marriage. The theme comes up again in *Four Weddings and a Funeral*, in a different way. Hugh Grant is attracted to all these different women and can't bring himself to marry any of them, but the woman that he does almost marry or maybe marry is called "Duck-face." Duck-face brings in the duck, a most ancient symbol in China and other places, of eternal pairing. But he's terrified of Duck-face. So we are left with this dilemma again and again: the desire to be coupled or mated and the fear of it.

Marriage is riddled with the fear of one or the other breaking out of it. Here is another marriage poem, "The Dream," by Felix Pollak: "He dreamed of an open window. A vagina said his psychiatrist. Your divorce said his mistress. Suicide said an ominous voice within him. It means you should close the window or you'll catch cold said his mother. His wife said nothing. He dared not tell her such a dangerous dream." An open window suggests going out, unconfined, uncoupling. He dared not tell her such a dangerous dream because of the raging fury of Hera.

Now what about Zeus? Why is he always going out the window? He brought forth through Themis the Three Fates; through Eurynome, he brought forth the Three Graces; with Demeter, probably Persephone; with Mnemosyne, the Muses; with Maia, Hermes. He was also the father of Apollo, Dionysus, Artemis, Athene, Hercules. He appears as an inseminating bull, and in other animal shapes.

Yet they are a brother-sister in eternal embrace. In Paestum you can see a low covered shrine, with a huge heavy slab of roof on it, and there Zeus and Hera are underground in the dark making love and have been forever and forever and ever after. Eternally coupled and at the same time he's out the window. Why does it occur to the important, successful man to be philanderer or a womanizer? The main attacks on Zeus in the anti-pagan Christian writers is that he was a philanderer, hardly a high sky god! He was wanton pleasure, as they said, and he went with nymphs and goddesses and humans and anything going, and he put on all these animals modes. We have to connect the sexual, generative powers with his imaginative powers because out of the Zeusian imagination came such a variety of other forms. He was chief among the gods because he could imagine the nature of Dionysus and imagine the nature of Apollo and of Hermes and of Athene. His imagination could embrace all these various potencies. So there is something about the imagination in that little poem of Pollak—his imagination is an open window. It goes beyond the confines of the house; and Hera, I believe, is a great literalist. She cannot imagine in the same way: just look at Typhaon! So if he goes out the window, then he is disserting the depths of the coupling, and their story is a constant struggle between the fixed and the volatile (to use that alchemical language again). It doesn't mean that one or the other partner must go out as a bull or a swan, but it does imply that the imagination must go out, must follow its dangerous dream. One of the Hera mistakes in our culture is the moral censoring of the imagination.

Another story from the classics, this one is from Virgil's *Aenead*. The story of Dido, and mentioned again in Shakespeare's *The Merchant of Venice*: "In such a night stood Dido with a willow in her hand upon the wild sea-banks, and waft her love to come again to Carthage" [V.1.9]. Dido was the queen of Carthage who fell in love with Aeneas, a son of Aphrodite/Venus (so we get where he's coming from, as they say—"Where are you coming from?" "I'm coming from Venus."). When he lands in Carthage (after the fall of Troy and on his way to found Rome), she uses a little ruse to get them together. She takes his little son on her lap. Metaphorize that. Through the relationship with "his little boy" they begin their amour.

She, however, is under the patronage of Juno (Hera). The lovers arrange an assignation in a cave and they go off into darkness to fulfill their union. They couple—or do they? Can they? If we don't know the myths, we don't understand what fantasies we have when we go into a union. When we go into the bedroom we don't know which myth we are enacting. He goes into the cave with the fantasy of a child of Venus. For him this is a pleasurable, delightful experience. But she is under the guidance of Juno. She goes in with the marriage fantasy of deep coupling. Soon after he gets a message from Hermes that he must get on with his job which is to go found Rome, and so he sets sail. She's absolutely destroyed. Desertion, betrayal. For him it's not a betrayal because he came with a different fantasy. For her, it is a radical violation of the laws of the universe, the very Queen of Heaven. And she never forgives him, because she appears in the Underworld still enraged, embittered forever. There's a lot of instruction in that story. What is the fantasy that governs a relationship? What myths are at work when lovers meet? Are their fantasies coupled?

Perhaps I have been making Hera rather heavy. So, we have to realize that she also belongs to the basis of comedy. The classical form of comedy presents ending in a coupling. *A Midsummer Night's Dream* would be the perfect example. All four pairs get coupled. Many of the movies that are called light romantic comedies are about boy gets girl or girl gets boy. They end in the union of the two. This was the classical form of comedy. A comedy has a much deeper meaning; all things are now in order because heaven and earth are joined, and comedy also means that when two people get together there's a lightness to life itself. If one could play those two parts of the marriage instead of the practical verses the ideal. If one could take marriage both lightly and seriously, play the comedy and the depth, put those two together (rather than the two that I mentioned at the beginning). How do you live the comedy and the depth—not only how do you live the practical and the ideal.

We come now to a few further essentials of Hera. To begin with, the house. The first object, the oldest temple to Hera, is a stone house: one door, two windows, and a low roof. Like the little drawings you may have drawn as a child in kindergarten. At Paestum, which is near Naples, there are three Hera temples. Paestum was a very sacred place to Hera, and these superb temples are still standing, despite the shaky nature of the earth there. If you think back to all the times you play house as a child, or had a dollhouse, or made little houses out of cartons and boxes, this is an archetypal move going on. We forget that the house is not just something made by an architect and sold you by a developer. House-keeping is taking care of Hera. In Christian thought, Platonic thought, New Age thought, the body is a house; the temple of a soul. I like to think the house is also the body of Hera. What one does for the house, to the house, with the house, is taking care of Hera. Housekeeping is a Hera activity. Our culture recognizes this. Think of the enormous quantity of house magazines: House and Garden, House Beautiful, Home Decorating, Architectural Digest, World of Interiors, the home section of newspapers, home improvement on TV, supposedly a best-selling TV show or one of the most watched, "This Old House."

Realtors are a most important political organization in the United States with huge influence. This realm of Hera almost dominates the economy because the house is the main financial asset of the citizen. Here we have to make clear a distinction between Hestia's interiority and focus, and the *domus* or *oikos*, the management of domesticated life. The household economy, living together under one roof, being able to provide for all, including visitors and strangers. Juno Moneta (from which our word "money" derives) was a cult title of the goddess and refers to the temple in Rome where money was coined.

Still, in the Middle Ages Hera's influence continued. All products given to the lord of the manor together with the fees that were levied on slaves and taken into the royal household, or the duke's household, or the count's household, were placed according to the domestic rules under the supervision of the Lord's wife who, being a woman, managed the private sphere. She managed the household. The household was the house, and it was also the people, the animals, and the things, and the caring of all of that. Today we feel managing the household to be such an enormous burden, without recognizing that all those things are forms of power and gratification. For many people, caring for things of their house is a most pleasurable activity. Maintaining, renovating the house, redecorating the house. Every few years getting new curtains and starting the whole thing again. For other people this seems absolutely insane, but that's a drive of Hera, to maintain this temple.

I know a woman who decorates people's houses. You pick out the furniture and the fabrics—then she'll lay out the paintings you should have, what repros you should have on the wall, and the bric-a-brac and what colors the walls should be and so on. She told me that in every one of the cases that she works with (of married couples), the woman picks out everything in the house and the entire house belongs to her except for the husband's desk and his playroom and maybe the garage. He has his little area and the rest of the house is hers. He makes no decisions about what color the upholstery should be or the kinds of window shades.

Often when you go to people's houses the wife shows off the house while the husbands talk shop. "Come, let me show you my house; I want to show you the house." She's showing a part of her Hera nature.

In Switzerland, they say that as soon as a couple begins to talk about moving and building a new house (that is, they've moved up the economic ladder), it is the first hint of divorce. When they break up their house they've broken up their marriage. The house is more than just a thing you move from here to there. It is a symbol of Hera's mating. A man stood up at one of the men's retreats at which I used to teach and said that they were building a new house, and his wife went off with the builder. The builder was closer to the feeling for "house." So don't underestimate what you do around the house and how important it is. Coming back from a business trip you stop and, like a Greek hero, you bring back something for the house. Caring for the house, the house begins to care for you. You find that it gives you pleasure to come home. Or it gives you pleasure to take care of it. And I think that's where Hera is, in giving back something to you, for you giving to her body in the house.

There are these old sayings (whether you go with the gender of them or not): a woman likes a man who can do things around the house, and she hates it that she always has to pick up after him and he leaves things in a mess. By desecrating the house that way, he insults Hera. And a man likes a woman who's a good housekeeper. These are Hera statements. Another one: She loves the house more than me. And the jokes: A man is making love to a whore and she says, "You're the greatest;" and when he's making love to his mistress, she says, "I love you so much." But when he's making love to his wife, she says: "I wonder what color we should paint the ceiling." Now, that is a nasty gender joke, but it isn't! She really loves the house. That's crucial and shouldn't be treated as just a kind of obsession. Her obsession with the house equals his obsession with sex.

So, in a sense, Hera is also the goddess of maintenance, keeping up the appearance. In the movies done by Merchant and Ivory, it's all household stuff: scene after scene of household stuff. All the silver polished and all the furniture polished and everybody so happy watching those beautiful interiors. The house responds to gifts, to flowers, to *objets d'art*. It's filled with memories. On the one hand, it's all cleaning up, fixing, endless repetitive routine; let's get away. On the other hand, the pleasures of these routines, the deep satisfaction that the furniture gives.

One last thing about Hera and clothing. The great goddess in the temple of Samos, says Kerényi, did not begin to look like a goddess as imagined by those who wanted to please her until they had dressed her, pleased her with the clothing. Dressing Barbie dolls is a beginning of that. Buying all those little things that you put on and take off the little figure. That's part of the cult of Hera, and is not only Aphrodite—who anyway is more often depicted partly unclothed.

I mentioned Juno and that her element was Air and a special place of her body was her brow. A person had a clear forehead, a beautiful brow. But it's not simply an unfurrowed brow and the well-separated eyebrows; it's something more to do with the upper regions that Hera aspired to. There's a social climbing aspect to Hera as well. She grants social status by taking someone into her world. Her metal at Paestum was silver. Think of silver wedding presents and the place of silver in the bourgeois household system. This brow thing further implies an overview over the entire establishment.

A married woman had social status and could display her lofty position by receiving guests. We still use the word "reception": "We're having a reception. She's giving a reception." Corresponding with Zeus's great imagination is her great capacity for reception which expands her dominion by taking in all comers. When one has a house, when one is married, we can receive guests, give dinner parties, receive all kinds of people from everywhere and show hospitality. That's one of Hera's great virtues.

I want to repeat that it is a mistake to assume that this pair must be a mother and a father and remind you that Hera was not called "mother." In myth her mothering is rather monstrous: the figures that she brings forth, and how she treats her son Hephaestus. Probably mothering in the usual sense gets in the way of the social function, the political function, the hostess function, the reception that the Hera life is.

Sex, however, is part of the coupling. It's not something independent of the coupling. Mating is with the mate for the sake of the couple.

It belongs to their life together, Zeus and Hera's, a life more a snuggle and struggle rather than some aphrodisiacal paradise or ecstatic Dionysian abandon.

There's one final thing to mention. The first day of every month in the Roman calendar was called *Kalends* from which we have the word calendar. The first of the month meant the first of the lunar month and therefore was associated with the menstrual period. That day belonged to Juno, so the structure of the schedule of the calendar, the organization of the official, social laws of the state, and the interior rhythms of the woman's body were all connected. In Rome, *juno* was the word referring to a woman's *genius,* or inner daimon.

It's not merely an external thing, what goes on in society. Society is intimately connected in Hera to the psyche and to biological laws. In that way she is the upholder of civilization, of providing the homestead, the economy, the household, the domestication, the husbandry of civilization, so that marriage becomes something dedicated to service to principles higher than personal happiness. The house stands for both civil society *and* my personal property. If he husbands the house, she rules the house beyond their own personal happiness.

References

The Homeric Hymns, translated by Charles Boer (Dallas: Spring Publications, 1970).

Louise Cowan, "Hera," in *The Olympians: Ancient Deities as Archetypes,* edited by Joanne H. Stroud (New York: Continuum, 1996).

Adolf Guggenbühl-Craig, *Marriage Is Dead—Long Live Marriage!,* translated by Murray Stein (Putnam, Conn.: Spring Publications, 2008 [1977]).

Karl Kerényi, *Zeus and Hera: Archetypal Image of Father, Husband, and Wife,* translated by Christopher Holme (London: Routledge & Kegan Paul, 1975).

Philip Elliot Slater, *The Glory of Hera: Greek Mythology and the Greek Family* (Princeton, N.J.: Princeton University Press, 1992 [1968]).

Murray Stein, "Hephaistos: A Pattern of Introversion," *Spring: An Annual of Archetypal Psychology and Jungian Thought* (1973): 35–51.

——, "Hera: Bound and Unbound," *Spring: An Annual of Archetypal Psychology and Jungian Thought* (1977): 105–19.

Robert M. Stein, "Coupling/Uncoupling: Reflections on the Evolution of the Marriage Archetype," *Spring: An Annual of Archetypal Psychology and Jungian Thought* (1981): 205–14.

⟜✠⟞

11

HERMETIC INTOXICATION

Millennial Psychology

A the end of a century, a *fin de siècle* mood with its foretellings and forebodings hangs over these last years of an eon that stretches back to the beginning of our calendar. Yet we must not forget that a millennial psychology is specific to a Christianized world. Mohammedans have another myth affecting their calendars, as do the Jews. The rest of this great globe filled with archaic and sophisticated tribal peoples, nomads and pagans of all sorts, Hindu villagers in Bihar and Mysore, the billions of bodies living in East Asia, in tropical Africa and America—all do not have the same millennial myths and millennial psychologies. All these peoples may use our imposed calendar, and though its dates have been missionarized—f not by religion, certainly by business—their worlds do not threaten with an end of time, because they do not date a beginning of calendar time with the appearance of Jesus.

Millennial thinking about the end of the nineteen hundreds, the end of time itself, belongs to our Western sacred book, and that final chapter of fearful horror, *Revelations,* with its catastrophic vision of world conflagration. This anxiety about the millennium and what comes next is a Christian phenomenon, since much of official dogmatized Christianity belongs to this city, it is appropriate that we discuss this theme in Milano. Constantine and Constantius (enemy of the pagan, Julian); Ambrose, the

---

Under the title "Millennial Psychology," parts of this lecture were delivered to a general public, Banco Populare Commercio, Milan, May 1996, and expanded into "Hermetic Intoxication," at the Department of Psychology, University of Turin. A revised version was presented at the Center for the Rocky Mountain West, University of Montana, Missoula, October 1996, under the title of "Intoxication by Hermes: The No Place of Cyberspace," as a contribution to the series *Human Place and Cyberspace.*

great defender of the dogma; and Augustine himself taught here. If we wish psychologically to work our way through the anxiety constellated by the end of this century, we do well to begin in this particular place.

By situating the millennium within a global context, I am attempting to make two psychological moves. Both derive from the foundational work of C.G. Jung. The first move Jung called "relativizing the ego," that is, by situating our Western concerns within the broader context of world myths with many different calendars and dates and ideas of time and eschatology, the Christian perspective becomes only one among many, only relative rather than ultimate. As well, our futurism—projections about what lies ahead—become statements of a Western ego, casting its own shadow forward. As the ego does not represent the whole psyche, so the Western mind cannot speak for the whole world.

The self-importance we give to our worries about the end of the century and the futuristic projections we make about what will come next, in fact the very agenda books we buy with dates already printed: December 31, 1999 and January 1, 2000—all this is relativized by the awareness that these numbers have little significance when one steps outside one's own fixations predetermined by the basic myth of Christianized time-consciousness.

This inclusion of global variety is my second move. It derives from Jung's notion of collective consciousness—the attitudes, anxieties, opinions, tastes, desires, habits of mind and heart that we all share. They are in the air we breathe, the light we see by.

Basic to collective consciousness today is global awareness, multiculturalism, planetary thinking, multinationalism—the sense that all things private and personal and local are always being impinged upon by what others are doing everywhere. The music on your radios blows in from London recording studios, the bananas transport their toxic insecticides and preservatives from Ecuador, the shrimp bring with them Gulf of Mexico, as the computer chips import onto your workstation molecules from Ireland, India, Texas, and Korea.

Multinational consumerism, tourism, and the worldwide web of Internet communications are the evident and superficial levels of this collective consciousness, this globalism. Within it, and permeating globalism as a subliminal mood, is a sense of diffuse identity, an anxiety about borderlessness, what we in clinical psychology refer to as borderline personality disorders, panic attacks, paranoid defenses, and narcissistic rages. That is, diffuse borders and paranoid purisms, as well as retreats into intense, isolated self-centeredness, worries about one's immune system, with hatred for everything invasive (including immigrants), a syndrome of characteristics owing to the loss of personal certitude, self-definition and location within well-defined borders.

Globalism and Futurism translate in the individual to panic anxieties and narcissistic retreats.

To find again these personal and local borders we sometimes revert to hostile measures of exclusion. We try to resist the incursions of the Other into our private sphere. We join separatist movements, pledge allegiance to cults where the Other merely mirrors me, thereby avoiding the challenge of difference.

These regressive defenses against dissolution attempt to recapitulate the older security structures of the ego, prior to its displacing and deconstructing by globalism. These moves take political form in xenophobia, ethnic cleansing, genocide, or in retreating to a Lombard League with its echoes of earlier Italian and Mediterranean city states, or walls and fences at the U.S. border and the Israeli border. All these moves attempt to achieve what Jung called the "regressive restoration of the persona" or *status quo ante*, by means—in the political sphere—of literal localism. We see this in Israel, in Chechnya, in Bosnia and Croatia, in Cyprus, and among the Basques and Catalonians in Spain.

Enter Hermes

From the perspective of an archetypal psychology, the fascination with exchange between peoples everywhere, the hypercommunication of globalism, the emphasis on trade and finance, the instantaneity offered by electronics, the compulsion to travel—all this indicates the mythical cosmos of Hermes-Mercurius, the fleet-footed god with wings on his feet, cap of invisibility, and winged thoughts.

Globalism feels like an overdose of Hermes, just as the age of reason suffered from an overdose of Apollonic sunlight and an excess of the normalizing rationality of Minerva. Or, for another example of divine hypertrophy, the madnesses of Mars that so seizes a people that any common man and woman can become an enraged killer.

As the century turns, a monotheism of Hermes holds us in thrall. Not only his new instrumentarium, but the acceleration with which each new generation of these tools and devices is developed—obsolescence within eight months, each device surpassed by increasingly expanding improvements, ever wider reach, ever quicker connections.

A second area where Hermes rules is the marketplace—the stock-market place. Mutual funds, speculations in currencies, commodities, futures, options, derivatives, hedges. The markets of the world connect today by instantaneous communications, allowing for giant shifts of money from one place to another, one currency to another, one market to another. What once was chronic long-term investment is now quick Hermetic turnover. The market as a game; as we say "playing the market."

These giant shifts of money are shadowed by giant scams and thefts, by laundering and deceptions. Accounting systems can no longer keep up with the fast moves of the bankers who handle millions and billions of dollars per transaction. Governments cannot control the multinational corporations or govern the fluctuations of currency, the price of gold, and basic commodities, or the value and amount of their own money supply.

Once Saturn ruled money. In the old books of symbolism, Saturn was called a moneybags. He was depicted with a tightly closed purse and declared god of the mint. Now, with this hypertrophy of Hermes, money is no longer solid coin nor backed by gold, only words and numbers, mere messages sent by electronic data processing and represented by a little oblong of embossed plastic.

In many places where Hermetic finance has reached its apogee, the fundamental importance of home and land have fallen to Hermetic intoxication. The earth and its buildings that give stability and shelter find their value determined by speculative development and mortgage rates. Hermes, who himself has no resting place or permanent abode on earth, has brought his impermanence and quick turnovers of value directly into our human habitations.

One aspect of Hermetic intoxication deserves special psychological attention. I refer to the appetite for information. If you recall, Hermes was the messenger of the gods, and an indiscriminate messenger. This because he carried all messages without actively entering into the content of what he carried. He had no opinions, values; he made no editorial comments; he did not censor. His task was to make communication possible, even communication with the realm of the dead and the world below.

We may find Hermes as a painted and sculpted image in Greek pottery and marble, in easy association with both Apollo on the one hand and Dionysus on the other, with Aphrodite, and with Athene and Artemis, with Zeus and Hades, and even Hercules, though Hermes himself was not heroic by any means. Information takes no positions, carries no grudge, and thus has no limits—it is *toujours disponible*.

In a culture that has lost the gods, a culture from which the gods have withdrawn, we have the messages but they do not carry the gods' meanings. Mere "information." Yet Hermes, in his dutiful faithfulness to his archetypal role, passes on the information, indiscriminately facilitating the messages regardless of their content, which may as easily be a blog, a joke, an ad, a sexual come-on, or a revelation of crucial political significance. The word "information" itself has become so inflated that it carries the code of an individual's DNA identity and destiny. Not wisdom, not knowledge, not inspiration, not learning, not comfort, not truth, not prophesy, not moral value or aesthetic beauty. Instead of messenger of the gods, Hermes has become servant of the Internet.

When we say, as in the popular guides to mythology, archetypal psychology, and astrology, that Hermes is the "god of communication," we must recognize that communication cannot belong to only one god. There are many modes of communication. For instance, there is the connection—wordless, intimate, and sensate—between lovers, between mothers and babies, between patient and nurse, between animals and their caretakers. There is communication by means of the daily delights of life: flowers, cooking, drinking together. There is communication on the level of a Dionysian "participation mystique" when all rock together at a large outdoor pop music concert, laughing together at comedians on the screen. There is the communication of the thunderbolt of Zeus, the flash of inspiration, of enlightenment, the *coup de foudre* of falling in love with an utterly unknown person. There is the gestural communication among warriors in formation, even between enemies in the battling contests whether in warfare or on the football field, and between a cruel Saturnian prison guard and his prisoners.

There is also the communication of teaching and learning, slow, painstaking, and without the flash and fun of Hermes. Communication also proceeds through art and craft, whether through a piece of artwork that communicates by means of a spark that leaps from the artwork into the eye and heart of the beholder, and then to his or her hand to make another artwork.

Hermes, please, is not the only means of connection. It sins against the pantheon of polytheism to assume that Hermes is the sole god who governs communication. This monotheistic usurpation of all these different modes into the Hermetic elevates the electronic media to prime position in our *instrumentarium*. Moreover, this Hermetic intoxication gives an exclusive definition to communication, neglecting the arts, the body, the subtleties of sensate silence. And this hypertrophy of Hermes assumes that your PC, iPod, Blackberry, PlayStation, Xbox, ATM, or whatever else has become your "server," have actually become indispensable *chirungas* for "getting the messages," "keeping in touch," "enabling" you to be in life and enjoy it. Besides, the degradation of Hermes to convenient instruments of clever wizardry degrades the god to a chip. And if the chip is programmed to work on the 1-or-0 principle of either/or, then Hermes no longer is the god of "go-between," of ambiguity, as the myths present.

To make this degradation clearer, let me use a parallel regarding the hero. The ancient hero served the city; in fact it was on the tomb of a hero that an ancient city was founded. The original idea of hero meant one who was between the human and the gods, and who helped bridge the difference between the mortals and the immortals. Whether mythical like Hercules and Aeneas or human like Alexander and Julius Caesar, heroes were imagined to have a human and a divine parent, thereby incorporating both natures in one figure. Jesus Christ is imagined in this same archetypal pattern.

Now, as Hölderlin, Rilke, and Nietzsche have said, the gods are no longer with us; they have found this modern human world not quite to their liking—or if not withdrawn or dead, they are certainly less among us than before.

Instead, "all the gods are within," as Heinrich Zimmer said. They have become psychologized, functions of the human psyche. So the hero becomes internalized as a psychological component, renamed "the ego," that figure in the psyche who leads the way, decides the course of action, and overcomes the monsters of unconsciousness. But this hero, without the gods, without the limits set by them, is merely secular ambition, careerism, brutal strength, misogyny, and an enemy of nature. Ego incorporates all the qualities of the ancient hero, but has lost his *raison d'être*—the service to the gods, the founding of civilization, and the bridging between human life and the transpersonal myths and values. Nothing remaining but the overweening heroic pride, the egotistic hubris of Western secular culture.

Drawing the parallel with the hero as secular ego, we find that Hermes has become secular messenger. No longer of the gods, and instead infiltrated with the monotheism that has lost its viable credibility as lord of all dominion. The former Omniscience has become the overall broadband reach; Omnipotence, the virtual reality that can stimulate all things; and monotheism's divine Omnipresence, the instantaneity of ethereal connections and satellite photography that can observe and map every phenomenon of the planet.

Hermetic intoxication may also delude us. After all, wasn't Hermes the master of deception? He is a thief, a conniver, a trickster, a surreptitious nightwalker. Is it Hermes who suddenly drops the call, makes the computer not function, neglects to back up what I just wrote, finds ways to infiltrate bugs and viruses that destroy whole programs and irreplaceable data banks? Perhaps it is Hermes, the god of merchants, who convinces the consumer that one needs more capability, faster processing and more peripherals than one will ever use, selling us the latest software before we have fully utilized what we already have. Is it Hermes who inspires young hackers to penetrate corporate secrets, police files, government records, science labs, and to steal information or jam the hard disk and magically transform the precious into the senseless.

Perhaps it is Hermes who invented identity theft, stripping us of our collective cover, leaving us as a nameless, naked soul. As he leads souls (*psychopompos*) to the underworld, perhaps he makes use of the underworld to lead our souls from the legal identity we hold in our wallets. As *psychopompos* he is also a *psychogogos,* a teacher of the psyche, a psychologist, whose main instruction is ambiguity, duplicity like the twin serpents entwined on his staff. Is he undoing our ego-identity for the sake of the soul which is often only experienced first through loss.

A great question haunts me: If my mythical diagnosis is correct and Hermes is the god in the disease, then could Hermes be playing a computer/video game with the whole world? Is the future necessarily electronic, the New Age an information age of media, e-mails, spin, infotainment, virtual reality, cyberspace? Or could we be caught in a Hermes game...I do not mean the games the computer plays, but is Hermes, by means of the silicone chip, playing games with our human civilization?

These suspicions come to mind. That they come to mind is further indication of the presence of Hermes/Mercurius, for deceit is as much his business as is business. We are suspicious not because we are Luddites and against technology, we are suspicious because part of hermetic awareness is to be awake to deception. *Simul similibus curantur*: Like cures like. To catch Hermes is to catch a thief and not only to catch a quick flash of inspiration.

Because Hermes's interactive devices facilitate the mating game of Aphrodite and the tactic of war, the calculations of construction and agriculture, the connections among family, the solitude of Saturn, providing even Jovian enjoyments, no other principals impede Hermes's dominion. With the whole wide world available to you individually, personally, by yourself alone, intoxication follows. One click and I am turned on, the epicenter of a worldwide web.

Google, Internet Archive, Wikipedia resurrect the ghost of ancient Hermeticism, that vast collection of occult wisdom literature, mnemonic images, symbols, and magical practices aimed at the mastery of all knowledge.[1] Its followers from Renaissance Italy to Elizabethan England attributed the teachings to Hermes himself, or to another god of world-knowledge, Thoth of the Egyptians. By means of allegorical, symbolic, and mathematical reductions, hermeticism sought to transpose the physical world into mental space. Data becomes message; the world is angelic; the cosmos hermetic, that is, sealed until disclosed, and the disclosure was also the world's redemption through knowledge. Does this motive still lurk in our contemporary intoxication?

1. For wide-ranging parallels between ancient hermeticism and contemporary cybertheory, see Erik Davis, "Techgnosis: Magic, Memory, and the Angels of Information," *South Atlantic Quarterly* 92, no. 4 (Fall 1993), and also his "Trickster at the Crossroads: West Africa's God of Messages, Sex, and Deceit," *Gnosis* (Spring 1991).

Yet even while Hermes gives this miraculous access, what does he as well take away? Remember, Hermes is god of both finding—and losing; of giving—and stealing.

Imagine a party. A dinner party, a dancing party, a birthday party. Dressing and fashion and interior decoration, anticipation before the event and gossip after the event; imagine the cooking and serving, the wine and the flowers, the bodies and their motions, the flirtations and seductions, the sudden encounter with an old friend, or an old enemy; then think, too, of the subtleties of gesture and language, the tones of voices and peculiarities of speech, regional dialects and little phrases. The perfume.

At the computer an extraordinary array of sophisticated social skills that have taken centuries to elaborate no longer play any role whatsoever. One of the most Hermetic figures of our day, Brian Eno, who has taken part in so many levels of media invention and performance, and thinking about it, said: "The trouble with the computer is that there isn't enough Africa in it." Body. Rhythm. Soul. Social Ceremony.

Civilization depends on its Africa, on the social skills that belong with communication—unless communication be merely dots and dashes sent over a Marconi telegraph. Communication is multileveled interaction, a complex impinging of souls, not merely interactive messages. Moreover, communication is ultimately for the sake of knowing—knowing not only the message, but also the sender and the receiver—who the other is and what bearing the message has specifically for you.

A message is an angel from the Greek *aggelos* (message), through the Latin and theological meanings of a divine message. The angels were many; they had particular names, shapes, depictions. A true message announces something, reveals something, alters something; it brings knowledge of high significance. The voice of the angel was shattering, a trumpet blast, a whirl of black wings in the night. What cellphone can transmit an angel?

Is there a cure for Hermetic intoxication? What can free us of this addiction to instant access and delivery, this delight in the invisible passage of anonymous words through the air, this privilege of possible connection to everyone anywhere?

Neither his father Zeus nor his brother Apollo could truly tame Hermes; he deceived them both. Nor could the goddesses, nymphs, and humans with whom he mated change his ways. With these many female figures he produced offspring, but his copulations did not result in coupling. Only one of all the mythic figures appeared as his counterpart: Hestia. In the Greek world, and then the Roman where Mercurius was paired with Vestia do we uncover an answer.

The Focus of Hestia

Before we begin to talk about Hestia, we should toast her: Before any event, the old Romans said: *Vesta!*, as we, raising our glasses say: *Salud, Kampei, Cheers, Prost, Santé, L'chaim*...She came first, before Zeus, before Hera, Gaia, Demeter.

In other words, first one must be focused, at home in oneself, present here and now. *Focus*, our word in English for the concentrated attention, the interest that warms to life all that comes within its radius, originates as the Latin word for *hearth*. And hearth was Hestia. The place where the home fire glowed was Hestia. This *Focus* was not her symbol; it was Hestia herself.

The name Hestia/Vesta probably derives from the Indo-European *vas*, "inhabit." Another derivation, according to philologists, is from the root, "essence." In short, she is not only "in," as inside the home or in its hearth. She is in the focused intensity and warm interest that we call attentive consciousness. And, like Hermes, she is a quality of mind, an invisibility. He is invisible in his quick passing, "the Hermes moment;" she is invisible as consciousness itself. If Hermes brings possibilities to mind, Hestia centers them and gives them focus. Elemental mercury scatters everywhere into a million bits, whereas salt, her elemental stuff, is the alchemical principle of fixation and immutability.

With Hermes's expansion and placelessness in mind I ask you now to hear these attributes and habits of Hestia.[2] For instance: ancient judges wrote down at the end of each day all things germane to a criminal case and left the writing on Hestia's "altar." Hermes, too, had a connection to writing—but Hestia's writing is exact record-keeping, pinning things down. She governed contracts; Hermes made deals.

Hestian consciousness circles around itself. It goes nowhere, intends nothing outside of itself. So, Hestia was always seated on circular elements, and the places where she was worshipped were always circular.

---

2. See the above "In: Hestia's Preposition" for a fuller phenomenology with references of Hestia.

In Plato's *Phaedrus*, when the eleven gods travel to Olympus, Hestia "alone abides at home." To her is attributed the invention of domestic architecture. Not only the house, the place, the absence of movement—but as well the family: the life and law of the clan. The only actual service performed in her honor was the family meal. The *Homeric Hymn* to Hestia says, "Without you, humans would have no feasts."

How different from Hermes, always moving, no images of him sitting down and passing time with family, sharing food with others. With the laptop, cell phone, iPod, and TV come grabbing a bite, slurping, and snacking on the run. Hermes goes to the restaurant with the world in his bag.

So it was to Hestia that one went for sacred asylum, where one could find refuge and stillness.

Supposedly, the combination of a fixed stationary electronic screen inside your home and its worldwide reach replicates the Hestia-Hermes union. A common altar; a focusing hearth. Inside and outside joined: supposedly, as you sit there, you serve this ancient pair equally.

This argument omits the deeper sense of Hestia. She becomes merely a fixed service station for Hermes, as if the wife who maintains the foyer so that the husband can fly in and out between appointments. She has no value in herself; a mere servo-mechanism. The PC notion of Hestia omits the disciplined devotion to *inwardness,* less to message than to meaning, less to connection outward than to the processes of inwardness themselves, their virginal uncontaminated nature.

Only those processes that have no direct functional use, those that make no connections, communicate nothing, but come before all possibilities—the inwardness of focused life that cannot fall to the seductions of outward temptation, that purity, that *askesis* even, of disciplined attention, self-enclosed as the circle—offers the *gravitas* and counterweight to Hermetic intoxication.

The fact that the Internet, or its equivalent in each country and system, quickly became a pornography exposition and that it is used for many sorts of "virtual" sexual interactions gives further evidence of its solely Hermetic association. Hermes of myth had a strong sexual component. The cock and the ram were especially his animals. He was configured primordially as a phallic herm.

When we look at the carved images of Hermes, we see his sculpted head sometimes with its cap of invisible winged thoughts above, and his well-defined member below. Between head and phallus—only a stone slab. The mind and the sex—two great generative and autonomous powers; but the body of inwardness, of reception and digestion, the heart and stomach and gut, all this is blank. Or sometimes his body is presented as a very slim, very unwounded youth. Hermes, an adolescent hacker?

That the Internet became so quickly sexualized makes it easier to understand the puritanical moves to put controls on cyberspace programs and on television. The censoring against "virtual sex" and the sexual content of television show again the counterweight of Hestia to the lascivious side of Hermes, where communication and connection also mean intercourse.

Hestia, it is said, is "immune to Aphrodite's power and to Eros's arrows." And it is said, "Sexuality must be hidden from Hestia." Her servants, the Vestal Virgins, could be put to death, and were actually buried alive, if they gave off one sign of Venusian allure with their eyes, their gestures, even their dress or their walk.

When Hermes and Hestia are not in a sympathetic rhythm, then they push each other to extremes. Sexuality becomes a major area of their contention, and puritanical asceticism rigidly overrides the fantasy and freedom of desire.

Our electronic generation has already discovered its need for Hestia and puts into practice each day, along with its worldwide hermetic intoxication, deliberately dull and repetitive activities of quiet and intense focusing—gymnastic exercises on aerobic machines, isolated jogging with earphones, as well as Zen, Taoist, Yoga, and other centering rituals of meditation. These behaviors provide counterweight; they offer a Hestian antidote to the Hermetic addiction. We move back and forth between messaging and meditation, between Hermes and Hestia, much as soldiers and sailors used to move back and forth between battle station and whorehouse, between Mars and Venus.

Therefore, deep, prolonged psychotherapy (which I have previously raised questions about) can serve as a Hestian ritual for holding Hermes within the here and now. Classic psychotherapy as proposed and practiced by Freud and by Jung was consistently located in one physical location (Vienna's Bergstrasse and Zurich's Seestrasse on the lake). This long-term, ongoing discipline, interminable and without future, introverted, slow, careful, and intensely focused on inwardness becomes, in this quick digital age, more necessary than ever before.

Here and Now

I want now to explore with you another aspect of millennial psychology, one that follows logically upon what we have already said regarding Hestia and the significance of place. The desire for place, the retreat to homeground, the search for sanctuary—what the Jungians call the *temenos* or vessel of containment—suggest a radical alteration in our thinking and feeling, one that elevates place as a refuge against time.

By place I do not mean space. Let us be clear. Since Newton and Descartes, and especially since Kant, we have conceived a world built upon two principles, space and time. Both are abstractions without palpable contents, sheer vast containers of emptiness without meaning or value, without qualities or differences in themselves. The one like a universal room into which anything can be located by means of geometric coordinates; the other, an endless river of discrete units, each exactly equal to the next, mere contiguous ticks of an invisible tyrannical clock.

Yet now, at this millennial turning, we observe our world engaged in vicious struggles about *place*. People the world over are ready to lay down their lives for particular places, the suburbs of Sarajevo, the rocky villages of Chechnya, city districts of Belfast, blocks of Los Angeles, Kurdistan, Chiapas, trans-Jordan settlements. Of course this is not only a phenomenon of today. Wars over territory are archaic and animal. I am suggesting, however, that these current battles belong to our current symptoms, and it is always to the symptoms that psychology looks for where consciousness is emerging, where paradigms are shifting. The symptom is the first source of psychological insight.

The symptoms of ethnic cleansing and racial hatred (xenophobia) say: "preserve the purity of this place." Allow no alien gods be honored here. Xenophobia is monotheistic in its psychology and literal in its belief in turf, soil, home and Hestia. We may understand its protests best if we seek their mythical roots, and hear their claims as archetypal expressions.

Within the construct of the Hermes-Hestia pair, ethnic cleansing, the extermination of native populations and the demolition of houses and scorching of soil in a frenzy of self-protection are excesses of Hestia paired with the excesses of Hermes—worldwide web of cyberspace and globalism Hermetic communications, where anywhere is everywhere, and the very idea of place has become irrelevant.

As Hermes can go mad with hermetic intoxication when severed from Hestia, so a monotheism of Hestia becomes only fanatical purity, fanatical devotion, the single-focus upon home, homeland, and family relations. No contacts with others; they become an evil empire, an axis of evil. Communication becomes contamination. No nuance, no ambiguity, no Hermes. "Robert McNamara reported that during his seven years as Secretary of Defense there were not even seven minutes of direct communication between Presidents Kennedy and Johnson and President Ho Chi Minh."[3] Under Hestian notions of purified security, Hermetic diplomacy is allowed only through back-door channels, illicit, unscrupulous, undercover and stealth spying. Hestian defense of the "good old local ways" provides a gated barricade against the onrush of a miscegenated multicultural fantasy of the future. The symptoms of ethnic cleansing, tribalism, and xenophobia attempt to hold back this "future." They affirm "place" as protection against the changes that come with "time." They reassert the primacy of place over time as the most important ruling principle for ordering existence. They try to put an end to time.

And this—end of time—is precisely what our current millennial anxieties are about. We imagine an end of time in a literal and spatial manner, a giant cataclysm affecting the whole earth, a global epidemic like ebola and AIDS, warming of the ice caps and flooding, nuclear winter, ozone depletion, universal cancer, universal famine, a universal gaseous night.

I am therefore suggesting that the return to place frees us from the desolation of spatial thinking and the anxiety of time. In fact, we may then deliteralize the Christian "end of time" and its terrifying sadistic vision of *Revelations* into a metaphor. Yes, time comes to a stop as the millennium ends—not literally; the old clocks will continue their little mechanical circles and the calendars continue to have their pages torn off and thrown away. But where we are, and its effects on how we are, becomes the essential consideration of a life. For each place will reveal its local determinants, the gods and *daimones* of the place, whether as a

3. "Briefings," The Watson Institute for International Relations, Brown University (Summer/Fall 1999), 2.

bioregion, as a deposit of tradition, as an architectural composition, as a landscaped mood, a psychic climate. The place you are becomes the essential truth of a life, rather than getting on and moving forward. This psychological way of an "end of time" promotes an ecological, embedded way of life, and one that is also animistic and polytheistic. It also returns Hermes to the pantheon from which he seems to have sprung free and detoxifies that inflation of one god above all others.

The hypertrophy of Hermes fills our days with hurried anxiety, fearing to fall behind. We seem never able to catch up; time is so fleeting, life so fast. We cannot be where we are and instead live in a future, our heads leaning forward, our feet trying to wear his airborne sandals. So we live our schedules, not our days; our appointments and not our rhythms.

The shift of paradigm from time to place, this restoration of Hestia as first among all gods and goddesses, would naturally affect all therapy because the soul would no longer be measured by the time of the body and the time of the world—stages of growth, age in years, our generation, and our period in history. The soul's symptoms of slowness, such as depression, resistance, forgetting, repetition, fixation, could be revalued as rejections of time, motions away from the pressures of time and into the stability of place.

One of the major maxims of the Renaissance was, "Look back to see forward." It was also expressed as *retrocedens accedit,* advancing by retreating. When Brunelleschi designed the dome of the Florentine cathedral, he looked back to move forward, saying "Not even the ancients raised a vault so enormous as this one will be." His notion of progress was governed by ideals of the past, not fantasies of a future, utterly new and independent of precedent.

The backward look reveals the patterns that show themselves repeatedly. They indicate archetypal realities. It is not history that governs the future, but the projections forward of these archetypal patterns. Thus, when Futurology reports hope, progress, and greening, and supports these optimistic prognostics with evidence from space science, biotechnology, lowered rates of infant mortality, more cell phones, refrigeration, longer life expectancy, new ecological awareness—we believe we see reality. We imagine these are the determining facts.

But the reality lies in the eyes that see, not in what they see. For precisely the eye of the Futurologist, informed by another archetypal more Saturnine vision, looks into the future and sees doom and gloom, destruction of habitat and species, floods and famines, civil insurrections, terrorism and plagues—a world described by the great saturnine pessimist Thomas Hobbes as a war of "all against all," and human life as "nasty, brutish and short."

We look back to gain information about the archetypal forms of our insights so that we may understand that all futurisms are fantasies—no matter the evidence.[4] Because present trends are multiple and contradictory, extrapolations from them into the future can lead only to multiple and contradictory predictions. No single vision can prognosticate. Objective realities beyond here and now remain unknown and cannot be known, for that is the meaning of the word "future": that which *is* not and cannot be stated in the present tense. There "is" no future. Future is merely another name for unconsciousness in the mirror of which we see our own subjective proclivities.

Ending as Continuing

It is time to conclude. Time still urges and pushes and presses; we are still in this millennium. Time would move us quickly along, force us out of here, away from this place, so that we may go to another place, a bar, a cafe, a bed.

Or maybe Hestia is calling us home.

So, I shall conclude by saying once again: millennial thinking about the future is an archetypal fantasy. This fantasy seduces us from confronting two fundamental facts of all human existence, of all cosmic existence. First, any actual moment occupies an actual place; and second, life depends on a deep faith in existential continuity. Futurism escapes from the first, always leaving here for elsewhere; and futurism denies the second, by evacuating the certitude of the actual with speculations about a vague and vast unknown.

For the great catastrophe that the future brings is not the future as such, but the effect of Futurism on present life, how it turns attention from what is to what is not, drawing focus from the daily bread and salt and water of the actual to the unknown and conjectural, thereby negating Hestia, and making us all "homeless."

---

4. For five radically different projections of the future, see my *Kinds of Power* (New York: Doubleday, 1995), 226–32.

I have been doing my utmost to restore the centrality of Hestia who can locate us, wherever we may be, in concrete physical life. The hearth is wherever you are actually focused, as hers was also in the midst of the city, in the *Prytaneion,* or common city hall. For whatever the century on the calendar and the time on the clock, this time always takes place somewhere—in a bed, at a table, in an office, on a street. We are all homeless when living only in space and time; and no one is homeless when Hestia is present. She gives each environmental situation a sense of being here, *Da-sein.*

The certitude of the actual—that it is because it is here, and given an eternality that cannot go away and is not subject to time—is similar to what George Santayana, the old Spanish philosopher who lived his last days in "the eternal city," calls "animal faith." It is that feeling in our bones that the earth is beneath my feet, that the sun sets this evening, that the world—whether fearful, tragic, unjust, or senseless—nonetheless does not go away. This animal faith is like the consciousness of animals themselves who have no futurology. Instead, their possibilities of existence are always grounded—that the air is there for the bird's wing, the water there for the fish's pleasure. This ground is always "here," not virtual but utterly here, allowing us the possibility to live at all, allowing us to sleep at night knowing the sunrise will find us in the same place, allowing us to tidy up with faithful gestures of animal certitude after disaster, to bury the dead and serve the mourners a warm and friendly meal.

12

A NOTE ON HERMES INFLATION

Despite our postmodern, polysemiotic, ironic, avant-garde, deconstructed, psychoanalytical sophistication, it is still so damned difficult for us to shed our historical monotheism. I once heard Karl Kerényi, who taught me mythology in Zurich almost fifty years ago, say it was impossible to return to the Greek style of mind. We cannot escape two thousand years of Christianity and its pervasive monotheistic psychology, which favors an abstracting, cohesive, unifying, and centrally organizing viewpoint—or what psychology has baptized as "ego." We seem unable to escape obeisance to "one-sidedness" (Jung's definition of neurosis, by the way), which raises one or another perspective above all others. Thus it is not Hermes who has caught the psychology of our times, but the perdurance of monotheism. Hermes and his computer is merely the fashionable front-man.

The shifts in gods influencing twentieth-century psychology do not indicate a true displacement of the monotheistic model in favor of a polytheistic consciousness. One god rises to the foreground to vanquish all others and then subsides. For a while it was the Great Mother. Neumann, Bowlby, the Kleinians took over the entire pantheon. Earlier there was the dominance of the heroic ego: "where id was there ego shall be," draining the Zuider Zee like Hercules cleaning the stables, resisting the regressive monsters and sirens of the id, like Ulysses tied to the mast, a good-enough husband heading home. We have also had a monocular focus on Artemis and on the Amazons with anti-phallic combative feminism. And, we have had, or been had by, a one-sided identification with the abandoned child, victimized, abused, and sentimentalized.

This response to Bernard Neville was first published in Italian translation by Bianca Garufi and Pierre Denivelle in *Rivista di psicologia analitica* 4, no. 56 (1997), and in English in *Spring: A Journal of Archetype and Culture* 65 (1999).

These vagaries in the patterns of myth influencing psychological theory are merely slight twists in the same kaleidoscope of monocular vision. Each is a point of view, interpreting phenomena in terms of one god or goddess only. Changing the gods, their names, or their locations (from Judah to Attica), or gender (from upward phallic arrow to descending pubic cross) does nothing to the unifying insistence of Western Christianized consciousness (*our* cultural psyche) and its faith in singleness. The shift to Hermes is one more such turn, as if the contemporary psyche were desperately trying to writhe free from the ouroboros of Western History that swallows every emerging potential back into the same unifying loop. Remember what the patristic thought-police said in their debates with the ancient polytheistic texts: "We take prisoner every thought for Christ" (Gregory of Nazianus).

Though Bernard Neville[1] admirably explicates the manner in which Hermes has become the one high god of the contemporary scene, dominating our world from market economics to information-age communication, Neville's discussion remains monotheistic, willy-nilly. For instance, when he accuses Hermetic consciousness of "radical relativism," he misses the psychological experience that while engaged in any conflict, there is no relativism. We are torn between calls; caught, challenged. There is emotional involvement, immersion in and penetration by the issue at hand, called problem, conflict, ambivalence, opposites, whatever. The pathologized moment is always radical yet never relative.

Only when stepping back and theorizing in the reflective stance about polytheistic consciousness can we speak about radical relativism. Only when one has assumed the old ego position of evaluation and choice outside the engagement of myth in life, then many alternatives can seem equally possible. Then one feels able to choose among the myths or the gods. But that posture, too, is mythical; consciousness is reflecting Hercules at the crossroads or unsure Paris asked to choose among the goddesses, or enlightened Apollo musing at a distance. In other words, only the "ego" can speak of mythical complexity as "radical relativism," rather than as dramatic tragedy or the constellation of fate.

The Classical and Renaissance solution to identification with one god, i.e., the monotheistic affliction, was not resolved in syncretism, or

---

1. "The Fascination with Hermes: Hillman, Lyotard and the Postmodern Condition," *Journal of Analytical Psychology* 37 (1992): 337–53.

"getting it all together" by worshipping all the gods, as if standing in a circle and bowing to each in turn. This keeps the old "I" in the center, apportioning attention according to the principle of equity (Apollo? Saturn and his scales? Athene and justice?...) A pantheon is a Roman idea, appearing in a culture that still today gives home to the One True Universal Church (i.e., Catholic).

No, the Greek and Renaissance solution to identification with any single god was the profound realization that never does one god appear alone. The gods are not so much distinct units as interwoven patterns implicating one another. May I refer you here to *Revisioning Psychology*, Part 3, but even more to one of its sources, Edgar Wind's chapter "Pan and Proteus" in his masterful work *Pagan Mysteries of the Renaissance.* There he lays emphasis upon the duplicity of the gods and their inherent involvement with one another. He writes: "The mutual entailment of the gods was a genuine Platonic lesson."[2] He recalls Schiller's verse: *"Nimmer, das glaube mir, erscheinen die Götter, / Nimmer allein."* (Never, believe me, never do the gods appear alone.)

The myths place the gods always in a *complicatio*, that is, internally necessary to one another, often expressed as trinities. Hermes, for instance could be "sided" with Dionysus, with Zeus his father, with Apollo his brother, and with his own underworld aspect. As well, he was closely linked with Hestia and Aphrodite. There was no single Hermes, like a lonely, bare, white marble statue. The epithets of the gods portrayed and betrayed their affinities and polythematic complexities.

Besides, their myths have them squabbling, as Neville says. As we know from our own lives, squabbling is a major form of relating, of being involved with one another, especially where relationships are entangled as among families and close colleagues. To squabble is to be affected, afflicted, even infected by the other. Myths present patterns of contagion, and gods appear first in myths and rituals, only later as isolated figures separated and hardened into symbols. Hermes cannot be singled out and treated alone without falling into a monotheistic consciousness that contradicts the very origin and nature of Hermes in a polytheistic cosmos. The Hermes we are indulging today is one fallen from the

2. Edgar Wind, *Pagan Mysteries of the Renaissance* (Harmondsworth: Penguin, 1967), 198.

brotherhood and sisterhood. He is no longer in divine company. He has lost his association with the gods, become profane.

This is no longer the ancient Hermes, the polytheistic Hermes, but a mercurial mask disguising the same old monotheism of our civilization. This Hermes offers neither help for the wayfarer nor guidance of souls, nor can he link human life to its depths in the underworld and its Shades. Instead, this Hermes is a salesman of the usual salvational program and its grandiosity of hope and faith in progress to kingdom come, now by means of postmodern (de-)constructions, electronic universality, deregulated "free" marketing by players in the "game," and invisible molecular recombinations. What Neville calls the inflation of Hermes is the conflation of Hermes with the secular and singular Western ego.

At the risk of going on too long about a theme I have already written too much about in the course of too many years, I want to discern one crucial difference between archetypal *psychology* and those writings with which Neville has placed mine (Lyotard, Foucault, Baudrillard, Maturana, Derrida) and make clear my alignment with Jung. Because images are the primary mode of thinking and devotion in monotheism's pagan rivals, Hebrew, Christian, and Muslim psychology has been wary of images. "Image is psyche," said Jung. Moreover, Freud began depth psychology by investigating the dream image. This is the *via regia*, he said, the royal road for the return of the repressed.

If images are essential to pagan polytheism and are the stuff that monotheistic consciousness represses, and if images are the way in which the repressed returns, then images are the mode by which the pagan psyche becomes visible, and sticking to them becomes the first step of a polytheistic method. Imagining better describes the method for engaging the repressed than analyzing into meaning or moralizing into positive and negative.

It further follows that conceptual language fails the image and the method of imagining. Therefore, terms Neville uses for critiquing Hermes consciousness such as "relative," "multiperspectivism," "positive and negative" drop from hermetic discourse while the search for a substantial "reality" apart from the image becomes vainly chimerical. Once we stick with the image, it draws us in, iconically fascinating, a resonance of souls. For if image is psyche, then image is soul. (Please note that I use a Jungian word here, a word hard to find in Lyotard *et Cie.*

Hence archetypal psychology is a psychology and not an exercise of the ironic French intellect.)

Despite the unfathomable depth (Heraclitus) to which an image opens and from which our more narrow and fearful consciousness tries to rescue the image by means of interpretative schema, we are solidly founded in a true reality when sticking with the image. It is psyche in its primordial originating shape. That's why archetypal psychology requires no foundation in another so-called reality and why it is not dependent upon an external philosophy, science, or metaphysics. It relates to them, benefits from them and exchanges with them, as Hermes with his Olympian family and friends. But Baudrillard and Neville are quite right: the image requires for its significance no direct relation with any reality posited as more real, more foundational, than the image itself. For psychology, the image *is* the thing itself. Even archetypes, gods, and myths are knowable only as images.

Again, let us keep in mind the fact of our ingrained iconoclastic bias. Of course we have trouble grasping the nature of images. We fear them. We hate them. We kill them. Subliminally we know they are ambassadors of alien gods. If conquering cultures reduced the threat of other gods by physically smashing images, psychology does the same work more subtly. We reduce the image to rationalist explanations and personal history. If we cannot squeeze an acceptable meaning from an image—one that is coherent with our world view—we discard the image as meaningless and wait for the next dream to come along. By separating the image from its divine message, the analytical method for all its fawning on Hermes and hermeticism actually keeps him and all his company at bay.

To work through the Hermes inflation, we have first to restore Hermes to his polytheistic authenticity. This requires restoring images to their primary place as carriers of many kinds of divine messages. Hermes *psychopompos* transmitted the gods' messages by *psychic* means, via the soul, to the soul. Since images are soul per se, the medium of Hermes's message is the psychic image.

For us in practical psychology this means respecting the image as *logos spermatikos,* a spark of divine intention, igniting imagination. The invisibility of Hermes the messenger within the image means that an image is neither a replica, a simulacrum, a representation, nor a derivative of any other reality. It generates out of nothing that we already know, which in no way assumes a nihilism but, rather, an autochthonous source as myths themselves. An image calls out to imagination. Or as Jung said of his interpretative method: dream the myth along.

As Neville says, the grand narratives have been voided. They have been taken to the Underworld; deconstructed, deliteralized, depotentiated. All the way down, neither turtle nor supportive elephant. We no longer look to big integrative ideas from, say, Hegel, Teilhard de Chardin, Toynbee, or even Einstein for living our lives. Hermes has taught us to treat ideologies hermeneutically (to meet them with suspicion) and hermetically (to search theories for their secretly hidden images). Hermes as God of Invisibility has become Master of Paranoia. And so all the old virtues of intellect prized by other gods (Saturn, Athene, Apollo, Metis, Zeus)—coherence, universals of explanation, laws of logic, axioms, verification, and deep thoughtful construction—have become deceptions, a white patriarchal con game. Hermes-Mercurius who once was a god of the versatility of word and mind and writing is his own undoing, deconstructing his own virtues, cheating the human world of any true grounding.

This leads Neville to say we are floating in a sea of images. Suppose, however, these images are life preservers after the shipwreck of titanic modernism, each grand narrative, such as Marxist economics, social Darwinism, Freudian Oedipal theory, is competitively more inclusive, more inflated than the next, each supposedly unsinkable as permanent truths.

Instead, suppose or imagine each image floating by contains its depth, its story, and its values. We need but take hold of one and not let it go, letting it prove the eternal buoyancy of myth and its beings. We have never given the image a chance to realize all it can offer in our iconoclastic culture, traces of which still besmirch even Neville's excellent article which speaks of images as "only" images. Have we not yet realized that all depth lies on the surface and that the gods display in the detail, the phenomenon itself, and not the overarching philosophy from which the profound and distinct eachness of the phenomenon must be saved. Images may keep us afloat in the actuality of life, our actual lives lived without fundamental anchor and without hope of being fished from the sea by some godly fisherman in the salvational net of a grand narrative.

Sometimes my polytheistic intoxication lets me imagine things from the other side. Then it seems to me that the gods have been deprived of images for so long that they have been going quite mad, finding only concepts and abstractions and formulae in which to settle down. And they are uncomfortable there. Not enough fun, not enough fantasy; too much definition, their *complicatio* and ambiguity too easily brought under human control.

I find myself believing that the immortals—as the Greeks spoke of the gods—desire visibility among the mortals. They long for adequate images. Otherwise they remain literally invisible and are homeless on earth. They seem always to have had an affinity with, and a desire for, images. From the earliest cave paintings, history everywhere shows our recognition of their desire. Wherever humans have gone, we set up their images to support our cultures, much as we now set up electronic, media, and mercantile images, as an impoverished way of honoring Hermes.

I like to believe that the gods in their frustration try in every which way to awaken our imagining capacities by forcing images upon us—in dreams, in fantasies, in memories, in fears and pornographies. Since the secular world no longer invites the gods into its images—having banned beauty from its schools of image-making and confined the invisible powers to "religious" art, "outsider art," and the art of the "insane" and their therapies—what can these powers do but press their presence upon us in distorted forms, such as the current obsessions with Hermes that Neville catalogues. Their desperation, their imageless homelessness drives them into the last place available: the human mind. As Heinrich Zimmer said years ago, "All the gods are within." And as Jung continued, "The gods have become diseases." Their insanity has become the root of ours.

A major sign of this insanity is the insane way our times uses the word "image." Having been severed from its immortal associations, it can be affixed to any transient mortal event from pixels to personas to pop pictures. Images require a cosmology that gives them value and holds them in order from within. That's why Vico said that the *vera narratio*, the truth of myths, are important for ordering the imagination.

At its beginning, depth psychology must surely have pleased the gods. It invited the repressed to return. But the repressed returned within an utterly secular and scientistic cosmology. Thus Hermes, deprived of his depth and his divinity, became secularized, merely slippery, deceiving, seductive, commercial, a thief and a liar, as Neville writes, and his inventiveness and invisibility became electronic technology.

I imagine him urging us to find more valid images to hold the invisibles; he is asking to be freed of the glass and plastic altar of our PC monitors and be given a more welcoming and beautiful place on earth. The construction of such image receptacles means depth psychology must not fail the battle in the mind launched by Freud (against the illusion of religion) and Jung (against the one-sided Christ). This essential battle against Western history's monotheistic unconsciousness necessitates a battle against monotheism's professional minions of its secularism and scientism, today's thought police, who, in the name of mental health and therapy of soul, apply ego psychology to the diseases of the gods.

13

MOSES, ALCHEMY, AUTHORITY

There is a peculiar but strong strand in the complex history of European and Arabic alchemy that founds the field upon the authority of Moses. By claiming Moses to be its first practitioner, alchemy dresses itself in that patriarch's virtues—his nobility of spirit, his stalwart ethical values, his humility, his redemptive heroism, and above all the orthodoxy of his unwavering monotheism. How could alchemy be a "devil's art," pagan in its references to many gods and planets, sinful in its gold-lust, and why must its devotees be persecuted if the founder of the one law upholding all three monotheistic religions also founded alchemy?

Despite such eminent intellectual pursuers of alchemy as Thomas Aquinas, Roger Bacon, John Evelyn, and Isaac Newton, and such powerful patrons of the "black art" (as it was often called) as James of Scotland, Emperor Rudolf, and Charles the Second of England (who had a secret alchemical laboratory built under his bedchamber), alchemists were marginal, if not outlawed, in medieval society, unorthodox in the Renaissance, and ridiculed when alchemy finally lost its faith in itself during the Enlightenment. A gnawing need for authority that would fortify its authenticity plagued alchemy all along the way, a need that is partly responsible for its defensive, self-defeating exaggerations, which of course led to more need for backing and grounding in the validity of an orthodox and rational tradition, exemplified superbly by Moses.

The kind of authority Moses offers, in fact, the very idea of authority in relation to Moses, we shall come to later. But first, Moses the alchemist.

Contribution to the Conference *Mosè: conflitti e tolleranza*, Accademia di San Luca (Rome, 2001) and in part published, in Italian translation by Silvia Ronchey, in *Domenica, Suppl. Il Sole/24 Ore* (December 16, 2001).

The *locus classicus* for Moses the alchemist is Exodus 32:20: "[Moses] took the calf [of gold] which they had made, and burnt it with fire, and ground it to a powder, and strewed it upon the water, and made the children of Israel drink of it." Alchemists seized upon this passage as overt evidence of three well-known alchemical operations: calcination (the reduction of a substance by heat to a dry powder), solution (the mixture of a powder with a liquid), and the potability of gold (when changed from its ordinary or vile nature to a sophisticated or subtle nature as an elixir or *aqua permanens*).

Alchemists were widely called workers in fire. "Would you know the perfect Master?" wrote the English alchemist Thomas Norton in 1450, "It is he who understands the regulation of the fire, and its degrees." Moses knew fire: by means of fire he transforms the golden calf; a pillar of fire leads him through the nights of the Wilderness (Exodus 13:22), and a fiery bush speaks to Moses, a bush that "burned with fire, and the bush was not consumed" (Exodus 3:2).

Besides the alchemical readings of the Exodus passages, Moses enters alchemy via innumerable compression of figures and writings. For instance, Maria Prophetessa or Maria the Jewess was sometimes identified with the Biblical Miriam and called the "Sister of Moses." A traditional formula for doubling the weight of gold was called the Diplosis of Moses. A confirmed historical person named Moses who lived in Hellenistic Egypt wrote several alchemical tracts. This author was easily confounded with the Biblical Moses. Zosimos, the major textual source of Western alchemy, refers in his *The Divine Water* to a long treatise, *The Domestic Chemistry of Moses* (preserved in the Leiden papyrus, third century AD). Zosimos definitely associates this text with the Biblical Moses, "thereby endowing it" as Raphael Patai says, "with an aura of antiquity and authenticity" (Patai, 31). Our very topic to which I promised to return, that is, if time allotted allows me to enter the promised land of fulfilling promises.

The incorporation of Moses into the patrons of alchemy belongs to a wider tradition of syncretistic Hellenism (cf. Gager, 1972)—that is, Mediterranean thought and culture from, say, the fourth century BC through the fourth century AD. This habit of mind could easily assimilate Moses into Greek wisdom and Egyptian sciences, identify him with Orpheus and interchange him with Hermes, and even find that a vague figure of Greek myth, Museus, was the Biblical Moses, a blurring that gave

Moses the added authority of founding the Greek mysteries of Eleusis and inspiring all the Muses, their sciences and arts (Roscher, "Musaeus"; Patai, 33).

Moses the Magician finds Biblical support in the plagues inflicted on the Egyptians, the parting of the Red Sea, bringing forth water from a rock and food from heaven, Moses' brass serpent that heals—to mention but a few of the more familiar events reported in the Bible expanded in legend and *midrashim*. The major early Arab alchemist Jabir or Geber refers to Moses as alchemy's founder. This tradition continues through the Medieval period, through Paracelsus, and becomes ever more fervid so that "by the seventeenth century, the belief that Moses was a great alchemist was so widespread...that more critically minded writers... found it necessary to combat it" (Patai, 37). The crux of the evidence for and against was always Exodus 32:20, the burning of the calf. There was another seemingly quite rational link: alchemy (born in Egypt like Moses), the word deriving from an Egyptian syllable *khem*, black. Alchemy, the black art.

This brings us to the Moses of Michelangelo, for this Moses incorporates both the patriarchal and the magical—the beard, pointed finger and elongated stature of lawgiver, yet with the horns of the animal-man. Another alchemical transformation: the bull, not destroyed but restored and emblematic in Moses himself. Even should we interpret away the horns as symbolic of the radiant spirit, as a nimbus or halo, the power of mind made evident, or reduce them to an error of translation of Exodus 34:29 where the Hebrew *karan*, beams, from Moses's face becomes *keren*, horns, emanating from his forehead (Margaret MacLean, 97–99). Nonetheless, those horns placed there whether by God or by Michelangelo restore to Moses what he had rent asunder: God and animal, law and instinct, duty and pleasure, Hebrew monotheism and Egyptian polytheism.

For the burning of the golden calf is that moment in mythical history, in the civilization of the psyche and in the monotheistic theology of nature that ruptures the sacred fusion of the holy and the animal, denying animal nature to divinity and divinity to animal nature (Giegerich, 281–93). This fusion is boldly restored in the horned Moses, which also restores him to his Egyptian origins (cf. Gager, 113–33), a theme brilliantly and thoroughly examined by Jan Assmann.

Here we may recall that Moses was born in Egypt, that the mother who claimed him and raised him was Bithiah, the Pharoah's daughter, and that when courting Zipporah, a *midrash* says, he was explicitly named an Egyptian, which Moses did not deny (Ginzberg, 2: 293).

Moses the Egyptian!—a no lesser myth-maker than Freud concurs. For Freud's late essay, "Moses and Monotheism," his last, completed when the old man was two years away from entry into the promised land, stakes much on the hypotheses that Moses was indeed an Egyptian. Therefore, in a nutshell, may we consider his monotheism to be that of a convert, doubly intense, maybe fanatic, because it must hold in check the return of the repressed: pagan polytheism, the black tide of the occult, alchemy. This repressed pagan announces itself in the fury that smashes the tablets of the law (Exodus 32: 19).

The Moses of Michelangelo turns his eyes away from the tablets at his side, seeming to let them even slide from his hand. This Moses with horns on his head bears resemblance to Pan—as Freud notes—a nature figure, or demon, of sensuality and powerful emotion.

A Jewish legend expands upon this rougher, uglier Moses, characterizing him as "covetous, haughty, and sensual, disfigured by all possible ugly traits." (Ginzberg, 2: 275) The legend goes like this: After the miraculous escape from Egypt, a king of Arabia sent an artist to Moses to paint his portrait. The king assembled his wise men and physiognomists to judge the character of Moses from the image painted. They agreed unanimously that the man was disfigured by every sort of ugly trait. The king was much vexed, castigating his experts for reading villainy in the countenance of one so holy, so heroic. The wise men put the blame on the painter for falsifying Moses's image. But the painter insisted that the image was a true likeness. The king had no other recourse than to go to Moses directly. He immediately saw that the painting was indeed a true likeness and that his counselors were wrong to claim the painter falsified.

But then Moses himself intervened: no one was wrong. Neither the painter nor the judges of character from the painting. This, because Moses said, "If my fine qualities were a product of nature, then I were no better than a log of wood (wood, by the way, was the old Greek *hyle* and an alchemical term for transformable matter) and would long remain just as nature produced it. Moses went on to say, "I make the confession without shame. I did possess all the reprehensible traits that the experts read in my face—and perhaps to a degree greater than they surmise. But I mastered my evil impulses, and the character I acquired through severe discipline has become the opposite of the disposition with which I was born" (Ginzberg, 2: 275–76). Of course, "the character with which I was born" obliquely or directly refers to his original Egyptian nature.

This legend hardly supports the spiritual interpretation of the horns of the statue—unless we shift our idea of spirit from elevated bodiless abstractions to the chthonic spirit, such as the spirit of the shaman who was at once man and animal healer and dancer, magician and wise man, exemplified by the famous primordial horned figure of cave art (*Les trois frères* in the Pyrenees).

Some of the sins that the *midrash* legend attributes to Moses—covetousness, arrogance, sensuality, as well as the killing rage notorious in Moses's character, are the very sins enumerated in the tablets Moses brings down from Sinai. Here it is crucial to note the sequence of events. Moses goes up the mountain, returns with tablets, finds the people worshipping the bull, falls into a rage, destroys the tablets, slaughters the backsliders, again goes up the mountain, and returns with new tablets, which we know as the Ten Commandments.

The first laws, the laws Moses smashed, remain a mystery, and have been subject to Jewish mystical speculation for centuries, according to Gershom Scholem. Is the second edition a mere copy of the first? A revision of the first? Decreed in light of the behavior of the people and in reaction to the behavior of Moses, which the second version enumerates and forbids? All we know is the second version follows directly upon the dancing in the desert and the murder of the dancers.

In short and in conclusion: Michelangelo's Moses is indeed an alchemist because this image restores a golden value to his pagan origins, which began to emerge in the Biblical tale with the outbreak of anger that waxeth hot, releasing Moses from the discipline of the commandments, the raging bull now he himself, ordering the killing of thousands (Exodus 32:28) who had lost faith in the man in favor of the animal.

The text is most shocking: "And he [Moses] said unto them 'Who so is on the Lord's side, let him come unto me...' And he said unto them [the priestly group of Levi]: 'Put ye every man his sword upon his thigh, and go to and fro from gate to gate throughout the camp, and slay every man his brother, and every man his companion, and every man his neighbor.' And the sons of Levi did according to the word of Moses; and there fell of the people that day about three thousand men." Moses then rebukes the people for having sinned a great sin—the sin of "having made a god of gold," the golden calf—not the sin of killing his son and his brother, his companion and his neighbor! Worship of the animal worse than civil war, fratricide, bloody murder.

That animal, that bull, after all, rules the Mediterranean world as Apis of the Egyptians, Dionysus and Zeus of the Greeks and Cretans, appears in the Roman cults of Attis and Mithra, and is holy as well in African cultures beyond Egypt and in the ancient Mideast beyond Canaan to Assyria and Sumer.

It can be conjectured that this moment in the desert replicates the great divide presented in many mythologies where the animal is severed from the divine. Theology is born, and religion as we know it, its piety, its spiritual abstractions, credos and laws, its enmity of the instinctual flesh. In Greece it was the great mythologems of Hercules, slaughtering the Boar and the Crab and the Lion and the Hydra, the Stymphalian birds, the Bull of Minos, the dog Orthos; in Rome, Mithra slayed the bull, in Babylonia, Gilgamesh overcoming the animal-man Enkidu. Egyptian myths do not show this radical separation of the divine from animal except perhaps in the short period of Akhnaton's ascendancy. Curious is it not that in the Mediterranean world of antiquity, in the Renaissance, and in alchemy into the eighteenth century, Egypt was the deepest source of wisdom? What is that Egyptian wisdom for us today? Could it be the resurrection of the oldest images of divinity humans have ever imagined and constructed: the animal; and does not Michelangelo's Moses present just such an image of religious authority?

In the marble of Michelangelo we see both the control and the fury, or as Freud notes in his 1914 paper on the sculpture, both the law and the rage. But now we can take a hazardous step further along, along with Michelangelo, into an alchemical Moses who joins in this figured stone, this *lapis philosophorum*, the tablets of Law and horns of Pan, divine word and divine animal.

Moses as composite of logos and animal shows up in a most curious and not irrelevant example from antiquity that I doubt was known to Michelangelo. Diodorus Siculus (34.1) reports that "when Antiochus was making war against the Jews, he entered the sacred shrine of god...he found a stone image of a thick bearded man seated on an ass and holding a book in his hand. He assumed it was a statue of Moses..." Another early Alexandrian tradition, explaining the origins of the letters of the alphabet, associates *alpha* or *aleph,* shaped like the head of a bull, with Moses, the first lawgiver (Gager, 129).

The integrity of the animal-man, conjuncted man and animal, the shaman (Eliade, *passim*), the Adam Kadmon or primordial man rejoins what Moses had split apart in the desert, giving Moses an added authority beyond that from the Law alone. The *terribilità* of Michelangelo's sculpted stone redeems Moses from patriarchal sanctimoniousness whose authority lies only in severe orthodoxy. Here, however, authority emanates from his horned head and fiery glance that knows nature from within the fire of his own nature. This Moses is impassioned by nature, is part of its instinctive unruly force, its *calor inclusis,* knows of killing and coveting, of false witness and theft, of denying God, and of other gods. This Moses, because of his horns, is unnatural and supernatural, an *opus contra naturam*—one of the widest definitions of alchemy—a figure who embodies Ostanes's ever-quoted maxim for the alchemical process: "Nature enjoys nature; nature wars with nature; nature rules nature."

In brief, Michelangelo's Moses affords an image of the alchemical Moses, whose authority derives from the underlying alchemical principles of *solve et coagula*: what is fluid must be solidified and what is solidified must be dissolved. Law-making yields to law-breaking requiring law-making, again and again. Authority consists in the practice of both. The authority of the horned Moses resides in both the Laws he handed down and in letting them slip from his hands. He lets slip the fixity of literalized monotheism by admitting in his very person the presence of other gods, just as the Torah's second commandment declares (Exodus 20:3). As idols must be smashed, so Moses smashes the stone tablets lest they become idols and the law abiders become idolaters of the laws— which today many have become.

Thus Michelangelo's graven image addresses our world in which the prohibition against other gods has become itself a graven image, fixed and solidified in the fundamentalist minds of the three monotheistic faiths— all three of which Moses is a founder. If we follow alchemical method, then religious consciousness can move through this destructive condition only when coagulated monotheism has thoroughly dissolved.

References

Jan Assmann, *Moses the Egyptian: The Memory of Egypt in Western Monotheism* (Cambridge, Mass.: Harvard University Press, 1997).

Diodorus Siculus, "Fragments of Books," translated by Francis Walton (Cambridge, Mass.: Harvard University Press, 1967).

Mircea Eliade, *Shamanism*, translated by W.R. Trask (London: Kegan Paul, 1964).

Sigmund Freud, "The Moses of Michelangelo," in *CP*4: 257–58.

——, "Moses and Monotheism: Three Essays," in *SE*23.

John G. Gager, *Moses in Greco-Roman Paganism* (Nashville: Abingdon, 1972).

Wolfgang Giegerich, *Die Atombombe als seelische Wirklichkeit* (Zurich: Schweizer Spiegel/Raben-Reihe, 1988).

Louis Ginzberg, *The Legends of the Jews* (Philadelphia: Jewish Publication Society, 1928).

Margaret MacLean, "The Horns on Michelangelo's Moses," *Art and Architecture* 6, no. 2 (August 1917): 97–98.

Ruth Mellinkoff, *The Horned Moses in Mediaeval Art and Thought* (Berkeley: University of California Press, 1970).

Thomas Norton, "The Chemical Treatise or The Ordinal of Alchemy," in *The Hermetic Museum*, vol. 2, edited by A.E. Waite (London: Watkins, 1953).

Raphael Patai, *The Jewish Alchemists* (Princeton, N.J.: Princeton University Press 1994).

W.H. Roscher, *Ausführliches Lexikon der griechischen und römischen Mythologie* (Hildesheim: Georg Olms, 1965).

Gershom Scholem, *Alchemy and Kabbalah*, translated by Klaus Ottmann (Putnam: Conn.: Spring Publications, 2006).

14

THE CALL OF THE GOD OKEANOS

Born in a room that gave directly onto the ocean, among the very first sounds I must have heard was the crash of waves breaking on the shore. Classic psychoanalysis would be pleased with this testimony, affirming their orthodox symbolism that claims a symbiosis of ocean, mother, infant, and bliss. Psychoanalysis enjoys the idea of oceanic feelings, of melting and floating on the rhythmic breast of the sea, of being carried into its embracing womb.

There is, however, another sea of Father God Okeanos from whose seed came thousands of springs, streams, and rivers, and whose daughters, the Nereids, present the ocean's ever-changing moods and shifting colors. These daughters of the ocean are enchantresses. One was named Calypso, another Callirhoe, the beautifully flowing. It is they who give the one single engirdling sea its multitude of names. They beckon humans ever outward and deeper. As the old-fashioned English poet-laureate John Masefield wrote so famously:

> I must go down to the seas again, for the call of the running tide
> Is a wild call and a clear call that may not be denied;
> And all I ask is a windy day with white clouds flying
> And the flung spray and the blown spume, and the sea-gulls crying.

> ("Sea Fever")

Masefield hears the call of Okeanos: the call to Jason and Ulysses, the call heard by that strange Ligurian fantast, Cristoforo Colombo, and by Vasco da Gama, by the Uskok pirates and Venetian and Genovese admirals, and by Drake and Cook and Bougainville, and the characters

---

Talk on the occasion of the annual Regatta and Conference *Man and The Sea,* sponsored by Fondazione Zegna (for Mediterranean conservation), Portofino, May 2000.

in the novels of Herman Melville and Joseph Conrad, and by Sir Francis Chichester, out across the wide seas, their lurking monsters and furious winds blowing from all quarters as depicted on the old maps, and the sudden rocks, reefs, and riptides.

Okeanos invites the human world to adventure. He draws forth our skills. Aeschylus (*Prometheus Bound*) calls him a "schoolmaster." For we did not master the arts of boat construction, of sail rigging, of navigation alone at home thinking in a chair. We had to set forth, risking.

The Greeks spoke of Okeanos as a great encircling horizon at the far edge of the world. Okeanos evokes desires for what lives in the distance, a yearning to go beyond, to the very edge. He offers a limitless vision of possibilities which can only be realized by human skills and cunning: to tie fast knots and slip knots, to lay a keel, chart a channel, shape a prow. From the schoolmaster of the sea we learn another kind of reading and reckoning: how to taste the wind, look deep into the color of the water.

The mind plumbing the darkest deeps or theorizing far out about the origin of the cosmos—that, too, is prompted by Okeanos, *"theon genesis,"* origin of all, father of all the gods (*Iliad*, 14: 201, 304). Okeanos breeds forth mythic figures of every shape and visage, as if to say all the possibilities of the archetypal imagination arise from his primal fecundity. Okeanos, writes R.B. Onians, "can be explained as the imagined primal cosmic psych☐ or procreative power, liquid and serpent...the name appears to mean 'circling.'"[1] Though generator of the gods, he is not one among them. He is rather their imageless, ever-moving source, so when they all assemble on Olympus, only Okeanos is not there (*Iliad*, 20: 7).

Human hubris makes us believe *we* mastered the seas with our marvelous human intelligence. But human intelligence awakens only to challenges. Our earliest habitations settled by his waters along the sea coasts, river banks, mountain streams. Okeanos's limitless horizon offered endless fantasies to human imagination, puzzling our wits with ever-circling life-or-death problems. It is the sea that tests our wits, fathers the mind that maps by the night sky, the angle of the sun, and the instruments that give prudence to human adventure. After all, smart intelligence, called Metis by the Greeks, is one of his daughters, as is Elektra, clarity.

---

1. Richard Broxton Onians, *The Origins of European Thought* (Cambridge: Cambridge University Press, 1952), 249.

Degrees of latitude and longitude arose from confronting the sea; the pitch of propeller blades, the cut and trim of sails, the weight and angle of keels—even hurricanes gestated in the warm equatorial seas each come tagged with numbers and a name. It is as if Okeanos generates accuracy in response to his fearful immensity.

The root meaning of *sophia* (wisdom), still contained in words like philosophy, sophistication, sophistry is simply "skill" or "clever handling." Or, "skilled in seamanship," according to the ancient poet Hesiod. *Sophia*: the helmsman at the tiller with an eye on the sails, making continual adjustments that keep the boat close to compass course. Okeanos teaches the humility that we are always somewhat off course and that life requires continual trimming, correcting to port, then starboard, then port again... This *sophia,* this skill of the helmsman, can be learned on board ship, in the arts, or managing the business of living. This is also the *sophrosne* or mindful attentive noticing that Okeanos advises Prometheus. Sailors still call that most important duty "being on watch."

That crafty sailor, Ulysses, was opposed all the way home by another sea god, Poseidon. The conflict with Poseidon brought out Ulysses's native skills, as if intelligence sharpens its wit against ever more difficult challenges.

The unbounded immensity of the sea contrasts with the nestling enclosure of its harbors, and gives to them their psychological meaning as the place of return, of homecoming, journey's end. As the ocean is limitless, so the individual tiny harbors, like Portofino, are innumerable. We each find our own journey's end. And, "to multiply the harbors/ does not reduce the sea," wrote one of America's greatest poets, Emily Dickinson, though she herself hardly ventured from her upstairs bedroom, her tiny harbor into which the oceanic powers of imagination flowed.

Contemporary cravings for the sunny beach, the tropic isle, and tourist ship avoid the challenge of Okeanos. Tourists neither confront the sea, nor feel the harbor, neither the exhilarating terror nor the relief. Adrift, waterlogged, capsized, rudderless, shipwrecked refer only to their personal psyches without objective reference to actual risks. They know nothing of coming into a snug port, anchored, moored, docked, the foot again on land; or of setting sail beyond the harbor lights into that vast tumult of waters which psychoanalysis has given the pseudo-scientific and pejorative name—"The Unconscious." What! Okeanos, unconscious? The sea is not unconscious—it reflects the light of the stars and the moon; it is peopled with luminosities at the crest of each wave, and flashes the phosphorescence of the spirits who are there at home.

Okeanos may be endless, but I may not be. I must bring my windy excursion into port, which I shall do now with a brief surprising passage from Nietzsche's *Fröhliche Wissenschaft* called "Knowing How to Find the End":

> Masters of the first rank are recognized in a perfect manner how to find the end...be it the end of a melody or a thought...a tragedy or a state of affairs. Masters of a lesser degree always become restless toward the end, and seldom dip down into the sea with such proud, quiet equilibrium, as for example, the mountain-ridge at *Portofino*—where the bay of Genoa sings its melody to an end. (281)

15

ORPHEUS

I

The question is: Have the gods truly fled? Is this a *dürftige Zeit*? Even should this indeed be a time of need, a time of impoverished soul, does it necessarily follow that therefore the gods have fled? Can they leave the world at all? That is an even more necessary question. If they are the world as the powers within its variety, how can they be separated from it? Are they not the immortality, the *athnetos*, of the world, giving every item of this world its inherent transcendence, its sublime enchantment and beauty which is at once also fearful, cruel, and profoundly intelligible?

Why has the modern age accepted the thesis that the gods can simply up and go? Certainly their absence, if that is the case, cannot be due to us, to our having deserted their groves and altars, failed their rituals and sacrifices, forgotten their mysteries. They surely cannot be that dependent on what we do nor not do. If that were the case how could they claim their supra-human authority in the cosmos? If *their* presence or absence depends on *our* behavior regarding them, the gods of myth are really nothing more than what secular enlightenment insists: fictions of human fantasy.

So the question turns again: who and what benefits from declaring the ancient gods fled, or dead? Who wants them gone; and with their absence all pagan feeling, all pagan style of consciousness gone as well.

Presented at the conference *Il viaggio di Orfeo: Mito, Arte e Letteratura,* Università degli Studi di Torino, April 2003. First published, in Italian translation, as "Il complesso di Orfeo," in *Orfeo e le sue metamorfosi: mito, arte, poesia,* edited by Giulio Guidorezzi and Marxiano Melotti (Rome: Carocci, 2005).

One thing is sure both historically and logically: the absence of the gods allows the world to become *res extensa,* a mathematical space calculable in forces, adrift with the litter of soulless objects, all soul, all mind, all consciousness condensed inside the human brain, putting nature at the disposal of the human will. The absence of the gods is not only a secular convenience, or an industrialist opportunity for exploitation, or a hubristic inflation of mortal humans; much more, the declaration that the gods have fled is also a Christian convenience. Their absence leaves the world open with plenty of room for the presence of Jesus the Savior who gives his redemptive answer to the *dürftige Zeit.*

There have been many scholars of religion and history, of myth and literature, of arts and philology who have intimated the survival of the pagan gods, hidden, and not so hidden, within the Christian *mythos,* disguised presences despite their official and evident absence. There have been many as well who have attempted the revival of the pagan gods by imitations, by invocations, and by hermeneutical interpretations.

Myself, I have followed a method that springs from two famous sentences often used by and quoted from C.G. Jung: The first comes supposedly from Delphi. It is a saying cut in stone and placed as the lintel over the front door of the house where Jung lived and worked for most of his long life. "Called or not called, the god will be present." *Vocatus atque non vocatus deus aderit.*

The second: "The gods have become diseases; Zeus no longer rules Olympus but rather the solar plexus, and produces curious specimens for the doctor's consulting room, or disorders the brain of politicians and journalists who unwittingly let loose psychic epidemics on the world." (*CW* 13: 54)

The interiorization of divinity, the move from transcendence to immanence had already been argued by Spinoza for which he was banned from his community; the move was further presented by Heinrich Zimmer, the indologist, who said—again famously—"all the gods are within." These moves—Jung's, Spinoza's, Zimmer's—are each different, and different Jesus's (Luke 17: 21), "The Kingdom of God is within you." The differentiation of immanence is not to our point here; but it is important to recognize the crucial twist that Jung's psychology gave to the immanence of the gods. They have been interiorized into pathology; they live in our symptoms, irrepressibly demanding recognition and observances. They bear new names borrowed from the textbooks of psychiatry and abnormal psychology. Their refuge is no longer the altar and temple fanum, the site of oracle and mystery cult. Instead, they inhabit the interiority of the psyche where they make themselves very present indeed as the powers in the background of the soul's infirmities. Since the repressed returns in the strangely inventive form of symptoms, the gods have indeed become diseases, both in the individual and the collective psyche of the *anima mundi*. To find the figures of ancient myths today we turn to the pathological, rather than the idealized, following Jung rather than Winckelmann. The practice of depth psychology as I understand it provides a method for welcoming the return of the gods.

I do need to add that Jung is neither the only nor the first of this confluence of the mythological and the pathological, the gods and diseases. Already in 1900, W.H. Roscher's monograph on Ephialtes is subtitled "a pathological-mythological treatise."[1] Concurrent with Roscher, Freud moved Oedipus from a theatrical figure we may watch on the stage to a drive in your personal intimate body. As well, Freud elevated the mythical personifications Eros and Thanatos, to be the dominant gods of all psychological happenings. It is fashionable today to bypass or surpass Freud for all sorts of reasons—sociological, feminist, scientistic. But one gift from Freud we ought never neglect: his return to the sources of culture in Mediterranean myths, rooting psychology not in the brain or genetics or blind evolution, but in the poetic basis of mind, whose imagination is structured by mythical configurations, or *universali fantastici* as Vico called these archetypal presences.

These forerunners, and Nietzsche, too, of course, laid the groundwork for a psychological approach to Orpheus, searching for him or noting his absence, in the confused soul of personal privacy and in the soul of the world as the larger harbor of the shipwrecked.

The recognition of the intimate and subtly differentiated connection between myths and pain, between the gods and diseases is the greatest of all achievements of the Greek mind, singling out that culture from all others—despite its flaws, its faults. That achievement? The Greek perfection of tragedy, which demonstrates directly the mythic governance of human affairs within states, within families, within individuals. Only the

---

1. "Ephialtes: A Pathological-Mythological Treatise on the Nightmare in Classical Antiquity," in my *Pan and the Nightmare* (Putnam, Conn.: Spring Publications, 2007).

ancient Greeks could articulate tragedy to this pitch, and that achievement has not been equaled since.

I do not want to overlook the fact that the psychological method I am pursuing gives scant attention to the historical time-frame of the myths and their geographical locations, to the philological analysis of the texts where they are recounted, to the authenticity of their transmission, to the visual evidence from archeology and art, to the sociological and political implications of their themes either then or now. In other words, the psychological method I am advancing is shamefacedly syncretistic and may offend the patient devotion to scholarly research by those who come at the same tales with different intentions. To uncover ancient myths in behavior, in the phenomena we unthinkingly absorb as usual reality and utterly un-mythical—that is the revelation an archetypal psychology seeks. We ravage the scholarship of others and pilfer whatever we can, justifying these violations in the name of bringing deeper understanding to psychological afflictions.

Besides our aim of tying a human mess to a wider myth, we are also attempting to connect present experience to historical culture, hoping to open a long closed door, bolted from two sides: history and its scholarship bearing witness only to the dead, past, and gone; psychology utterly contained within the subjective soul, all too close and personal. I am attempting to show how antiquity can be relevant to the life of the psyche and how psychic life can vivify antiquity. When scholars speak only to documents and psychologists only to patients, culture languishes, its soul shallow and unrooted in historical knowledge, its knowledge without soul.

II

Now to Orpheus. Which Orpheus? Whose Orpheus? We do not need to specify. My prolonged preamble on method dispels these questions. In what follows now "Orpheus" refers to a compact intertwining of eight well-known mythemes which together comprise the main perduring features of this figure, and I borrow this distillation into eight from Friedman's study, *Orpheus in the Middle Ages:*[2]

---

2. John Block Friedman, *Orpheus in the Middle Ages* (Cambridge, Mass.: Harvard University Press, 1970). Martin P. Nilsson gives a similar list of identities in his

1. Orpheus, of Thrace, descendent of a Muse and a wine god, and/or possibly Apollo.

2. Orpheus among the Argonauts, but not quite one of them, not a hero, not a killer, but the one who played "the rowers a measure for their long sweep of the oars."

3. Orpheus "whom the trees disobeyed not and the lifeless rocks followed, and the herds of the forest beasts" because of his music.

4. Orpheus the priest, first of Dionysus and then of Apollo, student of Moses, prophet, simulacrum of Christ, giver of religion, author of dogma and hymn, idol of a sect, teacher of a *Lebensweg.*

5. Orpheus, poet, especially cosmological poet, technician of poetry to whom the invention of both alphabet and varieties of poetic measure are attributed

6. *Orpheus-cum-Eurydike:* sojourner to the Underworld; lover extra-ordinaire; failed hero yet psychopomp; untrusting lover; disconsolate and lonely sufferer.

7. Orpheus, misogynist; torn by furious women, limb from limb — for any number of reasons, including disdain for them, exclusion of them from his cult, and preference over them for the love of boys.

8. Orpheus, whose singing head washed up on the isle of Lesbos sings on after his dismemberment and is worshipped there, together with his lyre, and also in the heavens as the constellation, Lyra.

As for whether or not there was a "real" Orpheus, a historical figure to whom the stories cling, a *theologos* whose words and deeds collected accretions and embellishment that have formed the "myth" of Orpheus, I could not enter this dispute. From my psychological perspective, a "real" anything has always a mythic, archetypal component, or can be viewed archetypally. Even were the bones of the man and the skull of his head found and preserved, along with tablets of his preaching and scrolls affirming his Thracian ancestry, all signed and dated with his seal, and so forth and so on, the "myth" of Orpheus could not be dispelled any more

---

Opuscula Selecta (Lund: Gleerup, 1960): "In der klassischen Zeit wurde dem Orpheus fast alles angehängt. Er ist ein großer Sänger, Musiker, Dichter, Zauberer, Stifter von Mysterien, der Held bekannter Mythen, er ist Vegetarier, er schreibt Reinigungen vor (In classical times almost everything was attached to Orpheus. He is a great singer, musician, poet, magician, founder of mysteries, the hero of well-known myths, he is a vegetarian, he prescribes purifications)" (3: 296).

than can the evidence supposedly establishing the existence of a histori-cal Jesus evacuate or diminish the power of the mythical Jesus. If "real" is determined by characteristics such as powerful, effective, actual, fecund, enduring, and emotionally moving, then the real is the mythic.

From the cluster of eight Orphic themes I would like to comment brief-ly on three because they seem to show his presence and absence in the psyche today. These are, in short: Orpheus in the midst of nature; Orpheus and music; and *Orpheus-cum-Eurydike*.

Let us look first at Orpheus in the midst of nature, the Orpheus to whom the animals, the rocks, and the trees listen in rapt attention, the Orpheus whose cosmological hymns reach to the stars and beyond. This Orpheus is a nature god, master of the beasts, and also of the supposedly inanimate rocks and trees. These natural settings imply his mythical ori-gins in the wildernesses of Thrace; but Orpheus comes to life, enters the world, wherever there are animals, rocks, and trees. Orpheus, God of the Environment, as we now name the natural world. That anthropocentric word "environment" comes from *environs,* surround (a word which places the human in the center), a stage setting for human willfulness, nature only a background, a mere *res extensa,* the animals, rocks, and trees noth-ing but raw materials and natural resources.

Sometimes I like to think one man alone, Jesuit-educated René Des-cartes, drove Orpheus from the world, leaving it as dead matter to be used and abused to the profit of one species only. Of course, much earlier, as Plutarch reported, the great god Pan was dead, and with his death the world lost its hidden internal life, the sudden wildness that brings panic and spontaneous desires. With the arrival of Christian-ity, Orpheus, too, and the polytheism that acknowledged the soul in nature was eliminated by the assimilation of Orpheus into Christ. The absence of Orpheus belongs to the symptoms of the *Weltbild* that West-ern Christian society continues to export with missionary, military, and commercial zeal throughout the planet even in remote and pagan and polytheistic places of animals, rocks and trees like the Amazon, West Irian, and the sub-Sahara, which may be new to Christ but where nature gods similar to Pan and Orpheus have always been present.

Absent, but present too. Let us imagine a case. An adolescent girl from one day to the next joins an animal rights campaign against furs, vivisection, against animal testing, against zoos. She converts to vegetarianism, prefers beans, and won't touch eggs, just as Pausanias reported of the Orphics. She collects crystals and fossils and rocks, and wears kinds of stones according to their innate powers. She joins other young women in the forests to protect the trees from felling. She is a pacifist, reads Eastern religious texts. And she writes poems and songs, which she plays on the stringed instrument she is learning. She may also bear an angry contempt for men.

Do these sudden awakenings, conversions come from friends? From pamphlets? From a nature film seen by chance? Or indeed have the gods become diseases, that is, is it Orpheus who has struck, an "Orpheus complex" to use the language of Gaston Bachelard? Could we not as well imagine the presence of Orpheus, very much alive in the psyche, drawing even today new members into his cult.

Despite the evident, if subliminal, presence of Orpheus in contemporary movements of "neo-orphism," that is, environmentalism, Orpheus is nonetheless woefully lacking in these very movements. He may be present in their ideals, their practices, their inspiration, but lacking in their language.

The relation between Orpheus and the natural world was by means of language, the hymns, the *ars poetica*, for he was the son of Calliope. Orpheus reaches into the heart of the natural world by means of his art, and via this art nature enters speech, becomes poetry. If the speech of environmentalism does not awaken nature's sublimity, its beauty and its terror, if the rocks and trees do not speak, they remain mere objects, not ensouled subjects with whom the human is bound in *"biophilia,"* the "sympathy of all things" in older terms.

This aural gift of Orpheus is absent today. *The Orphic Voice*, as Elizabeth Sewell called her inspired study, does not sound in the language of ecology. The very word "ecology" remains Cartesian: it is atonal, mathematical, economic, hyper-rationalized. Ecology speaks the language of oil depletion, sustainability, zero population, energy efficiency, climate measurement, pollution particles, desertification, gene pools. Yet it is the aesthetic response to the world that keeps it alive for us and makes us want to keep it alive. Orpheus is lacking as well in the Christian language of environmentalism, where the emphasis is on morality—we should feel guilty for what we have done to the world and make reparations; we have a duty; we are to be good shepherds.

Neither of these languages, Cartesian or Christian, reaches to the heart which is the heart of the environmental disorder. It is the aesthetic response to the world's suffering, its ugliness, its abuse and exploitation—and its sublime beauty—that brings the phenomena of the world to life; the aesthetic response that sees and feels and speaks of the world as alive, ensouled, pagan. I am arguing that the environmental movement must find the Orphic mode of *poiesis* to enchant the human ears to hear the singing of the world, ears that have become stone deaf, and human actions that have become boringly wooden with ecological rationality.

My second exhibition of the presence of Orpheus is music. Perhaps music belongs in first place: how many concert halls are named for him; how many images show him with his instrument; how many lyrical poems, operas, book titles bring him together with song and sound.

I want, however, to place this music within a wider category covered by a phrase that Guthrie uses for a chapter title, "Orphica and the New Age."[3] The New Age to which Guthrie refers is not the contemporary popular movement referred to by that name. Guthrie's book came out originally in 1935 long before hippies, pot, and peace. He is referring to the period of Greco-Roman syncretism when Orpheus was a major cult figure. Nonetheless, that syncretism bears comparison with the mood, interests, and beliefs of our "Age of Aquarius" as our contemporary New Age has been called, and which crystallized in the 1960s. Music was a communal force and message-bearer sounding through societal unrest, feminist liberation, politics of protest, idealistic reform, bodily freedom with banners flying for racial justice, community, love, youth, and imagination.

To sort out today's New Age themes is as complicated as differentiating them in the early centuries of our era. Parallels are nevertheless striking: "Syncretism and the mingling of religious traditions," says Guthrie (255), "were the order of the day." "One mark of the new age was the spread and increased importance of private esoteric cult-societies" (254). Of the cults (Mithra, Osiris, Christ, Bacchus/Dionysus) many claimed

3. W.K.C. Guthrie, *Orpheus and Greek Religion: A Study of the Orphic Movement* (Princeton, N.J.: Princeton University Press, 1993 [1952]).

descent from, incorporated aspects of, or showed similarities with the cult of Orpheus. The reference to Orpheus in the Christian context brings us again to music.

Christianity came with a New Song, according to Clement's *Exhortation to the Greeks.* Christ, the second person of the Trinity, brings the word of God, which is a New Song; this trope makes use of the New Song mentioned in the Psalms, but it was more familiar to the populace in the syncretic atmosphere of the time as an indirect, and even direct, reference to Orpheus. And, as you all well know, a great deal of study has been given to the Orpheus/Christ identification. I am only stressing the presence of Orpheus as music—where he continues to this day to inspire Christians from Bach to Gospel.

The 1960s New Age also came with a New Song: Joan Baez and Bob Dylan, the songs of the black marchers in Alabama and South Africa, the sweet love songs of the Beatles, the dancing Dionysian pelvis of Presley. As this music took hold, its infectious energy incorporated instruments, harmonies, and dissonances in a syncretistic fashion—Andean flute, Indian and Persian strings, Latin guitars, African rhythms, Brazil, Tibet, blue grass, rhythm-and-blues, country-and-western...the last is especially Orphic not in its syncretism but in its wailing over lost separations, Eurydike; mistakes, departures, as the blues too tell of longing for a love that's gone.

"The mingling of religious traditions," as Guthrie said, was a mark of that New Age then as it is of ours now: Kabbala, alchemy, Zen, Burmese monasteries, Nepal, Pondicherry, the Apocrypha and Dead Sea Scrolls, rebirthing, sufism, shamanism, magic, meditation and asanas of yoga, Chinese healing, and wandering as a way of life: "Increased importance of private esoteric cult-societies," then and now. The liberating universality of the 1960s New Song infiltrated the old redoubts—even the Churches had nuns with guitars singing hymns to the congregations, delivering the religious messages. Transistors and boom-boxes the world over carried the New Sound; just like in Jericho, music brought the walls tumbling down. It has been said that the pope's Polish influence did not do as much to transform Eastern Europe locked behind the Iron Curtain as did the New Song sounding through the tiny transistors. Orpheus, liberator, whose music brings new life.

A simplistic equation based on the happy coincidence of two New Ages and two syncretisms is far too literalistic. In fact, the music of Orpheus in our times began decades before the 1960s, already at the end of the nineteenth century, and not in a concert hall, not as music as such, but in the art of listening. Orpheus is a phenomenon of the ear—a point made beautifully by Elisabeth Sewell.[4] Remember: the animals and trees are held in suspension by the faculty of hearing.

The faculty of hearing, the art of listening, receptivity to the music in the voice went through a radical change in the Viennese consulting rooms of Dr. Breuer and Dr. Freud, when the "talking cure" as Freud came to call his method, first appeared. They listened to the singing of the souls telling of their strange afflictions. The doctors gave a nuanced ear to what was said, hearing the overtones of what was implied and the undertones of what was not said; they listened for repetitive choruses and double entendres and metaphors. They initiated a method of musical listening which today has become so refined that the practitioner listens for changes of key, breathings, rests and stops and quavers, *sub voce* asides like recitatives that move the plot along; listens for crescendos in volume and glissandos of escape. The psychotherapist brings an attention to the patient's performance much as one does to a musical recital, a story-teller, a poetry reading. This ear is specifically Orphic, I would claim, because it listens for the absent in the evident and for the tiniest involuntary indications of the spontaneous spirit inflecting speech, breaking through the humdrum monotone of recounting quotidian events—those sudden transcendences that recompose the ordinary into the extraordinary, into revelation.

III

Finally, Orpheus and the loss of Eurydike. This strand of the Orphic weave has come more to the fore in modern times; it is perhaps the favorite way of imagining him: losing his beloved on their wedding day; he, winning an exceptional permission to descend into the netherworld to retrieve her, liberate her, from the halls of Hades and Queen Persephone, providing he meet one folkloric condition (that

4. Elizabeth Sewell, *The Orphic Voice* (London: Routledge and Kegan Paul, 1960).

he not look back); his last moment hesitation, the glance over the shoulder to be sure she was following, and her slipping away and back into the shades, irretrievable—because of his, well, doubt? His distrust of her? Distrust of woman: a disobedient independent who belonged to nature rather than civilization? Or a careless, neglectful *puer aeternus*? Unconsciously such "slips" are intentional and not a mere slip of the hand. Or, was it her intention to remain *not* with him, giving him the slip? Perhaps, he was right to lose her, as many Medieval versions and moralizers would have it: she was a no-good woman to begin with! She belonged to the realm of darkness all along, which he suddenly recognizes as they emerge toward daylight.

Or did she deliberately make return to life impossible? "Did she will herself more deeply into death?" asks Beverky Zabriskie. "After being amidst the dead, how could she live among those who had not died?"[5] Apart, she nonetheless remains his eternal and constant bride, the handmaiden maintaining fidelity with death.

After all, how could it have happened that Orpheus, Master of Animals—and depictions do sometimes show a snake among his rapt audience of beasts—would allow that mortal bite by a snake in the boot of his bride. The gods have their chthonic and animal epiphanies: so, was this snake just a snake, just an accident, or was this fateful snake an emissary from the netherworld stating its claim on Eurydike-Agriope, her alliance with those below preventing a misalliance with Orpheus?

Perhaps the snake was Asclepius arriving as a guest at the wedding to save her from the toils of a wifely existence, or healing her of simple unconsciousness by the bite that in an instant revealed her to be one of the twice-born and the death of the maiden, that idealized anima image that Orpheus, the poetically musing, divinely inspired, vegetarian pacifist could no longer hold on to and had to relinquish to fulfill his own destiny that has kept him present ever since.

This final thread is both tragic as echoed by the *Alkestis* and romantic as it afterward became—a paradigmatic tale of lost love, lost soul, eternal separation, sadness ever after—and also as enigmatic as a Noh drama. An enigma is a goad to wonder, to speculation. An enigma is like a Her-

5. Beverly Zabriskie, "Orpheus and Eurydice: A Creative Agony," *Journal of Analytical Psychology* 45 (2000): 432.

akleitean gnomon, a koan, an invitation to the hermeneutical pleasures of uncovering, to dig more deeply, thereby breaking the mind of its primary habits and easy apercues.

Marie Delcourt[6] writes: "An *ainigma* refers to all things with a second sense, symbols, oracles, Pythagorean sayings..." This second sense, the *hyponoia* below the evident fatal flaw, is given by his dedication to otherwise and elsewhere: to his lyre, to his singing head, to his cult, to *poiesis*. In this world there was no place for Eurydike, except as enchanted listener, a follower that, he recognized, she could not be. As he let go, or she let go, as he looked back[7] because she was letting go, did he see that it was not her he desired but the longing inspired by her image. It was her image he needed to hold on to rather than her hand. To keep the loss of her, loss as keepsake—that is what sounds through her Orphic voice.

At that moment begins Orpheus's fateful chastity—not as abstinence and frustration, or misogyny and homosexuality (the conventions that would explain it), but chastity as that energizing fidelity to the beloved image—like Petrarch, like Dante—the chastity of longing required by the poetic calling, giving it its wings that expand through the widest cosmos and make possible a cosmological, an Orphic, imagination.

Longing for what is not here, what is beyond, transcendent, cannot be grasped, an imagined beauty, this *pothos*[8] that aches for an *epistrophē* to a further shore—this is the source of Orpheus's poetic enchantment. As Rumi said in countless verses, what we long for is the longing itself. To be filled with longing—that is fulfillment. Tell me what you long for, said the German Romantics, and I will tell you who you are. *Sehnsucht.* From this divine longing come the songs; and Eurydike's absence is present in lyric love poetry, the undying arias of Italian opera, in immediate appeal of Romanticism from Ovid's wry and sophisticated love stories to Shakespeare's allusions to Orpheus, *Anna Karenina*, Bovaryism, and Hollywood.

Orpheus is the god of our all-too-human disease of *Sehnsucht*, afflicting us with lonely nostalgic remembrances, our ache for an absent beauty, our heads afloat and tossed by waves of ungoverned emotions,

6. Marie Delcourt, *Œdipe ou la légende du conquérant*, Bibliothèque de la Faculté de Philosophie et Lettres de l'Université de Liége, fasc. 104 (Paris: E. Droz, 1944).

7. Cf. Christine Downing, "Looking Back at Orpheus," in *Spring: A Jopurnal of Archetype and Culture* 71 (2004): 1–36.

8. See my "Pothos," in *UE* 3: *Senex & Puer.*

singing of what cannot be and never was, estranged on a distant shore far from any home and unable to cease from poetizing the rending pains of human life.

16

GOOD MOTHER EARTH:
IMAGINAL OR LITERAL

I

With your permission I shall begin my contribution to this conference with a biographical fact. I was born onto this planet Earth in a location where there is no earth. The town of Atlantic City in the state of New Jersey is constructed upon a sand bar in the Atlantic Ocean, a place made by waves of water. It is an island of sand; below, of course, is the coastal shelf of rock, which supports the foundations of its great hotels. All the earth, the soil for gardens, for trees, flower beds, and grass had to be brought onto the island by trucks.

The second confessional phenomenon of my biography is that my astrological horoscope announces, at the moment of my birth in this earthless place, I was not granted any planets at all in any of the three zodiacal signs of earth. Earthless in fate as earthless in place.

So I am here today as an "earthless" phenomenon addressing the question of literal and imaginal earth, about which, because of my own peculiar fate, belongs to my psyche and lies close to my heart.

When I arrived in Europe shortly after World War Two, a strong early impression was the sense of *terroir,* the sense of belonging to very specific locations, of the depth of physical earth—granite and flint, sand-

---

The version printed here incorporates passages from "The Good Earth: Imaginal or Literal," originally presented at the conference *Corpo spirituale, terra celeste: La rinascita dello spirito nella materia,* organized by the Associazione Culturale Holos International, Campione, Italy, October 2003, and published in Italian translation in the acts of that conference, Melide, Switzerland, 2004; and from "Mother Earth: Nobody Knows the Troubles I Cause," a talk first delivered at the second international conference on the work of Gaston Bachelard at the Dallas Institute of Humanities and Culture, 2002.

stone and limestone, the alluvial soils with vineyards and fruit trees, and the attachment of the people to their earth. And, the qualities of the different earths seemed to attach to the food and wine, gestures and feelings, and to the very natures of the different peoples.

Physical earth as place became a life-or-death conundrum during the Hungarian Revolt in 1956 when refuges fled into Switzerland. If the Russians were to come, would one flee or hold to one's own land? Motherland. Fatherland. What did these terms mean? During this time I recall the film *High Noon* figuring intensely in psychological conversations and my personal analysis. The hero: does he stand or leave? I remembered then the initiation rite of a Plains Indian tribe where the young brave drives his stake through his bison hide, pinning him onto one spot on the earth, letting the stampeding herd crush him into the earth or divert around him as he stands his ground.

Was I therefore ungrounded, earthless, a vagabond, wanderer, uninitiated, shifting like sand in water, without *terroir*? Moreover, I was in Zurich with Jung where the imaginal emphasis lay upon rocks and soil, on historical ancestors buried in the deep valleys, of hillsides with heavy earth and heavy cows, avalanches and tunnels, underground vaults of gold—a nation of earth identity. It was in this situation that my rebellion began, and my pursuit of earth of another kind.

By "rebellion" I refer to my refusal to be caught in any literalist or materialist thought structure that attempted to ground the psyche in anything beyond itself. My search began for a psychic ground, an ontology of the soul for itself, rather than the usual systems of thought, which ground the psyche in sociology, genetics, physiology, philosophy, or metaphysical transcendences of a literalized spirit.

There is another contributing factor, also biographical. In the early 1950s in India, I had by chance met a man, Gopi Krishna, in whom the Kundalini serpent had awakened, causing him all sorts of physical troubles and psychological anguish and insights. Returning to Europe, I studied Kundalini a bit and benefited from the record of Jung's seminar comments on Kundalini Yoga, and myself wrote a psychological commentary of Gopi Krishna's experiences.[1] Central to our theme of earth is

---

1. "Commentary," in Gopi Krishna, *Kundalini Yoga* (London: Stuart and Watkins, 1970).

the understanding of the Kundalini image of the elephant, which is the animal carrier at two chacras of the Kundalini anatomy: one at the base of the spine and perineum, *muladhara*, the other in the throat and speech center, *visuddha*.[2]

The first elephant at *muladhara* implies the earth as support system, the ground on which you stand, the base of the sitting body, the community, the family; let us say, the roots in the literal earth. The second elephant suggests another support, the word, the figures and images of speech that the breath produces, the expressions of language.

This too has the strength of an elephant, and can be thought of as another kind of earth, the imaginal earth, the *terre pure* as it is called in Buddhism, like the *terre celeste* of Henry Corbin's Persian and Islamic studies, and the fields of Elysium in Homer and Hesiod.

You have been patient to listen to these biographical details, and I believe you understand the dilemma that they expose: How does the sand-bar man find the solid footing of earth, if he refuses to accept the usual ontological groundings that are, each one, literal in one way or another.

The answer is in the work of Gaston Bachelard (1884–1962) who was a student of both poetry and chemistry, both an academic and a freethinker, a member of the highest French intellectual circles and also a recognized scientist.

Bachelard elaborated earth as one of four metaphorical elements. In two books,[3] *Earth and the Reveries of Will* (*Earth I*), and *Earth and Reveries of Repose* (*Earth II*), he laid the poetic foundations for the most conundrum-filled of all archetypal ideas that feed and puzzle the imagination. His work offers an illumination: perhaps there is a depth, a solidity and facticity of matter without earth, an earthiness without soil. Perhaps it is possible to be grounded and to materialize fully without any literal earth.

---

2. C.G. Jung, "Psychological Commentary on Kundalini Yoga: Lectures Three and Four—1932 (from the Notes of Mary Foote)," *Spring: An Annual of Archetypal Psychology and Jungian Thought* (1976): 1–31. Cf. Arthur Avalon, *The Serpent Power* (Madras: Ganesh & Co., 1931), pl. 6.

3. Gaston Bachelard, *Earth and the Reveries of Will: An Essay on the Imagination of Matter*, translated by Kenneth Haltman (Dallas: Institute of Humanities and Culture, 2002) and *Earth and Reveries of Repose: An Essay on Images of Interiority*, translated by Mary McAllester Jones (Dallas: Institute of Humanities and Culture, 2011).

From Bachelard I gained the radical insight that my own dilemma about earthlessness originates in a *literalization* of this element. The poetics, the image, the idea of earth had become congealed with and stuck into the idea of this physical planet. I was now able to grasp that earth as an element of course had its repercussions and expressions in physical forms just as does air and fire and water, but that elemental ideas are not things. Moreover, Bachelard opened an even more subtle door of understanding: the fact that the archetypal idea of earth does literalize and concretize into the physical stuff of the planet is a function of this particular element. It is earth itself that produces this idea of itself—that it is solid, palpable, dense. So dense in fact that we can't see through its literalism into its metaphor. Thus the first psychological task for me became to see through and de-literalize this first element, earth, and turn it, as Bachelard was doing, into psyche, rather than to attempt to turn psyche into something earthy, concrete, physical.

Let us now turn to three areas of current concern—Therapy, Environment, and Violence—and examine, in brief, ways in which the ideas of earth affect our present confusions and sufferings.

II

T*herapy.* We begin first with therapy. By distinguishing earth from an identification with matter, and then placing this element in the imagination, matter as an archetypal idea and earth as an archetypal image, Bachelard corrects Descartes. For it was Christian Descartes who conflated matter with *res extensa,* and thus with the earth of the world and our physical bodies.

Lots of troubles when body becomes Cartesian. It then becomes our earth and our ground, and a dumb passive instrument subject to our will. Then it is but a short mental step to blame the unwilling, inert, or sensuous aspect of body for its sluggish refusal to follow the upward drive of spirit. In fact, body becomes the seat of all resistance to "improvement." Body and mind become opposed, opening the way to Christian asceticism, or just the reverse, New Ageism where body is the wise teacher and the source of freedom and redemption.

Indeed the body does suffer, not because it is earth, the pliable material to our will, but because this earth element has been *literalized into the physical body.* The body's sufferings can as well be poetic, i.e., afflicted by reveries of air, desires of fire, the ebbs and flows of our restless tidal waters. The body is a citadel of metaphors, a repository of images—and this poetics of body scientific medicine can only call psychosomatics.

The term "psychosomatics" attempts to join psyche and soma. Psychosomatics as a practice attempts to uncover the *suksma* in the *shtula,* the subtle in the gross, the poetics of the physical. Bachelard offers modern therapies, and the sufferings of the body, a differentiation of understanding, a way of seeing the material body as held within a poetic imagination called the *ochema* or "vehicle" by the Neoplatonists.[4]

Bachelard's therapeutic contribution to psychosomatics invites us into the body as foci of intimacy—less bones and organs, physiology and genetics, but as psychic qualities of interiority. Inside the earth; the earth inside. Kinds of places where the body hides or is hidden, qualities of lostness, of entanglements, sources and replenishments.

Moreover, the imagination of the earth frees the body's innate desire for repose—Freud's death-drive toward static equilibrium—giving more value to inertia, resistance, fixation, so that the body can follow Alfred Ziegler's idea of morbidity.[5] This Swiss psychiatrist of psychosomatic conditions wrote, in various studies, that life is inherently death oriented. All life follows Hermes *chthonios* who takes souls to the underworld's deep invisible earth, the earth as *chthon* below the earth of Gaia, and below the more seasonal naturalistic earth of Demeter. *Chthon* is the deepest interiority where Hades and Persephone receive the souls, and whose messages we receive as symptoms.

III

Environment. Bachelard's imagination of earth is free from moralism. It is a true phenomenology. The earth escapes the Christian condemnation. As the great Jesuit scholar Hugo Rahner said, the New Testament stresses that "Earth and world become the embodiment and symbol of the moral remoteness from God." "The darkness, inertia

---

4. E.R. Dodds, "Appendix II" in Proclus, *The Elements of Theology* (Oxford: Clarendon Press, 1963).

5. Alfred J. Ziegler, *Archetypal Medicine* (Thompson, Conn.: Spring Publications, 2020 [1974]).

and heaviness that we call earth and matter become the tangible image" of this fall. "Satan and his demons are spirits of the 'depths'... their drive downward... to the depths of this dark earth." [6]

As that element which invites *volonté*, will power, we must remember to keep that power intimately inherent *in earth itself* and not as an opposite, a human activity applied to a passive paste or clay. *It* wills. Earth is a seminal force, the "force that through the green fuse drives the flower," in the words of Dylan Thomas. As the actual earth throws up its forms, hurling rocks and spewing lava, remembering shapes in fossils and compacting jewels and fuels, so the imagination of earth shows its animal force as the bugs in Navaho myth at the bottom of the world, the Turtle below everything in Sanskrit legend, the Serpent in American Indian, the Fish in Japan, and in Hebrew legends the most bottom place below is where reside Behemoth and Leviathan.

Though an active principle, earth is not demonic as in Christianism or necessarily female as in Feminist Revisionism wants to believe. For instance: ancient Egypt, where earth, Geb, is male. It is the stubborn force of earth that teaches the potter and leads the miner to follow its veins. The imagination of earth is tough as anyone knows who tries to work it—not merely in concrete representations like potting or mining or gardening, but anyone who tries to go deep, or lay foundations of thought, or excavate for etymological roots. Earth is a *spiritus rector*, a teacher of the hand and the mind to not move too fast, of the eye to note palpable differences, of the body to sit still and weigh and sound and measure and ponder.

It is very hard for us today, after Descartes—who lay the philosophical groundwork for the exploitation of the environment by declaring it dead without soul, without activity of its own—very hard for us to imagine the actual literal earth to be inspirited. Peoples of many other cultures feel the soil on which they live and from which they live not merely as a nourishing and exacting mother, but also as directly infused into their own personal souls. The inner soul and the outer soil have a permeable osmotic connection, so that where there is forcible expulsion, migration,

6. Hugo Rahner, "Earth Spirit and Divine Spirit in Patristic Theology," in *Spirit and Nature: Papers from the Eranos Yearbooks*, edited by Joseph Campbell (New York: Pantheon, 1954).

or radical destruction of the actual earth—for mining, damming of a river, deforestation—they feel their own souls deteriorating, the life goes out of them, and they die. This is not merely for economic reasons: that they have been deprived of their subsistence—animals, plants, water. Rather, their spirit world has been disrupted; they have lost their protectors and their reason for being and serving. Where we in our "civilization" can live without gods in a secular society, functioning quite well as lost souls in a soulless condition, from their point of view we are already walking dead, zombies, unreal. Only in this way, detached from the ground, are we able to be as successful as we are. Successful within the madness of a philosophically dead planet.

When we pray "Thy Will be done," it is to an abstract transcendent god who lives far away from the earth, if he "lives" at all. When animistic, polytheistic, pagan peoples pray "Thy Will be done" they are speaking to the rain and the river, to the plants and the insects too, to the earth's own willing powers.

Earth II investigates the very reverse of the autonomy of the earth's Will: Repose. Here Bachelard takes us into the poetic depths of the earth's interiority, tracking inward as roots and tubers move, into slowness, darkness, labyrinths—the very companion, or cancellation, of the aggression offered by *volonté*. Rather than action and concrete mineral riches, Bachelard presents in *Earth II* the imagination of qualities, tonalities, sensations, rhythms. It is from this second volume that environmentalism will be able to draw thoughts for a reverent, responsive, aesthetic approach to the planet. For environmentalism today (regardless of the side you are on, exploitative or protective) is driven by activists, the imagination of Will.

There is far more to ecology than attention to the destruction of Mother Earth and the urgency of doing something to protect her. The Will is only one side of a caring and intelligent response. Green activism, green politics, green restoration are the energies of the earth expressing itself through the heroic activists, the Mother's sons.[7] Unless, however, the intimacy of repose, the listening to the earth with a poetic, contemplative ear accompanies the activity, we are running the same danger:

---

7. Cf. my "The Great Mother, Her Son, Her Hero, and the Puer," in *UE 3: Senex & Puer.*

heroic hastiness. The earth, whether literal or imaginal, has one common trait: slowness. Even an avalanche begins slowly. Earth's solidity, deep resonance, and pull inward and downward work like a magnet of gravity. The density of earth smothers fire, dams water, clouds and clogs air. The *terre celeste* of heavenly earth, described as a throne of precious stone, a blue *caelum* or covering vault, eternally fixed or as an unending geography of a heaven with its own mountains, is equally solid! The imaginal earth offers as much ground for psychological action, the action of contemplation, as physical action in the literal field of green environmentalism. Mother Earth, both green and blue[8] can constellate heroics of the spirit, and both theaters of redemptive efforts may be pleasing to her.

IV

Violence and War. The Roman god of war, Mars, was also a god of agriculture, and the early Roman legions, before the incorporation of non-Italic men from transalpine tribes, were farmers. The plowshare and the sword belong in the same image (Isaiah 2:4) as do brass church bells and the cannon barrels into which the bells have been smelted. Nowhere do Bachelard's two aspects of earth show more clearly than in the battlefield. There we encounter violent extremes of desperate Will and fallen bodies in complete Repose. For millennia wars have been fought over territory. Thousands of dead to gain or hold a few feet of sodden terrain as in Flanders.

Even today it is the oil fields in the earth of Iraq and the spread of bases in the lands of the Near East and Central Asia that are the hidden agenda of "regime change." Machiavelli insisted that the best general knows topography and by mastering the lay of the earth where an engagement takes place he could win the battle.[9]

Since no theory of the origins of war has been put forward to everyone's satisfaction, and since wars have existed since humans populated the earth, perhaps it is the earth itself that initiates the violence. Perhaps the earth does not like humans and might do better without us. Maybe

---

8. For data on the green/blue contrast, see my "Alchemical Blue and the *Unio Mentalis*," *Spring: A Journal of Archetype and Culture* 54 (1993): 132–48.

9. Niccolò Machiavelli, *Il Principe*, translated by L. Arthur Burd (Oxford: Clarendon Press, 1968), ch. 14.

Mother Earth wants us to pay in blood for our offensive use of the land even long ago as planters and settlers. Perhaps Earth is the active principle of violence, demanding continual sacrifices—not only with toil as the Bible says—but blood sacrifices, as if Mother Earth impels her children to wars.

Let us turn to a terrible example of earth causing violence: 'Am ha-eretz Israel. 'Am ha-eretz equals the land, the earth of Israel as a people, a dream and a place. The Bible names on page after page places of the land and of battles. The Bible is Bachelardian; it is a book of Earth and Will. In the prayers for the State of Israel there has been a fusion of connotations of the term ha-eretz, so that is means land or earth, *and* the Holy Land, *and* the Promised Land, *and* Zion or Jerusalem, *and* Return from Exile of the Jewish people after the destruction of their Temple, *and* also actual geography. This merging of religious vision and physical geography in the Hebrew word for earth is a cause of the greatest trouble.

Recently, alternatives for a new prayer have been proposed with phrases that imply a distinction between actual geographic earth on the one hand, and on the other, the messianic salvational Zion—the physical location of which, by the way, is strongly disputed—or Holy Land, and that imaginal place similar to the *terre pure* in Buddhism and the nowhere (*Na-Koja-Abad*) in Persian mysticism.

It is important here to recall the mythical crossing of the Red Sea so essential to Jewish legend and cult. It presents a dividing line between the land of Egypt and the Promised Land, between the past and future. The literal and sensate on the one side, and the imagined and redemptive on the other. To achieve the promised earth at least two conditions must be fulfilled. First, forty years of wandering. Wandering in a hostile, unfriendly desert; the earth of deprivation and of fulfillment. Second, longing for the old earth of Egypt and its physical realities must be suppressed. The privation of the people during the wandering years was great, says the Bible; the earth gave them nothing to eat. And the people longed back to Egypt, to the fertility of the sensate geography of the Nile valley, saying,

> We remember the fish which were we wont to eat in Egypt... the cucumbers, and the melons, and the leeks, and the onions, and the garlic; but now our soul is dried away; there is nothing at all.
>
> (Numbers 11: 5–6)

The Red Sea crossing marks the division between *kinds of longing;* longing for the *land of imagination,* the land of promise, of milk and honey, and the *actual geography* of Egypt, the melons and cucumbers, the literal historical, sensate longings of memory.

As the Biblical people were driven and scattered into many parts of the globe, and migrated from place to place, this imaginal earth of the promised land became their foundation. Their earth was to be found in their books and commentaries, their rituals and community customs, the words of promise in the Bible and the longing for return from exile. These longings for return tended to incorporate nostalgia for the fertile geography left behind, thereby literalizing *both* earths into the place of Israel, both imaginal milk and honey and literal melons and onions.

The image of the Red Sea crossing recapitulated annually in Jewish ceremonies of Pessach clearly distinguishes two kinds of earth. But this distinction is unacceptable to fundamentalists of various persuasions who take the Bible—that amazing tome of legend, story, family, poetry, wisdom, puns, moral lessons, wonders, heroics, love, and cruelties—as literal history and the actual word of God. Whose god? Which god? Such questions are heretical, anathema to the literalist mind.

Although 'Am ha-eretz as both imaginal and literal has proven precarious to sustain and politically not fully possible, the literalization of Mother Earth into a place has also tended to literalize the idea of exile into placelessness. Exile became a literal condition rather than the "wandering" that fosters imagination, as the wandering in the desert fostered visions of milk and honey.

Plato described a wandering principle or "errancy" as another archetypal basis, second to the dominance of reason, to be a cause of all things (*Timaeus* 47e–48e). Is it not this irrational "wandering" of the Jewish soul without permanent "home" among the ruling domination that lies in the background of the Jewish soul's haunting sense of exile? Has not exile also provided the wide-ranging freedom and cross-cultural fertility of the soul's imagination, an imagination that has in fact been the grounding home of the Jewish diaspora through the ages? That earth gives the Will to fight all obstacles and shape ever new adaptations and also the Repose of the stubborn solidity of tradition from which the soul draws comfort and support.

V.

Finis. Now at the end it may perhaps seem that I have been too topical, discussing such mundane issues as therapy, the ecological predicament, and the violence of the Middle East. These are major issues of our time and they cannot be set aside while we pursue more universal questions of the spirit. The soul lives in the valley, not on the mountain top. As a psychologist I feel called by the soul's entanglements. Many of these entanglements are the result of ideas, not only personal relations, feelings, and societal conditions. Ideas. Unconscious or half-conscious ideas. Ideas that we have and do not know we have, have us; we are caught in them and suffer from not weighing them carefully.

So I consider these few remarks to have been a therapy of ideas. I have attempted to show the relevance for the suffering of violence when an idea of earth is literalized into a specific earth; for the suffering of the body when we imagine the body to be only matter and not also metaphor, for the suffering of the environment when we neglect its own autonomous Will and its chthonic spirit and intentions.

Hence I have been emphasizing the Will. I have wanted, also, to keep in our minds the common language about the "good" earth's shadows: soil and dirt; fears of being buried alive; quicksand, sinkholes and dust bowls; earthquakes and avalanches; the parched desert, the quagmire, the foxhole and battle trench, slag heap and rock wall; bats in black caves, spiders and serpents lurking, ghouls rising from graves; dust to dust...the unfathomable autonomous depths.

Of these shadows, the figure of Mother Earth herself is the deepest. As Sam Gill contends, the collapsing of many female goddess figures into a single goddess named Earth Mother "at least for North America would seem to be historically and ethnographically an error."[10] Though an *idea* of Mother Earth, says Gill, is "primordial and archetypal," it took on actual life among native peoples only in the nineteenth century after anthropologists and scholars had used the concept to understand native practices and sayings mainly in relation with official "white" institutions. It is as if Mother Earth activated the imagination in defense of

---

10. Sam D. Gill, *Mother Earth* (Chicago: The University of Chicago Press, 1987), 151–52. Cf. 120.

native Americans in many areas of the United States concurrent with the insinuation of "white" thinking into native minds parallel with the encroachment of "white" invaders into their lands.

My main aim is to draw us away from imagining the earth as a good mother, passive, nurturing, and supportive, and to recognize the *idea* of earth to be a complex phenomenon requiring efforts of thought and imagination. This because the poetic element of earth itself imagines itself into our actions. It is the factor that wills us to concretize and literalize and to posit grounds as heavy as the elephants, whether physical ontologies of *muladhara* or metaphysical of *visuddha*. This elemental earth urges upon us a terrible *furor agendi,* that curiously, ironically leads to the very destruction of the actual earth (in the name of "development" and in defense of "our land"), even in the Holy Land itself, such as we see each day, and in the exploitation of the body and the environment.

The earth that we need to recover so that we may be less vulnerable to our unthought thoughts is the earth above this one, the *terre celeste,* where the roots of the Kabbalah tree draw their strength, and the earth that is deeply below in the chthonic underworld imagination, the cold, still depths where the images move in silence, yet which keep our invisible minds inquiring and poetizing.

The recovery of the imaginal dimensions of earth is of singular importance. For too long we have been Cartesian, assigning to earth nothing but blankness; or Newtonian or Einsteinien, that it is a soulless material force field; or Romantic as a mother whose bosom continues to offer fruits and flowers and sad graveyards for eulogies; or as Christians, regarding the earth as the place and source of the Fall from which we must all one day ascend to a new and better world by the conflagration of a fiery Revelation. My turn to Bachelard was to escape these other fantasies of earth in order to grant earth its dignity and autonomy as an elemental maker of our imaginations about it. For that is all we know: that we are no more than passing occasions standing on and over and under its great expanse, attempting to form images that give the earth its full due.

17

APOLLO, DREAM, REALITY

I

We begin in the ruins. Nothing stands. The marvelous edifice constructed by Freud in 1900—the thickest book of all his writings—did not last even one hundred years. Ethnologists showed the universality of his claim to be invalid; feminists exposed the misogynist distortion that faulted its bedrock; Marxists demolished its bourgeois bias, while social historians placed the entire construction within late nineteenth-century colonialism, so that contemporary environmentalists are able to plow fragments of Freud back into the ground to start all over with a new "natural" discourse of the dream as the psyche's reflection of the given world.

Even more, the dream itself, beyond any theory about it, is generally ignored by psychotherapies where once it was the *via regia* to understanding the realities of the soul. Little bands of restorationists and devotees of Freud and Jung, trained in their schools, still hold conclaves where dreams have prominence. Also, the old Romanticism that heralded dreams as revelations of truth continues in the contemporary affectations of shamanism and spiritualism. Nonetheless, for the wide consensus the dream refers to, depends upon, or is reducible to something more real than itself—linguistics, brain activity, biogenetics. *Au fond*, dreams are defenses against reality and escape from it.

Invitational Lecture (originally titled "Dreaming: an Escape to Reality") in the Kacalieff Visiting Artist and Scholars Program, *Dreamweaver: The Science and Culture of Escape, Fantasy, and Reverie*, Cleveland Institute of Art, January 2006, and revised into the present form for a *lectio magistralis* by "Nine Masters" under the auspices of *Torino: Capitale mondiale de libro*, Turin, Italy, September 2006.

The task today as I see it is not to resurrect Freud's edifice by rearranging the ruins into contemporary deconstructive shape. Rather it is to expose the idea of reality to which the dream is opposed and can be reduced.

Before we go any further into dreams, we must first reduce ourselves to where we are: in the "reality" of the consensus, the usual ordinary day-world. Our trip to the moon begins here on earth. And—this earth is flat. Even before the bulldozers and steamrollers flattened the earth into our daily urban "reality" of highways, driveways, and foundational concrete slabs. The earth had already been quite flattened by Western philosophy's first supreme developer, René Descartes (1596–1650) who named the world of material things—rocks and trees and our daily bread— *res extensa*, an extended thing, material, public, objective. The great wide world, "so beautiful, so various, so new" (as Matthew Arnold sang of it), Descartes flattened into a monistic geometry to be further comprehended and measured as space by Isaac Newton in the next century. Specific places became abstract locations, coordinates on a map, surveyors plats, while all the elves, wood spirits and river nymphs belonging to this place and that, the little people of ghosts and ancestors, the aboriginal inhabitants of the earth, were renamed, baptized into our Western tradition, or banned into the territory of the unreal, mere fables and myth, the province of witches and necromancy, superstition, heathen paganism, expected only in the fantasies of little children and the reveries of madmen in the asylum.

By the middle of the nineteenth century the mind of science had so taken over the notion of reality that the dictionary could define it as "that which constitutes the actual thing as opposite to what is merely apparent." Reality is "what underlies and is the truth of appearances." What underlies things as they appear? The laws and mathematical formulae of microphysics and microgenetics. These don't appear, but they constitute the dictionary's reality. Dreams and fantasies may appear privately, but only their public measurable reality—the brain?—is their truth. Moreover, what you and I taste and see, the aromas arising and the spill of colors are by definition not constitutive of things, mere secondary qualities as empirical philosophy declared, superficialities like soft covers pasted over truth. Sounds and sights, and especially dreams, are merely subjective. The world itself and its ultimate underlying *real* reality consist in the motion of the tiniest nano-impulses jostling randomly.

Since dreams and fantasies are neither hard, real, public, objective things nor reducible to mathematical formulae, they are unreal and untrue. Hence eminent scientists like Crick and Monod can regard them as mere garbage of the brain's electrical processing during sleep.

The Italian intellect, already in the figure of Giambattista Vico, recognized the ruinous effect on human phenomena not suited to Cartesian scientific method as it became science and epistemology. Vico's *New Science* says that the study of knowing and how to gain knowledge of reality and certitude of truth cannot begin in logic and mathematics and introspection, but in what is prior to them—historically, psychologically and philologically—the study of myth. The first science is the understanding of fables.[1] In them we find the *universali fantastici,* which stand within and before all concept formation that the Cartesian mind wrongly uses to know reality and state truth.

Vico's *First Oration* (1699 at age 31) already presents *phantasia* as a primary generative power. Knowledge of reality requires the "poetic wisdom," as he called it, lodged in the universals of imagination.

If we place our topic Dreams/Reality against Vico's thought and what I have earlier espoused as the "poetic basis of mind,"[2] dreams, because they are by nature not clear and distinct, become closed to understanding by Cartesian method, a method forced by its own epistemology to oppose them to "true reality."

II

More potent perhaps than even Descartes is the deeper distrust of dreaming that comes from the Christian Bible. The verb "to dream" does not appear in the New Testament, and the noun "dream" occurs only three times in Matthew. This dismissal of dreaming is part and parcel of the Christian relegation of the word "psyche" in the sacred texts in favor of "pneuma," the windy, airy, elevated spirit. The word for soul (*psychē*) is used fifty-seven times, but *pneuma* occurs two hundred and seventy-four times![3] Paul uses "soul" only four times and,

---

1. Giambattista Vico, *The New Science,* translated by Dave Marsh (London: Penguin Books, 1999).

2. *Re-Visioning Psychology* (New York: Harper & Row, 1975), xi.

3. David L. Miller, "Achelous and the Butterfly," *Spring: An Annual of Archetypal Psychology and Jungian Thought* (1973): 14.

says Miller, refers to *psichikoi* as bad and *pneumatikoi*, good (1 Corinthians 2: 13–15).

What does this matter? Who cares what Descartes wrote centuries ago, and hasn't the Reformation taught us to read the New Testament each in our own fashion? By exposing the background to our notions of reality and imagination I am saying we cannot get away from our tradition. Every kid playing his push-button games, entering virtual reality, falling behind in his math homework, and noticing his dreams have started down the slippery slope to perdition. He or she is escaping from reality, seduced by the irrational underworld of pagan powers who lured good Christians in Descartes's times with magic and alchemy and in earlier times of the great desert Saints with the temptations of the night. These holy men lived solitary lives in caves and kept vigils through the night to prevent falling asleep lest they dream.[4]

Distrust. Suspicion. For example: A major psychology textbook, *Psychology and Life*,[5] used for the college introductory course by at least 1,000 students each year in the Ohio University system, a book that weighs in at over 600 pages, costing students over two hundred dollars and is now in its twentieth edition, and written by a national authority who holds top professional power—this book makes one reference on one page only to "imagination," and that under "memory." On the same index page, words such as "internet," "intimacy," "infancy" receive multiple entries.

What do we discover in that textbook about imagination? It interferes with remembering reality; it fills in gaps. Imagination falsifies factual witness. You can't trust it. Imagination becomes by authority a confabulator and leads us astray. University students in psychology lecture halls to which hundreds of thousands flock all over the United States, and colonizing globally, in hopes of awakening to themselves and to the psyche in the grand spread of life are given the Cartesian-Christian message disguised as the latest textbook science: beware of imagination. It is hardly worth mentioning. I ask you to keep in mind this American textbook example regarding the absence of imagination. We shall return to it, and how it affects the reality of the world we all live in.

---

4. See my *The Dream and the Underworld* (New York: Harper & Row, 1979).

5. Richard Gerrig and Philip Zimbardo, *Psychology and Life* (Harlow: Pearson, 2012).

III

We come now to the third factor forming our world view that divides reality from reverie. First, Cartesians and objective positivists ever since gave us an idea of the real as the day world of reliable hard objects ultimately measurable and subject to science's reason. Second, the Christian Bible warned us against the night world as untrustworthy and dangerous to the soul. If the first support for our current popular notion regarding dreams is metaphysical and second theological, the third factor governing our relation with dreams is mythic. I refer specifically to the figure of Apollo.

That Greek god most influences our attempts to connect the day world of waking life with the night world of dreaming life. Apollo, in brief, and as you all well know, was the god who ruled the Delphic oracle, a god of prophesy, of healing, a god of youth and visible radiant beauty, very very male, violent and failed with female figures, and a killer of serpents and dragons; and, most relevant for our theme now, he was the favorite god of Artemidorus of Daldis, the person who authored in Greek, around the year 270 of our calendar, a full study of dreams. His *Oneirocritica*[6] presents a theory, an interpretive method, and a compilation of dreams gathered by him in the ancient world, both from literature and from actual dreamers. It was Apollo he declares who told him to do this work and write his book (II, 70). This book is his offering to Apollo. The *fons et origo* of dream study in our culture begins under the aegis of Apollo.

Describing the effects and qualities of the major gods, Artemidorus considers Apollo a helper of seers and philosophers. He gives them wisdom and brings renown and success. Apollo uncovers hidden things for he is identified with Helios, the personified sun, and called Phoibos—the shining light. As Helios, Apollo wakes us each from our sleep and cheers us on to our work. Further, he brings ruin to underworld thieves and underhanded swindlers because he reveals all things in public view (II, 35–36).

---

6. Artemidor von Daldis, *Traumbuch*, translated by F. S. Krauss (Basel and Stuttgart: Schwabe Verlag, 1965). Translated into English by Robert J. White (*The Interpretation of Dreams* [Park Ridge, N.J.: Noyes Press, 1975]).

The idea that the dream is a disguise, yet that its hidden meaning can be brought to light, comes originally in our tradition from Artemidorus, and behind him, Apollo. Nietzsche, in his way, continues the idea, calling Apollo, god of dreams, because in dreams we have direct apprehension of form without matter, forms lit by their own light. Pulp manuals of dream symbols as well as sophisticated texts like Freud's still follow the Apollonic method of converting the obscure into daylight. Freud, in fact, said a dream uninterpreted is like a letter unopened. From antiquity until today the Apollonic method of translating the enigma of the dream into *useful* knowledge has prevailed. (For Artemidorus, useful for prognosis and prophesy; for Freud, useful for self-knowledge, much as at Delphi: "know thyself.") We do not realize the overwhelming power of Apollo ingrained in our mental set, and the blinding consequents of that light.

We should of course not undervalue this light. Civilization, and culture too, still bathe in it. The Enlightenment: science, clear and distinct ideas, inquiry, intellectual discourse, the ideals of an educated public free of priestly power and terrorizing superstitions, a high culture of classical style with individual egoistic luminaries from Louis, Sun King of France, to the painters, dramatists, poets, scholars, musicians and other devotees of Apollo's Muses.

But are these clarifying virtues pertinent to the obverse half of the psyche,[7] imagination's night world of dreaming? For instance: during the night you are held within the dream, one figure—not always the chief one—among others walking around in its inscape. Then, with the first ray of morning consciousness, you believe the dream is in you—in your mind, your head. You say, "I had a dream," a statement of having and owning.

Yet during the night the dream had you in *its* possession. Just because something comes to you doesn't make it yours. If you see a horse in a field, a plane in the sky, they are not yours because you saw them. The Greeks said, I *saw* a dream; we say I *had* a dream. The verb "have" is a favorite of Captain Ego; I think we would do well to dispossess ourselves of it except for possessions picked up at UPIM and GAP.

---

7. Cf. Gilbert Durand, "Psyche's View," *Spring: An Annual of Archetypal Psychology and Jungian Thought* (1981): 1–19.

This seizure of the dream and claiming it as yours helps account for the resistance of the dream to being owned. It asserts its independence by refusing to be recalled. One needs a softened will, a gentle sinking, to let the dream return in daylight. It asks to be invited.

The interpretative method regardless of school turns images into words and then the words into concepts. The yellow dog baring its teeth and keeping you out of your own house in a dream becomes your nasty snarling impulses that prevent you from "being at home," whether at home in your day world house with your family or at ease in your own interiority. The snake in the grass of which you are so fearful in the dream becomes, through interpretation, magical bad fortune, an unsuspected enemy, slippery sexual entanglement, the mother complex, poisonous hatreds, a hidden deceit, which you are afraid to notice but which lie right at your feet with each step you take. This is all Apollo, bringing the concealed to light. The original is lost in translation. Once you know the meaning, you can throw the dream away. In search of its meaning, we demean the dream.

And, this is Apollo giving you healing and personal importance. The dog, the snake came to you so they are yours with a personal meaning for you, reinforcing your sense of individuality. Apollo, writes Nietzsche, is "the genius of the *principium individuationis.*"[8] The Apollonian gives the sense of singular individuality with a "biographical portrait" according to Nietzsche.

One more Apollonian influence: we feel less darkened and perplexed, clearer, brightened, whitened, even cleaner after a "good" interpretation. Again Apollo, for the root of *phoibos* means both prophesying and cleansing.[9] Apollo was the main divinity of purification rites.

There is madness, too, in this method. Oedipus, when asked by the Chorus "O doer of dread deeds...What daimon drove you on?" replies, "Apollo it was, Apollo, friends/Who brought these ills." (1318–21). Another clarifier and purifier, Orestes, was directly driven to his murders by Apollo. The mantic German poet Hölderlin, asked about his later madness, supposedly said, "Apollon hat geschlagen."

8. Friedrich Nietzsche, "The Birth of Tragedy," in *The Philosophy of Nietzsche,* translated by Clifton Fadiman (New York: Modern Library, n.d.).

9. Henry George Liddell & Robert Scott, *Greek-English Lexicon* (Oxford: Clarendon Press, 1890), 1685a.

Apollonic inspiration today does not rave, nor do the interpreters of dreams in the well-tempered sessions of therapy perform foretellings as if seized by a *theiamania*. Much has been tamped down since the gods-filled ancient world. Inspired revelation today by, for the most part female, analysts may be more quotidian, but no less certain. The simple act of turning to dreams to see what might be in store for the client and "guiding them aright" constellates the Apollonic background. It is a kind of seeing, writes Thomas Aquinas "like sunlight in the atmosphere." *Prophetia* and *raptus*, Thomas writes, "is being raised up by a higher power—away from what is proper to nature, toward what is contrary to nature (*contra naturam*)."[10]

The essence of interpretation remains the revelation of hidden meaning. Freud called it the "latent" meaning in distinction to the "manifest" content, which is "only natural" (*ganz natürlich*), the evident and ordinary residues of daily life. Jung's entire reading of psychic materials emphasized that the work is *contra naturam*—one of his favorite phrases. I too have often laid waste to the "naturalistic fallacy" in favor of "seeing through." Apollo seems unavoidable so long as we want to know.

IV.

What then do we do in our daily life with a dream? May I offer some practical counsel? First of all, try not to escape from it. Let it stay around, puzzling you, affecting you, haunting your feelings with its images. Live with the yellow dog, the snake. Keep an eye on the grass.

Second, resist knowing. Stave off the knowledge drive, the ancient Apollonic urge to read the dream for enlightenment, prediction. A "warning dream," a "blessing dream," a "bad dream." You don't know what it wants, why it came, what it means. Watch out for conceptual formulations. Heed the great French master of imagination Gaston Bachelard, who wrote: "Images and concepts are formed at opposite poles of mental activity: imagination and reason. A polarity of exclusion plays between

---

10. *Questiones Disputatae de Veritate* 12.1 and 13.1; cf. Josef Pieper, *Love and Inspiration: A Study of Plato's* Phaedrus, translated by Richard and Clara Winston (London: Faber & Faber, 1964), 55f.

them…" "Between the concept and the image, there can be no synthesis." "The image can only be studied through the image, by dreaming images…in a state of reverie."[11] And Vico: "The weaker its power of reasoning, the more vigorous the human imagination grows."[12]

Third, don't try to bridge straight into the day world or connect the dream with a day world worry. Of course a dream may sometimes offer a direct solution to a problem. Inventors, novelists, mathematicians stuck and sweating finally take to bed, beaten, only to find an answer come to them during the night, benefit of a dream. But this is fortuitous, and we thank the gods in the morning for providing this help. Fortuitous, yet possibly unfortunate: by reading the dream directly in terms of the problem, we may miss what other intimations could be coiled into its images.

Remember: application of a dream to a day world problem uses the dream for personal purposes, supposing the fundamental mistake of the Apollonic mind: that the dream is individually *yours*, a servant reinforcing your notion of *your* individuality.

Since you can't avoid the sense of the dream being meant for you, let the visitor in. Open the door; put out the welcome mat. Teach your children to be happy they dreamt and to tell the dream at the breakfast table, letting the night demons share the coffee, the sugar, and the bright orange juice. The dream becomes part of the communal household. In fact, smaller children more closely participate in dreams told at table. The *phantasia puerilis* is more scary because it is more present, as it is present, according to Vico and Herder and the Romantics, in fables and fairy tales, in "primitives" and visionaries, the deliria of the possessed imagination, and the child.

You may ask questions of the dream but withhold those interpretive remarks that could cause its images to wither. Be sensitive and sensible. Let a dream speak in its own language. For Freud this language was "associations": let associations come to mind without censorship, he said. For Jung, the dream spoke in images that needed support with cultural references from tradition, symbolism, ritual, folklore. For Vico, I suppose, the dream speaks its "poetic wisdom" in the "poetic logic" of

11. Gaston Bachelard, *On Poetic Imagination and Reverie*, selected, translated, and introduced by Colette Gaudin (Thompson, Conn.: Spring Publications: 2022 [1971]), 63.

12. Vico, *The New Science*, 89.

the universals of imagination. All its figures transform into their archetypal backgrounds or heroic configurations, no longer simply representing their day world counterparts. Vico, I suppose, would agree with Jung who nourished the dream, feeding it with cultural riches, placing its images among similar ones. Jung called his method "amplification," increasing its volume and value, taking it out of the personal and individual toward the archetypal and collective.

Fifth—if that is where we are—assume the dream is all one piece, any part of it belongs with the rest of it: The old tree in your childhood garden uprooted; the movie star telling you something you can't remember on waking; the sense that your dead mother or a woman like her was somewhere around in a little boat... these bits belong because the dream jumbled them together like a mosaic, like a collage, and, when any one of them is present, the others are also present. It is Apollonic to make acute distinctions, to select and discard, in order to know each bit.

Sixth, let the dream move along. If it does move, let it become a reverie, an active imagining that Captain Ego addresses with his or her day world intentions, and watch its response to your investigations. Like an author, let the characters in your theatre of the night speak for themselves. Don't put words in their mouths. Trust that what they say are *their* utterances and not made up by you. The dream may, however, not want to move on, but instead stay fixed, unbudging. Its blank enigmatic refusal to reveal anything further, by the way, can teach you just what *your* intentions are. It is revealing *you*, interpreting *you*. By sticking with its images of the dug-up tree, the movie star speaking and the mother-like woman in a canoe or kayak—that is precisely what it wants to show.

What *it* wants—that is the key. Turn yourself right around. The dog from which I am running in the dream—turn to it. What does it want? Why did it come to scare my sleep? What does *it* feel, not only that I feel scared. That strange landscape in which my dreams place me repeatedly, so familiar and yet unknown, a landscape I try to leave, find my way through, backtrack, awaking anxious, after trying so hard to get out. What is this country in which I pass so many nights? What draws me there? Again, what does it want with me?

Perhaps, the "me" in the dream is another me, just beginning to learn how to live among the creatures and terrains of imagination.

This takes us to the seventh piece of my counsel, most important of all. Stay involved in the dream. The key word: *participation,* rather than interpretation. Immersion, as plunged in music, wrapped round. "Caught in that sensual music, all neglect/Monuments of unageing intellect," wrote W.B.Yeats,[13] contrasting in his way the Apollonian attempts at static identifiable form with Dionysian immersion.

We have traveled widely and circled back to Nietzsche's attempt to discover the birth of tragedy, and from that the birth of art from the Dionysian imagination—despite Apollo and his lyre, the nobility of his inspiration, his youthful beauty, his manifestations in the formal disciplines of the Muses.

We are back in Delphi of primordial *phantasia* before Apollonic divination, when oracular inspiration emerged from the serpent Python and the place was Dionysian. And I am back with Nietzsche, calling up Dionysus and his troop of dancers, Dionysus-*zoe* as he was called, the animal rhythm of vitality *before* comprehension, *before* appearance in the light. Or, a dark light of subtle unreflected awareness, neither prophetically ahead of the dance nor digestively after, consciousness in the movement itself, like song breaking out of the throat, words from the tongue. Dionysus liberates fantasy; he was called "the loosener," the imagination that emboldens the autonomy of art and enlivens any moment of the world.

He was no Olympian, nor was he noble as Apollo, but Dionysus was perhaps the people's favorite; his presence, and the presence of the gods, in all things was the ancient reality, and can be ours as well once we recognize with Nietzsche: "the terrible historical need of our unsatisfied modern culture...the consuming desire for knowledge—what does all this point to, if not the loss of myth, the loss of the mythic home." This mythic home is the actual world around us as imagination gives it to us, the world filled with enigmatic potentials that the arts resonate with and reply to. Potentials reside in the hard, reliable things we call reality, Freud's day residues (*Tagesreste*), wherever, even in UPIM and GAP, things not sheerly such but as repositories of quickening fantasies, fertile images that reverie can turn into song.

Loss of the mythic home returns us to Vico again and to the deeper consequences of his obsession with the Cartesians. "Descartes made no

13. "Sailing to Byzantium," in *The Poems of W.B.Yeats* (New York: Macmillan, 1928).

secret of the very low esteem in which he held languages and rhetorical, literary, and historical studies, and in general the classical humanities," writes Elio Gianturco.[14] These studies were precisely the path (*methodos*) to knowledge that Vico pursued, a method more appropriate to understanding phenomena of imagination than direct observation, logic, optics, and geometry from which the Cartesian idea of understanding derives.

Moreover, the very idea of "understanding" must be re-conceived. To begin with, the dream presents itself as "un-understandable." "The dream is not meant to be understood," said Freud. Obscurity is of its essence. It's home is the mythic underworld, in the house of Hades who has no visibilities in the day world. Dreams (*oneiroi*) like *somnos* and *hypnos* and *thanatos* belong to the "brood of night," including, says Hesiod's *Theogony,* old age, envy, strife, doom, lamentation, deceit.[15] These phenomena are not clear and distinct. Cartesian method that cannot perceive them can therefore not understand them. Instead, says Vico, they require a "poetic logic." Understanding requires assimilation into their obscurity. "Man becomes all things not by understanding (*homo non intelligendo fit omnia*)... for when he does not understand, he makes them out of himself, and by transforming himself, becomes them."[16]

"Transforming himself into them"—that seems the key. This operation begins with the bare facts of the dream images. There they stand, fully exposed, yet utterly obscure. Since, according to Vico, *verum ipsum factum,* the incoherent images are the same as the dream's truth, its whole truth and nothing but the truth. The truth of the dream is not its "true meaning" awaiting revelation, but is the bare facticity of the dream itself. The student of dreams gains understanding by an effort of suppression, refusing any notion that the dream's truth lies elsewhere. You remain benighted, dedicated to your own opacity, steadfast in the inability to make anything coherent of the images.

Most important: avoid the seduction of a meaning brought to light with a sudden click of recognition. The "aha" experience that feels as if

---

14. Elio Gianturco, "Translator's Introduction," in Giambattista Vico, *On the Study Methods of Our Times* (Ithaca, N.Y.: Cornell University Press, 1990), xxxi.

15. Cf. Hillman, *The Dream and the Underworld,* 32–34; 123–33.

16. Vico, *The New Science,* 160.

you have "got" the meaning belongs to the elusive truth of the dream: its innate deceit! (Remember, Apollo is easily deceived as he was by his little brother, Hermes, by Cassandra, and by Daphne.) Instead, your operations with the images, your further imaginings, and your loss of certainty sophisticate your consciousness. What you do with the dream begins your assimilation into it, so that the way to its truth is not epistemological but psychological, its transformative effects in your soul.

A transformation has begun. The effort of withstanding the knowledge drive, resisting Apollo's enlightening clarifications, leaves one only with the dream. That's all you have and all you know. Yet this abdication grants iconic power to *phantasia*. The images gain value, they are rich with implications. The autochthonous generativity of the psyche, its *poiesis* or natural ability to make intelligibility, has begun to shine forth in the obscurity that you are allowing. Night has not yielded to daylight, and understanding now speaks with a darkened tongue: the devious occulted language of analogy, allusion and metaphor. Metaphor, says Vico, "confers sense and emotion on insensate objects,"[17] so that every thing in the dream becomes a "miniature myth"[18] (Vico's definition of metaphor), full of analogous truths, restoring you, the dreamer, to the underlying poetic imagination from which all mental life springs.

V.

We have moved from the hard-crusted flatland of our usual notion—or is it a fantasy?—of reality to the terrain of the animated imagination. We have crossed over from the fantasy of reality to the reality of fantasy, aiming at the activation of dream, reverie, myth, and ultimately the imagination of the arts, and a re-vivification of the world.

I like to think that we are also engaged in a politics of imagination, The immediate crimes of our times are political. I refer to *impetuous war, social injustice,* and *environmental neglect.* All indicate the impoverished imagination in the minds of policy, the heads of corporate power, the heads of state. Especially in the United States.

17. Ibid., 159.
18. Ibid.

Robert McNamara, Secretary of Defense during much of the Vietnam War, looking back, writes: "we can now understand these catastrophes for what they were: essentially the products of a failure of imagination." Another Secretary of Defense, Donald Rumsfeld, says that surprise, panic, and terror are due to "poverty of expectations—the failure of imagination." Michael Hayden, director of the National Security Agency, when comparing the disaster at Pearl Harbor with that of the Twin Towers, declared that "perhaps it was more a failure of imagination this time than last."[19] John Lehman, former Secretary of the Navy and member of the 9/11 Commission, said of that event: "The greatest failure of imagination by all of us."

More precisely, what is the nature of the present failure? After all, planning a military invasion half the globe away takes quite a fantastic imagination as do the visionary statements about transforming the entire Middle East. Wolfowitz, Rumsfeld, Cheney, and Rice were blinded by Apollonic reality: their factual appraisals of American hard power compared with their notion of the fantastic fanaticism of the Muslim mind that, they say, had not been through a Reformation or an Enlightenment. The Middle East had not found Apollo; not the sun but the moon waves on their flags. The planner's focus on logistics, hierarchical command and air power, their dependence on night-vision, high-altitude satellite surveillance and long-range missiles all bespeak Apollo, anciently and frequently called "the far darter," "he who killed at a distance."

Wolfowitz, Rumsfeld, Cheney, and Rice were out of touch with imaginative reality. They did not imagine the real — the ancestral ghosts; the chthonic force of xenophobia (fear and hatred of the outsider); the love of one's own house, neighborhood, land; the degradations of poverty, the inspirational poetics of the Arab language (versus computerized military Pentagonese); the importance of history and culture. It did not occur to American command to protect the museum of Iraq's antiquities. It should not surprise us that the heavy tread of war machines have crushed fragile sites of Mesopotamian civilization. The prophesies of Wolfowitz, Rumsfeld, Cheney, and Rice were too rational and unimaginative to foresee the horrors of war and its uncontrollable extensions. In short, a vision of a bright future for a society cleansed of evil is not the imagination of

---

19. James Hillman, *A Terrible Love of War* (New York: Penguin Press, 2004), 15.

archetypal passions such as those that arise from dreams. Quite possibly the suppression of imagination in psychology in younger years (e.g., the Ohio textbook) could trickle up and through the American population as a whole resulting in the failure of imagination in high places.

As for the other crime, environmental neglect, there is only this to say. As long as the planet is simply measurable matter and a place from which Christians should be delivered because Jesus's kingdom is not of this world, the planet is to do with as we want. Apollo's attempt to seize Daphne shows, among other things, the refusal of nature to yield to and be possessed by Apollonic intentions. Daphne fled and, as he was about to lay his divine hands on her body, she transformed into a tree. No matter how intensely the knowledge drive would penetrate nature, something in it eludes our mind's grasp and remains inviolate.

The Apollonic knowledge drive expressed in the sciences serves to harness the planet's spirits for human benefit. Anything is justified that increases knowledge. Imagination says otherwise. To imagination, dream, and reverie, the world speaks with intimations of a soul in things. "Nature alive," Alfred North Whitehead called this appreciation. To imagination, ecology is the study of the spirits in things, all sorts of things, affirming *their* animation rather than *our* advantage. Animals live in an animated world. From that reality they need no escapes. For animals, as for the ancient peoples, all things are full of gods. When nature is alive, there are little oracles everywhere.

Let us beware of things, facts and information as evidence of reality. The world out there conforms with our ideas about it. It can as well speak to the soul, to the imagination, to art as well as only to the Apollonian mind. The facts of the news, the objects on sale, the medical and financial statistics, the science and sentimentalisms about nature, images of the starving and sick...these are artifice, distraction, addictive soporifics that keep us entranced, or enchained. To consider this "reality" keeps us in the Cartesian cemetery, flat and soulless, and gives over the world to the Christian Devil so we must pray to be risen from it. Dreaming is no escape but a return to a reality of universal, ageless, recurrent, primordial themes—the *universali fantastici*—given with each psyche as its native prerogative and innate activity.

The reality of the dream does not yield even to Apollo, whose answers at Delphi were always ambiguous, enigmatic, teaching hesitation and pondering in face of urgency. Dream intelligence transcends ours and can transform ours, else we become dumber and blinder than we need be—and blind and dumb is the royal road to tragedy, as the Greeks taught us. Despite Nietzsche and Freud and Artemidorus, the dream encloses itself in an envelope of concealment. *This is the essence of its reality.* So, dreams are hard to decipher, tough in their emotional effect, resistant to the human will, lasting in memory. Are not these words—hard, tough, resistant, lasting—the very words we attribute to reality?

In Plato's famous myth of the cave in Book 7 of his *Republic*, the people are fettered since childhood and seated with their heads fixed to stare straight forward, able to perceive only the back wall of a darkened cave. The light behind them, which they know nothing about, casts shadows on the wall. They believe these shadows are real figures, real events. Only when they are freed to turn radically around do they waken to the truth that their idea of reality has been a manipulated illusion. But to awaken they must first turn from the fixed positions and false perceptions they had come to believe.

What I have been suggesting—no, pleading for—is that we must distrust our habitual beliefs, imagine in order to discover reality, and dream to be awake.

I am now at the end of my harangue, or was it a confession, or a sermon? I leave you with a passage from one of the lesser wise teachers of the Hebrew Bible, the Book of Joel, "your old men shall dream dreams, your young men shall see visions." Visions, grand schemes for the future, Apollonic enlightenment, and war for men in the grips of the young god. Old men dream dreams.

18

JOSEPH CAMPBELL: MYTH AS HERO

To appreciate Joseph Campbell we must stretch our minds. In fact, we may have to go out of our minds in order to imagine, for it is in imagination that we best meet Joseph Campbell.

First, imagine the extraordinary extent of this one man's research and collections from the earliest evidence of prehistory and the enormous corpus of Hindu philosophy to *Finnegan's Wake*, C.G. Jung, and George Lucas. Then, second, imagine the devastating effect of his work on the idea of "religion," not religion established in dogma and sectarian creed but rather as presented through images and rituals, myths and carvings, masks and dances, universal in its themes and shattering in its immediacy. Yet, third, his target was not the theologians of any particular orthodoxy, but the imaginative life of everyday human beings—college girls, moviegoers, TV watchers. He did not retreat academically or shy away from popular culture, because he showed that the life of mythic imagination was truly entertaining, truly enjoyable, and available to all—believers in religion or not. In this one popular aspect, Joseph Campbell carried on, fourth, the great tradition of the *mytho-logos*. He was himself a grand teller of tales, as was Homer and Plato, Ovid and Shakespeare and Cervantes. He carried on the tradition of the Irish bards, the Hindu and Persian imaginers, the scholarly Jewish fantasts.

From the large comprehensiveness of his undertakings, I want to select one particular work, perhaps his most famous book, *The Hero with*

Combined from "Campbell's Impetus" and "The Truth of Myth," two presentations at the Mythic Journey Conference Celebrating Joseph Campbell's Centenary, Atlanta, June 2004, and including passages from a talk to Friends of the Campbell Library, Pacifica Graduate Institute, Carpenteria, California, December 1993.

a Thousand Faces.[1] I do this for several reasons. From what I have already said, Campbell's own lifestyle and person has a heroic dimension, a *mythic* dimension. He was a foot racer who ran for Columbia University and he almost made it to the Olympics—one of his few great disappointments. In the old Olympic stadium, the runners originally ran for a quarter of a mile. (Campbell was a miler). Only later did the Olympics include chariots and physical combat. And, originally, the winner of the footrace was crowned with bay or laurel (in some races with parsley, wild olive, or pine). The runner had before his inner eye the mythic possibility that should he be crowned, he would be transported to immortality, and cults developed around this swiftest among mortals.

Campbell followed the labors of Hercules in his servitude to scholarship, performing with Sisyphean devotion. Imagine teaching undergraduates for thirty years! That is Sisyphus, rolling the boulder up the hill of ignorance year after year after year, and each September starting again. One of the names of the hero Hercules was "the beef eater," and I recall a dinner with Campbell before the conference in San Francisco "The Inner Reaches of Outer Space" in which we both took part. I had got off the plane exhausted, nervous, complaining, (that set of characteristics belonging to a psychoanalyst), while Joseph Campbell ordered a double thick steak, drank a couple of whiskeys, and retired to bed in great spirits—a hero of Herculean and Irish dimension.

Beyond the man and his deeds, the theme of the Hero is most relevant to our country and our civilization for its very continuation. This because "the work of the hero," writes Campbell, "is to slay the tenacious aspect of the Father/Dragon/Ogre/King, and release the vital energies that will feed the Universe."

A civilization requires the Ogre be slain. Who is the Ogre? The reactionary aspect of the *senex* who promotes fear, poverty, and imprisonment; who tempts the young and devours them to increase his own importance. The Ogre is the paranoid King who must have an enemy. He is the deceitful, suspicious, illegitimate King whose Nobles of the Court are sheltered in gated communities (already having locked themselves away or, rather, committed themselves to the enclosed asylum of security) where they nourish their world-devouring megalomania,

1. Joseph Campbell, *The Hero with a Thousand Faces* (New York: Pantheon, 1949).

but use the language of the legitimate hero to free the world from evil though they themselves are the carriers of lies, cruelty and death. The Ogre is the Sick King—a figure in myth, alchemy, and tribal ritual since the beginning of history.

Civilization requires a hero myth—in fact, is built upon that myth. Though the hero himself is nonexistent, a figure of legend, of another age past and dead. The ancient city is built upon the burial tumulus of that figure. The dead hero is thus never dead but lives on as the ideals and virtues of civilization. He is the imaginal force within the inspiration of great deeds of public good.

A dead hero upon whom the city is founded is represented in the American civilization by its capital, Washington, named for its dead liberator. The freethinking, secular state, wary of Imperial King and dogmatic Prelate, relying upon the inherent reason of the People and intending their common good, marks its other heroic dead founders in the capital with memorials to Jefferson, Lincoln, Roosevelt, and the dead of Vietnam. In Atlanta, this burned and conquered city, was re-founded on those earlier heroes and those founding principles by the community that re-fought, in the 1960s, the abolitionist heroic ideals of the 1860s.

The myth of the hero slays the Ogre by revealing the pattern in the paranoia, the myth in the mess. But it is not the hero as such who slays the old King, it is the effect of myth itself. Not myth *of* the hero, but myth *as* the hero. The heroic function of myth. This is the astounding gift Campbell has bequeathed to our civilization.

A mistake in my attacks on the hero has been to locate this archetypal figure within our secular history after the gods had all been banished. When the gods have fled or were declared dead, the hero serves only the secular ego. The force that prompts action, kills dragons, and leads progress becomes the Western "strong ego"—capitalist entrepreneur, colonial ruler, property developer, a tough guy with heroic ambitions on the road to success. I had lost the archetypal background in the secular foreground.

The original hero served culture and civilization. He saved the city, rebuilt the city, founded its myth and served its gods. Campbell's recovery of myths and their images, their literature, their arts fits the heroic pattern: founding culture by revivifying the archetypal imagination displayed by peoples the world over. By recovering the myth of the hero and restoring myth itself to primary place in cultural importance, Campbell has protected the city from the nihilism of materialist science, from Christian otherworldly redemption, and from the tyranny of capitalist commodification of all values. The panoply of materials that Campbell catalogued shows that the hero wears a thousand faces and cannot be reduced to the modern ego. Especially important in recognizing him is recognizing the heroic liberating function of myth—that it speaks truth to power, even the Ogre's power.

What is the relation of myth to truth? What is the truth of myth? This question is particularly important since the modern secular notion of "myth" usually means falsehood and fantasy, anything but the truth.

In old Greek, the idea of truth (*aletheia*) supposedly had three root meanings, three ways of understanding the word. First, truth is not *pseudo*, that is, truth differs from or opposes lies, deceits, and falsities. The second version derives from the word itself, *a-letheia*, "not Lethe," where Lethe refers to the River of Forgetfulness. Truth includes *memoria*, an imagination that holds and is enhanced by the past. Truth bears witness not merely to facts, but to the *archē* within the facts, the resonances of memory that facts (the "bare" facts as we call them) tend to forget and so cannot tell the whole truth. Third, truth is frank, direct, clear, evident perception; seeing things straight, closely corresponding with the actual world of things as they are.

Myth speaks truth because it fulfills all three of these supposed meanings of *aletheia*.

Myths tell a "just-so" truth. They depict happenings, including falsehoods and fantasies that form myth's ambiguous complexities. They resonate with ancient implications, the interweavings of plots and characters and locations, worldly and otherworldly, and with extraordinary pathologies and extraordinary miracles. The truth of myth is never single, never simple, never general. Their truth is descriptive, becoming prescriptive only when they are used to argue a fundamental meaning, when myth serves allegory or when called on to validate a preconceived opinion or belief. Such simplifications distort the truth of myth into prescriptive literalisms and moralisms—this is what the myth means; *this* is the truth it is telling. Any myth, no matter how sacred, how profound, loses its purchase on truth and becomes *pseudo* once it is simplified to fulfill a truth supposedly more fundamental than the myth itself.

Finally, myth speaks the frank truth of the world as it presents itself to our senses, clearly, evidently, directly as a world alive—animated, intentional, intelligible, and at moments, vividly beautiful. Myths let plants and animals speak, endow rivers and rocks with names and beings, trees with spirits, mountains with gods, and the underworld alive with ghosts and ancestors below, each footfall shadowing every thought and feeling. Myth tells the truth because it is utterly of this world, in this world, and for this world, no matter how preposterous its range of fantasy. No matter what ogres appear in its tales, myths show the world as it is and always is. Never can myth say, as in the gospel of John, "My kingdom is not of this world."

⸺✻⸺

www.ingramcontent.com/pod-product-compliance
Lightning Source LLC
Chambersburg PA
CBHW031424270326
41930CB00007B/559